A Geological Companion to Greece and the Aegean

A GEOLOGICAL COMPANION TO GREECE AND THE AEGEAN

Michael Denis Higgins
and Reynold Higgins

Cornell University Press

Ithaca, New York

First published 1996 by Cornell University Press.

Library of Congress Cataloging-in-Publication Data

Higgins, Michael, Denis, 1952–
    A geological companion to Greece and the Aegean / Michael Denis
Higgins and Reynold Higgins.
        p.   cm.
    Includes bibliographical references and index.
    ISBN 0-8014-3337-1 (alk. paper)
    1. Geology–Greece. 2. Geology–Aegean Sea Region. I. Higgins,
Reynold Alleyne. II. Title.
QE271.H54 1996
554.95–dc20   96-18855

Note

The numbers cited in superscript in the text refer to the
numbered bibliography. Numbers in the figure captions
(e.g. 'after 260') also refer to the bibliography.

Printed in Great Britain

Contents

Contents

Contents

Contents

Contents

14. The Dodecanese and the Carian Shore

15. The Cyclades

Contents

x

Preface

After a visit to a major library or a large bookstore, even academics may be inclined to feel that there are too many books. However, I feel that this book really does fill an unoccupied niche. This was especially apparent after a visit to the library of the British School at Athens. Despite the huge collections of material on the Aegean region, archaeologists were using declassified British Secret Service documents from the first half of the century for their geological background.

Few guidebook authors can actually visit all the places they write about, and this geological companion is no exception. Most places have been visited by the archaeologist (Reynold Higgins), but the geological cover is a little thinner. We had to rely on maps and scientific publications for parts of Macedonia, Thrace, the islands of the northern Aegean and the Ionian islands. Elsewhere, bibliographic research has been generally complemented by site visits.

The transliteration of Greek place names has presented its usual problems. No overall system has been used, just what 'sounded right' to Reynold Higgins, or what has been most commonly used in publications. However, the reader should have little difficulty in identifying the places referred to in the text.

The region covered by this book straddles two modern countries, Greece and Turkey. As is commonly the case, few geological studies extend across the border, hence many geological boundaries are artificially placed close to the political boundary, rendering correlations across the region difficult: we therefore ask the reader to bear with us if the geology appears to change so rapidly in the eastern Aegean Sea.

This book is the result of a collaboration between an archaeologist (Reynold Higgins) and a geologist (Michael Higgins). Reynold Higgins provided the original impetus for the book, selected the sites, decided on transliteration of the names and wrote the first draft of the cultural introductions. He helped with some of the bibliographic research, especially that concerning marbles and other decorative stones. He also read through much of the geological text and tried to reduce the amount of jargon. Sadly, Reynold Higgins, my father, died before the completion of the book. I would like to remember particularly his balanced view of the Aegean: one hot day we were visiting the mines of Lavrion when he spotted a tree laden with ripe figs. He immediately began to eat the fruit as fast as he could with the comment, 'Bother the archaeology, I'm only here for the figs.'

Classical authors

A number of classical authors have been referred to in the text: the *Geography* of Pliny the Elder, the *Histories* of Herodotus, the *Geography* of Strabo and the *Travels* of Pausanias have been particularly useful.

Cultural bibliography

The best overall cultural guides to this region are the three Blue Guides to Greece, Crete and Turkey (Barber, Cameron and McDonagh; Black and Norton). Turkey is well covered by *Aegean Turkey* and *Turkey Beyond the Maeander* (Bean; Benn, London). The ancient history of this region is described in the *Oxford History of the Classical World* (Oxford University Press) and *A Traveller's History of Greece*

(Burn; Pelican). Other pertinent books are *The Seven Wonders of the Ancient World* (Clayton and Price; Routledge, London); *The Acropolis* (Hopper; Weidenfeld and Nicolson, London); *An Introduction to Greek Art* (Woodford; Duckworth, London); *Studies in Ancient Technology* (Forbes, Leiden).

Acknowledgments

First, I would like to thank Claude Dallaire for carefully and patiently drafting the maps and diagrams, and Denis Côté for his help. Next come those who helped us in our bibliographic researches: the staff at the libraries of the Institute for Geology and Mineral Exploration, Athens (IGME), the British School at Athens, the Geological Survey of Canada, and the inter-library loan services at Université du Québec à Chicoutimi. Most of the text was read by Georgia Pe-Piper and David Piper, together with Vronwy Hankey, John Underhill, Ian Whitbred, Ursula Roberts, Carol Lister and George Koukis. Many others have helped with advice, including Dov Avigad, W. Vetters, Guy Saunders, Susan Walker, L. Lazzarini, Ayhan Erler, Bernt Schröder, Lucilla Burn, Gyorgy Ozoray and many others. However, I reserve the errors for myself. Finally, we would like to thank Patricia Higgins, Judit Ozoray, Ester Higgins and Zoe Higgins for their perseverance.

Further information

Bibliographical references in the text, which appear as superscript numbers referring to the numbered bibliography, include most of those associated with ancient quarries and mining, but only those most recent, most complete or most accessible for other subjects. For brevity, geological maps published by the governments of Greece and Turkey have not been referenced in the text or acknowledged in the figures, but they have been of immense help. I hope those authors not cited will forgive my omission.

Aerial photographs of many of the sites have been published in *Ancient Greece from the Air* [242] and the *Aerial Atlas of Ancient Crete*.[187] Cultural information comes from many sources, but the Blue Guides to Greece, Crete and Turkey have been invaluable. A useful compilation of data is in the *Gazetteer of Aegean Bronze Age Civilisation*.[249]

Other references to recent published research articles and abstracts of conference presentations can be found using bibliographic databases such as Georef, available on-line or on CD-ROM, at most geology libraries. However, there is much unpublished information only available at the offices of IGME for Greece and MTA for Turkey (for addresses see below).

Geological maps: Greece

A geological map at a scale of 1:500,000 covers the country in two sheets. There is also a seismotectonic map at the same scale, with earthquake and fault information, as well as simplified geology, at the same scale. Most of the country is also covered by geology maps at a scale of 1:50,000. There are also some hydrogeological maps at the same scale. All these are available from IGME, 70 Messoghion Street, Athens 115 27, Greece.

Geological maps: Turkey

The whole of Turkey is covered by geological maps at a scale of 1:500,000, each accompanied by a short explanatory text. Unfortunately these maps do not always give much information on the types of sedimentary rocks, just their age. The regions described in this book are covered by the Istanbul, Izmir and Denizli sheets. The country has been mapped at a scale of 1:25,000 but these maps have not been published, although a limited number of 1:100,000 compilations of these data are available. All these maps can be obtained from MTA Genel Müdürlügü, BDT Dairesi Nesriyat Servisi, Ankara, Turkey.

To Judit, Ester and Zoe

LEGEND FOR THE MAPS

--------- *Fault*

▲---▲ *Thrust fault, teeth on upper side*

• *Spring*

⊙ *Sink-hole*

.... *Ancient shoreline*

....400.... *Bathymetric contours in metres*

▲ 166 *Peak and altitude in metres*

⌒ *River*

⌒ *Road*

⚲ *Monastery*

⟩⟩⟩⟩⟩⟩⟩⟩ *Ancient city walls*

⚒ *Quarry or mine*

Archaeological time in the Aegean region

Palaeolithic	
	10000 BC
Mesolithic	
	6000 BC
Neolithic	
	3000 BC
Early Helladic (E. Bronze Age)	
	2300 BC
Middle Helladic (M. Bronze Age)	
	1600 BC
Late Helladic (Mycenaean, L. Bronze Age)	
	1100 BC
Geometric	
	750 BC
Archaic	
	500 BC
Classical	
	232 BC
Hellenistic	
	146 BC
Roman	
	330 AD

Plates

(between pages 80 and 81)

1

The Geological Background

Geology influences our lives and our communities in many ways: its clearest influence is in the production of wealth from the exploitation of minerals and oil. However, we must not underestimate the effects of rock composition and the availability of water on the productivity of soils and hence on agriculture and stockbreeding. Geology also influences the shape of the land, and thus the distribution of human populations. All these factors are important today, and were important in the past. The aim of this book is not simply to describe the geology of Greece and the Aegean, as that has already been done,[34, 127] but also to comment on how geology influenced the development of the ancient civilisations of this region.

Before discussing these topics, a word on geological methods. The classical procedure, as practised in the nineteenth century, was essentially descriptive: a catalogue of what could be seen on the surface of the earth. Some attempt was also made to predict what could be found in areas hidden beneath the surface or concealed beneath water. Although the descriptive method is still an important part of geology, recent work has been more directed towards an understanding of the processes involved, and this has necessitated extensive borrowing from both physics and chemistry. This expertise has also been passed on to archaeology, giving rise to the new discipline of archaeometry.

In this chapter we will give an outline of the geological background, especially as regards the Aegean region. Many of these ideas are treated in more detail in subsequent chapters. We have tried to simplify some of the geological controversies, but geology is an active field of research and ideas and interpretations change

with time. There are many good books covering various aspects of geology, such as *Geology in the Field*,[42] *Rocks and Rock Minerals*,[59] and *The Holocene: an environmental history*.[235]

Geological time

The earth is about 4,500 million years old, and was formed at the same time as the sun and the other planets. Geology is distinguished from most other sciences by its study of this immense period of time. However, geology is also concerned with processes on much shorter time-scales, and eventually blends into those of archaeology.[31]

Initially fossils were used to establish the relative age of different rocks. A limited number of geological periods were defined in terms of these fossils and given special names. More recently it has been possible determine the age of rocks in years, using naturally radioactive elements. However, we continue to use the named geological periods for a number of reasons, not least being that it is easier to refer to names instead of numbers. (See Fig. 1.1.)

The structure of the Earth

The outer core of the earth is largely composed of liquid iron and is the source of the magnetic field (Fig. 1.2). Above the core lie the lower mantle and the asthenosphere, which are the largest part of the earth, and are largely made of magnesium and iron silicates. The uppermost part of the solid earth is the lithosphere, comprising the uppermost mantle and the crust (Figs. 1.2, 1.3). The continental crust is 30-80 km thick and is rich in silicon and aluminium. It extends out underwater to the edge

Uniform Time Scale	Subdivisions based on time	Epochs	Time (millions of years)	Evolution of living things
0			( )	
PHANEROZOIC / **CENOZOIC** — Quaternary	Recent or Holocene / Pleistocene	0.01 / 1.6	Homo sapiens
575 CENOZOIC — Neogene (Tertiary)	Pliocene	6	Later hominids / Primitive hominids
	Miocene	22	Grasses grazing mammals
Paleogene	Oligocene	36	
	Eocene	58	Primitive horses
	Paleocene	65	Spreading of mammals
MESOZOIC — Cretaceous		145	Dinosaurs extinct / Flowering plants / Climax of dinosaurs
Jurassic		210	Birds
Triassic		250	Conifers, cycads, primitive mammals / Dinosaurs / Mammal-like reptiles
PALEOZOIC — Permian		290 / 340	Coal forests, insects, amphibians, reptiles
Devonian		365	Amphibians
Silurian		415 / 465	Land plants and land animals
Ordovician		510	Primitive fishes
Cambrian		575	Marine animals abundant
PRECAMBRIAN — PRECAMBRIAN			Primitive marine animals / Green algae
~4550 Birth of Planet Earth		4550	Bacteria, blue-green algae

Fig. 1.1. Geological time.

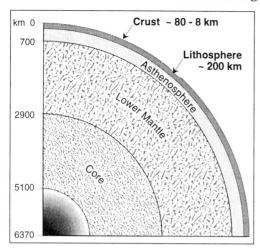

Fig. 1.2. The structure of the earth. The magnetic field is generated in the core. Convection in the mantle drives plate tectonics. The upper part of the earth is divided into the asthenosphere and lithosphere, which includes the crust. The crust is all that we normally see on the earth's surface.

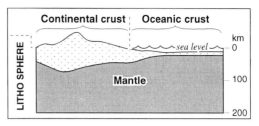

Fig. 1.3. Section through the lithosphere (not to scale). The continental crust is much thicker than the oceanic crust, and has a different composition.

of the continental shelf. The oceanic crust is much thinner, typically 8 km, and is poorer in silicon and aluminium than the continental crust. Another difference between continental and oceanic crust is their age: the continental crust tends to be much older. Some crust, such as much of the eastern Mediterranean sea, is intermediate in properties.

Below the first few metres temperature increases with depth in the earth by about 3°C per 100 m. This is because heat is continually being produced in the mantle and crust by the decay of the naturally-occurring radioactive elements potassium, uranium and thorium. Rocks conduct heat very poorly, so heat escapes from the mantle by convective movements of rock. These movements are transmitted through to the surface of the earth, where indirectly they produce many of the large-scale structures of the earth (see next section).

Plate tectonics

Some time ago it was observed that certain widely-separated coastlines could be fitted together, for example the east coast of South America and the west coast of Africa. These observations were incorporated into the theory of continental drift, according to which various supercontinents had existed in the past, to be split apart and amalgamated again many times. These ideas were not widely accepted, partly because of the lack of a convincing mechanism for the process. Geological and geophysical exploration of the ocean floors in the 1950s and 1960s produced the first evidence that these regions are drastically different from the continents, both in their relative youth and their composition. This proved to be the key to the problem and led to the modern theory of plate tectonics.

In this theory the lithosphere of the earth is divided up into about twenty major rigid 'plates', all in motion with respect to adjoining plates, at speeds of several centimetres per year. The upper part of each plate may include both continental and oceanic crust, but the plate extends downwards into the mantle to a depth of 200-400 km. Here the plates glide over the underlying rock, lubricated by a small amount of molten rock (magma).

This theory contrasts with that of continental drift in that the continents do not move on their own, but are merely carried along by the underlying plates. This suggests that geological processes will be concentrated along plate margins rather than continental margins. The driving force for plate motions is convective movements of the mantle as it tries to rid itself of internally-produced heat.

Although many plates contain both oceanic and continental crust, these two parts are not created and destroyed in the same way: new

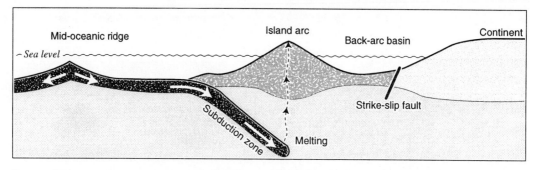

Fig. 1.4. Plate tectonics (not to scale). New oceanic crust is generated at a ridge in the oceans and eventually goes down a subduction zone beneath another plate. Melting of the plate and the overlying mantle produces magmas that rise up to form the volcanos of an island arc. Spreading behind an island arc produces a basin, commonly with some volcanism.

plate is always oceanic (Fig. 1.4). It forms along the margin and moves away in opposite directions at rates of several centimetres per year. Currently no new plate is being formed in the Mediterranean region. Oceanic portions of a plate are consumed in subduction zones. Here the oceanic plate dives underneath the adjacent plate and descends into the earth to a depth of up to 600 km. During the descent parts of the plate and the overlying rocks melt and the liquid rock rises towards the surface. It may solidify before it reaches the surface or it may erupt onto the surface to form volcanos. Where the opposing plate is oceanic the magmatic activity will produce a chain of islands, usually in the form of an arc, such as the Japanese islands, or, less typically, the volcanic islands of the Aegean. Buckling of the crust in front of the volcanic arc may produce a chain of non-volcanic islands, such as Crete, Rhodes etc. Diffuse extension of the crust behind the volcanic chain may produce a basin intermediate between true oceanic and continental crust.

It is not possible for continental crust to descend into a subduction zone as it is too light: any attempt will clog it up and throw up a mountain range. When a small block of continental material, possibly with islands, collides with a subduction zone, a mountain range is formed and the subduction zone shifts to the other side of the former block. During these collisions part of the ocean floor, especially that in the basins behind volcanic arcs, may not go down the subduction zone, but be thrust up onto the land. These slices of sea-floor frequently include peridotite from the uppermost mantle, which is commonly metamorphosed into serpentinite, a dark-green mottled rock named for its resemblance to snake-skin. Other characteristic components of the sea-floor are basalt lavas (see below) that have been erupted underwater as a series of pillow-like blobs, and the sedimentary rock chert. Such isolated remains of former oceanic floor are sufficiently common to have been given a name – ophiolite suite rocks (from the Greek for snake – *ophis*).

Plates may also slide past one another along major faults that can cross both continents and oceans. Here plates are neither created or destroyed. In the Aegean region the North Anatolian fault zone is of this type: the European continent is moving to the right with respect to the Anatolian plate. Plate boundaries may also be transitional between these cases, and their character can change along their length.

Local tectonics

The subject of plate tectonics attempts to explain the large-scale structures on the earth's surface; the detailed structures are the domain of local tectonics. Broadly, two different regimes occur: overall compression and extension (Fig. 1.5).

Compression of the crust must be accommo-

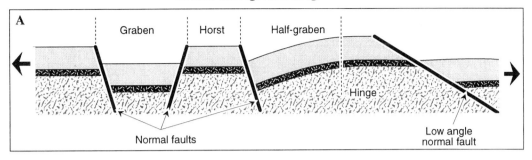

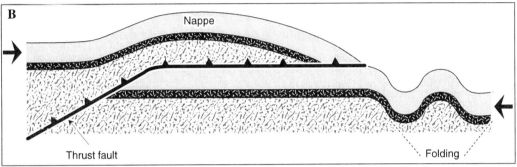

Fig. 1.5. Geological structures produced (A) during extension, (B) during compression. Faults can be reactivated and move in a different direction. Folding tends to occur at greater depths than faulting.

dated by folding of the rock strata or by faulting, i.e. movement along cracks in the rock. Which mechanism dominates depends on the strength of the rock and the depth at which the compression is occurring: at great depths the rocks are weaker and will tend to fold rather than fracture. The faults must accommodate shortening, so the upper block moves over the lower part, thickening the pile of rock. Such faults are commonly almost horizontal, and are called thrust faults. The rock unit bounded by thrust faults is called a nappe.

At the boundary between two colliding continents (see above) the crust is partly folded and partly cut up into nappes, which are piled on top of one another to form a thickened crust. The crust 'floats' on the underlying, denser mantle, hence a thicker crust will ride higher and more will project above the sea as mountains.

Nappes can be very variable in thickness and rock components. For example, some nappes are dominated by ancient sea-floor (ophiolites), whereas others are dominated by

limestones deposited in shallow water. Large nappes or groups of nappes with similar rocks and geological histories are called isopic zones, and those of the Aegean are described in Chapter 2.

Extension of the crust can produce a single new plate boundary or it can be distributed over a wide region, as in the Aegean. Extension is accommodated near the surface by faulting. In this case the upper block drops down with respect to the lower block, and the mechanism is termed normal faulting. If the faults are steep then extension will produce tectonic valleys called grabens, separated by mountain blocks called horsts. Very commonly there is a fault on only one side of the graben and the floor has hinged downwards, to create a half-graben. In some areas the normal faults are almost flat-lying, resembling thrust faults, and do not produce grabens and horsts.

Earthquakes

Earthquakes are vibrations of the earth that

are produced when rocks juxtaposed across a fault slide past each other. Some faults slide very easily so stress on the fault is dissipated continually. However, many faults are 'sticky' and the stress can build up to much higher levels before the energy is released in an earthquake.

The magnitude of an earthquake (the well-known Richter scale) is not a measure of destructiveness but merely indicates how much energy is released. It varies according to the amount of movement of the rocks (from a few centimetres to several metres) and the surface area of the fault that moved (from a few square metres to tens of square kilometres).

The amount of vibration felt at a particular place on the earth, and hence the local destructiveness of an earthquake, is called the intensity. It is measured on the Modified Mercalli scale and varies with location. Each earthquake therefore has only one magnitude but many intensities. The intensity depends on the distance to the centre of the earthquake, its depth and the local geology. Many sediments, especially those in recently drained lakes, can amplify considerably the earthquake vibrations and increase the intensity.

Joints

Most fractures in rocks do not have any significant movement of the two sides: these fractures are called joints, and several different sets can be seen in most outcrops. Some joints are formed by the same regional stresses that form the faults, others by contraction during cooling of igneous and metamorphic rocks. However, many form as a result of stresses produced during erosion or quarrying: at depth in the earth the stresses are more or less equal in all directions. When material is removed stress in the vertical direction is reduced, but the horizontal stresses are unchanged. Therefore, expansion can only be accommodated by upward movement, and joints parallel to the earth's surface will form. This effect can aid quarrying operations, as large blocks will naturally split off horizontally after a trench has been excavated around the block. It can also cause blocks to split during excavation.

The basic rock cycle

Rocks are naturally occurring materials made up of distinctive components, minerals, that have a limited range of composition and struc-

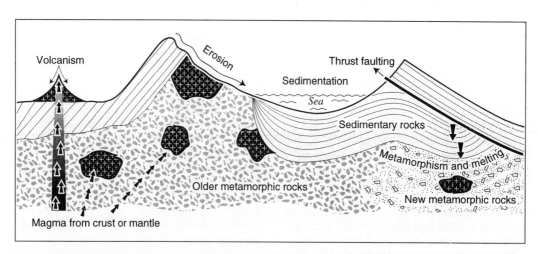

Fig. 1.6. Simplified rock cycle. New igneous rocks crystallise from magma produced by melting of the crust or mantle. They are eroded, along with existing rocks, and the sediments are commonly deposited in the sea or lakes. Thrust faulting thickens the crust, forming mountains and forcing the rocks downwards into regions of higher temperature and pressure, where they are transformed into metamorphic rocks.

ture. Rocks can be divided up into those that
were at one time molten, termed igneous, those
that formed on the surface of the earth, termed
sedimentary, and existing rocks that have
been transformed by heat and pressure,
termed metamorphic. The interchange between these three groups of rocks is illustrated
in Fig. 1.6.

Igneous rocks

All igneous rocks have crystallised from molten rock, termed magma, formed in the interior
of the earth. Magmas poor in silicon and rich in
iron and magnesium, such as basalt, form at
depths of 100-200 km by the melting of rocks in
the mantle. Magmas rich in silicon, such as
granite, commonly form at much shallower
levels in the crust by the melting of sedimentary, metamorphic or existing igneous rocks. In
each case only part of the original rock melts,
so that the magma has a different composition
from its source.

The names of different igneous rocks reflect
both their composition and the level at which
they crystallised: slow cooling of magma below
the surface of the earth produces rocks with
mineral crystals that are readily visible to the
unaided eye. Such rocks are termed plutonic
(after Pluto, the Greek god of the underworld)
and an example is granite. Faster cooling on
the surface of the earth produces volcanic rocks
(after Vulcan, the Roman smith god), which are
generally fine-grained. These rocks may contain large crystals, called phenocrysts, but
these formed at depth before the magma was
erupted.

Volcanic rocks are further subdivided into
lavas and pyroclastic rocks. Lavas were still
liquid when they were extruded, generally quiescently, onto the surface. Pyroclastic rocks are
produced during explosive eruptions. Liquid
magma is blasted into the air where it solidifies
before it hits the ground. The finer-grained
material is called volcanic ash or tuff (not to be
confused with tufa, a soft limestone). Volcanic
breccias include blocks of pre-existing rocks
and pumice, a solidified volcanic foam.

Sedimentary rocks

Sedimentary rocks are produced on the surface
of the earth by accumulation of rock fragments
and biological materials or by crystallisation of
minerals from water.

Many sedimentary rocks, such as clay, shale
(the term schist is used in some older texts),
siltstone, sandstone and conglomerate, are accumulations of rock fragments, and are termed
clastic rocks. Weathering breaks down existing
rocks into smaller pieces (sediments), which
are transported by wind or more commonly
water. These sediments accumulate in dunes,
river valleys, lakes or most commonly in the
sea. Crystallisation of calcite, and other minerals, from fluids percolating through the loose
material cements the grains together. Harder
rocks are produced by more cementation. This
process can continue even after the rock is
quarried: as it dries out further crystallisation
of the interstitial liquid will strengthen the
cement.

Two series of clastic rocks have been given
special names that reflect the environment in
which they form. Flysch is a series of rocks
deposited in the deep sea adjacent to a rapidly
rising mountain chain. It is dominated by
sandstone, with finer siltstone and clay. Molasse is another type of clastic rock associated
with mountain chains. However, it is produced
after the mountains have formed and it is
deposited in shallow lakes or river beds. It is
dominated by conglomerates, with sandstone
and siltstone.

The term clay applies to both a group of
platy minerals, and a rock dominated by these
minerals.[179, 116] As mentioned above, clay can
form by weathering, but it can also be produced
by the alteration of rocks in contact with hot
water (200-400°C) associated with volcanism
or the emplacement of intrusions. The amount
of clay minerals is increased when the rock is
eroded, transported by water and redeposited.

Most clays are mineralogically unsuitable
for making pottery as they are too stiff or they
do not fire well. However, suitable clays are
commonly associated with layers of lignite, a
low-grade coal.[283] The original environment
was a shallow lake in which fine clay accumu-

lated. Eventually the water was sufficiently shallow for plants to grow abundantly. The plants died but did not decay in the stagnant water and their remains were transformed into lignite. Red pottery clays were also obtained from 'terra rossa' soils (see below) by washing and settling of the liquid.

Limestone is a sedimentary rock formed almost entirely of the mineral calcite and can form in a number of ways: many limestones are accumulations of marine shells, some microscopic in size. These rocks are generally formed in shallow seas, but can also form on the ocean floor, or even accumulate in sand dunes. Under certain conditions calcite (or the similar mineral aragonite) can crystallise directly from the sea to produce accumulations of calcite-mud, which is then cemented into solid rock. Finally limestone can be precipitated from freshwater in caves and around springs to form stalagmites, stalactites and travertine (tufa). Part of the calcium in calcite may be replaced by magnesium to form dolomite, a rock very similar in the field to limestone, but slightly more resistant to erosion. Marls are soft, impure limestones with large amounts of clay and sand.

Some organisms, such as sponges, have a skeleton made of silica. These skeletons can recrystallise to form the hard rock chert (flint), which commonly occurs as nodules or layers in limestone.

Prolonged evaporation of seawater in enclosed basins or irregularly flooded coastal flats can produce sedimentary rocks called evaporites. The first mineral to crystallise from the brine is gypsum, followed by common salt (sodium chloride) and then potassium and magnesium salts. Evaporites are too soluble to be generally observed on the surface, except for gypsum rock (alabaster), and even this is weathered very rapidly.

Fossils are an important part of many sedimentary rocks. Fossils are the remains of animals and plants or of their activities, such as worm tubes, tracks or faeces. Some fossils, such as shells, are essentially unchanged since formation. Others, however, have been chemically or physically changed during fossilisation: carbon, silica or calcite may replace organic matter or the organism may rot away and the hole become filled with fine-grained sediments.

Metamorphism and metamorphic rocks

When rocks formed under a certain pressure and temperature are moved to a different part of the earth with a different pressure and temperature, either higher or lower, then some of the minerals in the original rock may become unstable and new minerals will be formed. In some cases the only change is the recrystallisation of minerals to form larger grains. This is the process of metamorphism, and it can act on sedimentary, igneous and already metamorphosed rocks. Many metamorphic rocks have a distinctive layered structure, produced by deformation of the rock when it is weakened by the metamorphism.

Metamorphism of clay-bearing sedimentary rocks initially produces a platy mineral, mica, which gives a sheen to the rock, termed phyllite. With increasing pressure and temperature the size of the mica crystals increases and their good cleavage gives a fissility, or ability to be split into sheets, to the rock, which is now called schist, from the Greek *schizein*, to split. Mica is not stable at higher temperatures and pressures and is replaced by other minerals, such as amphibole. The resulting rock, which does not split very well, is termed gneiss (pronounced 'nice').

Rocks rich in iron and magnesium, such as basalt and gabbro, are metamorphosed into dark-green to black amphibolites, i.e. rocks made up of amphiboles. Metamorphism of peridotite at low temperatures yields a rock rich in serpentine minerals called serpentinite.

Very high temperature metamorphism can produce melting. If the magma is retained in the rock then a streaky rock called migmatite is produced. At higher degrees of melting so much magma is produced that it can not be retained in the rock and will start to separate. When it crystallises it will form an igneous rock, commonly a granite.

A 'typical' major volcanic eruption

Although every volcanic eruption is different in detail, many of the large explosive eruptions that have occurred in our region have similar features. The eruption begins with a plinian phase, named from the eruption of Vesuvius in AD 79, as observed by the Roman writer Pliny. An initial explosion, or possibly a landslide, opens up a pathway for the magma from a temporary storage chamber (magma chamber), at a depth of several kilometres, to the surface. The first magma to use this pathway is from the top of the magma chamber, where it contains much dissolved water. The water boils as the pressure is reduced and produces a light froth which accelerates upwards, fragments and leaves the volcano as a high-speed jet of ash. This rises into the atmosphere, sometimes to a height of 30 km, and takes the form of an umbrella-shaped cloud. Deposits from this stage of the eruption are called ash-fall tuffs. Their thickness will depend only on the distance from the vent and the prevailing wind direction and will not be affected by local topography.

As the eruption continues, water in the magma chamber is reduced and there is less force in the jet. Eventually the jet is unable to support the weight of the ash column and collapses. When the collapsing column hits the top of the volcano the ash has nowhere to go but sideways. The result is a strong lateral blast of ash and gases in all directions, termed a base-surge, and it can occur several times during an eruption. A base-surge is so fast that it is not deflected by topography, such as valleys, and will deposit equal amounts of material on both the valley floors and the ridges.

During the final stages of the eruption the magma does not normally have sufficient power to overflow the rim of the crater. Periodically, the activity increases and a hot mixture of fine ash and gas may roll down the side of the volcano. This mixture behaves like a liquid and will generally flow down valleys like a snow avalanche, leaving deposits that are thicker on the valley floors than on the sides. If the flow is very hot then it may glow, and the particles may weld themselves together to give a hard, dense rock called ignimbrite. This type of flow is termed an ash flow or nuée ardente (glowing cloud).

Lava flows are generally produced by magmas with smaller amounts of water. This may arise either because they have lost it in earlier eruptions or because they are naturally poor in water, as is basalt, for example.

Weathering and soils

When rocks are exposed to rain, frost and sun many of their minerals are no longer stable, and new minerals form, a process called weathering. Part of this process is physical, as cracks develop due to thermal expansion and contraction; part is chemical, reactions between the minerals and the air and water; and part is biological, caused by the growth of roots, bacteria, fungi and lichens. Generally minerals formed at high temperatures, such as pyroxenes, olivine and feldspars, are replaced by minerals stable on the surface, such as quartz, iron oxides and clay.

Soils are one of the materials produced by weathering. The nature of the soil and its thickness depend on the nature of the original rock, the climate and the time available before the soil is removed by erosion.[47, 30, 84] Stony or thin soils are produced where there is rapid erosion of weathering products, such as on steep hillsides where there is little vegetation. Such erosion may have occurred in the distant past, or it may be related to recent climate change or human activities. Red and brown Mediterranean soils cover large areas of Greece and western Turkey. These fertile soils were probably produced during the last glacial period, when the climate was wetter and cooler. They can be produced from a variety of different rocks. Soils in recent volcanic areas are usually very thin as there is not sufficient time for the breakdown of the rocks. However, where the streams flow into closed basins that have little or no access to the sea, the sediment may stay there long enough for chemical weathering to produce soil. Old volcanic areas may have deep fertile soils. Weathering of pure limestone or marble produces a thin red soil called terra rossa. This soil is produced by weathering of the impurities in the original rock and is rich in iron oxides (hence the colour) and clay. Although fertile, it is usually too thin on the hillsides for successful agriculture. One of the best soils in the Aegean region, known as rendzina, is produced on marl and flysch. However, the most productive soils are alluvial soils, formed in river valleys and former lakes. The amount of these soils available for agriculture has been greatly increased by drainage programmes, both recent and ancient, but they are also lost to urban development.

Soils in dry regions commonly develop a hard crust rich in calcite just below the surface. This crust is a type of soft limestone and is commonly called caliche or calcrete (from its common resemblance to concrete). Caliche develops where evaporation exceeds rainfall. Under these circumstances groundwater from deeper levels percolates upwards and evaporates below the surface. Small amounts of calcite in solution in the water are deposited at this level and form a harder layer. Subsequent erosion by rain or wind may remove the overlying softer soils and leave a pavement of 'fossil' caliche. Some of the rock locally termed 'poros' is caliche, but this term also applies to rocks with very different origins.

Extreme weathering of limestones under tropical conditions (in the Tertiary period in the Aegean) gives bauxite, a loose, red rock that is the ore of aluminium. In a similar way weathering of peridotite or gabbro can produce a loose, brown rock called laterite, used in antiquity as an ore of iron, and now also as an ore of nickel.

Groundwater

Rainwater or melting snow either flows along the surface into rivers and lakes, or is absorbed into the underlying rocks, where it is called groundwater (Fig. 1.7). Water can move through permeable rocks such as sandstone, or along cracks in less permeable rocks such as granite or limestone. Clay is impermeable as the material is weak and will reseal any cracks which could transport water.

The water descends until it reaches the water-table, which is the upper surface of the zone of rock completely saturated in water. This is the level of water in wells which are not being pumped. The water-table may be quite close to the surface, especially in valleys, where

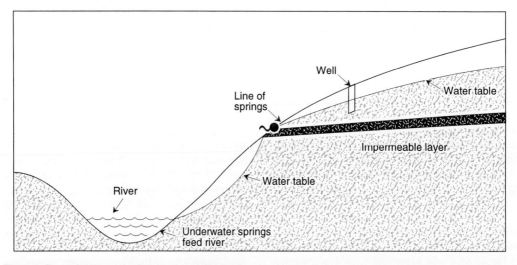

Fig. 1.7. Groundwater cycle. Some rainwater falling on land runs off along the surface and some percolates into the rock, where it descends to the water-table, the zone of permanently saturated rock. Loss of vegetation can increase the amount of run-off, and hence decrease the amount of water absorbed and available for springs. Springs form where the water-table intersects the surface, such as above an impermeable layer. Most springs debouche underwater and directly feed rivers.

10

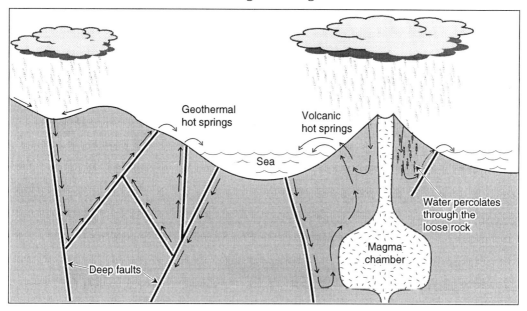

Fig. 1.8. Geothermal springs. The source of heat for most hot springs is the natural increase in temperature with depth of about 3°C per 100 m. For some springs in volcanic areas the heat source is cooling magma. Seawater or freshwater descends one fault or percolates through loose rocks, is heated and returns to the surface as hot springs.

it can be tapped with wells. However, in limestone or marble the water-table may be very deep (see below). Water can sometimes be perched on top of layers of less permeable rock, such as clay.

Where the water-table intersects the surface groundwater will rise as springs (but for karst springs see below). Although we usually think of springs discharging on land, most debouche directly into river beds. The passage of water through rock can be interrupted by an impermeable or less permeable layer of rock. This can lead to a line of springs at the boundary between the two rocks.

Hot springs

Most hot springs are related to deep faults, and not to volcanism, as is commonly supposed (Fig. 1.8).[1, 180] As mentioned above, temperature increases with depth everywhere in the earth. Two intersecting faults are necessary to tap this source of heat. Cool surface water (seawater, rivers or lakes) descends one fault

to a depth of several kilometres. There the water is heated by the surrounding rocks, expands and starts to rise up the other fault, creating a convection system.

These hot waters can dissolve parts of the surrounding rocks, especially limestone and marble. As the liquids rise to the surface their temperature falls and minerals, commonly calcite, crystallise in the upper parts of the faults and around springs to form travertine (but note that travertine can also form around cold springs). These deposits tend to clog up the faults, and consequently in many areas periodic movements of the faults are necessary to maintain the flow of hot water.

The glacial period and recent climatic change

The climate of the last 1.6 million years, the Pleistocene and Holocene periods, has been marked by dramatic fluctuations. Within this period, loosely called the Ice Age, the climate has been generally cool, with warmer conditions typically lasting for about 10,000 years every 100,000 years. During the cooler periods temperatures were about 5-8°C lower, the glaciers advanced and covered much of northern Europe, and the climate of the Mediterranean region was generally wetter.

We are now in one of the warmer intervals, called the Holocene or Recent period, which started about 10,000 years ago.[235] It began with rapid warming, but about 8,000 years ago the climate became more stable. Since then climatic variation has been less extreme, especially during the last 4,000 years,[235, 237]

Sea-level

Although the sea is often viewed as unchanging, its level with respect to the land was often very different in the past (Fig. 1.9).[261] These differences reflect both global changes in the level of the sea and local changes in the height of the land, and the history of sea-level changes is therefore different at each location.

During the cooler periods of the last few million years much water was stored on the continents as ice-sheets, lowering sea-level by as much as 120 m (Fig. 1.9). The last glacial maximum was about 20,000 years ago. This water was released as the climate warmed up, returning the sea-level to its earlier condition. Since then this mechanism has had little effect on sea-level.

Local changes in the height of the land are commonly related to large-scale tectonic movements, commonly along faults. The Aegean is the most active region of the Mediterranean, and hence tectonic control on ancient sea-level is the most important process.[85]

Evidence of ancient sea-level stands (periods of static sea-level with respect to the land) can be found in coastal landforms, in the occurrence of recent marine fossils on land and in archaeological remains. Erosion by the sea is strongest where the waves break on the shore, hence prolonged action of the waves produces a notch in the sea-cliffs and a surf bench (see Plate 1A). The absence of significant tides in most of the Mediterranean means that these effects are concentrated in a narrow zone, and lowering of sea-level will preserve these fea-

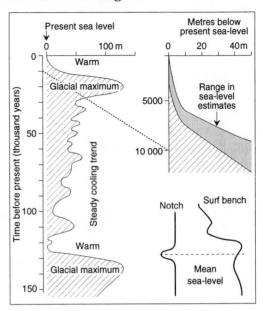

Fig. 1.9. Global sea-level variations during the last 150,000 years have been controlled by global climate: during cold spells water was tied up in glaciers and sea-level dropped. Estimates of recent global sea-level changes are complicated by local tectonic effects, so only a range in sea-level estimates is given. However, most estimates agree that there has been little global sea-level change during the last 5,000 years. When sea-level is maintained at one level for a period of time then a notch or surf-bench develops. In regions with little tide the roof of the notch is about 30-40 cm about sea-level.

tures from further erosion. The occurrence of marine fossils on ancient platforms serves to distinguish them from terraces produced by faulting, and can be used to determine the age of the sea-level stand. Archaeological remains that were once at sea-level can also be used to determine the height and age of ancient sea-levels.[256]

Rivers and alluvium

Rivers are a major force in shaping the land. It is easy to underestimate their effect during the dry Mediterranean summer, but winter floods can rapidly reshape valleys. It is not only water that moves in a river, but also sediment, from clay particles to boulders. When deposited on land this material is called alluvium.

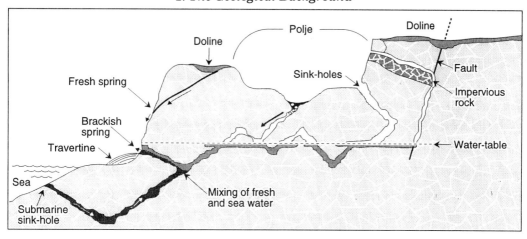

Fig. 1.10. Karst features. Rainwater or snow-melt is drained into dolines or sink-holes whence it flows underground, through fissures and caves, to reappear at karst springs.

The upper, steeper and straighter sections of rivers tend to erode their beds, and the eroded material is transported to the lower parts of the river where it is deposited to form alluvial plains. Rivers flowing across alluvial plains tend to follow a sinuous pattern, termed meandering after the river Meander (now the Büyük Menderes). Alas, this river now runs in a straight canal.

Rivers can cut down into old alluvial plains if the bed of the river is steepened by tectonic movements, a drop in sea-level or other causes. The old alluvial plain will be preserved as terraces on the sides of the valleys. Conversely, an increase in the amount of erosion in the upper parts of a river can rapidly bury old alluvial plains under new alluvium.

Limestone and marble (karst) landscapes

The ability of limestone and marble to dissolve in and crystallise from water has led to the development of a distinctive landscape called karst (Fig. 1.10), named after a region of Croatia where it was first described.[86] The gas carbon dioxide dissolves in water to produce a weak acid that can dissolve the calcite (and dolomite) in limestones and marbles. Calcite crystallises from these waters when the concentration of carbon dioxide in the water drops.

In karst regions there are few streams or rivers and most rain or snow-melt sinks directly down into the rocks, to appear as springs, commonly far away.

We start with a small-scale surface feature of limestones and marbles: the ridges and grooves produced by weathering. A great variety of different types have been described, but the most distinctive are razor-sharp ridges produced by solution of the limestone in rainwater. The effect occurs immediately after the raindrop hits the rock. Smoother grooves are formed underneath soils and sediments.

On a larger scale closed, cone-shaped basins 2-100 m deep and 10-1,000 m in diameter, commonly floored by sediments and soils, make up an important part of the surface of most karst regions, and give it a pitted relief. These basins are called dolines and may be widely separated or occur as swarms. Rain and snow-melt drain into dolines and then into the underlying rocks, hence they take the place of valleys in non-karst areas. Dolines form by solution of the underlying limestone along cracks, and the settling down of the smaller blocks. Solution may be enhanced by higher levels of carbon dioxide in the soils, produced by plant decay.

Dolines absorb rainwater, but rivers and streams disappear into sink-holes (swallow-holes). These may just be areas of loose sediments where the water sinks away, rather like dolines, or they may be caves in a cliff or holes in the ground. Most sink-holes develop from dolines. Sink-holes generally lead into cave systems, but these may not always be accessible.

Valleys are not completely absent from karst areas. Major rivers that originate outside the region can cross in a valley. Blind valleys end when the river drops into a sink-hole. Some valleys are normally dry, but may contain water when flow exceeds the capacity of the sink-holes.

Flowing water may dissolve the walls of cracks and faults to produce caves. Once established, caves can also be enlarged by the abrasive action of sediments in the water. In the upper parts of caves water commonly flows only in the lower part of the passage, and processes similar to those seen in rivers on the surface, such as meandering, beaches etc. may occur there. In the deeper parts water completely fills the caves, like water in a pipe. Here the cave tends to have a different shape: it is commonly rounded in section and much straighter.

Caves are guided in direction by existing structures in the rocks, such as joints and faults. However, most caves have one or more prominent levels, corresponding to ancient water levels in the cave system that were maintained for a long period. There are many reasons why solution should be most active near the water level, but the dominant effects are flow speed and the time available for reactions: below the water surface flow is slower, so that dissolved material is not removed so fast. Above the water level most of the rocks are not continually immersed in water, hence there is less opportunity for solution.

Although karst caves are formed by solution it is the opposite process, crystallisation, that has decorated them, and is the main reason for their interest. In most caves calcite crystallises in response to loss of carbon dioxide rather than evaporation of the water. A slow drip rate promotes formation of stalactites from the roof, and a faster rate favours production of stalagmites on the floor. Continuous flow produces sheets of calcite on the walls, called flowstone,

and curtains of rock from the roof. Seepage of water too slow to form drops, can produce weird shapes like springs, called helicites, and irregular branching forms 2-5 cm long, called cave coral. Water flowing along the floor also deposits calcite in areas where more carbon dioxide is lost. This occurs where water overflows a barrier, such as the edge of a pool. Deposition of calcite builds a small dam, and the pool deepens with time. Such processes can also occur on the surface, producing a series of pools and deposits of calcite called travertine. Most of the decorations in Greek caves formed when the region had a wetter climate, probably during the last glacial period.

Another distinctive feature of karst landscapes is the formation of large basins, known as poljes, surrounded by hills that slope quite steeply to a flat floor. No rivers or streams leave these basins, instead they are drained by sink-holes in the floor, or at the edge of the plain. Drainage is commonly inadequate so that many poljes are flooded in winter but dry in summer. Poljes commonly develop by differential erosion along contacts with less readily weathered rocks, or by tectonic movements along faults. Once they have started to form, the ponded water will dissolve away the limestone or marble of the floor, and the solution will be drained away into the sink-holes. This is why the floors are commonly so flat.

Water enters the rocks of a karst region at many points, but tends to leave at only a few major springs.[146] Some springs rise underneath alluvium, but others flow from an open cave or rise up a steep conduit to the surface. Loss of carbon dioxide from the waters as they leave the ground can lead to crystallisation of calcite and the production of travertine terraces. Some sink-holes can become spring outlets during heavy rains, especially those around poljes. Some springs debouche offshore in the sea.

Beach-rock

Many beaches in the Aegean have a gently shelving platform of well-cemented beach sand and gravel that resembles concrete (see Plate 1B). This is called beach-rock and it can form extremely rapidly, in 25 years or less. The sediments are commonly cemented by calcite, but the origin of the cement is not always clear.[115] Some may originate through evaporation of fresh groundwater in a process similar to that which produces caliche. It has also been suggested that the cement forms from evaporation of seawater, aided by small variations in the level of the sea or by mixing of sea and fresh water. In any case cementation takes place below the surface and the beach-rock is exposed by subsequent erosion.

2

Geological History of the Mediterranean

The Mediterranean has a very complex geological history, mostly spanning the last 200 million years. Interactions between the European/Asian and African continents have created and destroyed several seas, of which the Mediterranean is but the most recent. The geological complexity, the landscape and the climate of this region have long attracted geologists. The best compilation of their work, at least for the European side of the Mediterranean, is *The Geology of Europe*.[2] The geology of Greece and Turkey has also been treated in detail in two books,[127, 34] as have the mineral deposits.[172,24] Here we will give an outline of the geology of the Mediterranean, but will deal in more detail with the Aegean and adjacent areas. More details of the geology are given in the regional chapters 3-16.

The geological framework

The Mediterranean region has a complex internal geological history, but the external events that controlled the development of this region are simpler to explain, and we will start there. Our history begins 190 million years ago, in the Mid-Jurassic period. Although there are many rocks older than this in the region, we are uncertain of the position of the continents in earlier times, and hence cannot reconstruct the earlier history of plate tectonics.

The North Atlantic Ocean did not exist in the Early Jurassic period and both Africa (more correctly Gondwanaland: Africa with other continents) and Eurasia (Europe and Asia) were united with the North American continent to form a super-continent named Pangea (Fig. 2.1). Between the future continents of Africa and Eurasia there was a wedge-shaped ocean, named Tethys (after the daughter of the earth-goddess Gaia), which opened out to the east where it joined the other oceans. This state of affairs changed when the North Atlantic Ocean began to form about 190 million years ago.

A new plate margin started to form with the rifting of the continent along huge normal faults, following closely the position of an older ocean that had closed up to form the Appalachian, Caledonian and Scandinavian Mountains. New crust was created in the rift, forming a new ocean, the North Atlantic. Initially this rifting was concentrated in the south, separating Africa from North America, and moving it to the east. The position of continental rifting, and new ocean formation, moved slowly to the north, like a tear, and by about 110 million years ago Eurasia had started to separate from North America.

During the next period, the southern parts of the Atlantic Ocean continued to form more rapidly than those in the north, forcing the African plate to rotate in a clockwise direction about an axis in the Atlantic off Gibraltar, closing up the Tethys Ocean. This rotation slowed down considerably when the Arabian part of the African continent hit Eurasia, producing the mountains of Turkey, and has now almost ceased. Of course, within this framework there is much detail. For example, continental fragments originally attached to Africa, such as much of Italy and parts of Greece, have broken off, crossed the closing ocean and hit Eurasia. It is this part of the story that will be expanded below. But first we must deal with some of the special terms commonly used in Alpine and Aegean geology.

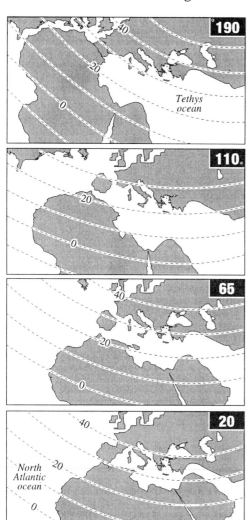

Fig. 2.1. Overall evolution of the African, Eurasian and North American continents during the last 190 million years.[56] Dashed lines indicate the approximate latitudes. The modern outlines of the continents are shown here so that places may be easily located, but these were not the actual coastlines at the time.

Isopic zones and massifs

The overall geology of the Alpine region has traditionally been described in terms of isopic zones and massifs. Isopic zones are groups of widespread rocks that share a common history, both in the ancient environments of deposition of sediments (deep ocean, shallow sea, continent, etc.) and their faulting and folding. They were originally continental fragments, islands, oceanic ridges or parts of the ocean floor. Isopic zones may be hundreds of kilometres long, and up to several kilometres thick. They are bounded by faults, commonly shallow-dipping thrust faults, formed during regional compression, and are hence nappes or groups of nappes. These compressions have also stacked the isopic zones up onto each other and against the massifs.

Massifs are blocks of metamorphic and plutonic rocks, formerly assumed to be much older and more resistant to folding and faulting than adjacent sediments. Nowadays the distinction between massifs and rocks of the other isopic zones is not so clear: some of the metamorphism is quite recent, and parts of the massifs may not be much older than adjacent sedimentary rocks. Massifs are better considered as slightly lower levels of the continental crust exposed by faulting or erosion.

The isopic zones and massifs of the Aegean were once a series of continents, continental margins, deep troughs and ocean basins (Figs. 2.2, 2.3, 2.4). The present geographic distribution of these zones is now very different as they were piled up on top of each other during the Alpine crustal compression (see later). The various groups of rocks will be described in order from the 'internal' zones of the north-east to the 'external' zones of the south-west.

The most extensive area of metamorphic and plutonic rocks in the Aegean region is the Rhodope massif in Greek Thrace and Bulgaria, and the adjacent Serbo-Macedonian massif to the west (Fig. 2.2). These massifs may continue under the Thrace basin into north-eastern Turkey, as the Sakarya zone (or Western Pontides). All these massifs have long and complex histories, which may stretch back into the Precambrian epoch over 600 million years ago. They were partly metamorphosed and faulted during the Alpine compressions. More recently granites have been emplaced and volcanic rocks erupted.

The Vardar (Axios) isopic zone lies to the west of the massifs, and continues northwards into the former Yugoslavia (Fig. 2.2). To the

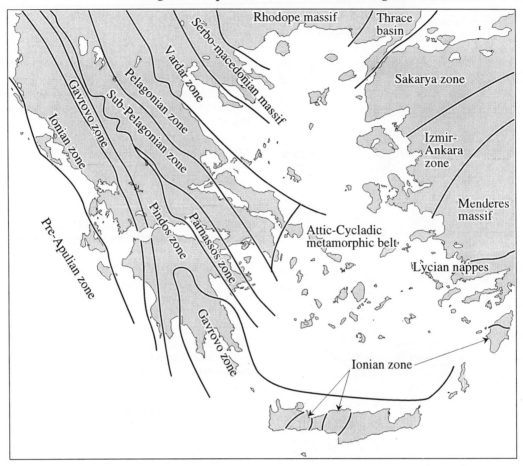

Fig. 2.2. Isopic zones and massifs of the Aegean region.

east it sweeps under the Aegean Sea, possibly to reappear in Chios. It may continue on the Turkish mainland as the Izmir-Ankara zone. It is a complex zone that has been sub-divided by some geologists into separate zones. However, it is dominated by Mesozoic deep-water sediments and ophiolites, and is hence an old ocean basin, part of Tethys. Within this basin were a number of older continental fragments, expressed as ridges.

The next isopic zone is the Pelagonian, which is exposed in much of eastern peninsular Greece. During the Triassic and Jurassic periods shallow-water limestones were deposited on this continental fragment, in an environment similar to that of the Bahamas today.

Some geologists consider that the Pelagonian zone continues to the south as the Attic-Cycladic metamorphic belt (or massif). The oldest rocks are schists, gneisses and granites some of which may be Palaeozoic. However, many of the rocks are similar in age to those of the adjacent zones, and some metamorphism was the result of the Alpine compressions.

The Menderes massif starts near the Aegean coast and extends far into central Turkey (Fig. 2.2). It is geologically similar to the Attic-Cycladic metamorphic belt but also shows some affinities with metamorphic rocks in Africa. It is not clear if it was separate from the Attic-Cycladic metamorphic belt, or merely a lateral extension.

The Sub-Pelagonian zone is the great belt of ophiolites and associated rocks (limestones, cherts) of the Aegean, and continues to the north into Albania (Fig. 2.2). It may continue to the south-east within the Lycian nappes of Turkey. These rocks were originally part of a continental margin, between the Pelagonian continent and the Pindos Ocean. The region was lifted up during the Late Jurassic and Early Cretaceous. After a period of emergence, reef limestones were deposited during the Late Cretaceous. During the Oligocene and Miocene a deep continental trough developed, which filled up with up to 5 km of continental and shallow-water sediments, called molasse, and deep water flysch sediments.

The Parnassos zone is only exposed in south-central Greece. For most of the Triassic to the Palaeocene this small continental fragment was under shallow water, and limestones were formed. When the region was dry land tropical weathering produced bauxite deposits. These rocks were followed by flysch, which terminated with conglomerates in the late Eocene, indicating nearby mountain-building.

The Pindos zone crops out in central Greece and the Peloponnese, but is much more extensive as it underlies or rode over much of the other zones. Its sediments were mostly deposited in a deep oceanic trough, but there are no ophiolites in this zone. During the early part of its history it was a true ocean basin.

The Gavrovo zone (in places called the Tripolitza zone) is narrow along the coast of Albania and in central Greece, but widens out in the Peloponnese. Like the Parnassos and Pelagonian zones, this region was a continental fragment for the early part of its history. Initially, during the Mesozoic, thick shallow-water limestones were deposited. However, in late Eocene times mountains had been formed and they shed flysch sediments onto the limestones, almost completely covering them up.

The Ionian zone comprises much of Epirus, and parts of the Ionian islands and Peloponnese. Like the Pindos zone, in early times this zone was an area of deep water, but probably floored by thin continental crust. Again it contains Mesozoic limestones deposited in a trough. As in the Gavrovo zone, and for the

same reasons, flysch makes its appearance in the Eocene.

The most external (westerly) zone is the Pre-Apulian, and it barely touches our region. It comprises little deformed sediments of both deep and shallow water origin, and is really part of the Apulian platform of Italy. It is a block of continental crust.

To these zones and massifs we must add the Thrace basin of north-western Turkey. It is not a true isopic zone as it was formed after most of the Alpine compressions, in response to movements of the North Anatolian fault zone, which divides the Eurasian plate from the Turkish plate. A large thickness of sediment was deposited here from the Early Tertiary onwards, but recently sedimentation has ceased and depression of the crust has shifted southwards to the Sea of Marmara.

Thus overall the various zones and massifs represent an alternation of micro-continents, deep troughs on continental crust and true ocean basins (Fig. 2.4). Next we will trace the interactions between these units and their assembly into the present Aegean region.

The geological development of the Aegean

There have been many different reconstructions of the history of the Mediterranean region, but here we will follow that of Dercourt et al. [56] which is the most comprehensive. The overall history is that of the closure of an ocean basin filled with islands and underwater ridges and the thrusting of each component onto the adjacent parts generally to the north and east (Figs. 2.3, 2.4).

In the Early Jurassic, 190 million years ago, the Rhodope and Serbo-Macedonian massifs and the Sakarya zone lay along the north shore of the Tethys Ocean. These rocks are considered to be the southern margin of the Eurasian continent. To the south a subduction zone plunged northwards under the continent. All the other zones lay further south, adjacent to the African continent. Between was a wedge of true ocean, part of the Tethys Ocean.

The Pelagonian, Parnassos and Gavrovo zones were continental platforms, covered by

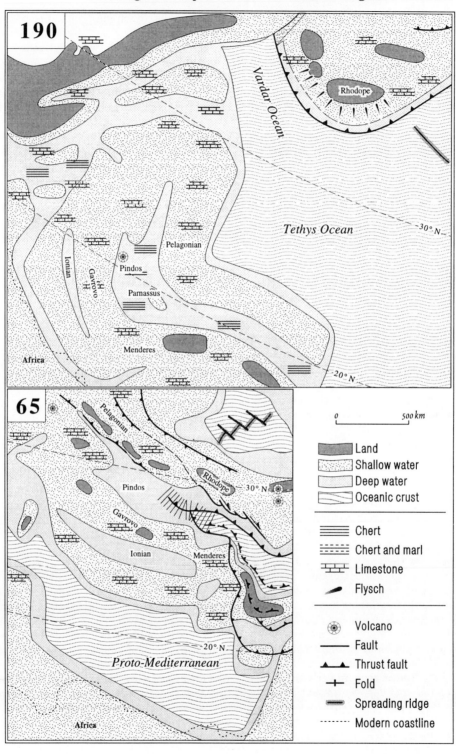

Fig. 2.3. Ancient positions of the isopic zones of the Aegean region for 190, 110, 65 and 20 million years ago.[56] Most of these zones, except the Rhodope massif, originally lay adjacent to the African continent. The abundant limestones of the Aegean region formed in these warm, mostly shallow, seas. Convergence of Africa and Eurasia forced the Tethys sea to close up, but at the same time a new ocean basin, the early Mediterranean, opened up to the south. Expansion of the basin separated the Aegean isopic zones from Africa and helped to force them against Eurasia.

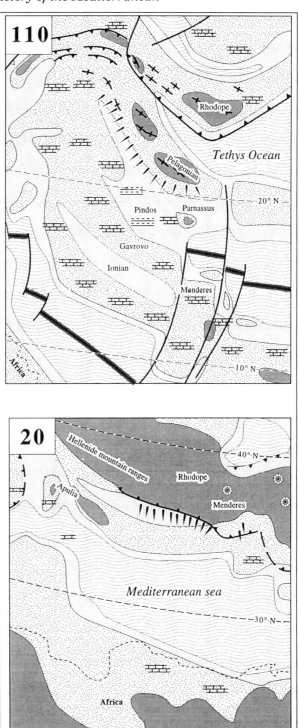

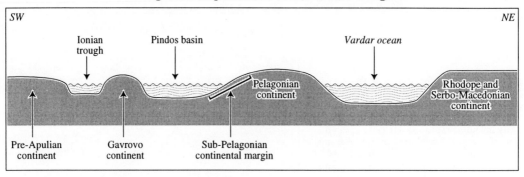

Fig. 2.4. Schematic section across the Aegean region before compression. The Pre-Apulian, Gavrovo and Pelagonian continental zones were covered with shallow seas for much of the time.

shallow, warm tropical seas, where limestones were deposited in an environment similar to that of the Bahamas today (Fig. 2.4). The Ionian zone was a deep trough on the African continental shelf and the Pindos basin was floored by true oceanic crust. The Sub-Pelagonian zone was the continental margin adjacent to this basin. This arrangement was relatively stable until the end of the Jurassic (130 million years ago) when parts of the Sub-Pelagonian continental margin and Pindos basin were thrust eastwards onto the Pelagonian continental platform.

A major change had occurred by the Mid-Cretaceous, about 110 million years ago; a new plate boundary had formed south of the Pre-Apulian zone and an ocean basin, the Proto-Mediterranean, was growing. This new ocean detached from Africa the zones that would later form the Aegean region and Apulia (southern Italy). As there was relatively little change in the positions of Eurasia and Africa, the Tethys Ocean basin to the north had to close up. It was partly subducted beneath Eurasia and partly piled up against the massifs as in the Vardar zone. As the Pelagonian zone neared Eurasia the regional compression was converted into uplift by movements along thrust faults. Parts of the Pelagonian zone above water shed flysch sediments into the Pindos Ocean basin to the south-west. Similarly the Parnassos continental fragment was raised above sea-level and intense tropical weathering produced bauxite and laterite deposits.

During the next period the Aegean isopic zones were forced to the north by expansion of the ocean to the south. Ocean basins were subducted and/or thrust westwards over the adjacent zones. Continental fragments were similarly stacked, one on top of the other. By 35 million years ago all that remained of the vast platform once attached to the African mainland were the Ionian and Pre-Apulian zones. Even the Menderes massif had been welded onto Eurasia. By 20 million years ago the Ionian zone had almost been completely consumed, and continental crust, albeit thinner than normal, linked Apulia and the Hellenide mountain ranges.

The overall process of regional compression has continued in the Ionian islands to this day, but elsewhere in the Aegean major regional expansion became important. This expansion has shaped much of the landscape of the Aegean and continues today.

Subduction of oceanic crust northwards beneath the Aegean started during the Miocene, or possibly a little earlier, initially along an east/west line (Fig. 2.5). The crust above the subduction zone arched upwards to form the non-volcanic Hellenic arc, now represented by the islands of Crete, Karpathos and Rhodes, the western edge of the Peloponnese, and south-eastern Turkey.[13] Further north melting of the subducted slab, and the overlying mantle, produced the volcanoes of the South Aegean volcanic arc and the more diffuse, but important, Early Miocene volcanic rocks in the western Aegean and Turkey. Volcanism con-

60 to 16 million
years ago

12 to 5 million
years ago

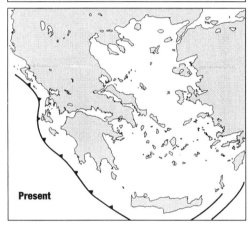

Present

Fig. 2.5. Evolution of the Hellenic arc over the last 60 million years.[137] Initially the arc ran almost straight, east/west. The curvature developed by expansion of the crust north of the Aegean arc, forming the present Aegean Sea.

tinues now on the islands of Thera (Santorini) and Nisyros.

Crustal extension associated with the subduction was concentrated in the region north of Crete, above the subduction zone, so that the initially straight subduction zone was inflated into the curve we see today (Fig. 2.5).[137] This extension was coupled to overall plate motions, so that a large part of the region has experienced Neogene extension. At the surface the crust has responded to this extension by developing grabens and horsts. The orientation of these structures is rather variable, but many are approximately north-west/south-east, al-

though some of the youngest faults in the Peloponnese and Crete are north/south. It is these grabens and horsts that have produced many of the mountains and valleys, as well as the islands.

Mention should be made of an unusual event that occurred about six million years ago: The Mediterranean sea almost completely dried up.[117] This happened when tectonic forces closed up the Straits of Gibraltar. Rivers flowing into the basin, principally from the Black Sea, were insufficient to maintain sea-level and the sea dried out, except for a few saline lakes like the modern Dead Sea. There may even have been a salty waterfall at Gibraltar, also feeding the lakes. Evaporation of water from the lakes produced deposits of gypsum and other minerals.

The present plate tectonic configuration of the Aegean region is rather complex and the details are much disputed (Fig. 2.6, Plate 2).[260] The African plate is moving north-east with respect to Europe and descending along a subduction zone underneath the Aegean plate. To the east the plate motions are almost parallel to the plate boundary, hence the relative motion is taken up by strike-slip faulting. Still further east, towards Cyprus, the subduction zone resumes. In the north the Anatolian plate that carries much of Turkey is moving westwards with respect to Europe, and most of this motion is taken up by a strike-slip fault, the North Anatolian Fault zone. This fault runs across the northern Aegean Sea, as the North Aegean Trough, and fades out somewhere near Volos. The motion is also taken up by a number of parallel faults to the south in western Turkey and the Aegean. There are no simple plate boundaries within peninsular Greece to link up the major structures; motions are shared between a number of smaller faults of all types.

Geologically recent events

During the last cool interval of the glacial period, about 130,000 to 20,000 years ago, the climate of the Aegean was moist and cool. Glaciers were restricted to the highest mountains on the Greek and Turkish mainlands, and the island of Crete. Sea-level was considerably

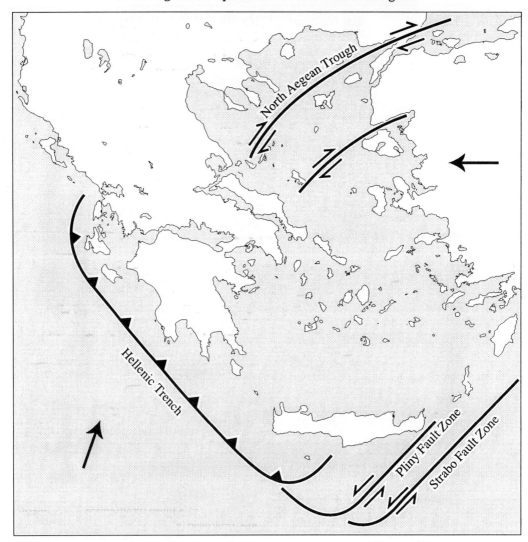

Fig. 2.6. The present-day plate tectonics of the region (after 260).

lower that it is today, and hence the river-beds were steeper and there was rapid erosion. Mountains were deeply incised and broad, flat valleys were developed. It is this landscape that we see in Greece today, modified by postglacial effects. Many of the red and brown soils were produced during this period.

At the end of the last glacial period the warming was accompanied by a rapid increase in sea-level. The sea invaded the valleys, form-ing deep inlets, which were rapidly filled in by sediments transported by the rivers. The alluvial sediments that fill most Mediterranean valleys have been divided into the 'older' and 'younger' fills, originally thought to have been two synchronous events.[277] However, it is clear that in many places there are several different younger fills, which are not synchronous. The older fill was produced by erosion associated with the post-glacial warming, but the cause of

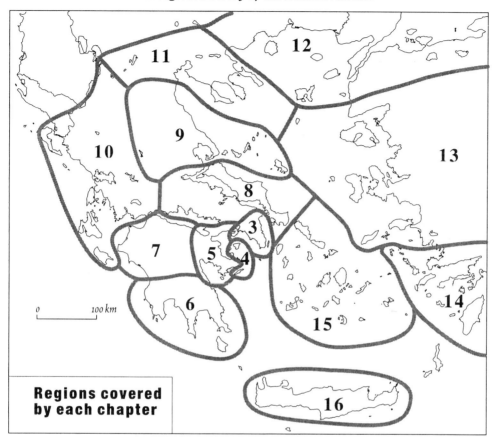

Fig. 2.7. The regions covered by Chapters 3 to 16.

the younger fill(s) is more problematical. It was originally suggested that it was due to the climate becoming drier, but there is little evidence for significant changes over the whole region.[191,235,237] A more likely cause is deforestation produced by people and maintained by grazing animals.[270,271]

3

Attica

Attica is currently the wealthiest and most densely populated part of Greece. It consists principally of a number of interconnected plains, floored by alluvium and Pleistocene sediments, and cut off to the north-west by the great mass of Mt Parnes (Fig. 3.1; Plate 3A). The Central Plain around Athens is bounded on the north by Mt Parnes, on the north-east by Mt Penteli, on the south-east by Mt Hymettos, and on the west by Mt Aigaleos. It connects with the smaller plains of Marathon on the north-east, Eleusis (the Thriasian Plain) on the north-west, and the Mesogeia on the south. The indented coastline provides a number of good harbours, of which Piraeus is by far the best. There are few rivers, apart from the Kephissos and the Ilissos, which run through Athens partly underground; all are dry in the summer.

The soil is generally poor. It is unsuited to stock breeding and, in general, to agriculture, except for olives, vines and figs. The territory is, however, rich in limestone and in the marble of Mts Penteli and Hymettos; in addition, there was formerly (until it was worked out) a copious source of silver and lead in the hills of Lavrion. Finally, Attica was (and is) blessed with generous supplies of potter's clay, to which the Athenians surely owed their pre-eminence in the craft of pottery. The best clay came from deposits near Athens, especially at the northern suburb of Amarousi (where it is still worked), and on Ayios Kosmas (ancient Cape Kolias), near the present airport.[130]

In early times Attica was made up of a number of independent communities. There is probably an element of truth in the legend that they were brought under Athenian control by the hero Theseus at about 1300 BC; but the process was probably not completed till the seventh century BC. Thereafter, the history of Attica is inextricably bound up with that of Athens.

The geological structure of Attica, as in much of Greece, is dominated by a series of nappes stacked up during Alpine compressional movements. The oldest rocks in the region occur in one of the higher nappes along the north-west borders of Attica, in the mountains of Aigaleos and Parnes. These mountains are dominantly made of Triassic limestones of the Pelagonian zone similar to those occurring as far north as Thessaly and western Macedonia.

The southern and eastern parts of Attica are underlain by schists and marbles of the Attic-Cycladic metamorphic belt similar to those in southern Euboea and the Cycladic islands. These marbles make up Mts Hymettos and Penteli, as well as the hills around Marathon and Lavrion.

The next highest nappe is made of schists, cherts and ophiolites, which is in turn overlain by lightly metamorphosed and unmetamorphosed limestones and flysch sediments of Cretaceous to Eocene age. The uppermost part of this series is called the Athens schist (see below).[173]

During the Neogene period compressional forces associated with Alpine mountain-building ceased. Erosion and faulting produced a series of basins which were flooded by the sea and filled with sandstone, shale, clay and limestone. These rocks are still in their original places of deposition, except that they have been raised above sea-level by geologically recent tectonic movements.

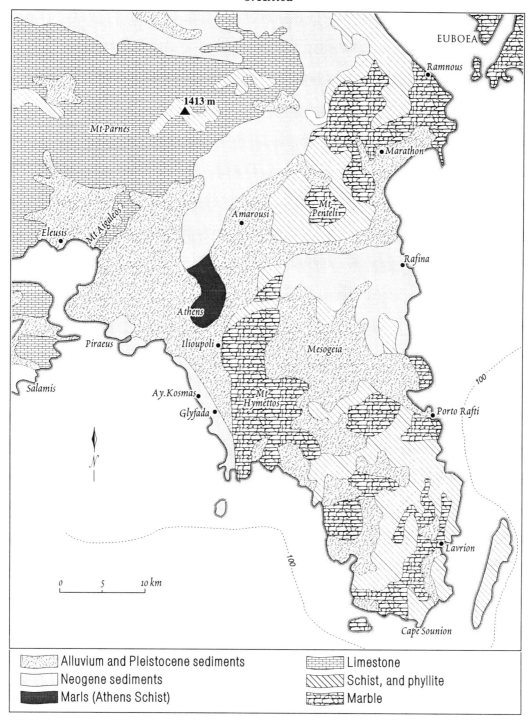

Fig. 3.1. Attica and Athens.

EUBOEA

1413 m

Mt·Parnes

Ramnous

Marathon

Amarousi

Mt. Penteli

Rafina

Eleusis

Mt·Aigaleos

Athens

Piraeus

Ilioupoli

Mesogeia

Salamis

Ay.Kosmas

Glyfada

Mt Hymettos

Porto Rafti

N

100

Lavrion

Cape Sounion

0   5   10 km

100

Alluvium and Pleistocene sediments

Neogene sediments

Marls (Athens Schist)

Limestone

Schist, and phyllite

Marble

Athens

The site of Athens has been inhabited for approximately 8,000 years, and from at least the beginning of Mycenaean times, around 1600 BC, it has been one of the greatest cities of Greece. Like Mycenae and Tiryns, Mycenaean Athens possessed Cyclopaean walls, a monumental entrance, a postern gate, a royal palace, and a secret water-supply. It is also to this period that the legends of the exploits of Theseus refer.

Around 1000 BC the Dark Ages were coming to an end in Athens, and the city became increasingly prosperous, reaching a climax between 600 and 500 BC. During much of this time Athenian pottery was the best in Greece and was widely exported for some 700 years. Another source of wealth was the silver from the mines at Lavrion, especially from about 500 BC. In 490 and 480 the Athenians defeated attacks by the Persians at Marathon and Salamis. Then followed fifty glorious years, which included the rule of the great statesman Pericles. But the Peloponnesian War, 431-404 BC, broke the power of Athens for ever. Henceforward, whether under Hellenistic or Roman rule, Athens, though artistically and intellectually pre-eminent, was politically reduced to the second rank. Neglected by the Byzantines, it regained a little authority under the Franks after the Fourth Crusade of 1204, but sank even lower when the Turks invaded in 1456. In 1834, however, Athens was designated capital of the newly liberated Greece.

The city of Athens stands in a great topographic basin surrounded by Mts Parnes, Aigaleos, Penteli and Hymettos (Figs. 3.1, 3.2). This basin was formed partly by faulting and partly by the erosion of the soft 'Athens schist', which outcrops or underlies the veneer of younger sediments in much of this area. The Athens schist is a slightly metamorphosed series of Cretaceous marls and shales, with lenses of sandstone and limestone. It is not a true schist by modern English usage.[173]

Many of the hills in the eastern part of the Athens basin, such as Lykabettos hill, the Areopagus, the Acropolis and the Philopappos hill, are made of Late Cretaceous limestones (Fig.

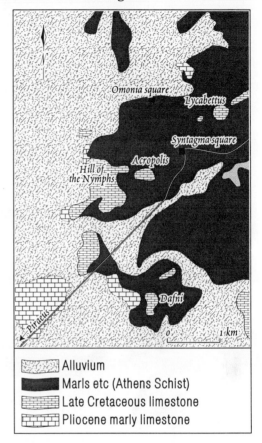

Fig. 3.2. Central Athens.

3.2). There is some debate about the geological position of these rocks, but most geologists consider that they are the upper part of the Athens schist series of rocks. They may not have been originally continuous over the area and minor tectonic movements have detached these stronger blocks from the weak underlying marls of the Athens Schist. Steep faults have since then dissected the limestones into smaller blocks.

The Athens basin contains a number of different Neogene sedimentary rocks originally formed in shallow lakes, such as limestones, marls and clays. The clay deposits were the basis of the ancient Athenian pottery industry, and are still exploited today. Finally, much of the central and western parts of the basin have been covered with a layer of alluvium up to 20

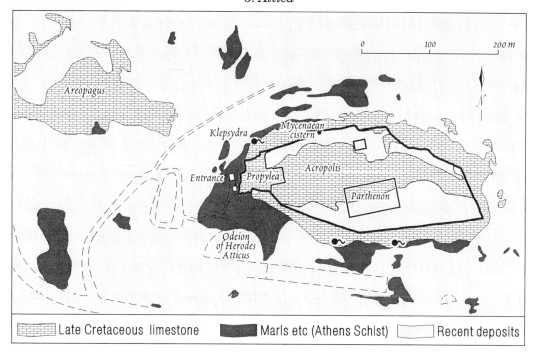

Fig. 3.3. The Acropolis and Areopagus (after 9).

m thick. Much of this deposition occurred during infrequent floods in the recent past.

The Acropolis

The Acropolis hill is a block of Late Cretaceous limestone resting on the marls and sandstones of the Athens schist rock series (Figs. 3.3, 3.4), which can be seen on the approach to the main entrance to the site, and just beneath the Propylea.[9, 10, 264] The grey limestone is well exposed on the top of the hill. It has closely spaced joints and some of the older fissures have been filled with red marl or coarse calcite crystals. The top of the Acropolis hill has been levelled with artificial fill up to 14 m thick which is

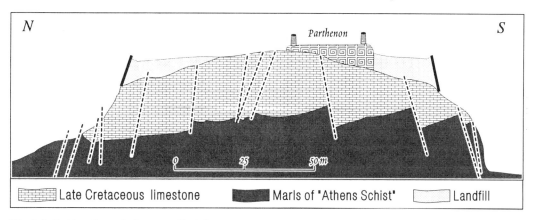

Fig. 3.4. Section through the acropolis (after 9).

retained by the walls.

Rainwater seeping into the faults and fractures on the upper part of the Acropolis has dissolved away the limestone to form caves and clefts. Such caves can be seen in the north-west and southern slopes of the hill (Plate 3B), but others, probably mostly choked with debris, undoubtedly exist in the interior of the hill. Much of this percolating water does not penetrate the underlying marls, which are less permeable, but reaches the surface at a number of springs around the base of the hill. One such spring, the Klepsydra, originally issued from a small cave in the north-west cliffs and attracted Neolithic settlers to the area. It was in constant use thereafter and has been subsequently considerably modified.

Towards the north-western part of the Acropolis percolating water has enlarged a fault in the limestone to produce a cave or cleft about 35 m deep. Percolating water fills the base of this cave to a depth of several metres, but the rate of inflow of water is low. The water level is about 4-5 m above that of the Klepsydra spring to the west. The Mycenaeans constructed a means of access to this water source but appear to have used it for only 25 years or so before it was abandoned. It is possible that the rate of inflow was too low to be useful.

Flow from these springs was probably stronger in antiquity. This may reflect climatic change, but is more strongly controlled by modifications to the geography of the hill. In the past the presence of plants, soil and loose materials on top of the bedrock would have retarded run-off so that the water could have time to be adsorbed. Recently, infiltration has been all but eliminated by sealing all the open cracks and fissures on the hill with cement. This has been done to reduce the rate of erosion, now enhanced by acid rain.

The sacred hill of the Acropolis was never defaced with quarries, but limestone for many of its buildings and the walls was quarried from several of the adjacent hills, including the Hill of the Nymphs.[57, 290] The foundations of many of the buildings on the Acropolis were made of limestone from Piraeus (see below) and Aegina. Marble from Penteli was used for the construction of all the great buildings of the

fifth century, including the Parthenon (see below). Limestone and conglomerate from Kara, near the base of Mt Hymettos (see below), were also extensively used.

Piraeus

Piraeus, the port of Athens, comprises three harbours (Fig. 3.5): the principal harbour, Kantharos ('Goblet'); a small circular harbour to the south, Zea (formerly Pashalimani); and another small circular harbour east of Zea, Mikrolimano (in antiquity Munichia, recently Tourklimano). At first Piraeus was not used as a port, since the Athenians preferred to beach their ships along Phaleron Bay. But in 493 BC the Athenian statesman Themistocles started to make the whole of Piraeus into a fortified port, joined to Athens by walls. The task was completed a generation later by Pericles, who also rebuilt the city on a chess-board pattern. The walls were destroyed in 86 BC by the Romans, and the port lost its importance until comparatively recent times.

The town of Piraeus stands on a series of low hills south-west of Athens. Although Late Cretaceous limestone underlies two small hills to

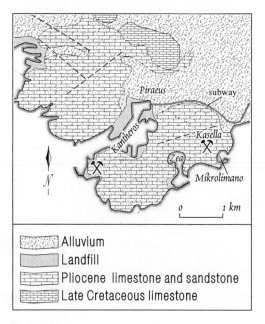

Fig. 3.5. Piraeus.

30

the north, the larger hills to the south are made of Pliocene marly limestone and sandstone. These rocks also occur along the coast to the north-west and south-east, past the airport. During the Pleistocene these rocks were uplifted about 80-100 m and eroded to form the present-day topography.

The soft Pliocene limestones, known as Aktites Lithos in antiquity, were quarried around the top of Kasella hill north-east of Mikrolimano harbour and also near the southern approaches to the main harbour. This rock is easily cut and hence was used extensively in Athens, especially in the sub-structures of the buildings of the Acropolis. It was also used in the Agora at the Stoa of Attalus, and indeed, the ancient quarries were reopened for the reconstruction of this building.

Eleusis

The present-day surroundings of Eleusis, polluted by industry, are far from prepossessing; but from 1500 BC to about AD 400 it was one of the great religious centres of Greece, second in importance only to Delphi. Here was the Sanctuary of Demeter, where the Eleusinian Mysteries were celebrated every September. The rites of initiation were kept secret, and we know nothing about them, except that the initiate was promised wealth in this world and

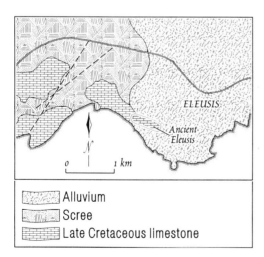

Fig. 3.6. Eleusis.

happiness in the next.

Eleusis is situated on the coast, in the southern part of a Neogene sedimentary basin that lies south of the Parnes range and west of Mt Aigaleos (Figs. 3.1, 3.6). Within this basin weathering and erosion of the sediments has produced fertile soils. In the western part of the basin there are a number of low hills of Late Cretaceous limestone that protrude through the Pleistocene sediments. Much of the ancient city of Eleusis was constructed on one such hill.

The acropolis hill rises to 63 m and runs parallel to the coast for about 1,500 m. It is composed of limestone and marl, variable in colour from pale yellow to grey. Some of the rainwater falling on the hill is adsorbed and reappears as springs and in shallow wells around the edge of the hill. One such water source is the sacred well called Kallichron, near the Greater Propylea.

Eleusis was also the source of a dark grey to black limestone used as a decorative element on some buildings in Athens. It was possibly extracted from a quarry on the north slope of the acropolis hill.[72]

Mt Penteli and Mt Hymettos

Mt Penteli (1,106 m) is part of a 20-km-long sector of metamorphic rocks north-east of Athens, extending past Marathon to the coast opposite Euboea (see Fig. 3.1). Mt Hymettos (1,037 m) is part of another sector of metamorphic rocks to the south-east of Athens. Both these mountains are part of the Attic-Cycladic metamorphic belt (see Fig. 2.2 and Chapter 15). Both schists and marbles occur here, but the marbles are most resistant to erosion and stand up much higher as mountains.

In both mountains there are two main marble layers:[162] the geologically upper layer is predominantly grey, while the lower is predominantly white (Fig. 3.7). Paradoxically the lower marble is exposed near the main summit of Penteli, and the upper marble is at lower elevations. The grey colour is produced by the presence of minute amounts of graphite, formed by metamorphism of plant remains in the original limestone. Some parts of the marble beds contain muscovite, which consid-

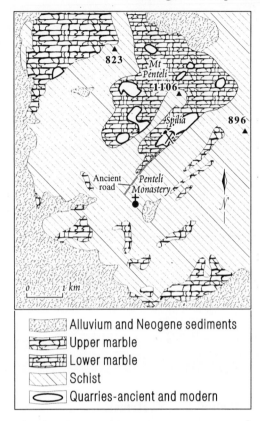

Fig. 3.7. Mt Penteli (after 162 and other sources).

erably reduces the resistance of the rock to weathering.

Although both white and grey marble occur on both mountains, in antiquity the best white marble was obtained from Penteli, and the best grey from Hymettos, a fact which has misled many modern scholars to refer (incorrectly) to the grey as 'Hymettan' and the white as 'Pentelic'.

The modern quarries are all around the main peak of Mt Penteli, and have partly obliterated the ancient quarries, which lie mostly to the south of the principal summit. About 25 of them have been found situated one above the other, many linked by an ancient, paved quarry road. One of the larger quarries, Spilia, about one third of the way up Penteli, is thought to have been the source of the marble for the Parthenon.

Although Pentelic marble can be very pure,

joints are relatively closely spaced, which restricts the maximum size of the blocks that could be extracted. This does not appear to have been a problem in classical times, but the Romans used other sources of marble for their larger pieces.

The ancient quarries for the grey marble on Hymettos are on the west side, near the former monastery of Karyes, below the Kakovevma gorge. It was not much used before the third century BC, but was quite popular in Roman times.

Two different rocks quarried near Ilioupoli (Kara), at the base of Mt Hymettos, were used for the foundations of many of the buildings in Athens.[290, 57] A Pliocene yellowish-grey freshwater limestone was mainly extracted during the sixth to fourth centuries BC.[72] A second rock was conglomerate formed by cementation of pebbles in alluvial cones shed off Mt Hymettos.

On both Mts Penteli and Hymettos weathering of the marble has produced a thin red soil (terra rossa) that has mostly been removed by erosion and redeposited in the valleys. The paucity of the soil has been compounded by the porosity of the rock to produce very poor conditions for plant growth, unsuitable for trees and most crops. By way of exception, the highly aromatic shrubs on Hymettos produced, and still produce, some of the best honey in Greece.

Marathon

The Bay of Marathon lies 42 km north-east of Athens and is famous for the battle fought there in 490 BC. The Persian army, some 25,000 strong, disembarked in the Bay with the intention of marching on Athens; for safety, they moved their ships to the eastern end of the Bay. Meanwhile an Athenian force of about 10,000 men set out for Marathon, where they were joined by a contingent from Plataea. They encamped in the foothills of Mt Stavrokoraki and waited until the Persians should withdraw their cavalry. When this happened they gave battle and soundly defeated the Persians. Altogether, 6,400 Persians were killed, many being drowned in the Great Marsh while trying to reach their ships. The Athenians lost 192; they were buried in a mound on the battlefield which still exists.

The Marathon plain lies at the foot of mountains of schist and marble of the Attic-Cycladic metamorphic belt (see Fig. 3.1). They rise steeply from the plain, suggesting that subsidence is still occurring to maintain this sharp relief against erosion. The straits separating Euboea from the mainland, including the gulf to the south-east of Marathon, are active grabens (see Corinth in Chapter 5) and the Plain of Marathon is, therefore, probably an extension of these structures into the mainland.

The plain is typical of other coastal plains in Greece and consists of alluvial fans, formed by the transport of sediment in torrents from the mountains, descending into a marsh (now mostly drained) which is separated from the sea by a scrub-covered sand and gravel barrier.[20] The plain is divided by the Charadra river which formerly meandered across the plain, but has now been channelled. Flow of this river has been reduced by the creation of the Marathon Lake reservoir, and the diversion of the waters to Athens, but it is not likely to have been a significant river in antiquity. Sediment samples have shown that the plain has alternated between marine and estuary conditions. In 490 BC the coastline in the eastern part of the bay was located further inland by 500 m and the north-eastern part of the plain was a densely vegetated muddy marsh. This is the Great Marsh in which many of the invading Persians died.

Lavrion

Lavrion is one of the best-known mining areas in Greece. Although silver was extracted here as early as Mycenaean times (1600-1100 BC) the really rich veins were not discovered or exploited before the fifth century BC. Lavrion then became the principal source of silver for Greece. That produced in these mines was used in the minting of silver coins, which were the source of much of the wealth of ancient Athens, as well as for plate and statuary. The lead by-product was widely exported throughout the ancient Greek world, and has been found in western Turkey and Egypt.[97] Lead was used for

Alluvium
Upper schists and phyllites
Marble in upper schists
Upper marble
Mica schists
Lower marble
Granite
x x x x Areas of ancient mines

Fig. 3.8. Lavrion and Sounion (after 171).

anchoring iron clamps, covering the hulls of ships, and for making sinkers for fishing lines and standard weights. It was added to bronze to improve fluidity for casting and for the attractive patina that such alloys develop. In Roman times plumbing became its most important use.[188] After this time mining activity declined and ceased altogether by the time of Christ. Activity recommenced at the end of the nineteenth century, but has now ceased.

The deposits were formed in two different series of metamorphic rocks (Fig. 3.8).[171, 44, 95, 97] The sequence starts in the Attic-Cycladic metamorphic belt with the lower marble, exposed in the west. This is overlain by mica schists, that then pass into an upper marble unit. Over this package have been thrust Jurassic schists and phyllites, with some marble. All these rocks are cut by a Miocene intrusion of granite and its associated dykes.

The ore occurs as replacements of the marble near the contact with the schists and intrusions. The primary ore consists of galena (lead sulphide), which contains the silver as an impurity, together with sphalerite and pyrite. Near to the surface these minerals have been oxidised and hydrated to form oxide and carbonate minerals of the same metals. The ore mined in ancient times contained up to 50% galena, and the lead smelted from this ore had 0.1-0.4% silver. Minor amounts of other metals, such as arsenic and gold, are associated with these ores, and it has been suggested that Lavrion may have been an important ancient source of copper.[96] Among other by-products was the flue-dust of the smelters, which was occasionally used as a medicament.[188] However, the 'emeralds' reported by Pliny are only zinc carbonate, an alteration product of the ore.

The ores crystallised from low to medium temperature watery solutions that were expelled during the crystallisation of granite intrusions beneath the region. These fluids migrated along existing cracks, such as the margins of the dykes and the thrust faults, and reacted with the marbles to form the ores.

The ancient mines are very extensive and over 2,000 shafts have been found. Most of the ore appears to have been processed locally and the remains of the ore washing facilities have been excavated in the Agrileza valley. 'Washing' of the ore was the process of removing the associated minerals, which did not contain metal. These are generally lighter than the ore and so could be separated in a current of water (Plate 4). It has been estimated that 1-2 million tonnes of lead and 8,000 tonnes of silver were produced from these mines in antiquity.[188]

The Lavrion mines have produced some fine mineral specimens, especially of secondary minerals such as smithsonite, adamite and annabergite, but this region is principally known by mineral collectors for its secondary lead slag products. In antiquity, slag from lead smelting was dumped in the sea, principally around the town of Lavrion, where it has reacted with seawater during the last 2,000 years. The most common new mineral is aragonite, but a large number of other products occur, principally as minute crystals in former gas bubbles in the slag, including laurionite, named after this region.[140]

Cape Sounion

Cape Sounion looks out over the Aegean sea to the Cyclades and is part of the same geological unit. The bedrock here is marble, geologically similar to that of Mts Penteli and Hymettos to the north and the islands of Naxos and Paros to the south. The temple of Poseidon was constructed of a grey-veined white marble, which was quarried at Agrileza 3 km to the north, a place also famous for its silver mines (see Lavrion).

4

The Islands of the Saronic Gulf, and Methana

The Saronic Gulf is, for the most part, a Neogene graben. It is closely related to the Gulf of Corinth graben on the other side of the isthmus of Corinth (Fig. 5.1). Both are similar in age and both are still actively forming today, although the rate of movement on the Gulf of Corinth graben is greater.

Two of the islands of the Saronic Gulf, Poros and Aegina, together with the peninsula of Methana, are partly volcanic (Fig. 5.1), and are the northernmost major expressions of the South Aegean volcanic arc. The ultimate origin of the volcanism is the subduction of the African plate beneath the Aegean plate. Earthquake locations show that the slab of old oceanic floor and its underlying crust lie at a depth of 200 km. Volcanism occurs here because of the deep graben faults of the Saronic Gulf, which have guided the magmas produced in the mantle through the crust to the surface.

Aegina

Aegina is a dry, infertile island, relying on wells for its water. While the interior is mountainous, much of the north-western part consists of a plain, producing chiefly pistachio nuts. For long the inhabitants have lived by seafaring, manufacturing, sponge-fishing and, recently, tourism.

Aegina has a long history of settlement, starting in the Neolithic, about 3500 BC. Around 2000 BC, at the start of the Middle Bronze Age, the island was enriched by two further waves of invaders: Mycenaean Greeks from mainland Greece and Minoans from Crete. They seem to have settled down happily together near the present town of Aegina, where the Temple of Apollo would be built, and above the Bay of Ayia Marina, where the Temple of Aphaia was to stand. About 1000 BC there was a further settlement of Greeks – Dorians from Epidauros in the Argolid – who established their capital, Aegina, where the town of Aegina stands today. By 600 BC they possessed the finest fleet in Greece, had founded many colonies, and struck the first coinage in Greece west of the Aegean. But by the middle of the fifth century BC their greatness was over, and they were subjugated in succession to Athens, Macedonia, Pergamon, Rome, Constantinople, Venice and Turkey. In 1826 the town of Aegina had its last brief hour of glory, when it became, for two years, the first capital of liberated Greece.

Aegina lies in the Sub-Pelagonian zone and much of the basement of the island is made of the characteristic Triassic-Cretaceous limestones of this zone (Figs. 4.1, 5.1).[60] However, these rocks are only exposed on a series of low hills in the north-central part of the island. Elsewhere in the northern part of the island they are covered with a layer of Pliocene marine marl and limestone, with minor andesite lavas and tuffs (see below).

In the southern and eastern parts of the island volcanos erupted large quantities of dacite tuffs, breccias and lavas about four million years ago.[205, 60] Following this event there was a pause until the end of the Pliocene, about two million years ago, when volcanism recommenced for a brief, but important, period. Initially, a small lava flow was erupted in the south-west and flowed into the bay of Marathon. Activity then shifted to the centre of the island: andesite lavas flowed from vents on

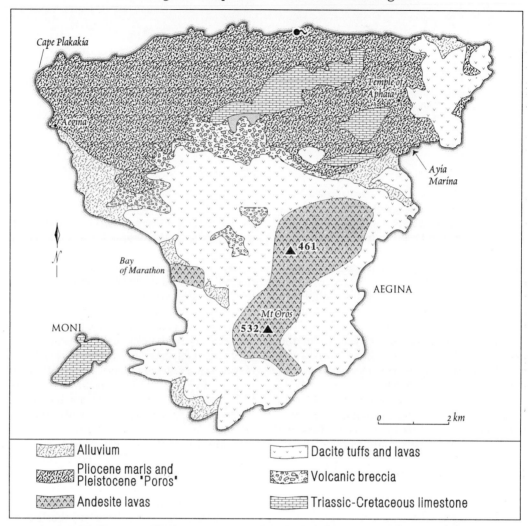

Fig. 4.1. Aegina (after 60 and other sources).

Oros and Lazarides to build the present edifices, now 532 and 461 m high. Since then volcanism has ceased on Aegina and appears to have migrated to Methana, 10 km to the southwest.

During the Pliocene, following the volcanism, much of the northern part island was submerged and yellow sandy marls and impure limestones were deposited. Relative sea-level fell during the Pleistocene, exposing wide beaches. Winds transported the exposed calcareous sands inland, and deposited them

at elevations up to 180 m, in a layer less than 10 m thick. Percolating rainwater dissolved part of the sand and cemented the rock to form a porous light-weight rock locally called Poros. This rock was widely exploited here, as elsewhere in the Aegean, for rough construction and sub-structures of buildings. That used in Athens may have come from quarries near Cape Plakakia.[217]

There is a warm spring (25°C) on the north coast of Aegina. This is not directly related to the volcanism, which is much too old, but may

36

be controlled by the same fault system that guided the magmas towards the surface.

The town of Aegina

The town of Aegina is constructed on Pliocene marly limestones that have been exposed where a small stream cut down through the Pleistocene Poros sandstone that covers Cape Colona, just to the north of the town, and much of the north-west of the island.

Ayia Marina and Temple of Aphaia

The bay of Ayia Marina was formed by the erosion of softer Late Pliocene sediments between two headlands of more resistant volcanic rocks. Above the bay lies the Temple of Aphaia, which was constructed on a ridge between low hills of hard limestone to the west and dacite lavas to the east. The oldest rock exposed here is a pale grey, hard limestone of Triassic age, which was covered with a thin layer of soft, porous, shelly yellow limestone during the Pliocene. In places both these rocks are covered with Pleistocene marls and limestone called Poros.

The temple was constructed largely of the local soft yellow Pliocene limestones. This rock has few joints, as it has never been deeply buried, hence many of the columns are monolithic. It was covered in stucco, partly for decoration and partly to protect the surface from erosion. The sculpture was carved from marble from Paros. Blocks of dacite were also used in the construction of the priests' houses. A well or cistern has been excavated through the Poros into the underlying Pliocene limestone. As on Delos the Poros layer is less permeable and reduces evaporation of groundwater from the underlying limestones.

Poros

The island of Poros, some 15 km south of Aegina, is separated from the Argolid by a narrow channel (Figs. 4.2, 5.1). Known in antiquity as Kalauria, it is composed of low rocky hills covered with pines, and is a popular holiday place for Athenians.

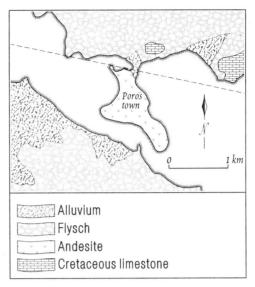

Fig. 4.2. Poros town.

The channel separating Poros from the mainland is 1-2 km wide, except where the town of Poros almost blocks it. It was formed by erosion of rocks adjacent to a fault running parallel to the coast. It continues to the west under the lowland that separates Mt Aderos (south of Methana) from the mainland and along the south coast of the Saronic Gulf to Palaia Epidauros (near Epidauros). This fault is part of a series which produced the Corinthian and Saronic Gulfs in geologically recent times (see Corinth).

The main part of the island of Poros has a very different geological history from that of the peninsula on which the town of Poros stands. The western and north-eastern coasts are made up of Mid-Cretaceous limestones (Fig. 5.1). Above these rocks, and exposed in the centre of the island, is a series of flysch sediments. Fragments of ophiolite suite rocks, now metamorphosed into serpentinite and other rocks, were incorporated into the flysch during closure of an ocean. The mainland opposite Poros is made up of similar flysch.

The town of Poros is built on a small ancient volcano connected to the mainland by a low isthmus. The rocks here are andesites with abundant phenocrysts of plagioclase and amphibole. The matrix is grey, except where the rocks were originally close to the surface. Here, loss of water has produced oxidation of the iron minerals which gives a pink matrix. The rocks formed as a series of lava domes, one of which developed a small flow to the south-east. These rocks were extruded about three million years ago, at the same time as lavas on Aegina.[94] The magmas were channelled to the surface along the fault that runs between the island of Poros and the mainland.

Hydra

Hydra is a long, narrow island south of the western tip of the Argolid (see Fig. 5.1). It is inhospitable, waterless, and infertile. For this reason the Hydriotes took to the sea in Turkish times and became famous mariners. During the Greek War of Independence they earned great renown for their feats of bravery.

The island of Hydra is almost completely made up of Triassic and Jurassic limestones, similar to those in the Argolid peninsula to the north (see Fig. 5.1). The massive and thickly-bedded limestones are resistant to erosion and make up the spine of the island. Permian and older sedimentary rocks occur sparsely on the south coast. Most rocks on Hydra have been tilted 20-30 degrees to the north to north-west, giving an elongation at right angles to this of the outcrops of the different rocks, the topography of the hills and indeed the island itself.

Methana

The peninsula of Methana is linked to the Peloponnese by an isthmus only 300 m wide (Figs. 4.3, 5.1). Unlike many narrow isthmuses this one is made of rock, a limestone, which continues to the first hill of the peninsula. The interior rises up to the barren volcanic slopes of Mt Chelona (742 m). The ancients were probably attracted to Methana for its hot springs.

Most of the rocks exposed on the peninsula are volcanic in origin, but this volcano, like the others in the Aegean, was constructed on a foundation of non-volcanic rocks: Mid-Cretaceous limestones and minor conglomerates of the basement are exposed on the isthmus and

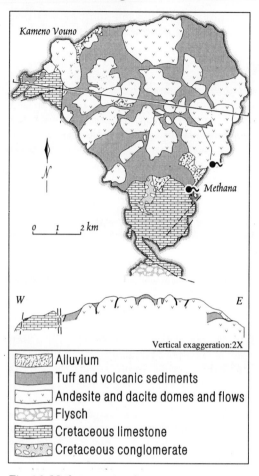

Fig. 4.3. Methana peninsula.

on the hill of Asprovouni to the north, whereas Triassic to Jurassic limestones occur in the western part of the peninsula. The latter are exposed here because they have been uplifted by movements of a fault since the volcanism started.

Volcanism started on Methana about a million years ago. Magmas rose up from the mantle and were guided by faults of the Saronic graben. The volcanic rocks of the peninsula are andesites and dacites, some with phenocrysts of plagioclase, amphibole and pyroxene. They occur as a series of domes and short lava flows which stand high above the minor ashes produced by these eruptions.[206]

They appear to have been extruded from a series of different fissures around the central peak of Chelona.

The last eruption was of andesite from a vent near the north-west coast of the peninsula, Kameno Vouno.[119] This eruption is thought to have occurred sometime between 276 and 239 BC.[258] Initially the magma formed a dome, which collapsed to give a crater after it was drained by a lava flow. The flow went towards the coast and into the sea, to give a lava field 2 km long and up to 1 km wide with a total thickness between 150 metres and 70 metres. Small amounts of ash from this eruption have been preserved on the limestones to the west. These young volcanic rocks can be seen clearly from the village of Driopi on the mainland.

Despite the small size of this eruption, it may have had a important effect on the atmosphere by the emission of large amounts of the gas sulphur dioxide. Layers of ice drilled from deep in the glaciers of Greenland are rich in sulphuric acid during the period 260 BC, with an error of 30 years, and this may be due to this eruption (see Thera). Also the winter of 270/269 BC was noted in Rome to be particularly cold. However, both these effects may have been produced other eruptions elsewhere.

There are hot springs on the north and south-west coasts as well as the well-known springs around the town of Methana, which issue at 34 and 41°C.[1] The largest spring issues south of Methana through the limestone near its contact with the volcanic rocks. All these springs may be related to the volcanism as the geologically recent eruption indicates that magma is present beneath the peninsula. However, it is also possible that they originate by circulation of rain and sea water down deep faults where they are heated by the normal increase in temperature with depth and rise towards the surface.

5

Corinthia and the Argolid

The Peloponnese

The name Peloponnese means 'the Island of Pelops', a mythical king of this region. Although an island in geologically recent times, it has not been isolated from the mainland within human memory, being attached by the narrow Isthmus of Corinth. However, in a sense the Peloponnese became an island in 1893 with the completion of the Corinth Canal.

Like all Greece, of which it is an epitome, the Peloponnese is very mountainous: mountains encircle the central district of Arcadia, where they attain a height of around 2,300 m, and radiate outwards till they reach the sea in almost all directions. The ancients compared its shape to that of the leaf of a plane tree. Perhaps a better comparison would be with an outstretched hand, with one finger missing. The thumb is the Argolid and the three fingers are in Laconia and Messenia. The seven modern departments of the Peloponnese correspond closely with the ancient political divisions. They comprise: Corinthia and the Argolid, which will be considered in this chapter; Laconia and Messenia (Chapter 6), and Elis, Achaea and Arcadia (Chapter 7).

Corinthia and the Argolid

The geological basement of Corinthia and the Argolid is dominated by rocks from two isopic zones (Fig. 5.1). Most of Corinthia and the eastern part of the Argolid is underlain by rocks of the Sub-Pelagonian zone, a band of rocks that were originally part of an old continental margin. This zone is characterised by ophiolite suite rocks and associated sediments such as Triassic to Jurassic grey limestones.

West of the Gulf of Argos and the Argive plain the Pindos zone is represented by thin-bedded limestones and flysch sediments. These rocks were deposited in a small ocean basin. During Alpine compression, the Sub-Pelagonian zone was thrust westwards over the Pindos zone.

The topography and geology of this area have been profoundly affected by the Neogene extension of the crust in the Aegean region. This stretching has created many grabens, of which the Gulf of Corinth, together with the lowlands to the south and its extension to the east in the Saronic Gulf, is a classic example. The Argolid is another graben, now separate, but originally connected to the early Corinthian graben (see Chapter 2).

Minor volcanism, part of the South Aegean volcanic arc, produced dacite lavas and small intrusions east of the Corinth Canal mostly near Sousaki about 4-2.7 million years ago,[94] as well as the Aegina and Methana volcanos (see Chapter 4). Hot springs associated with the Sousaki lavas are not heated by the volcanism, as it is too old, but are probably guided up the same faults as were used by the magmas.

Corinthia

Situated on the isthmus which bears its name, Ancient Corinth possessed two excellent harbours: Kenchreai on the Saronic Gulf and Lechaion on the Gulf of Corinth. So a strong Corinth would be able to control not only north/south land traffic, but also east/west sea traffic. And that is why, although the soil is very poor and earthquakes are all too common, there has been a settlement here or hereabouts for the last 7,000 years.

The first recorded inhabitants were Dorian

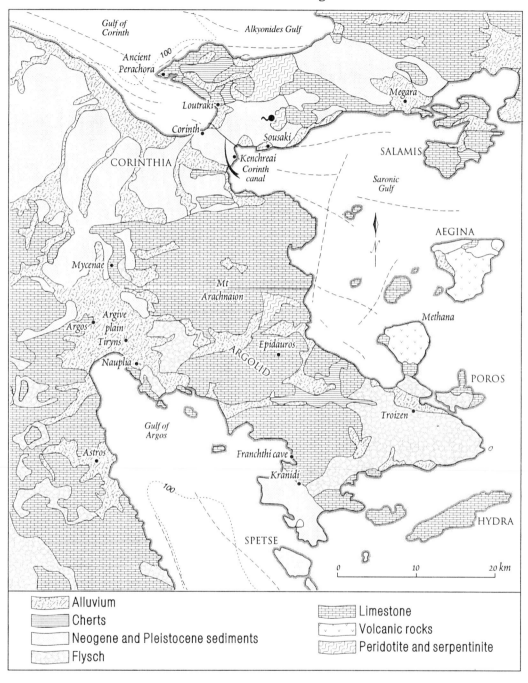

Fig. 5.1. Corinthia and the Argolid.

Greeks who united within their territory the two harbours and the citadel of Acrocorinth. In the sixth and seventh centuries BC the city gained importance and in 550 BC the great Temple of Apollo was built. Corinth continued as a artistic and commercial centre until 146 BC when the Romans destroyed the city. It was refounded in 44 BC and soon regained its previous stature, becoming a byword for worldliness and vice. Nonetheless, Corinth became the centre of the new religion of Christianity in Greece and was visited by St Paul. In the sixth century AD Corinth was laid low by two terrible earthquakes. Eventually a new city arose, to become the centre of the Greek silk industry. When this city was destroyed by an earthquake in 1858, New Corinth took its place and Old Corinth virtually ceased to exist.

The Gulf of Corinth

The Gulf of Corinth is a graben which has developed gradually over the last 5-10 million years.[125, 276, 66] It is a complex structure as movement has not been confined to two faults, but has occurred along a whole series of parallel faults, creating a series of huge steps parallel to the gulf. In addition the settling of the central part has been asymmetric, with much more subsidence towards the south, rather like a trap-door.[114] Initial faulting was confined to the region south of Corinth, extending all the way to the Argolid and a shallow sea or lake developed there. Sediments deposited there are now exposed in the walls of the Corinth Canal, in outcrops of the bed-rock in ancient Corinth and in the low hills that separate Corinthia and the Argolid. Later faulting switched to the north into the present Gulf of Corinth, and the southern area was uplifted above sea-level. The total subsidence of the graben floor during the last 5-10 million years is about 3 km and still continues.[256]

Before 250,000 years ago the Gulfs of Corinth and Patras were a lake, sealed off from the sea by a barrier that included the islands of Kephellinia and Zakinthos.[220] Rivers feeding this lake made large deltas that now survive as terraces, such as that on which Ancient Corinth stands. Similar terraces are present around Patras. Since movements of the land have opened up this region to the sea, though periodically the Rion straits north of Patras acted as a barrier and the Gulf of Corinth became a lake.

Three major earthquakes occurred in 1981: they were centered on an important fault that runs under the Alkyonides Gulf, but movements also occurred on faults on land on either side of the gulf. Earthquakes of this magnitude probably occur every 300 years in this area.[276] The Gulf of Corinth is also very susceptible to tsunamis produced by earthquakes (see Chapter 7).

The Corinth Canal

The Isthmus of Corinth, dividing mainland Greece from the Peloponnese, is only 6 km wide. Several attempts were made in antiquity to dig a canal across it, which would have saved a journey round the Peloponnese of some 300 km. On the last occasion, in AD 67, the Emperor Nero started digging operations, using 6,000 Jewish prisoners of war, but he was called away by troubles in Rome, and the work was stopped on his death the following year. As a second best, in the sixth century BC the Corinthians had constructed the Diolkos, a tramway cut out of the rock, for carrying warships, and the cargoes of merchant ships, across the Isthmus on wheeled transporters. After an interval of nearly 2,000 years the canal was finally completed in 1893.

A series of faulted Pliocene-Pleistocene marls, limestones, sandstones and conglomerates is beautifully exposed in the sides of the Canal (Fig. 5.2, Plate 5).[174, 41] These rocks were formed early in the history of the Gulf of Corinth graben when the southern part was below sea-level; they were uplifted relatively recently. The oldest rocks are best exposed towards the middle of the canal. They are a series of pale marls, with minor brown sandstones and conglomerates, and are Late Pliocene in age. These rocks were uplifted, eroded and then returned below sea-level for the deposition of the next series, the Pleistocene 'Tyrrhenian deposits'. These are

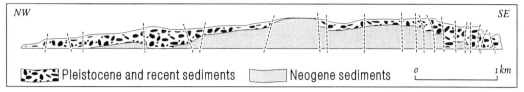

Fig. 5.2. The Corinth Canal (after 174).

conglomerates, sandstones, limestones and minor marls. The limestones make good building materials and were used in the construction of ancient Corinth (see below). Finally this whole package was raised above sea-level along a series of east/west faults.

These steeply inclined normal faults can be seen every few hundred metres along the canal (Fig. 5.2). The movement on these faults is symmetrical about the middle of the canal, which contains the oldest rocks. Therefore, the isthmus here has the form of a horst, as would be expected. Movement on each fault is relatively small, a few metres in most cases, and could have been accomplished in a single, large earthquake or at most very few.

The western end of the Diolkos is exposed near to the entrance to the canal (Plate 6A). It is partly covered with up to 30 cm of beach-rock, which has accumulated some time during the last 2,500 years, showing how fast these rocks can form. The beach-rock formed after the construction of the Diolkos, when the region was submerged by 80 cm, probably following an earthquake.[183] Subsequently the area was lifted up to close to its original level, exposing the beach-rock that we see today.

Ancient Corinth

The ancient city of Corinth lies on a terrace broadly parallel to the Gulf of Corinth (Fig. 5.3). The origin of this terrace is problematic, but it is probably a beach on the top of a delta formed in the Gulf of Corinth lake about 250,000 years ago.[220] The city was constructed on and largely of Pleistocene sandy limestones similar to those exposed in the upper parts of the walls of the Corinth Canal at either end. Outcrops of these rocks on the ancient site have well-developed beds which have the form of

ancient dunes. A good example can be seen on the side of the Fountain of Glauke.

Although the local stone is rather weak it does not have many joints as it has never been deeply buried, and hence could be extracted in huge blocks. Such blocks, faced with stucco, were used for the seven-metre columns of the Temple of Apollo. The quarry for these columns was adjacent to the temple and the city was subsequently constructed within it. Smaller columns and facings were made of imported

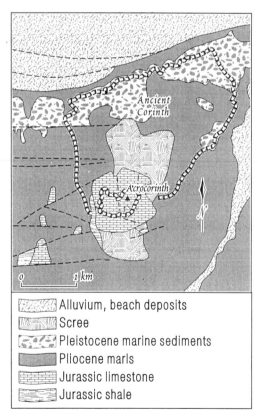

Fig. 5.3. Ancient Corinth and Acrocorinth.

Legend:
- Alluvium, beach deposits
- Scree
- Pleistocene marine sediments
- Pliocene marls
- Jurassic limestone
- Jurassic shale

stones, such as Cipollino (from Euboea), white/grey marble and a pink limestone breccia, which may be from the hill of Acrocorinth above the city.

There is a spring within the ancient city, the Lower Peirene Fountain. It has been extensively remodelled and cisterns have been excavated behind, but it is a natural spring, and now supplies water for the modern community around the site. The name links it with the Upper Peirene Fountain on Acrocorinth; both ultimately derive their water from rain that falls on the hill of Acrocorinth. The water descends within the hill and flows southward towards the spring within the scree deposits shed from the hill. Finally its passage is blocked by a fault that has brought down impermeable Pleistocene marls. The water then rises along this fault to the surface.

Ancient Corinth was an important centre for ceramic production.[289] The potter's quarter was situated about 3 km west of the city, on the edge of the Ancient Corinth terrace. A low-firing clay for fine ceramics may have been extracted nearby from beneath a layer of conglomerate that here caps the terrace. The clay used to make enormous quantities of transport amphorae must have been derived from another source. Analysis suggests that it may have been from a deposit associated with lignite, such as that at Nikoleto and Solonos, 3 km to the south-west and south-east of Ancient Corinth respectively. However, no quarries have been recognised. Another possible source of clay was terra rossa soil, produced by the weathering of hard limestone. The clay extracted by washing this soil gives pink ceramics.

Acrocorinth

The fortress of Acrocorinth stands on a barren, steep-sided hill (575 m) south of Ancient Corinth (Fig. 5.3). The ruins span many ages and different styles of construction: Archaic, Hellenistic, Byzantine, Frankish and Venetian. The hill is made of Mid-Jurassic limestone and minor shale, an eroded remnant of a layer of limestone now mostly seen in the hills to the south. During the Pliocene Acro-

corinth stood out as a island in the Corinthian gulf, then much wider. At this time the marls that now lie around the hill were deposited in the shallow waters.

The natural outcrops on the hill give the impression that it is made up entirely of limestone, but artificial exposures, such as roadcuts, show that there is also green and red shale. These shales erode much more easily than the limestone, and hence generate a soil which hides the parent rock. The colour of the shale reflects the chemical state of the iron in the minerals of the rock: red shale contains oxidised haematite but in the green shale the iron is present as black magnetite and the green of the other minerals shows through. Some of the silts have not formed individual beds, but have cemented together limestone breccias that were formed by the collapse of caves.

An important feature of this fortress was the presence of a water source within the walls. The Upper Peirene Fountain is about 5 m below present ground level in a small saddle towards the south-east of the summit. It is fed by rainwater seeping into the limestone of the higher ground on either side. From there it seeps downwards until its passage is blocked by a layer of shale. The water returns towards the surface along a north-south fault that bisects the hill. Preferential erosion of rocks adjacent to this fault has produced the saddle.

Kenchreai

In antiquity Kenchreai was the eastern port of Corinth, on the Saronic Gulf (Fig. 5.1). In classical times it was very active, but was abandoned around the sixth century AD, probably because of subsidence of the land.[33] This subsidence appears to have occurred over a period of at least 1,000 years: A classical sanctuary is now 150 m offshore in 2 m of water, whereas a Hellenistic building and an early Christian church are only slightly submerged.

Loutraki

The cliff behind the town of Loutraki is partly, at least, a recent fault scarp, which is why it is so steep (Fig. 5.1). The fault is exposed at the base of the cliff and inclines steeply towards the water. It is this fault that has channelled hot, deeply circulating rainwater towards the surface and produced the famous hot springs of this town. The main spring is slightly saline and sulphurous and has a temperature of about 29 to 32°C.[1] The spring area has been rather extensively altered, but there are traces of travertine in the area, though the spring no longer deposits this rock. Many other, smaller hot springs can be seen venting straight into the sea adjacent to the spring house.

Perachora

The peninsula north of Corinth terminates in a point near the ancient site of Perachora (see Fig. 5.1). Here, the sanctuary of Hera descends to a very small, charming bay.

A number of ancient sea-level stands can be seen in the cliffs around the Perachora peninsula.[224] The oldest is 3.1 m above present sea-level and formed before 4000 BC. The youngest sea-level stand, at a height of 1.1 m, formed during a period of a few thousand years until about 300-400 AD when this area was lifted up to its present level. These dramatic variations in sea-level reflect the extremely active nature of the Gulf of Corinth graben.

The Argolid

The Argolid is the north-easternmost of the promontories of the Peloponnese (Fig. 5.1). It is bounded on the north by the mountains which separate it from the Corinthia, on the east by the Saronic Gulf, on the south by the Gulf of Argos, and on the west by the mountains of Arcadia. Mt Arachnaion divides the Argolid into two sections: first, the tip of the promontory, with the ancient cities of Epidauros, Troizen and Hermione; secondly, the triangular Argive Plain. The rich alluvial soil is very fertile, and water is available from wells. In addition to the usual olives, figs and vines, cereals and citrus fruits are grown. Harbours are scarce; the only really safe one is at Nauplia.

Thanks to its fertility the Argolid was set-

tled at a very early date. The Franchthi Cave was inhabited from the Late Palaeolithic, about 8000 BC, into the Neolithic. At Lerna both the Neolithic and Early Bronze Age (3000-2000 BC) are well represented. This world came to a violent end around 2000 BC with the arrival of less civilised newcomers, probably the ancestors of the Greeks. They gradually settled down and by 1700 BC were in a position to trade with Minoan Crete, and also with Egypt, Syria and Asia Minor. Thus arose the impressive civilisation, based on Mycenae, which we call Mycenaean. This age, which ran from 1600 to 1100 BC, was the inspiration for the legends of Classical Greece and the Homeric poems. When it came to a violent end about 1100 BC, the Argolid was gradually overrun by Dorian Greeks, who ruled it from Argos. But Sparta always had her eye on this desirable land, and in the sixth century BC the Spartans defeated the Argives so profoundly that the district sank into an obscurity from which it never emerged.

The Argive Plain and Lake Lerna

The Argive Plain is a Neogene graben (see Fig. 5.1). The hills to the west are mostly made of Late Cretaceous limestones and to the northeast Triassic and Jurassic limestones predominate. These rocks are resistant to erosion and produce the high, rounded hills. The jagged hills immediately to the east are dominated by flysch sediments.

About 20,000 years ago, when the Ice Age was at its maximum, sea-level was about 120 m below the present level and the ancient shoreline was about 10 km further south.[83] Neolithic people probably lived on this coastal plain, but their remains have been buried by rising sea-levels and sedimentation. Melting of the accumulated ice caused sea-level to rise, and the coastline to advance north, until it stabilised during the Early Bronze Age at a height close its present level. At that time the sea was only 250 m from Tiryns, and the settlements of Temenion, Magoula and Lerna were beside the water.

While the east part of the Gulf of Argos was a sickle-shaped bay, the west half consisted of a beach barrier with a freshwater lagoon be-

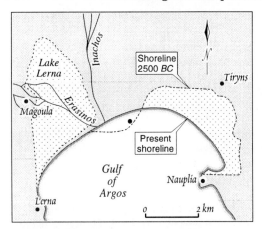

Fig. 5.4. The Lower Argive plain and ancient coastlines (after 83).

hind it (Fig. 5.4). This was the Lake Lerna that
figures in Greek mythology: it was here that
Herakles fought the Hydra. The maximum size
of this lagoon was about 2 by 5 km and was
assumed in antiquity to be bottomless. However, it was in fact quite shallow, about 6 m,
like many other 'bottomless' lakes.

About 2500 BC the coastline changed from
one dominated by erosion to one of deposition
of sediments.[226, 271] It is not clear why this occurred, but it could have been caused by a shift
in the place where the sediments were deposited from the deeper part of the ocean to the
plain, by climatic changes and the resulting
changes in vegetation or by human interven-
tion.[83, 271] At this time the plough was
introduced into Greece and the increase in
agricultural productivity led to an increase in
population. These developments could have
led to an increase in soil erosion. Similar
phases of soil erosion also occurred about 300
BC to AD 50 and AD 1000.

Sediments deposited by the rivers filled in
the shallow bay, forcing the shoreline to the
south until it was close to its present position
in about 1100 BC. However, not all the land
behind the coastal dunes was dry: paradoxically Lake Lerna in the west increased in size
in Hellenistic to Roman times, but subsequently became marshy. To the east there
were also marshes between Tiryns and the

coast that remained until recently when they
were artificially drained.

The shape of the land in the Argive Plain is
now controlled by the deposition of sediment
from the streams and by the activities of man.
The Inachos river in the west (Fig. 5.4) and the
Megalo Rema river north of Nauplia (Fig. 5.6)
are usually dry, but tend to flood every 15-25
years. These floods can move huge amounts of
sediment and have produced ridges on either
side of the stream bed (levees). In contrast, the
Erasinos river is perennial and one of the largest streams in the Peloponnese, but does not
deposit any sediment, because it is fed from
springs (see below).

Mycenae

Mycenae, the city which has given its name to
the illustrious Greek civilisation of the Late
Bronze Age, lies on a low knoll, protected by
hills to the north and south. This situation
controls the pass connecting the Gulf of
Corinth with the Gulf of Argos. It was the
greatest and wealthiest city in the Argolid from
1600 to 1100 BC, called by Homer 'Rich in Gold',
and the centre of many of the best known
Greek legends. It was from here that Agamemnon departed to Aulis to lead the expedition
against Troy to recapture the beautiful Helen,
and here he was murdered on his return by
Klytemnestra. Mycenae was burnt down in
1200 BC and again in 1100 BC. It was never
again important.

Mycenae lies on the hills that make up the
eastern wall of the Argos graben (Fig. 5.1, 5.5).
The knoll on which it is built is made of Late
Triassic to Middle Jurassic limestones, similar
to those that underlie the small steep hills to
the north and south and the mountain range to
the east. The walls of the city were built of this
limestone which was quarried from the adjoining hills.

Most of the valley between the hills and the
ridge which runs from west of the citadel towards the south is made of very different rock:
marls and conglomerates were deposited here
by rivers and streams that flowed into the
graben during the Late Pliocene to Pleistocene
periods. The upper parts of this ridge contain a

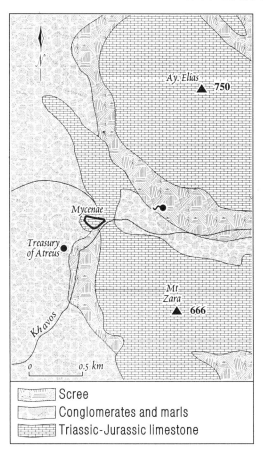

Fig. 5.5. Mycenae.

There is a spring 200 m east of the citadel, at the base of Mt Ayios Elias. It is fed from water that falls on the hill and descends underground. Its passage is blocked by Pleistocene marls that fill the valley bottom and it reaches the surface though ancient scree deposits shed from the hill. In Mycenaean times it was piped or channelled underground to the 'Secret Cistern' at the east end of the citadel beside the walls. It has supplied Mycenae ever since.

Tiryns

Though not nearly as rich in legend as Mycenae, the citadel of Tiryns presents an even grander prospect today. It has been suggested that in the Bronze Age Tiryns was not an independent kingdom, but was the port of Mycenae, which is not far away. It was inhabited from Neolithic times, but what we see today belongs almost without exception to the Mycenaean period, 1600-1100 BC. More than Mycenae, it is a sort of textbook of Mycenaean architecture, with its outer gateway, ceremonial entrance, forecourt, and palace. The citadel was destroyed about 1200 BC and again a century later.

The citadel stands on a small knoll of Early Cretaceous limestone that protrudes from the geologically recent alluvial deposits of the plain (Fig. 5.6). The hills a few kilometres to the east and south-east, both called Ayios Elias, are geologically similar and were quarried by the builders of Tiryns for material for the walls. These grey limestones contain marly layers and minor breccias cemented by marls. A conglomerate was used for the door-posts and lintels as it is has few joints and hence was available in large blocks. It was probably quarried from layers in the upper parts of the limestone of Ayios Elias or from flysch sediments in the low hills further east.

Like Mycenae, Tiryns had a secret water-supply for use in times of siege. Two corbelled stone galleries pass under the walls and run downwards and almost parallel in a westerly direction for some 30 m. The ends of the galleries descend below the water-table, hence the water sources are wells.

The position of the coastline has changed

very well-cemented conglomerate that was used extensively in the citadel and the best of the beehive tombs. This conglomerate has much more widely spaced joints than the limestones, as it has never been deeply buried, and hence was available in much larger blocks. These were used for lintels and door-posts, where the limestone could not provide sufficiently large blocks. Some of the largest blocks, such as those seen in the Treasury of Atreus, may be close to the original thickness of the beds.

The deep ravines around the citadel were excavated as a result of the rapid subsidence of the graben: the steep gradient of the water in the stream enabled rapid erosion. They probably follow minor faults.

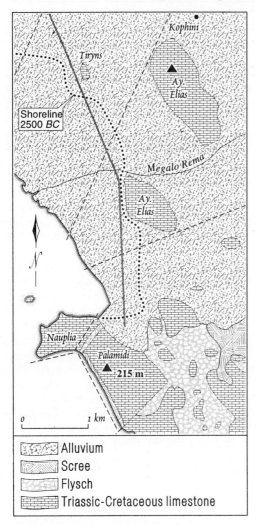

Fig. 5.6. Nauplia and Tiryns.

Argos

Argos lies 5 km from the sea, at the foot of two hills, both of which were used as acropolises: Larisa (276 m) and Aspis (80 m). It has good supplies of water. Although traditionally the oldest city in Greece, Argos was evidently not of the first importance for a long time; in the Mycenaean period it was certainly inferior to Mycenae and Tiryns. Under the Dorians, who arrived about 1000 BC, Argos was the first city of the Argolid for over 400 years.

The city is situated on the western edge of

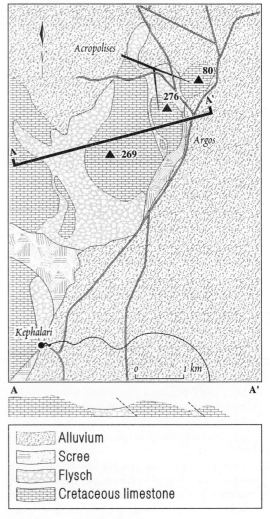

Fig. 5.7. Argos and Kephalari.

since antiquity. Its most landward position was at about 2500 BC, during the Bronze Age, when the sea was only 250 m from Tiryns. By 1100 BC the shoreline resembled its present appearance.[83] Another event also occurred at this time: catastrophic flooding of a stream near Tiryns resulted in the rapid deposition of about 5 m of sediments. This catastrophic event may have led to the construction of a dam a few km to the east near Kophini (Nea Tiryns) to prevent further flooding.

48

the Argos graben, just east of a promontory that projects into the Argive plain (Figs. 5.1, 5.6). This block of rock is bounded to the north by a fault that runs to the north-west along the valley of the Inachos torrent, and to the south by a fault follows the edge of the plain south-west past Kephalari. Both faults are related to the Argos graben. To the west rise hills of Late Cretaceous limestone and minor flysch, and behind these lie the plains of Arcadia.

The low-lying parts of the promontory are underlain by readily-weathered flysch, but the higher land is Triassic and Cretaceous limestone. The two acropolises are both blocks of resistant Mid-Cretaceous limestone that have been thrust over younger flysch sediments and isolated by erosion.

Kephalari and other karst springs

The source of the perennial Erasinos river is at Kephalari just south of Argos (Fig. 5.7). Major springs issue from in front of two caves to feed the river for its short journey to the sea, 6 km away. The caves have a long history of use, starting in Neolithic times. Later they were sacred to Pan and Dionysos and are now modified for use as chapels.

The spring water was traditionally thought to come from Lake Stymphalos, 51 km to the north-west, but water-tracing experiments show that it in fact originates from sink-holes that drain poljes at Alea and Scotini, just south of the lake (see Fig. 7.4).[182] The water flows underground through a series of fissures and caves until it reaches Kephalari. Here the flow of the water is blocked by a layer of less permeable flysch sediments exposed to the north, but also underlying the plain, and is forced to the surface along the fault that here defines the edge of the Argos graben. The flow of this spring is very variable, and has been known to dry up completely.

There are a number of other large springs along the western coast of the Gulf of Argos. The water of these springs also comes from the Alea and Scotini sink-holes as well as from the sink-hole that drains Lake Stymphalos (see Fig. 7.4). There is also a major contribution from the sink-holes that drain the northern

Tripolis polje, such as Kapsia, Milia, Kanatas and Nestani.[182] Some of the springs are brackish, from entrained seawater (see p. 102).

A number of springs debouche under the waters of the Gulf of Argos. The Kiveri spring group rises 15-50 m offshore, but has a low salt content. A retaining wall has been built so that these waters can be used for irrigation. Further south a large spring issues about 300 m offshore from Anavalos. The flow is so strong that it rises slightly above the level of the sea, forming two circles, known locally as *Lili to Mati* ('The Eyes of Lili'). The spring is fed uniquely from the sink-hole in the former Lake Taka, south of Tripolis.[182]

Nauplia

Nauplia is the safest harbour in the Argolid; it was occupied from a very early date, and served as a port in Mycenaean times. The Homeric hero Palamedes was associated in legend with Nauplia, and has given his name to the higher of the two hills that overlook the harbour, Palamidi (215 m). The other hill, Acronauplia, was preferred in antiquity as an acropolis, being easier of access. In 628 BC Nauplia became the official port of Argos, but soon faded into insignificance. It recovered under the Venetians (AD 1388 to 1540) and was briefly the capital of newly liberated Greece.

Nauplia is situated on the northern edge of a 10 by 4 km tectonic block that projects into the Argos graben (Figs. 5.1, 5.6). The main graben fault runs north-west/south-east, about 4 km to the east of the city. This block has been lifted up, with respect to the graben floor, along a series of faults that are buried in the plain just to the north of the city. This block is dominated by Triassic to Cretaceous limestones.

Both Acronauplia and the hill of Palamidi are made of Early Cretaceous limestone, faulted on almost all sides. The steep relief along the coast is due to movements along these faults, as well as differential erosion of the rocks on either side. The saddle that separates the two hills was produced by erosion of a layer of flysch and shattered rock along a fault. The fortified island of Bourtzi to the north is

yet another block of Early Cretaceous limestone, again probably fault-bounded.

Epidauros

The Asklepieion at Epidauros is situated in a
broad valley in the northern part of the Argolid. About 800 BC Apollo was worshipped
here, but by about 400 BC Asklepios had super-
seded him. The Sanctuary now became a
centre of healing and a fashionable spa, and
was adorned with suitable buildings. After sac-
rificing and taking a ritual bath, the pilgrims
would sleep in the Sanctuary in the expecta-
tion of awaking cured. Every four years a
dramatic and athletic festival was held in honour of Asklepios. The theatre for the dramatic
contests is in a remarkable state of preservation.

Much of the site of Epidauros is underlain
by green volcanic tuff of Triassic age (Fig.
5.8),[207] outcrops of which can be seen both
above and below the theatre. This rock is
closely jointed and weathers easily to produce
the gentle slopes and low relief of the site. The
hills behind the theatre are made of Triassic
yellowish cherty limestone, which overlies the
tuff and is more resistant to weathering. The
view to the north-west is dominated by the
distant hills of resistant Triassic to Jurassic
limestone.

The Asklepieion was supplied with water
from a number of wells and springs. The
springs are fed by rain that falls on the surrounding limestone hills and disappears
underground into caves and fissures. These
waters descend until they reach the tuff, which
is less permeable because of its clay content.
They are then channelled horizontally until
they emerge close to the upper surface of the

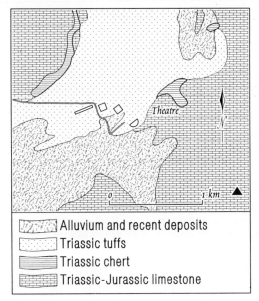

Alluvium and recent deposits
Triassic tuffs
Triassic chert
Triassic-Jurassic limestone

Fig. 5.8. Epidauros.

tuff as springs. They are now dry in summer,
possibly as a result of changes in land use that
has increased run-off of rainwater, and possibly because of a change in climate.

The foundations of many of the buildings
were made of a poorly-cemented limestone,
possibly from a local layer of caliche. This rock
has not withstood the high moisture levels in
the foundations and has frequently disintegrated, causing the collapse of the building.
The upper parts of the buildings and the theatre were made of grey and red limestone. The
seats of honour in the theatre were made of a
limestone breccia, with clasts of both red and
grey limestone. This breccia probably was
formed in caves by the collapse of the roof, and
the cementation of the debris.

6

Laconia and Messenia

The southern Peloponnese is bounded on the north by the high mountains of Arcadia, and by the sea on all other sides. Two lofty mountain ranges run parallel from north to south: Parnon, on the east, runs for more than 50 km, reaching a height of 1,937 m, and ends at the tip of the Malea peninsula; the Taygetos range runs down the centre and reaches a height of 2,300 m, the highest point of the Peloponnese. It separates Laconia in the east from Messenia in the west, ending at the tip of the Mani. Further west, the Messenian peninsula springs from the rather lower Mt Aigaleion. The Taygetos range also controls the climate: the rainfall in Messenia is double that of Laconia, which makes the former area more fertile than the latter. The land is rich in vines, olives, figs, cereals and pasture, and there are forests on the lower slopes of the mountains. There is, however, a scarcity of good harbours.

The history of Laconia, which we will consider first, is really the history of its principal city, Sparta (in antiquity Lacedaemon). Regular occupation started about 6000 BC, at the beginning of the Neolithic. The Late Bronze Age, 1600-1100 BC, is the period to which the Homeric poems look back. However, the city ruled by King Menelaus, husband of the beautiful Helen, seems not to have been near Classical Sparta, but may have been at the Menelaion, 5 km to the north-east, or perhaps at Amyklai, 8 km to the south.

Around 1000 BC, after the end of the Bronze Age, the area was settled by Dorian Greeks. At first rich and given to luxury, these Spartans gradually developed an austere way of life for which they became notorious. About 725 BC they conquered Messenia and reduced the inhabitants to a state of virtual slavery.

Henceforward, Sparta was always powerful but never popular. Their city was eventually destroyed by Alaric the Goth in AD 396. In 1248 it was succeeded by the city of Mistra.

To turn to Messenia, its early history runs parallel to that of Laconia. In the Late Bronze Age it was actually much richer than its neighbour, thanks to the greater fertility of their soil and closer contacts with Minoan Crete. Like Laconia, Messenia was occupied by Dorian Greeks about 1000 BC. But the Spartans always coveted this rich land; and when they conquered and absorbed it about 725 BC, that was really the end of Messenia for many centuries. In 369 BC, however, a new city, called Messene, was built as a capital for an independent Messenia. It remained important for many centuries, under Greek and Roman rule.

Laconia and Messenia, along with most of the Peloponnese, are dominated by rocks of the 'external' isopic zones of the Hellenides, the Ionian, Gavrovo and Pindos zones (Figs. 2.2, 6.1). Rocks of the Ionian zone were initially deposited in a deep-water trough, which became shallower as it filled with flysch sediments shed from an adjacent, rising mountain range. The Gavrovo zone was a region of shallow water, initially far from mountains, perhaps similar to the present Bahamas region. The Pindos zone was formerly a deep ocean basin. All these zones were stacked up against each other by the Alpine compressions during the Late Cretaceous to Palaeogene.

The overall topography of Laconia and Messenia is controlled by the Neogene stretching of the region. The Malea peninsula is a horst between two grabens. That on the east is the downthrown block of the Central Aegean; that on the west comprises the Vale of Sparta and

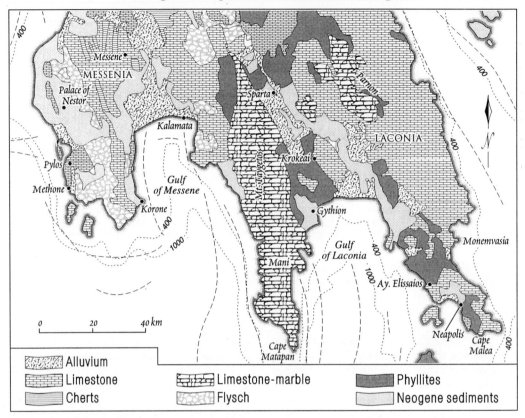

Fig. 6.1. Laconia and Messenia.

the Laconian plains and continues southwards under the sea. The Mani peninsula has a similar structure and is bounded on the west by a graben which starts in the Messenian plain and continues southwards under the sea.

Sparta

Sparta is situated in the fertile valley of the Eurotas, a river which flows from the Arcadian mountains in a southerly direction for the entire length of Laconia. The Vale of Sparta was aptly described by the Greeks as 'Hollow Lacedaemon', and indeed the Eurotas flows through a rich, fertile plain from Sparta to the sea.

The Vale of Sparta, with the town of Sparta at its centre, is a Neogene graben (Fig. 6.2). The western side of the valley rises rapidly to the

Taygetos mountains along a steep normal fault, which has been active very recently. The topography along the edge of Taygetos is controlled by the nature of the underlying rock: steeper slopes south and west of Sparta are largely made of hard Cretaceous-Eocene limestone and marble, which is strong and resists erosion, whereas the gentler slopes north of Mistra are composed of phyllite, a rock with little resistance to erosion. Deep, but short, gorges have been cut into the mountain front by this rapid uplift. Large fans of alluvial sediments have spread out from the point where each gorge debouches into the Eurotas valley.

Modern Sparta lies on a part of a Pleistocene alluvial fan, now dissected by the Eurotas and Magoulitsa rivers. Ancient Sparta, 1 km to the north, was constructed on a low mound of Pliocene-Pleistocene marls and clays, origi-

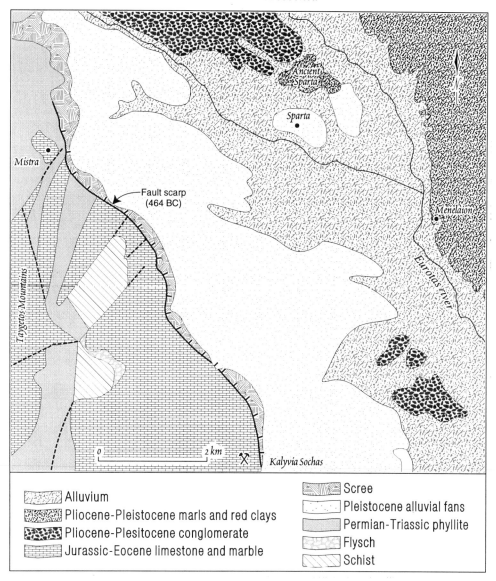

Fig. 6.2. Sparta and the Eurotas valley.

nally deposited in shallow lakes in the graben. As elsewhere the marls have provided a fertile soil, which may even be the origin of the name Sparta – 'sown ground'. The mound is surrounded by steep bluffs 1-6 m high, that probably aided defence of the site.[30]

A grey marble, much used in Classical Sparta, was quarried from the lower slopes of Taygetos, west of Kalyvia Sochas, about 6 km south of Sparta.

The Menelaion was constructed on a bluff of Pliocene-Pleistocene marls, clays and conglomerates, that rises about 50 m above the plain. The stepped topography of these hills reflects the underlying geology. Almost horizontal layers of conglomerate resist erosion and form the steps, whereas the more readily eroded marls and clays form the risers. This type of topography undoubtedly aided the defence of the settlement.[30]

The earthquake of 464 BC that destroyed Sparta was an important historical event of the classical period. It was produced by vertical movement on the fault at the base of the Taygetos mountains and had a magnitude of about 7.2. A fault-scarp 10-12 m high that runs for 20 km along the base of the mountains was produced by this and possibly 2-3 earlier earthquakes (Fig. 6.2). Similar sized earthquakes can be expected every 3,000 years.[15]

Mistra

In 1249 the Frankish Prince William de Villehardouin built a castle at Mistra in the foothills of Taygetos, 5 km west of Sparta. Ten years later he was forced to cede his castle to the Byzantine Emperor. A Byzantine town, adorned with splendid churches, soon developed here, and lasted until captured by the Turks in 1460. Between 1687 and 1715 it was ruled by Venice, and enjoyed a second blooming; but on the return of the Turks Mistra fell into a terminal decline.

Mistra stands in a dramatic position at the base of the Taygetos mountains, which rise in steps from the plains (Fig. 6.2). The Kastro hill is a block of hard Triassic-Jurassic dolomite, which is much more resistant to erosion than the phyllites to the north of the site and in the rounded hills to the west (Fig. 6.3). This block has been cut off to the south by a fault running at right-angles to the main graben fault. A steep gorge has been cut here, exploiting both the line of weakness associated with the fault and the phyllites immediately south.

Krokeai

Leaving the modern Krokeai (formerly Levetsova), you take the new road to Skala via Stephania. About 3 km beyond Pharos (formerly Alai Bey), at Psephi, on both sides of the road are lumps of a green porphyritic rock. This is the stone known to the Romans as Lapis Lacedaemonius (Spartan stone), to Italian masons as Porfido Verde Antico (ancient green porphyry), and to us as Spartan porphyry, basalt or andesite.

This rock is a porphyritic andesite and comes from a lava dome 2,000 m long by 500 m wide of Mid-Triassic age (Fig. 6.4).[211] Such domes form when viscous lava erupts quiescently onto the surface. This dome was a small, isolated eruption, with no large volcano nearby. However, there are small amounts of similar rocks scattered throughout the Peloponnese.

The prominent phenocrysts of the lava are plagioclase, now metamorphosed to a fine-grained mixture of albite feldspar and green epidote. In some parts of the lava several plagioclase crystals started to crystallise from the same point, to give rosettes of crystals. In parts of the dome the fine-grained matrix of the rock has been reddened by the oxidation of iron minerals to haematite.

Most of the blocks of this lava are small, less than 0.5 m across, as the rock has closely -spaced joints which probably formed during deformation and uplift of the rock. Indeed, Pausanias, writing in the second century AD,

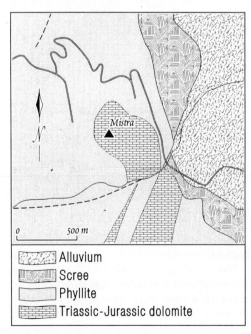

Fig. 6.3. Mistra.

- Alluvium
- Scree
- Phyllite
- Triassic-Jurassic dolomite

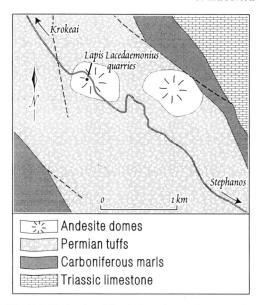

Andesite domes
Permian tuffs
Carboniferous marls
Triassic limestone

Fig. 6.4. Krokeai and Lapis Lacedaemonius quarries (after 211).

says: 'this is not a continuous mass of rock, but they dig out stones shaped like river pebbles, [which are] very hard to work'. Certainly, only comparatively small pieces seem to have been worked in Mycenaean and Roman times, although the Byzantines evidently had access to larger pieces (see below) probably from deeper quarries. Ancient quarry-pits, probably Roman, have been identified beside the road; the Mycenaean quarries were probably higher up the hill, where outcrops have been completely mined away.

Spartan porphyry was popular in Minoan Crete and Mycenaean Greece between approximately 1450 and 1300 BC, for stone vases and sealstones. In the Lapidary's Store at Knossos, Evans found a number of unworked blocks of this stone, and a partly worked block was also found at Mycenae. About 1300 BC the taste for such stones vanished, and did not return until the Roman Empire, in the early first century AD; this time for the decoration of walls and floors. Pausanias says that 'these stones were used for decorating temples, swimming pools and fountains'. The Byzantines made good use of Spartan porphyry. In the

Neonian Baptistry at Ravenna, of the early fifth century, are wall-slabs measuring as much as 1.5 by 0.5 m. Later, Roman and Byzantine stones were re-used on church floors, as in St. Mark's, Venice (twelfth century and later) and even Westminster Abbey (1268). Spartan porphyry was used by Renaissance architects and their successors as late as the eighteenth century.

Gythion

Gythion was the port of Classical Sparta, as it is of modern Sparta. South of the harbour, to which it is joined by a causeway, is a small island, the ancient Kranae, celebrated by Homer as the place where Helen and Paris spent the first night of their journey from Sparta to Troy.

Gythion is situated in the western side of a broad graben that extends north to Sparta and south into the gulf of Laconia (Fig. 6.1). The Kastro hill behind the town and the island of Kranae are made of Late Triassic, pale grey marbles, their age indicating that they predate the graben. The surrounding sedimentary rocks are Pliocene in age, deposited when the floor of the graben was below sea-level. Parts of the ancient city have been submerged below sea-level by movements of a fault, thus partly preserving the ruins that were created by the earthquake.[150]

Monemvasia

Monemvasia stands up, looking like the Rock of Gibraltar, off the barren east coast of the Malea peninsula. The name means 'single entrance', because it can only be reached from the mainland by a narrow causeway. In the sixth century AD, the rock became a refuge for Greeks from Laconia fleeing from the Slav invasions, and it soon became an almost impregnable fortress and a prosperous trading centre. By the thirteenth century it was the commercial capital of the Peloponnese. The English name for Monemvasia was Malmsey, and the wine shipped from here was the famous Malmsey wine. In 1464 Monemvasia fell to Venice, and in 1540 to the Turks.

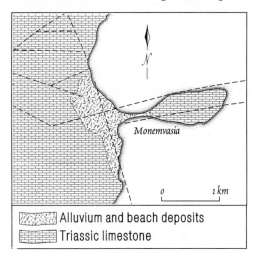

Fig. 6.5. Monemvasia.

Monemvasia is a steep-sided block of Trias-sic grey dolomite similar to the adjacent hills of the mainland (Fig. 6.5). The coastline here follows a steep north-north-west trending fault, part of a set that defines the grabens and horsts of the southern Peloponnese. A second set of faults, at right angles, has defined the block on which Monemvasia stands. The location of some of these faults can be seen, for example as a dolomite breccia cemented with brown silt, that crops out in the path at the base of the castle hill.

Cape Malea

The Malea peninsula is dominated by Triassic dolomites and phyllites, within which lie sev-eral economic deposits. A number of small iron deposits lie around Neapolis, in the phyllites or associated with the overlying thrust fault (Fig. 6.1). These deposits are dominated by haema-tite and limonite, and were probably deposited from hot, watery solutions that followed the fault. Ancient shards and other remains asso-ciated with slag heaps at Ayios Elissaios (10 km north-west of Neapolis) and at Neapolis itself indicate that they were exploited in an-tiquity.[25] Limestone, probably of Pliocene age, was also exploited here from Classical to Byz-antine times.[287] It was extracted from a number of quarries around Neapolis.

Mani

The Mani peninsula comprises the highlands which make up the southern 50 km of the Taygetos range, from opposite Gythion to Cape Matapan (Fig. 6.1). It takes its name from a Frankish castle built in 1248 and named Le Magne (the great). It is divided geographically into two regions. The general bleakness of the northern, or Outer Mani, is relieved by fertile gullies and small plains. The Deep Mani (the real Mani, as many would say) lies further south and occupies the Matapan peninsula. The coast is rocky and inhospitable. Inland, this hot and arid landscape grows nothing but olives and prickly pears, but is rich in good quality limestones and marbles.

The Maniots have long been famous for their warlike qualities; their boast is that they were never subdued by the Turks. Blood-feuds have long been endemic, and their tower-houses were built as a defence against each other.

Much of the Mani peninsula is underlain by Late Cretaceous to Late Eocene limestones (Fig. 6.6), parts of which have been metamor-phosed to produce marbles with a wide range of colours: although commonly grey, the upper parts of the unit may be coloured red, green or grey (see below). Within these limestones and marbles there are layers of clastic sediments, some now metamorphosed into schists.

North/south faults parallel to the main gra-ben structure are common and still active. Fault scarps are easily observed in many loca-tions, such as the peninsula near Kounos (Plate 6B). There is a particularly spectacular example on the west side of the Bay of Geroli-mena: here, towards the base of the cliff, there is a fault scarp 3-4 m high.

Pauses in the tectonic uplift of the area, or times when uplift and sea-level rise kept step, have produced plains or steps in the topogra-phy. The most extensive is at about 220 m and forms most of the arable land along the west coast of Mani and the valley west of Areopolis that transects the peninsula. The main road follows this level for much of its length, as many settlements were built at this level.

In other places three or four other steps can

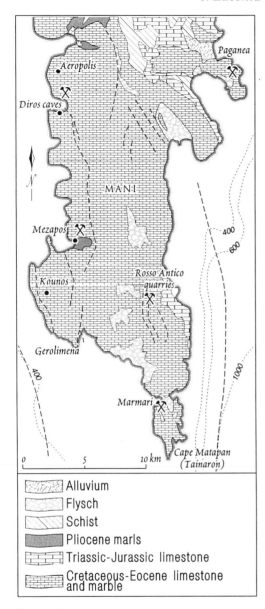

Fig. 6.6. Mani.

Legend (in map):
- Alluvium
- Flysch
- Schist
- Pliocene marls
- Triassic-Jurassic limestone
- Cretaceous-Eocene limestone and marble

fault-bounded block moves independently on a short time-scale.

Rosso Antico quarries

Thirteen km north of Cape Matapan, near the abandoned village of Profitis Elias, are some of the ancient quarries of Rosso Antico (Fig. 6.6).[74, 105] This marble was first employed in Minoan-Mycenaean times, between 1700 and 1300 BC, in architecture and for stone vases. It was not in regular use again until about AD 50, when it is found in Roman and Early Christian buildings, decorating walls and floors. The Romans knew it as Lapis Taenarius (Stone of Tainaron). Re-used pieces were popular in the Middle Ages and later for floor decorations, and were frequently mistaken for Imperial Porphyry (an igneous rock) from Egypt. The quarries were re-opened by an Italian company for a short period in the early twentieth century.

Rosso Antico is a fine-grained, red to purplish red marble, with some varieties streaked with white veins and patches. It occurs in the upper part of the main limestone unit of the Mani, where low-temperature metamorphism has converted the rock to marble. The red colour is due to the presence of minute haematite crystals, and the purple tinge indicates the presence of manganese. The white areas are pure calcite, produced by the solution of calcite in the original red rock and recrystallisation in cracks.[160]

The Profitis Elias quarries also yield white, grey and green marble, which were also exploited in antiquity.[105] In the green variant the iron has been reduced by organic matter in the limestone so that greenish iron-bearing silicates have formed in place of haematite. This stone was used by the Mycenaeans (e.g. in the Treasury of Atreus at Mycenae), but not subsequently. Ancient quarries of Rosso Antico have also been found Paganea, on the east coast about 16 km to the north.[160]

Cape Matapan and Marmari

The ancients regarded the large cave near the Temple of Poseidon on Cape Matapan (Tai-

be distinguished below this level. North of Areopolis the lowest step is about 5 m above sea-level. The uplift can also be identified by the location of the old marine cliffs, which are now set back from the sea. The 5-m level is not seen south of Areopolis, indicating that each naron) as one of the gates of the Underworld, through which Heracles descended to capture the three-headed dog Cerberus. The cave was excavated by waters following a fault that extends to the north in the limestone.

The Romans knew of a dark grey marble from the tip of the Cape, which they called, like the red, Lapis Taenarius (Fig. 6.6). The ancient quarry has been identified with a fair degree of probability on the west side. This marble was apparently known to Italian masons as Bigio Morato (dappled grey).

Six km north of the Cape, on the west coast of the Mani, is the bay of Marmari. Here ancient quarries of white marble have recently been discovered.[45, 113] It is virtually certain that the marble for the sculptures of the Temple of Apollo at Bassae came from these quarries. Nearby ancient quarries also produced a variegated marble with folded and deformed green, white and grey layers. All these different marbles are from the upper part of the main limestone formation of the Mani. Ancient mines of pure white marble have also been found near Mezapos, on the west coast of the Mani.[105]

Diros

At Diros, 10 km south of Areopolis, two well-known caves occur in Cretaceous-Eocene marble (Fig. 6.6). The Glyfada cave has a substantial flow of water (0.5 cubic metres per second) and can be toured by boat.[216] It was not used by ancient people, but must originally have had easier access as animal remains have been found. The adjacent cave of Alepotrypa was used by people in the Late Palaeolithic and Neolithic (25,000-3,000 BC). Finds include stone, bone and metal tools, jewellery, figurines and bones. There are also rock paintings and the remains of a potter's workshop.

Both caves have been excavated by the passage of groundwater that originally fell on the mountains to the east. This water was guided by a north-north-east fault towards the bay of Diros. The caves do not now exactly follow the fault as the waters have enlarged adjacent joints in the rock.

Rising sea-levels have caused an influx of seawater into both caves, so that the water is stratified, with lighter fresh water floating on denser seawater. This stratification continues out into the bay in front of the cave, where in summer, cool fresh water floats on warm seawater. Part of the fresh water in the cave of Alepotrypa is now pumped out for irrigation.

White marble is now produced nearby, but there is no evidence that it was exploited here in antiquity.[105]

Kalamata

Kalamata, under its original name of Pharai, is mentioned several times by Homer, and its antiquity is confirmed by the presence of Mycenaean walls on the acropolis and contemporary tombs nearby. In Classical times Pharai was used as an anchorage, but only in the summer. After Greek, Roman and Byzantine domination Kalamata fell to Geoffrey de Villehardouin in 1208, who built the imposing castle on the old acropolis. It is now the capital of Messenia and an important port.

Kalamata is situated on the eastern side of the Neogene Kalamata (Messenian) graben, which extends from the Gulf of Messene to the south into the Messenian plains (Figs. 6.1, 6.7). To the east the Taygetos range is made of limestones and marbles of the Gavrovo zone, whereas the lower hills to the west are underlain by many different sedimentary rocks (see Ancient Messene). The steep sides of the valley show that movements still continue.

The floor of the graben near Kalamata is underlain by Pliocene marls, sandstones and conglomerates, covered in places by alluvium. The conglomerate is the most resistant to erosion, and forms low, steep-sided hills, such as that of the Kastro.[143]

The Pamisos river proper rises from two large, perennial springs, Ayios Phloros and Pidima, at the foot of the Taygetos range. Surface water and springs are rare in these hills, hence much of the precipitation in the region must be channelled to these springs.[164]

Much of the present Messenian plain was the site of erosion during the height of the Ice Age, when sea-level here was more than 100 m lower than at present. As the glaciers melted

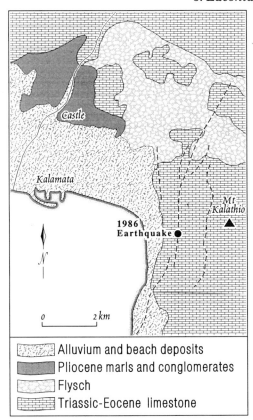

Fig. 6.7. Kalamata.

Korone

The site of Korone was briefly occupied in Classical times by a colony named Asine. In the Middle Ages the inhabitants of Korone (now Petalidi) transferred their city, and its name, 15 km southwards to this spot. The Venetians took it in 1206 and built one of their finest castles. Coron and its twin, Modon (Methone), were important military and commercial ports and were known as 'the principal eyes of the Venetian Republic'.

Steep hills of Jurassic to Cretaceous cherts and limestones descend to the north-east into a broad valley, floored with rolling hills of Pliocene marls, with minor sandstone, conglomerate and lignite beds (Fig. 6.8). This valley is now merely a step in the side of the Messenian graben to the east, but the area was below sea-level in Pliocene times and now has been lifted up. On the eastern side a north/south fault delineates a block that has been raised further from the valley floor to form the peninsula of Korone. The Castle of Korone was built on an outcrop of Pliocene conglomerate.

sea-level rose rapidly until the shoreline was up to 3 km further inland.[156] At this time the Early Helladic sites of Bouxas and Akovitika were on the sea. Since then sea-level has remained approximately stable and the valley has been filled with sediments washed in by the rivers. Large areas of the river valley were covered by swamps until recently when they were drained to provide agricultural land.

The destructive earthquake that struck Kalamata in 1986 had a magnitude of 5.8 and occurred on the Kalamata fault, 4 km east of the town, at a depth of only 5 km. The proximity of the epicentre and the presence of young, poorly consolidated sediments under the town both contributed to the severity of the destruction. Paradoxically this area has a low incidence of earthquakes, as compared to nearby regions, such as the Gulf of Corinth.[165]

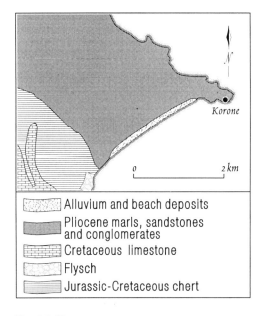

Fig. 6.8. Korone.

Methone

Methone was originally known as Pedasos, and, according to Homer, was one of the seven cities promised by Agamemnon to Achilles. The city was refounded about 700 BC under the name of Methone. In 1206 the Venetians occupied it under the name of Modon and built an enormous castle, matching Coron. In 1500 it fell to the Turks and mostly remained under their domination until 1828, when the French liberators of Modon evacuated the castle and rehoused the inhabitants at the present location of the town.

A narrow fault-bounded ridge of hard, grey Cretaceous-Eocene limestone runs south into the Methone peninsula (Fig. 6.9). From here the limestone continues as a series of shoals, before cropping out on the island of Sapientza, 7 km to the south. To the east of the Methone ridge lies a river valley, down which sediments are transported into the bay of Methone. The eastern side of the bay of Methone is also rocky, but it comprises a series of soft Tertiary flysch sediments: silts, unconsolidated sands and sandstones.[149]

At the climax of the last glaciation the bay of Methone did not exist and the coastline was about 4 km to the east of its present position. By Neolithic times the bay had formed, but it opened out to the sea south of Sapientza. Sea-level was probably only a few metres below the present level by 2100 BC, but the coastline was rather different: the sea had broken through the limestone barrier to the west, the bay of Methone continued about 5 km to the north and the east coast extended several kilometres further east.

Since that time the coastline of the Methone peninsula has changed little as these rocks are resistant to erosion and currents remove the sediments. However, the head of the bay has been filled up by sediments washed in by the river and transported along the coast from the east. The soft rocks of the east coast have been exposed to the full force of the waves and severely eroded.

The harbour now has considerable problems with siltation, partly as a result of the construction of a mole at the end of the nine-

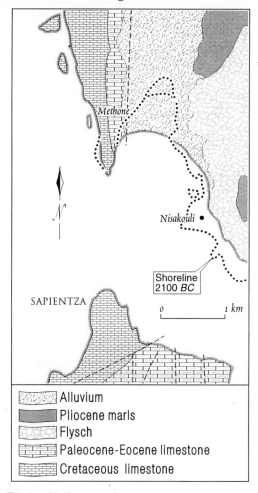

Fig. 6.9. Methone.

teenth century. Earlier moles had a hook shape, parallel to the shore, which limited the amount of sediment, transported from the eroding coast to the east, that was intercepted. The new mole stretched out 200 m directly east from the fortress and trapped much larger amounts of sediment.

Pylos and the Bay of Navarino

The Bay of Navarino, on the west coast of Messenia, is protected by the long island of Sphacteria, which makes it the safest harbour in Greece (Fig. 6.10). It is about 5 km long, 3 km wide and relatively deep. Classical Pylos (Palaiokastro) stood at the north end of the bay. However, the modern town of Pylos (formerly Navarino), is south of the bay. This site not inhabited in antiquity, but grew up around the Turkish castle on Mt Ayios Nikolaos.

The bay is celebrated for two battles. The first took place in 425 BC in the course of the Peloponnesian War. The Athenians made a sort of commando raid on the island of Sphacteria and succeeded in killing or capturing over 400 Spartan warriors. The second, the Battle of Navarino, was fought at sea in the Bay of Navarino in 1827. A force of 26 ships, British, French, and Russian, utterly defeated a Turco-Egyptian fleet of 82 ships and virtually ended the Greek War of Independence.

The western side of Messenia is dominated by a series of low, north/south ridges of Upper Cretaceous to Palaeocene grey limestone (Fig. 6.1). Towards the south these ridges protect from erosion the softer flysch sediments that lie inland. Near the Bay of Navarino these limestones have been breached by faults of the broad graben that extends to the east across the Messenian peninsula. Depression of the graben floor and erosion of the sediments have created an embayment about 10 km long and 4 km wide, and up to 60 m deep (Fig. 6.10). At present about 60% of this area is underwater, including the Bay of Navarino and the Osmanaga lagoon.[157]

Around the bay hard limestones form the hills to the south, and continue north as the island of Sphacteria and the smaller ridges of Palaiokastro, Profitis Elias and Petrochori. The eastern side of Sphacteria is very steep and plunges into deep water: it is a fault, parallel to the faults that shaped the hills and valleys to the south of the bay.

The plateau to the north-east is the 'Kampos', a Pliocene erosion surface and former coastal plain, which has been uplifted by about 400 m during the Pleistocene, and deeply incised by streams. To the east and south-east the bay is bordered by Miocene flysch.

Just after the end of the last glacial period, about 7000 BC, sea-level was 20 m below its present level and the bay extended all the way north to the head of the present plain, about 2

km north of Petrochori. The bay had three entrances: in the south and on either side of Palaiokastro, then an island. Rising sea-level and deposition of sediment from the Amoudheri and other rivers caused the shoreline to migrate southwards. By about 2500 BC it stood 2 km further south. Sea-cliffs to the north-east were probably formed at this time. The Helladic shoreline lay east of the present Bouphras bay, which may have remained an open channel at this time. It is possible that a port existed at this time on the northern shore of the bay. A sandy shore extending about 5 km to the north-west, and an inland dune-field west of Petrochori, were present at this time and could have been responsible for the Homeric epithet 'Sandy Pylos' (but see below). Certainly there were no other comparable areas in the southern or western Peloponnese. By Hellenistic or Roman times transport of sediment along the coast formed a sand-spit from Yialova to the Palaiokastro ridge, cutting off part of the bay to become the Osmanaga lagoon. Since then there has been little change in the position of the coastline.

The Sikia channel remained open until the battle of Lepanto in 1571. At that time the Turks blocked the channel with a line of sunken ships, which acted as a baffle for sediments transported along the coast. Accumulation of sediments has continued and the channel today is very shallow.

Coastal plains, such as that north of the bay, are generally very fertile as the fresh sediment is rich in nutrients and the water-table is close to the surface. It is no surprise that many efforts have been made to drain these areas for agricultural use. The first efforts may have occurred in Helladic times, as revealed by the route of the Amoudheri river. This river descends from the north, but instead of flowing onto the alluvial plain, it makes a sharp bend to the west and runs though a deeply incised valley to the Ionian sea. This diversion could have occurred naturally as a valley advanced by erosion eastwards from the coast, or it could have been diverted on purpose.[157] Certainly it removed major flood problems on the plain, and hence aided settlement. Diversions of this sort in antiquity are known elsewhere – a clear

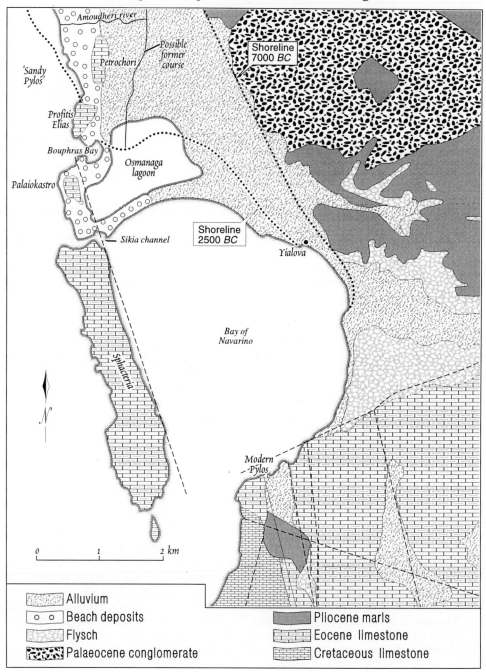

Fig. 6.10. Pylos and the Bay of Navarino (after 157).

example occurred during Mycenaean times near Tiryns.

Pylos

The modern town of Pylos is at the southern end of the Bay of Navarino (Fig. 6.10). It was largely constructed in a small north/south graben, between low hills of grey Eocene-Palaeocene limestone which support two castles. The coastline to the north of the town is a fault, an extension of a graben fault that cuts right across the peninsula.

The Palace of Nestor (Englianos)

The hill of Englianos lies 17 km north of modern Pylos, in the midst of a number of Mycenaean royal tombs (Fig. 6.1), where a magnificent Mycenaean palace may have been the home of that garrulous old man, the Homeric hero Nestor. It was built about 1300 BC, burnt down a hundred years later, and never reoccupied. Apart from its unwalled condition it is comparable in every way with the contemporary palaces at Mycenae and Tiryns.

This hill is a part of the Pliocene erosion and depositional surface known as the 'Kampos'. At that time this area was close to sea-level, and sands and silts, derived from the erosion of the Kyparissia mountains, were deposited here on a coastal plain. During the Pleistocene period the area was uplifted and the Kampos was dissected by streams that cut down into the weak sediments, creating steep-sided valleys. The Palace of Nestor was constructed on the Kampos, just above the geologically recent valley of the Amoudheri river. At the time of construction, the Bay of Naverino would have extended further north than at present, to within 7 km of the palace.[157] It has been suggested that the Homeric epithet 'Sandy Pylos' may not refer to the nearby beach, but instead to the sandy soils around the palace.[30]

Ancient Messene

The city of Messene was founded in 369 BC by the Theban general Epaminondas as a defence against the Spartans. The city stood on the

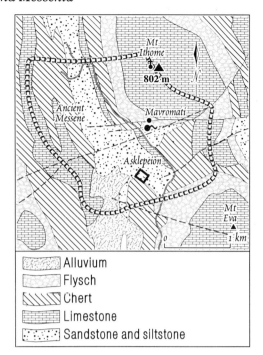

Fig. 6.11. Ancient Messene.

southern slopes of Mt Ithome above the fertile Messenian plains. The fortifications, of the fourth century BC, are excellently preserved; they guaranteed its independence until the Roman conquest of 146 BC.

Both Mt Ithome, above Ancient Messene, and Mt Eva to the south are made of hard Late Cretaceous limestone that has resisted erosion (Fig. 6.11). These blocks are the core of a syncline that runs north/south, hence the overall structure is the inverse of the topography. This limestone was quarried from the side of Mt Ithome facing Mt Eva for the construction of the walls of the city and most of the buildings.

A variety of different Jurassic and Triassic sedimentary rocks, including sandstone, limestone, red and green chert and red shale, occur underneath the limestone of Mt Ithome and are exposed throughout the ancient city. Most of these rocks, including the limestone, were deposited in the deep ocean.

A large spring issues from limestone in the centre of the village of Mavromati, on the north side of the main street, and flows into a modern fountain-house, which contains traces of classical construction. The spouts and water channels of the Arsinoe fountain-house, about 100 m south of the village, are thickly encrusted with travertine. These deposits are not present around the spring in the village, suggesting that a different spring, now extinct, once supplied this fountain. The presence of these springs was probably the reason for the cult of Asklepios here.

Both these springs are associated with east/west vertical faults. Some of the rainwater falling on the limestone of Mt Ithome descends into the mountain until its passage is blocked by the impermeable underlying sediments. The water then accumulates until it has sufficient pressure to rise to the surface along the faults, appearing as springs.

7

Elis, Achaea and Arcadia

This chapter is concerned with the districts of Elis, Achaea and Arcadia in the north-western and central parts of the Peloponnese (Fig. 7.1). As they differ geographically and geologically, they are best dealt with separately.

The western part of the Peloponnese is mostly underlain by the rocks of the Gavrovo and Pindos zones, which are seen also on the island of Corfu and the western part of the Greek mainland. These zones are the 'external' parts of the Hellenic collision zone and are, in essence, parts of the continent that impinged onto the Eurasian mainland. For much of its life the Pindos zone was a deep water trough, distant from land, where deep-water limestones accumulated. This was interrupted twice by deposition of flysch sediments, shed into the basin from adjacent mountain chains produced during regional compression.

The Gavrovo zone, south-west of the Pindos, was for a long time covered by shallow seas, distant from land. Reefs produced by accumulations of bivalve shells, algal encrustations and coral skeletons were eventually converted into limestone. Sedimentation in the Gavrovo zone ended with the deposition of marls and conglomerates. At this time regional compression raised the Pindos zone above sea-level and clastic sediments were shed into the adjacent Gavrovo zone. Finally, Alpine compression during the Eocene period thrust the Pindos zone south-westward over the Gavrovo zone.

As elsewhere in Greece this area was profoundly affected by the great Neogene phase of crustal extension (see Chapter 2). Here the direction of extension varied from north-north-east in the north, to north-east in the west. A series of grabens developed, including the Gulf of Corinth and the plains of Elis.

Elis

Elis is bounded on the north by Achaea, on the east by Arcadia, and on the south by Messenia (Fig. 7.1). Cut off by mountains from the Aegean, it tended to look westwards to the Ionian Sea. Olympia put it on the political map in the seventh century BC, and even in Roman times much of the Mediterranean world came to the games. The northern part, Elis proper, is divided into the Plain of Elis on the west, watered by the Peneios river, and on the east, the foothills of the Arcadian mountains. The Plain is good for livestock, and was traditionally renowned for its horses. It also grows flax and cereals. Further south, watered by the longest river on the Peloponnese, the Alpheios, is the district of Pisatis, which contained the Sanctuary of Olympia. Further still to the south is the district of Triphyllia, reaching as far as the river Neda.

The mountains inland from Elis are dominated by deep-water limestones of the Pindos zone in the east, and flysch of the Gavrovo zone in the west (Fig. 7.1). Neogene extension in a north-east/south-west direction produced the graben that is the broad valley of the Alpheios river, and the strait that lies between the mainland and the island of Zakinthos. A secondary Neogene extension, at right angles to the main direction, produced the north-west coast and plains of Elis, and continues into Achaea (see below).

In Pliocene times the graben of the Alpheios river and the north-west coastal plain of Elis initially sank faster than they could be filled up by sediments delivered by the rivers from the uplifted areas towards the centre of the Peloponnese. In these large bays or estuaries

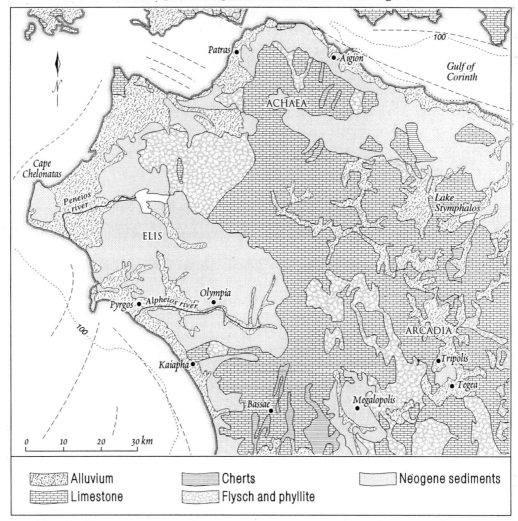

Fig. 7.1. Elis, Achaea and Arcadia.

marine and brackish water sediments were deposited, including the shelly limestones that were used in the construction of most of the buildings at Olympia. Subsidence slowed and/or the sedimentation rate increased during the Pleistocene and the bays became dry land. Recently, these deposits have been uplifted and strongly eroded.

Cape Chelonatas

The Elis Plain comprises a gravel-covered plateau and the alluvial deposits of the Peneios river. The plateau appears to be a Pleistocene erosion surface, originally at sea-level, but now lifted up by tectonic forces. The shoreline probably ran along the edge of this plain in Helladic times and hence the Chelonatas headland was an island.

For much of historical time the Peneios

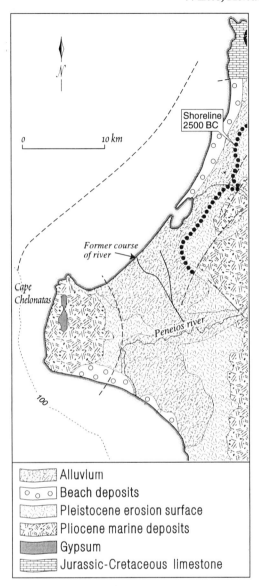

Fig. 7.2. Western Elis (after 148 and other sources).

Cape Chelonatas, is a series of low hills topped by the Frankish castle of Chlemoutsi (Fig. 7.2). This headland is a horst of Pliocene marine sediments, including gypsum, similar to those to the east on the other side of the graben.

Olympia

The panhellenic sanctuary of Zeus at Olympia takes its name from Mt Olympos in north Greece. It is situated in a lush green valley at the confluence of the river Alpheios and its tributary the Kladeos (Fig. 7.1). The site was first occupied in about 3000 BC. From 776 BC Greeks from all over the Greek world assembled every four years to worship Zeus and to participate in the Olympic Games. The Games were held regularly until AD 393 when the Sanctuary was closed by the Christian Emperor Theodosius 1. In 426 Theodosius II ordered the destruction of the Sanctuary; the process was completed by two terrible earthquakes in 522 and 551 (Plate 7A), followed by floods, landslides, and the attacks of the Vandals.

The most famous buildings were the temples of Hera (Heraion) and Zeus. The temple of Hera was built in about 650 BC of local shelly limestone, replacing an earlier building of wood and mud brick. The temple of Zeus was built between 466 and 456 BC of the same local limestone, faced with a marble stucco. The sculptures and the original roof-tiles were of Parian marble, but later some tiles of Pentelic marble were used as replacements. About 430 BC the sculptor Phidias made the colossal gold and ivory cult-statue of Zeus, a masterpiece which was one of the Seven Wonders of the Ancient World.

Olympia was built on the flood plains of the Alpheios and Kladeos rivers (Figs. 7.1, 7.3). The hills around the site are made of geologically young (Late Pliocene) uncemented sands, silts, clays and conglomerates. The best-known part of this unit is the Hill of Kronos which rises steeply to the north of the site. It is made of yellow, uncemented sands, which have been eroded to an angle steeper than their angle of rest and are only held in place by the trees. As a result there are numerous small landslides

river flowed north of the Chelonatas headland, depositing large amounts of sediments along the north-west coast. However, during the eighteenth century the river naturally shifted course to its present position south of the headland. This shift has starved the north-west coast of sediment and it is now being eroded.[148]

The westernmost part of the Peloponnese,

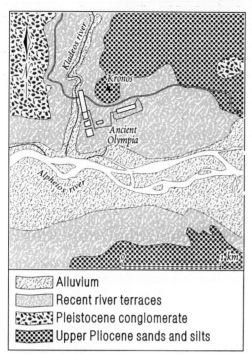

Alluvium
Recent river terraces
Pleistocene conglomerate
Upper Pliocene sands and silts

Fig. 7.3. Olympia.

But it is also possible that the burial was part of a cycle of sedimentation controlled by the interaction between the Kladeos and Alpheios rivers.[131]

The Alpheios, the major river of this basin, here occupies a bed about one kilometre wide. When it meanders near its southern limit the Kladeos must flow a further kilometre to join it, compared to when it is at its northern limit. A long river bed creates a shallow slope, so water flows more slowly. In these conditions sediments tend to be deposited and then form an alluvial fan upstream from the confluence of the rivers. A fan of this type from the Kladeos buried Olympia. Since then the Alpheios has migrated north and the bed of the Kladeos has become shorter. The more rapidly moving waters have now eroded the alluvial fan deposited earlier, and cut a 5-6 m deep trench which is the present bed of the river.

The form and position of the stadium suggest that it may have evolved from a natural feature: a channel of the Alpheios, when it was at its northern limit, would have had a similar orientation and topography. Such channels are abandoned when the river shifts, commonly abruptly, following a storm.

The buildings of Olympia, like the temples of Hera and Zeus, were mostly constructed from Pliocene and Pleistocene shelly limestones, or occasionally sandstones, deposited in the basin. The quarries were near the Sanctuary, on the opposite side of the Alpheios.[49]

Intense earthquakes are relatively common at Olympia, because of its tectonic setting and the local geological conditions. Unlike many sites in the Aegean, Olympia was built on river sediments rather than solid rock. Such sediments can resonate during earthquakes, amplifying seismic vibrations and considerably increasing the destructive force of earthquakes. This was well-known in antiquity and precautions were taken to mitigate the effects of severe earthquakes. The columns of the temples and other buildings could not be protected against violent shocks. The columns, thirteen on either side and six at the ends, collapsed during the earthquakes of AD 522 and 551, and can still be seen where they fell (Plate 7A).

along the lower slopes, especially along the modern road-cut, but they have not moved far. Similar landslides probably contributed to the burial of parts of the site adjacent to the hill, especially when the loosened material was further redistributed by surface water. The substantial retaining wall behind the Treasuries indicates that landslides from the Hill of Kronos were also a problem in ancient times. However, the amount of material shed from Mt Kronos was not sufficient to bury the site and most of the sediment must have been supplied by the rivers.

There have been many explanations for the deposition of alluvium here. Catastrophic draining of a temporary lake in the Feneos polje, 70 km to the north-east, is recorded to have produced flooding at Olympia (see Achaea), but it seems unlikely that significant amounts of sediment could have been deposited so far away.[148] Increased erosion during the fifth to seventeenth centuries has also been blamed for deposition of alluvium on the site.[277]

The Springs of Kaiapha

Two thermal springs rise 15 km south of Olympia (see Fig. 7.1).[1] The northern spring issues at about 36°C from a limestone cave, known in antiquity as the Cave of the Anigrian Nymphs. It is about ten metres deep and lined with flowstone, which is not caused by the spring itself but by seepage through the roof. Two faults, which can be traced into the limestone overlying the cave, probably guide the waters to the surface. The springwater contains about 30% seawater and issues from the rear of the cave, accompanied by a small amount of the gas hydrogen sulphide. This gas has reacted with the limestone to produce crystals of gypsum, which line the deepest part of the cave.

About 1 km south another sulphurous spring issues from the base of the hill in the Cave of Yeranion. This spring is much cooler, about 27°C, and is probably a mixture of deeply-circulating thermal waters and cool groundwater, with little seawater.[1] The walls of the cave are also coated with gypsum crystals, but these are much smaller than in the northern cave.

Achaea

The province of Achaea extends along the south shore of the Corinthian Gulf (Fig. 7.1). It consists of a narrow coastal plain, backed by the northern slopes of the Arcadian mountains. It is bounded on the east by Corinthia, on the south by Arcadia, and on the west by Elis.

The plain is very fertile, producing fruit, vines and olives; it is broken up and watered by numerous streams, most of which dry up in the summer. The higher slopes carry forests of oak and conifer. The coast is low-lying, with only one good harbour, at Patras.

Little is known of the early history of Achaea, but archaeology has established its importance in Mycenaean times (1600-1100 BC). Later, in the Classical period, Achaea became a federal league of twelve small towns until the fourth century BC. Helice, the sanctuary and meeting place of the Achaean league, was destroyed by a tsunami in 373 BC (see below). In the third and second centuries BC,

however, a reconstituted Achaean League became the principal power in Greece until it was swallowed up by the rising power of Rome.

The high mountains to the south, and those west of Patras, are dominated by deep-water limestones of the Pindos zone (Fig. 7.1). However, farther north the rocks, and the overall shape of the land, have been controlled by Neogene extension. The most important morphological feature of the area is the Gulf of Corinth. This graben started to form about ten million years ago and is still active (see Chapter 5). The western part of the Gulf of Corinth is, more accurately, a half-graben, as only the southern edge is descending along a fault.[114] The northern edge is more like a hinge. Initially the graben was much wider, and extended 15-20 km further south than the present coastline. During the Pliocene and early Pleistocene marine sediments were deposited in this trough. The graben migrated to the north in more recent geological time, uplifting these sediments to form much of the hilly area south of the Gulf.

Near Patras the tectonics have a different character: extension, or possibly strike-slip faulting, took place at right angles to the main direction. This produced an offset in the Gulf of Corinth, parallel to the coast of Elis to the south. The hills to the west of Patras are a block of Cretaceous and Jurassic limestone raised up by the combination of these two extensions. There are two prominent terraces near Patras, at 270 and 80 m.[220] The upper terrace is probably the top of deltas that were deposited in the Gulf of Patras when it was a lake, about 250,000 years ago (see Chapter 5).

Recent earthquakes along the faults of the Gulf of Corinth graben are concentrated towards the eastern end, along the northern shore and around the town of Aigion. Many earthquakes, notably those in 373 BC and AD 1402, were accompanied by tsunamis.[192]

The earthquake and tsunami of 373 BC was also responsible for the destruction of the city of Helice, whose exact location is still unknown, as nothing remains. It was probably 7 km west of Aigion, on the western gulf. Contemporary writers noted that wild animals and insects left the city during the five days preceding the earthquake, and this has often been cited when premonitory animal behaviour is discussed. The earthquake probably occurred on the southern graben fault:[184] this fault was reactivated in AD 1881, when it produced a scarp 2 m high and 13 km long. The city was submerged by movements on the fault, and its destruction was completed by the tsunami and further earthquakes along this fault. It is estimated that a total of 6.5 m of movement has taken place during the past 5,000 years.

Arcadia

The department of Arcadia, in the centre of the Peloponnese, is completely surrounded by a ring of high mountains. Much of it is drained by the river Alpheios and its tributaries; frequently the rivers, with no outlet above ground, disappear through sink-holes.

The most prosperous part in antiquity consisted of the eastern plains which, in spite of extremes of climate, grew vines, wheat and barley. Here were the substantial cities of Orchomenos, Mantinea and Tegea. The west is rough upland, and good for little but livestock. Here the shepherds worshipped the pastoral god Pan. Arcadia never achieved political importance, but was well known for its pastoral setting, and secondarily for the mercenary activities of its inhabitants. Their dialect, related to Cypriote, was the only version of Greek in the mainland which can be directly traced to the language of the Mycenaeans.

The bedrock here closely resembles that of much of the central Peloponnese. Cretaceous deep-water limestones of the Pindos have been thrust over flysch and Mesozoic shallow-water limestones of the Gavrovo zone (Fig. 7.1). The latter can be seen through windows in the overlying Pindos where it has been removed by erosion. Neogene faulting produced a series of grabens in the eastern part of the region. These grabens make up the interior plains of eastern Arcadia and most are poljes, i.e. they are drained internally by sink-holes (Fig. 7.4). Most of the poljes were originally valleys that drained westwards into the Alpheios river. During the Neogene period erosion of the river beds was unable to keep up with tectonic uplift

and the valleys become isolated. The waters ponded until they were able to widen existing fissures and escape underground.

The only waters that continue to flow westwards are those of the north-west poljes. Most of the water that enters the Feneos sink-holes reappears at the Ladon spring, near Likouria, whereas that from the Hotoussa sink-hole reappears at the Panagitsa and Daras springs.[182] All these springs feed the Ladon river, a tributary of the Alpheios. The connection between the Feneos sink-hole and the Ladon spring was well known in antiquity.[148] Several times the Feneos sink-hole was blocked and the polje became a lake. When it finally drained the flood was felt as far away as Olympia.

Water from all other poljes ultimately discharges into the Gulf of Argos. The Stymphalos polje in the northern part of Arcadia contains the only permanent lake in the region. At present the two major springs of the polje, Stymphalos and Kephalari, are fed by water from Mt Ziria to the north. The water accumulates in Lake Stymphalos, which is drained by a large, gate-like sink-hole. The water finally discharges from springs in the Argolid (see Chapter 5). Several attempts have been made to reduce the amount of marshy land in the valley; the earliest consisted of a canal cut between the spring and sink-hole. About AD 125 this arrangement was improved by the construction of a tunnel through the hills to the south, draining the spring waters into the Scotini polje. By the fifth century the tunnel had become blocked and the polje flooded, but it was repaired in AD 1885 and is still in use today.[182]

The Scotini and Alea poljes also feed the springs of the western Argolid, including the large spring at Kephalari (not to be confused with the Kephalari spring in the Stymphalos polje). The Alea polje periodically becomes a lake as drainage is insufficient to cope with the winter rains.

The largest polje is that around Tripolis. The northern part is a flat, treeless plain drained by five major sink-holes. The Kapsia sink-hole has an extensive cave system at least 2.5 km long that connects to the nearby Paleochori cave. In antiquity the city of Mantinea

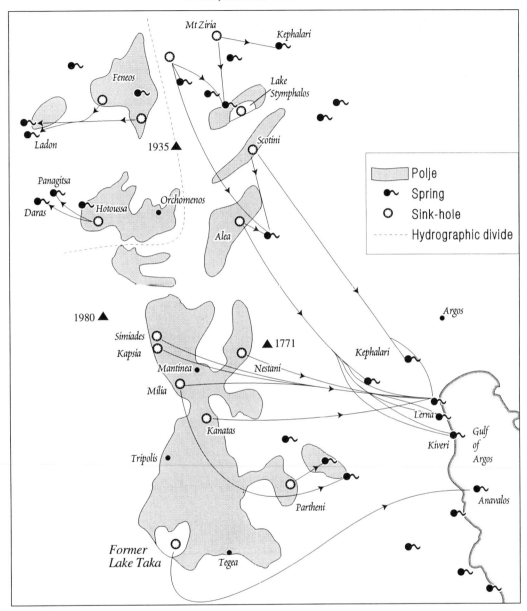

Fig. 7.4. Poljes, sink-holes and karst springs of Arcadia and the Argolid (after 182 and other sources).

stood here, and control of the sink-holes was very important. During one conflict, the sink-holes were blocked and the plain flooded. The mud-brick walls disintegrated and the city was taken. Today, the Kanatas sink-hole receives the sewage waters of the town of Tripolis, most of which are discharged into the Gulf of Argos at the Kiveri spring.

Waters from the southern part of the polje drain into the Taka sink-hole on the southern margin. They finally discharge directly into the Gulf of Argos at the submarine spring

Anavalos.[182] This alluvial plain was formerly a seasonal lake, until the sinkhole was cleaned out during the early part of this century.[182]

Tegea

As the most powerful city state in Arcadia, Tegea long resisted Sparta, but during the Peloponnesian War, in the late fifth century BC, it had perforce to ally its their ancient enemy. The city was most famous for the temple of Athena Alea, the finest in the Peloponnese. It was decorated with sculptures of marble of local origin.

The quarries for this marble, a sparkling greyish-white with a medium to fine grain, are situated on the northern slopes of Mt Parnon, near the modern village of Doliana, some 10 km south-east of Tegea (Fig. 7.1). The deposits are large, extending to 5 km by 1 km, but the marble was not much used outside Arcadia, owing to the difficulties of transporting it in Classical times.

Megalopolis

Megalopolis ('Big City') was founded in 371 BC in the south of Arcadia on the river Helisson, a tributary of the Alpheios. It was created from the amalgamation of 40 villages by Epaminondas of Thebes to be a bulwark against the Spartans. In this aim it succeeded for well over a century, until sacked by the Spartans in 222 BC.

The city was built in the centre of a small, fault-bounded plain, between flysch of the Gavrovo zone to the east, and Cretaceous limestones of the Pindos zone to the west (Fig. 7.1). This basin has existed since Pliocene times, and large amounts of sediments have been deposited here in shallow lakes and swamps. Lignite, a low-grade coal, formed here from accumulated plant remains. This rock is quarried in one of the largest operations in Europe and used to generate electricity.

Bassae

The Temple of Apollo Epikourios at Bassae, situated at an altitude of 1,131 m on the bare and windswept slopes of Mt Paliavlakhitsa (ancient Mt Kotilion) was built between 430 and 400 BC on the site of an earlier temple (Fig. 7.5). The Temple incorporated a number of unusual features, including the earliest recorded Corinthian capital. At first sight it appears to be comparatively well preserved, but was in fact seriously damaged in the Middle Ages, by people who tore the masonry apart to steal the metal clamps. Eventually, in AD 1811, the surviving sculptures were removed.

The bedrock beneath the temple is siliceous limestone of Late Cretaceous age. This rock is finely bedded and strongly jointed and folded, giving a low strength inadequate for fine construction. It was only used as rubble beneath parts of the foundations, and from the warping of the building appears to have been inadequate even for that purpose.[12, 46]

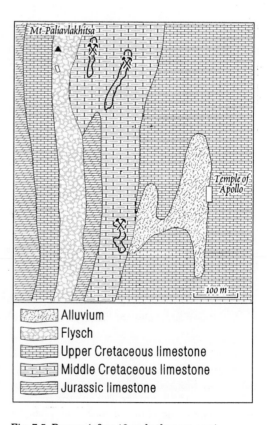

Fig. 7.5. Bassae (after 46 and other sources).

Most of the superstructure of the temple was built of slightly older, Mid-Cretaceous limestone that crops out in a band west of the temple. This limestone is purer, less folded and jointed than the bedrock beneath the temple, and so provided a much stronger rock, although still with well-developed bedding. The quarries for this limestone can be seen 200 m south-west and 300 m north-west of the temple.

The builders of the temple set the bedding so as to maximise the strength of the blocks. In a harsh climate, such as here, one of the most important mechanisms of rock weathering is the freezing and thawing of water absorbed into cracks, such as the bedding planes. The columns have best resisted weathering because the layering was oriented more or less horizontally, and hence little water was absorbed. The lintels were set with the layers in a vertical orientation, and hence have suffered most since the loss of the roof allowed water to penetrate.

The sculptures, architectural details, ceiling coffers and roof-tiles were made of white marble. Many sources have been suggested, but geochemical and textural evidence suggests that it came from near Marmari in the Mani (see Laconia).[45]

8

Central Greece

The term Central Greece is taken here to mean the Departments of Boeotia, Phocis and Euboea (Fig. 8.1). The area covered by this chapter spans four isopic zones and commences, in the east, with the rocks of the Attic-Cycladic metamorphic belt. These rocks underlie the southern, narrower part of Euboea, and adjacent parts of Attica. They closely resemble the rocks of the Cyclades, which are discussed in Chapter 15.

Further to the north and west lies the Pelagonian zone. Limestone is the dominant rock here, deposited in shallow seas during the Triassic and Jurassic periods. The Sub-Pelagonian zone further west was an ancient sea-floor (ophiolite), now composed of great masses of peridotite and serpentinite, as well as deep-water limestones and cherts. Further west lies the Parnassos zone, dominated by shallow-water limestone like the Pelagonian zone. Finally, in the west, the Pindos zone is here dominated by flysch sediments. The Alpine compressions stacked these zones onto each other: first the Pelagonian zone was thrust westwards onto the Sub-Pelagonian zone, then that package was thrust eastwards onto the Pindos and Parnassos zones.

During the Neogene volcanism was very limited, but important crustal extension began and is still taking place. The crust was stretched in a north-east/south-west direction, forming a series of parallel grabens. These are the Gulf of Corinth, the Kephissos valley (including the Copais basin) and the north and south Euboean gulfs. The faults defining the north-east coast of Euboea are also part of this system. The Spercheios valley cuts across this trend and connects two of the grabens, but is clearly part of the same system. Earthquake activity is concentrated along the Gulf of Corinth, which is the most active graben in this region.

Boeotia and Thebes

The district of Boeotia is completely ringed with mountains except on the south-east (Fig. 8.1). It is composed of a group of plains whose soil is unusually fertile for Greece, and is good for cereals and livestock. There are two principal plains, separated by an east-west range (an outlier of Mt Helicon) on which the city of Thebes stands. To the north, the Plain of Orchomenos is watered by the Kephissos river, which flowed into Lake Copais, now a drained area. To the south, the Plain of Thebes is watered by the river Asopos. Boeotia was a prosperous area in the Bronze Age and later periods, and provided the material base for the dominant city of Thebes.

The two principal Boeotian plains constitute a graben, set within hills of Triassic-Jurassic limestone (Fig. 8.1). This graben is probably associated with the Kephissos graben to the north-west (see Lake Copais below), but has been recently somewhat less active; large parts of the basin are underlain by Miocene, Pliocene and Pleistocene sedimentary rocks that were formed in lakes in the basin, but now have been lifted up and are being eroded.

Thebes was as important as Mycenae during the Mycenaean period. Its most famous king, the probably legendary Oedipus, killed his father and married his mother. Traces of a magnificent palace and tombs of royalty and nobility, all of Mycenaean date, have been found. From about 700 BC Thebes was leader of

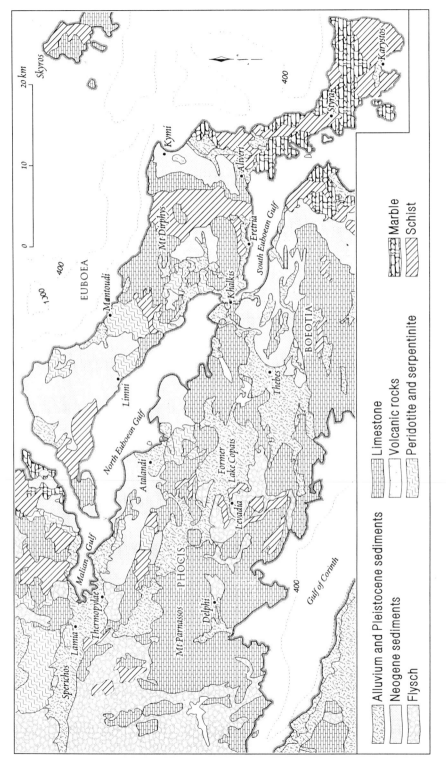

Fig. 8.1. Central Greece and Euboea.

Alluvium and Pleistocene sediments

Neogene sediments

Flysch

Limestone

Volcanic rocks

Peridotite and serpentinite

Marble

Schist

a Boeotian Confederacy until its destruction in 336 BC by Alexander the Great.

The east-west line of hills on which the city of Thebes stands is composed of conglomerates and sandstones deposited in lakes on the floor of the graben during the Early Pliocene to Pleistocene, and subsequently uplifted (Fig. 8.1). Thebes was constructed on a small plateau 60 m above the plain and still dominates the flat landscape. One reason why this site was chosen in antiquity was the presence of the copious springs in the two valleys on either side of the plateau.[259]

Lake Copais

In classical times Lake Copais was the largest lake in Greece, measuring 24 by 13 km. It was entirely surrounded by mountains and was fed by the rivers Kephissos and Melas and a number of springs, with the only natural outlets being a number of sink-holes on the north-east and east sides (Figs. 8.1, 8.2). For most of the year it was a swamp, but in the summer much of it dried out, and in the rainy seasons it became a true lake.

There were several early attempts to drain the lake in order to create good farm land. The Mycenaeans enlarged two sink-holes between 1400 and 1200 BC; but after their downfall in about 1100 BC, nature again took over. Two more attempts at reclamation are recorded, in the late fourth century BC and in the second century AD. Finally, after many centuries of neglect, drainage works were completed in 1931. The Copais area is now very fertile and is devoted to pasture, rice and cotton.

The Copais basin is bounded to the north largely by Triassic to Cretaceous limestones of the Pelagonian zone, and flysch sediments of the Parnassos zone to the south (Fig. 8.2). It is one of a series of basins that stretch from the Boeotian plain in the south-east to those along the Kephissos river in the north-west. This broad valley is a graben formed by the foundering of a slice of the crust during tension. This process did not occur evenly, but has left bridges of bedrock separating the different basins. This graben is parallel to similar structures in the gulf of Corinth and the North-

ern Euboean Gulf. All these grabens were formed during the last ten million years in response to north-east/south-west tension in the crust. The floor of the Copais graben is still subsiding, which is why the basin is floored by recent sediments.

Both vegetation and water levels have varied in the past: pollen studies indicate that before 3500-3000 BC oak trees were abundant in the region and Copais was a true lake.[5] After this time the oaks declined and soil erosion increased, possibly caused by or linked with increases in human activity. At the same time the level of the lake declined, marshes became widespread and peat was deposited in the basin. Therefore, by the time of the Mycenaeans, Copais was a marsh rather than a perennial lake.

There are many sink-holes along the eastern side of the basin, but the most important are those in the north-east, in Jurassic and Cretaceous limestone.[138] The Melas (Mavropotamus) river drains into the largest sink-hole, the Megali (Great) Katavothra. The water from all these sink-holes flows 2-4 km to the north and east, and feeds springs that discharge into the valley to the east and flow a short distance into the sea at Larimna (Fig. 8.2). Another group of sink-holes, to the south-east, feed springs that discharge into Lake Iliki. The bed-rock here is also mostly Jurassic limestone.

The Mycenaeans constructed a series of canals to drain the basin.[138] The canals terminated at the Binia sink-hole, north of Megali Katavothra, where a tunnel was excavated to augment the flow. Although over 2 km were dug, it was never completed. Another tunnel was started further south, to augment the flow into Lake Iliki, but was also never completed. However, it did anticipate the route of the modern drain, which passes under the National Highway.

Iron and nickel-rich laterite layers occur in the local limestones, both to the north and to the east of the Copais basin;[21] see below for the origin of the laterites. Pliny mentions an occurrence of iron ore near Hyettos, about 8 km north of Lake Copais, but it is not clear if they were exploited. Recently, the laterites have

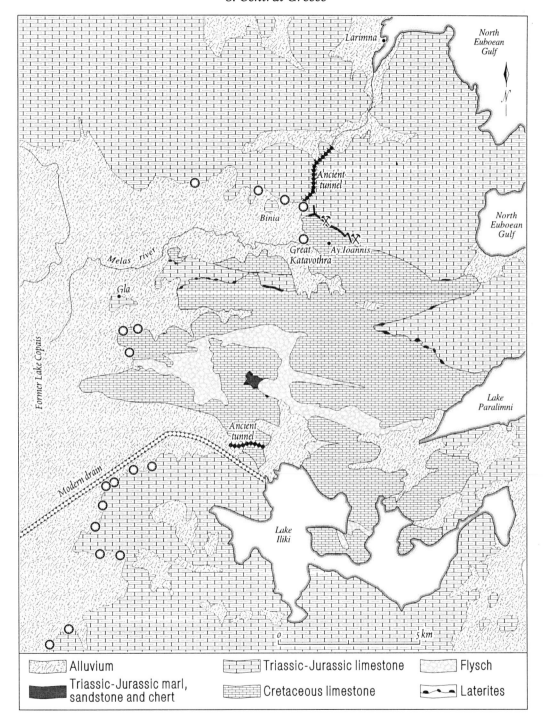

Fig. 8.2. The western part of the former Lake Copais basin (after 138 and other sources).

been exploited for nickel, especially around the village of Ayios Ioannis, near Megali Katavothra (Fig. 8.2). The ore was transported to Larimna where it was refined.

The Mycenaean stronghold of Gla lies in the north-east part of the Copais basin. Formerly an island, it is now a low, flat-topped hill. Ancient walls follow the edge of the cliffs for almost 3 km, and there is a Mycenaean palace at the highest point of the island. The hill is made of Cretaceous limestone, riddled with caves and abandoned sink-holes.

Levadia

Levadia was celebrated in antiquity for the Oracle of Trophonios, an institution second in importance only to Delphi. Trophonios was an old Boeotian god, later demoted to the status of hero. The oracular cave has recently been discovered on Mt Ayios Elias. In the deepest part of the cave were the Springs of Forgetfulness and Memory where the pilgrims bathed. Thanks to its strategic situation in the Erkina valley (ancient Herkyna), Levadia was of some importance in the Middle Ages, and today it is the capital of the Department of Boeotia.

Levadia is situated at the bottom of the gorge of the Kanellia river where it opens out into the plain of the former Lake Copais and joins the Erkina river (Fig. 8.3). The lower parts of the city are underlain by Palaeocene flysch, but the Kastro hill and the Kanellia gorge are faulted blocks of Late Cretaceous limestone. Further south flysch again reappears, this time above the limestone.

The gorge is a good example of a valley with incised meanders. The process starts with a slowly flowing stream meandering across relatively flat land. Rapid uplift causes the bed of the stream to cut down vertically into the bedrock, and it then incises the meanders.

Many springs feed the Kanellia river just above the Kastro walls turning it from a small stream into a significant river. On the east side of the stream a spring issues from the base of the cliff along a horizontal joint-plane, which has been enlarged into a small arch by the corrosive action of the water. The area above the spring contains many 'fossil' spring mouths

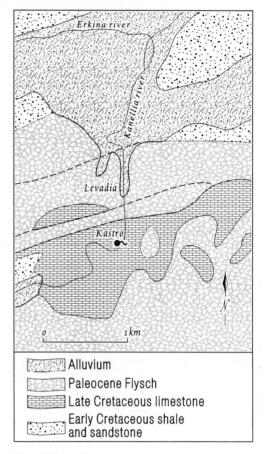

Fig. 8.3. Levadia.

which have a flat bottom and an arched top. Many of these have been further artificially enlarged into niches for religious offerings. The uppermost spring on the other side of the river feeds a reservoir for the city water-supply. Other springs issue directly into the bed of the river, some releasing streams of gas bubbles. These bubbles are air which comes out of solution in the water as the pressure is released.

Mt Parnassos

Mt Parnassos (2,457 m) has given its name to the Parnassos isopic zone, which crops out only in this area (Figs. 8.1, 8.4) and at Mt Olympos. The rocks here are a pile of shallow-water carbonates deposited from the Triassic to Palaeocene. These massive limestones are very strong and were not much broken up by the Alpine compressional movements, in contrast to the rocks in the adjoining zones, which is why today Mt Parnassos has such strong relief.

Three times during the Jurassic and Late Cretaceous this area was lifted up above sea-level. At this time Greece had a tropical climate, and under these conditions extreme weathering of the rock removes almost all chemical elements, leaving behind a layer of loose material rich in aluminium called bauxite. Similar processes elsewhere acting on other rocks produced a material rich in iron and nickel called laterite (see below). At the end of each weathering cycle the rocks sank again below sea-level and another layer of limestone was deposited, sandwiching the bauxite between layers of limestone. Bauxite is the major source of aluminium, and these deposits have been extensively exploited in Greece.

Delphi

Delphi, site of the most famous oracle of antiquity, is even today a place of mystery, wildness and beauty, perched on the mountainside, looking up to Mt Parnassos and down to the port of Itea (Fig. 8.1). Immediately above it are the twin peaks, the Phaidriades, and below it is the river Pleistos. It was believed by the ancient Greeks to be the centre of the Earth, and it is indeed just about at the centre of Greece.

Delphi was a holy place, and probably an oracle, from a very early period. According to legend, and corroborated by archaeology, the first presiding deity was the Earth Goddess, Ge, served by Cretans from Knossos. A little Minoan and much Mycenaean material has been found here, dating between 1600 and 1100 BC. At the end of the Bronze Age the god Apollo became dominant. Under his protection the oracle was very active from the eighth to the sixth centuries BC, giving advice and foretelling the future for public and private clients, through the voice of his priestess, known as the Sibyl or Pythia. After 500 BC its oracular authority declined, but Delphi functioned for

another 900 years, until it was abolished by the Christians in about AD 400. Christians, barbarians and earthquakes reduced the oracular site to ruins and eventually a village grew up here.

The dramatic topography of Delphi was caused by rapid uplift associated with the Gulf of Corinth graben (see below) and by the preferential erosion of rocks adjacent to a fault that runs along the valley of the Pleistos river (Fig. 8.4). This fault is almost parallel to the graben faults, and was probably formed by the same tectonic forces. The local topography of the site is also controlled by the nature of the underly-

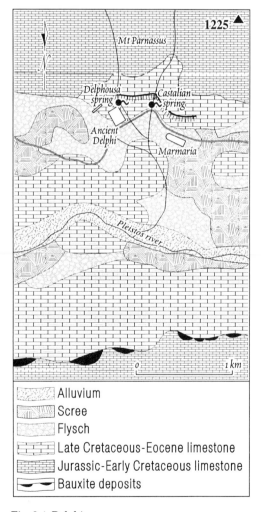

Fig. 8.4. Delphi.

ing rocks. Limestones are resistant to erosion and form steep cliffs, whereas shales erode easily and underlie the more gentle slopes.

Most of the rocks around Delphi have been turned upside-down by folding and faulting during the Alpine deformation of the area.[231] The oldest rocks are a series of dark Late Jurassic limestones and occur at the tops of the mountains. Below these rocks are a series of Middle Cretaceous pale limestones and slightly younger dark or black bitumen-bearing limestones. Finally, there is a thinly-bedded pale limestone, with layers of chert, of Cretaceous to Eocene age. The cliffs behind the ancient site of Delphi are made of the last three types of limestone. All these limestones are cut off by an almost horizontal thrust fault that runs just above the modern road. Most of the rocks below this fault are red shales of unknown age, as well as minor Cretaceous limestone and recent scree.

The south side of the valley has similar stratigraphy, but is offset by the steep fault that runs along the bottom of the Pleistos valley. On this side of the valley red-weathering bauxite deposits occur along some of the contacts of these limestones (see Parnassos).

The buildings of ancient Delphi were mostly constructed of local grey limestone.[194] Although some of this was cut from small quarries near the site, the supply was not sufficient and was supplemented by material from extensive quarries at Profitis Elias, about 5 km to the south-west. The quarries lie at an altitude of 210 m, in early Cretaceous limestones, with minor chert and calcite veins.

The Castalian spring was an important part of ancient Delphi. All who came here for religious reasons had to purify themselves in these waters. The spring issues from the eastern wall of the Papadia ravine, just above a thrust fault, where limestones overlie shales. The proximity of this fault is revealed by the well-developed cleavage of the rocks that dips 30° to the north. These waters originate as rain and snow which fall on Mt Parnassos and seep into the limestones. There the water descends until it reaches the less-permeable shale. Unable to descend further the water flows laterally until it reaches the surface as a spring. The flow rate

of the spring is rather low, and the water flows down the valley to join the Pleistos river far below.

The Kassotis fountain, immediately northeast of the Temple of Apollo, was also very important. The priestess drank from it before prophesying. This fountain was an artificial reservoir fed by waters from the Delphousa (Kerna) spring 70 m to the north-east, which issues from a cleft in the limestone. Small amounts of travertine have been deposited around the spring. Below the spring is a red limestone-breccia which is underlain by shale. This spring now supplies part of the water for the modern village of Delphi.

A greater deposit of travertine is present on the wall behind the temple of Apollo. Here up to 30 cm have been deposited since the site was cleared about 90 years ago. Traces of the travertine cone that once covered this whole area can be seen along the rear wall. This travertine probably comes from water channelled down from Delphousa spring or from a separate spring. The site must have been covered with abundant travertine deposits long before human habitation and these, now largely destroyed, may have first attracted people to this site.

The last temple of Apollo, whose ruins we see today, was built between 366 and 329 BC. Burnt in the first century BC, it was restored by the Romans and was finally closed in the fourth century AD. Subsequently earthquakes and human depredations took their toll.

The temple was built of local limestone, with columns of poros limestone covered with stucco. In the inner shrine, apparently an underground chamber, were the Omphalos (the navel of the earth) and the oracular chasm, over which the Pythia sat. Tradition holds that her utterings were induced by chewing laurel leaves and inhaling the emanations from the chasm. Of this chamber there is now no evidence and no emissions of gas are known today in this area. However, a sag in the middle of the temple floor suggests that it was constructed on artificial fill that has subsequently settled, perhaps into the chasm. Discharges of carbon dioxide are not uncommon in areas of limestone,[180] and such gas could perhaps induce a

1A. Sea-level stands near Ayia Roumeli, Crete. The highest is at 2 m above present sea-level.

1B. Beach-rock on Crete. The beds shelve gently towards the sea. The beach-rock here is being eroded.

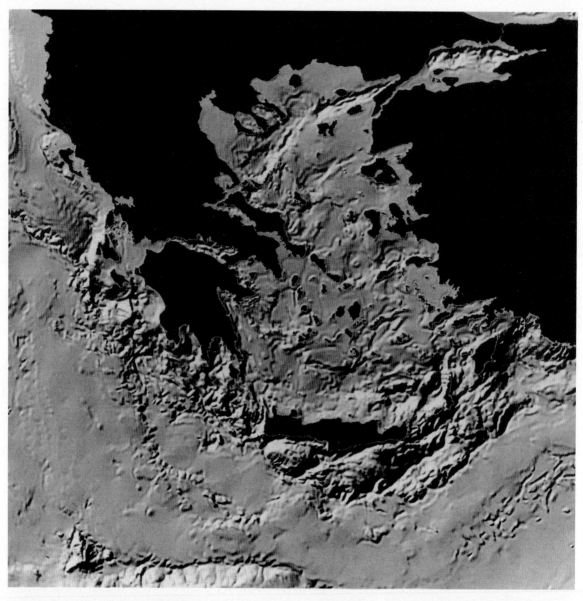

2. Computer-generated shaded relief map of the sea-floor around Greece and western Turkey.[175] Land appears in black. The relief is illuminated by a simulated sun to the north-west at an angle of 30°. Many of the modern plate tectonic structures show up well in this image.

3A. Space Shuttle photograph of Attica. North is to the top and the view is almost vertical. The city of Athens lies in the centre-right of the photograph. Clouds cover Mt Parnes to the north. (Courtesy NASA)

3B. The chapel of Panayia Chrysospiliotissa and the walls of the south side of the Acropolis hill, Athens. A natural cave was enlarged originally to accommodate a temple to Dionysos. Ancient water-level stands can be seen in the sides of the chapel.

4. Part of a circular washery for purifying lead ore, near Lavrion. The water flowed along the channel, dragging the lighter materials, while the heavy ore was trapped in the depressions.

5. The Corinth Canal. A series of normal faults is clearly visible in the walls.

6A. The northern end of the Diolkos, near Corinth. Beach-rock, visible in the background, partly covers the stone blocks of the Diolkos.

6B. Fault scarp near Geropotamos, Mani, 3-4 m high. This scarp was produced during one or several earthquakes. The age of movement is not known, but its steepness indicates that it was created recently.

7A. Fallen columns of the Temple of Zeus, Olympia. These columns were toppled during earthquakes in AD 522 and 551.

7B. The Kylindri quarry north of Karistos, Euboea. The cipollino marble columns are 12 m long and about 1.5 m in diameter.

8. Partially extracted column in the Kylindri quarry.

9A. The Meteora region, near Kalambaka, view west to the Great Meteoron monastery. The steep rocks in the foreground are conglomerate and sandstone of the Lower Meteora formation. The Upper Meteora formation, in the background, is more easily eroded, and hence supports more vegetation on less steep slopes.

9B. The Meteora. Most of the steep slopes are conglomerate, but the gently sloping layers are more easily eroded sandstone and siltstone. The vertical surfaces developed from joints.

10A. Ancient quarry face from near Kastri, Thessaly. The blocks were extracted by chiselling a trench, making the 'pecked' surface seen here, and then driving in wedges.

10B. Space Shuttle photograph of the Northern Aegean. The photograph was taken obliquely towards the south-west. The Sea of Marmara lies in the bottom left and the Thrace basin in the bottom centre. The deep waters of the North Aegean Trough, running up the centre, appear darker in this photograph as their wave patterns and currents are different from those of the shallower waters. (Courtesy NASA)

11. Space Shuttle photograph of the western coast of Turkey and the Greek islands. The top is towards the north-west in this vertical photograph. The island of Samos lies slightly left of the centre. The city of Izmir lies in the top right. (Courtesy NASA)

12A. The ancient site of Ephesus, view to the west. The street leads down to the ancient wharves (ruins and trees) and the flat, treeless area of the ancient harbour beyond.

12B. The phreatic (steam) explosion crater Stephanos on the island of Nisyros. The crater is 300 m in diameter and 25 m deep. The age of this crater is not known, but it is probably a few thousand years old.

13. The Temple of Pythian Apollo on Rhodes. The underlying layer of panchina can be seen in the foreground, with the softer sedimentary rocks underneath.

14A. Unfinished kouros statue 10.5 m long near Apollonia on Naxos. The statue was abandoned after it developed a crack caused by relief of natural stress in the original rock.

14B. Columnar jointed lava flow or dome on the Glaronissia islands, near Milos.

15A. Outcrop of obsidian blocks (dark) in crystallised and altered rhyolite (pale) near Demenegaki, Milos. The rock was originally completely glassy, but water entered along cracks and promoted crystallisation and alteration, leaving only small blocks of obsidian in the interior of the blocks.

15B. The caldera cliffs near Fira, island of Thera. Almost all the rocks visible are pumice and volcanic ash. The steeper parts of the cliffs are formed of ash that remained hot enough to weld together as it landed. Most of the houses are built on the loose, pale pumice of the Minoan eruption.

16A. Space Shuttle photograph of western Turkey and the Aegean sea. The photograph was taken towards the south-west. The sky was not completely clear, and there are ribbon-like clouds across the whole region. Turkey lies at the bottom right and Africa is barely visible at the top left. The island of Crete lies in the centre right, with a line of clouds across it. (Courtesy NASA)

16B. Ammoudha quarries at Phalasarna, Crete. This rock is a fossilised dune of shell debris, formed during the Pleistocene period.

trance. Earthquakes and construction activities can change the natural plumbing system, so the tradition of the vapours cannot be excluded on geological grounds.

A further spring or seepage appears below the temple of Apollo in the sanctuary of the goddess Ge (author's observation), adjacent to the Rock of Sibyl, where the first Sibyl was said to have prophesied.

All these springs have seasonal variations and also have been disturbed by earthquakes and construction activities. However, they all appear to fall along a straight line, which suggests that they are associated with a steep fault that runs about north-west/south-east.

Delphi is situated in an area much prone to earthquakes. Rockfalls associated with earthquakes have destroyed many of the monuments and have proved to be the decisive factors in several conflicts. The main reason for the frequency of earthquakes here is its proximity to the active Corinthian-Saronic graben. The walls of this graben have been uplifted and the floor has subsided to give at least 3 km of relative movement during the last 10 million years. Most of this movement has occurred during earthquakes.

The polygonal walls supporting the Sacred way were much better suited to withstand earthquakes than the square blocks of the temples, which needed reinforcing with clamps. Removal of these clamps during the Middle Ages led to the final disintegration of the temple of Apollo.

Thermopylae and the Malian Gulf

The only feasible route in antiquity along the east coast of Greece between Thessaly and Boeotia ran along the south shore of the Malian Gulf. The 6 km long pass between the cliffs of Mt Kallidromon and the sea was known as Thermopylae ('hot gates') from the hot mineral springs near the centre of the pass (see below). Here in 480 BC the Spartans earned immortal glory from their stand against the Persian invaders. A small force of 300 men held back the vastly more superior Persians for sufficient time for the bulk of the Greek forces to get away to the south. The Spartans were all killed, but by their delaying action they made possible the ultimate defeat of the Persians. The balance between sedimentation by the Spercheios river and subsidence of the land has changed the topography of the pass considerably since antiquity until now it is a broad plain. These variations in geography will be explored below.

The Malian Gulf is part of a graben that stretches from the North Euboean Gulf deep into central Greece (Figs. 8.1, 8.5). This graben probably began to form about ten million years ago when tension in the crust behind the South Aegean volcanic arc produced many grabens in the Aegean region (see Chapter 2). The grabens of the Gulf of Corinth and the Boeotian plain are parallel to this graben and were formed at the same time and in the same way. The topography of the graben has been controlled by three factors: sedimentation, subsidence and sea-level changes.[153]

The Spercheios river flows down the graben from the west, bringing large quantities of sediment formed by the erosion of the mountains. Other rivers also flow into the graben from the mountains to the north and the south. All these sediments are deposited when the river slows down as it enters the Malian Gulf. The deposits tend to fill up the bay and move the mouth of the river out into the Gulf. At least 800 m of sediments are present in the graben. Travertine formed around the hot springs has also contributed locally to the sediments in the gulf (see below).

The second factor, the subsidence of the floor of the Spercheios graben, began about 10 million years ago and still continues today. Movement is not generally continuous, but happens during earthquakes when movements of several metres may occur. Such events can drastically alter the coastline and the depth of the sea.

The third factor is the level of the sea: 18,000 years ago, near the end of the latest glaciation, sea-level was about 120 m below its present level. Rapidly rising sea-levels until 6,000 years ago exceeded sedimentation, flooding much of the former land that now lies beneath the Malian Gulf. It is possible that at this time the gulf extended right up to the cliffs on either side. After about 4000 BC sedimenta-

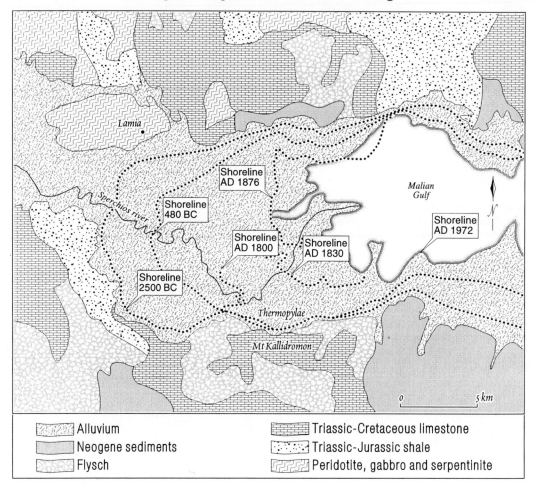

Fig. 8.5. Spercheios valley and the Malian Gulf (after 153 and other sources).

tion exceeded subsidence and rising sea-levels. This led to the formation of new land and the migration of the river delta into the gulf.

The Middle Gate appears to be the critical part of the pass (Fig. 8.6). At periods of high sea-level, possibly 1700 BC – 1300 BC and 300 BC – AD 1100, the sea lapped directly against the cliffs and the pass was effectively closed, while at other times it was open, but still very narrow. It was probably only 20-30 m wide at the time of the famous battle in 480 BC. During the nineteenth century the Spercheios river migrated or was diverted towards the southern shore, sedimentation increased and the pass began to broaden to its present width of 5 km.

Hot springs occur near both the Middle and West Gates, associated with the southern graben fault. The spring at the Middle Gate issues from beneath a boulder and scree at the foot of the cliff. The spring has a very high flow at a good bathing temperatures (40°C) but has been spoiled by the all too usual collection of decaying concrete, wire and pipes. The spring has deposited a large apron of travertine, on which the hotel and baths have been constructed. An appreciation of the rate of deposition can be seen near the parking lot, where a hot waterfall has deposited more than a metre of travertine. Travertine is limestone precipitated from the thermal waters as they

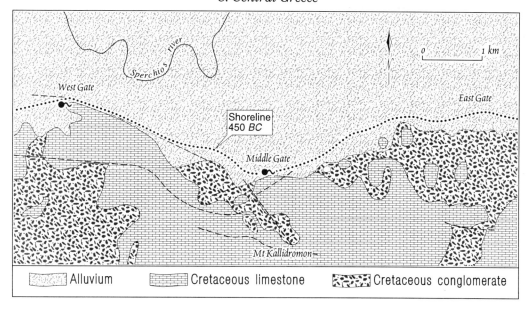

Fig. 8.6. Thermopylae (after 153 and other sources).

cool and lose carbon dioxide. The spring water is not very salty, which indicates that it originates as rainwater on the mountains to the south and is cycled along faults deep in the earth.[180]

The spring at the West Gate also issues from a scree slope below a series of low cliffs of limestone breccia. The original limestone has been shattered in place and recemented by circulating, mineral-laden fluids. This type of rock is characteristic of major fault zones. The spring has been recently dammed to make an attractive swimming pool. The thermal water is very salty, in contrast to the spring at the Middle Gate, and probably originated as seawater. Cool, fresh water enters at the edges of the pool and floats on the warm, salty thermal water which is denser. Small amounts of travertine have been deposited at the exit of the pool and along an old aqueduct.

Euboea

Euboea, the largest Greek island after Crete, is 175 km long (Fig. 8.1). It runs parallel to the Greek mainland, separated from it by a narrow strait, which contracts to 80 metres at Khalkis,

where it is bridged. The west coast is well provided with ports, while the east coast, with its steep cliffs, is only accessible at Kymi.

It is a mountainous island – Mt Dirphys in the centre is 1,745 metres high – and many of the mountains are covered with forests of sweet chestnut, pine, fir and plane. The coastal plains are fertile; they produce corn, olives and figs in abundance, as they did in antiquity. The island is also rich in minerals, especially lignite, nickel, iron, asbestos, magnesite and marble.

Habitation on a considerable scale began before 3000 BC, and several prosperous settlements from the Mycenaean period (1600-1100 BC) have been located. In the Dark Ages (1100-800 BC) Euboea was exceptionally rich and started a colonising movement. It was well-placed geographically for contacts with the north and east and was probably now exploiting the local supplies of iron, which replaced bronze for many uses. The principal cities were Khalkis and Eretria. At about 700 BC this prosperity was brought to an end by the Lelantine War when these two cities fought for possession of the fertile Lelantine Plain, which left both in a state of exhaustion. Prosperity returned about 300 BC and lasted throughout Hellenistic, Roman and Byzantine times.

The older rocks of Northern and Central Euboea belong to the Pelagonian zone and hence are linked with those of Thessaly, Boeotia, Corinthia and Laconia (Fig. 8.1). They comprise a series of older metamorphic rocks, currently exposed in a band north and west of Aliveri. During the Late Triassic to Early Cretaceous periods limestones were deposited in shallow water on these rocks. This activity came to an end when part of the Tethys Ocean closed and the ocean floor was thrust over these rocks to form ophiolites. Uplift of the rocks above sea-level was followed by tropical erosion and deep weathering, resulting in the formation of bauxites and laterites (see below). Another small ocean basin closed in the Late Cretaceous which resulted in the emplacement of more ophiolites.[236]

During the Neogene three basins developed in the northern and central parts of the island. The land in these areas subsided and sediments accumulated in shallow lakes in the basins. These sediments included marls, which have weathered to produce deep, fertile soils. Peat accumulated in swamps and was converted into lignite (see below).[135] The lower part of the sedimentary basin north of Aliveri is cut by minor andesite volcanic rocks that were erupted about 13 million years ago.[90]

The basement of southern Euboea is quite different from that of the north. The lowest rocks are exposed in a tectonic window south of Aliveri. Here the phyllites and marbles are part of an underlying nappe that is also seen on Mt Ossa. Overlying these rocks, above a thrust fault, are the marbles and schists of the Attic-Cycladic metamorphic belt that comprise the rest of southern Euboea.

The most recent phase of volcanism in this area was part of the Volos volcanic field to the north. The small island of Likhades off the westernmost part of northern Euboea is made of andesite which was erupted about 500,000 years ago.[90] Minor eruption of andesites on the adjacent mainland at Kamena Vourla occurred rather earlier at 1.7 million years.

The North and South Euboean Gulfs that divide Euboea from the mainland are Neogene grabens, in which most of the movement occurred during the last million years.[213] The South Euboean Gulf is separated from the Aegean sea by a sill only 55 m deep that runs from Ayia Marina to Stira island. At times of low sea-level, for example 25,000-18,000 years ago, this sill would have isolated the gulf and turned it into a lake.

Lignite and magnesite mines

Lignite is extracted from an open-pit mine at Aliveri and most of it is burned in the local power-station.[135] The lignite formed from decayed Sequoia trees that grew in a marshy area during the early Miocene period. Later on it was covered by limestones, marls, conglomerates and sandstones, which must now be removed to uncover the lignite seams. There are also deposits of lignite at Kymi on the east coast in the northern part of the basin.

Magnesite has been mined around Mantoudi and Limni in northern Euboea. It occurs as veins and irregular masses in serpentinites formed by the metamorphism of the peridotite parts of ophiolites. It is used to make refractory bricks.

Khalkis

The ancient city of Khalkis was situated west of Mt Vathrovounia (Greki), an isolated block of Triassic-Jurassic limestone, similar to the formations of the mountains to the east (Fig. 8.7). The acropolis was constructed on the south-west part of this hill. The low hills of the peninsula to the south-west of the ancient city are made of Late Cretaceous limestone. The plain on which the ancient city stood, and the modern city stands, is underlain by readily-eroded serpentinite. The Trokhos spring (in antiquity, Arethusa) east of the ancient harbour is brackish but drinkable. Seawater mixes with freshwater in the caves and fissures beneath the spring. The ancient water supply came from three freshwater springs on the northern edge of the mountain at Tris Kamares. The water for all these springs originates as rain on Mt Vathrovounia.

The Euripos or strait of Khalkis only opened

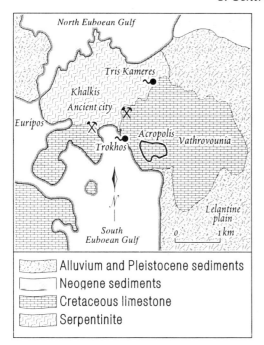

Fig. 8.7. Khalkis and environs (after 21 and other sources).

up about 6,000-5,000 years ago and is relatively shallow.[133] It is famous for the strong variable currents which reverse direction 6-14 times a day. Popular tradition holds that Aristotle, in despair at his failure to understand the phenomenon, threw himself into the Euripos. The currents originate in the interaction of tides in the North and South Euboean Gulfs. The tides in most parts of the Mediterranean are very small, such as in the South Euboean Gulf to the south of Khalkis which has a tidal range of 9 cm. However, in certain areas the configuration of the coastline combined with the depth of the water can cause a resonance which considerably increases the tidal range. The waters of the North Euboean Gulf to the north of Khalkis, where the tidal range is 42 cm, illustrate this phenomenon. Differences between the height and timing of the tides on either side of the strait at Khalkis produce the currents.[133] This phenomenon is a good example of a class of mechanical systems in which the interaction of periodic forces, in this case the tides, produce chaotic motions.

The Lelantine plain is a sub-aerial part of a long graben, mostly occupied by the South Euboean Gulf (see above), where less subsidence has taken place (Fig. 8.1). The plain is enclosed by mountains of Triassic-Jurassic limestones on the north and east. The ancient settlement of Lefkandi was situated on the southern part of this plain and was constructed on an eroding cliff of alluvium of the Lelas river.[133] Iron ore was smelted at Lefkandi around 900 BC.

Iron and nickel deposits

Euboea, and particularly Khalkis, was well-known in ancient times for its iron industry.[21] The iron deposits occur in the mountains north-east of Khalkis, near the Aegean coast (the range that includes Mt Dirphys), and on the adjacent mainland, in north-east Boeotia, between Lake Copais and the North Euboean Gulf (Figs. 8.1, 8.2). They can be seen as long, thin, meandering lines of dark-red rock between paler limestones or greenish serpentinites.

The iron deposits are laterites, ancient deposits rich in the iron mineral haematite and were formed during the Early Cretaceous when a tropical climate prevailed in Greece. Intense weathering of serpentinite rock removed most of the chemical elements in solution, leaving behind a layer up to 10 m thick rich in iron and nickel. In some areas the laterites were eroded and redeposited on top of Jurassic limestones. At the end of the Cretaceous the sea invaded the area and limestone was deposited on top of the laterites. The laterites can be found now as a layer beneath the Cretaceous limestones, and on top of serpentinite or Jurassic limestone. Some of these laterites have been exploited recently, but for nickel instead of iron. The main nickel refinery is at Larimna, on the North Euboean Gulf.

Eretria

Three kilometres north of Eretria are quarries of a variegated red, violet and white marble known to the Romans as Marmor Chalcidicum and to Italian masons as Fior di Pesca (peach

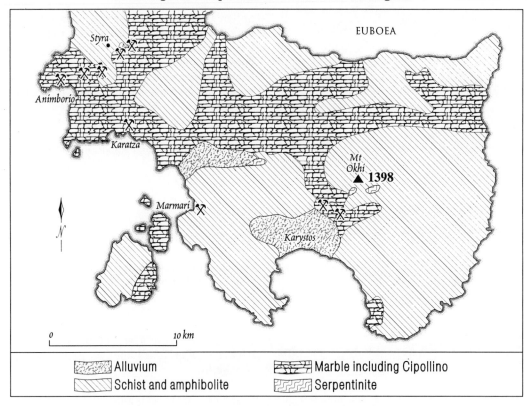

Fig. 8.8. Southern Euboea and the Cipollino quarries (after 159 and other sources).

blossom; Fig. 8.1). It was popular from the late first century BC into early Christian times, and was later used in Renaissance and Baroque architecture. This marble originated as Carboniferous limestone that was brecciated and infiltrated with iron-rich silts before it was metamorphosed and deformed.

Karystos and the Cipollino marble quarries

The area round Karystos was celebrated in antiquity for the veined green marble known to the Romans as Marmor Carystium and to us by its recent Italian name of Cipollino (onion). The name is apt, as a cut section of this marble looks very like an onion. It was used for monolithic columns, public fountains and wall-facings in Roman and Byzantine buildings from the first century BC to the seventh century AD. It was widely exported all around

the Mediterranean, and a piece has even been found in York.

There were five principal centres of exploitation (Fig. 8.8): Styra, Animborio, Karatza, Marmari, and Karystos.[159, 147] By far the best preserved is the quarry north-east of Karystos and east of the village of Myli, at an altitude of about 650 m on the south-west slopes of Mt Okhi. Here one can see no less than 13 roughhewn columns, many nearly 12 m in length, and one partly cut out of the rock face (Plates 7B, 8). It is hard to see how the monolithic columns were safely brought down for shipment.

Cipollino marble originated as Permian limestone, with layers of silt and clay. Metamorphism converted the clays into muscovite and chlorite, which gives both the green colour and the good cleavage of the marble. Quartz and feldspar are also present and stand out from the other softer minerals after erosion.

Euboea was also known for its asbestos which was used in antiquity for making fire-proof cloth. Asbestos is a fibrous form of serpentine minerals that crystallises in veins up to 5 cm wide in massive serpentinite. The crystals are generally lined up at right-angles to the direction of the vein, and form as the vein opens up. The ancient sources were veins in small patches of ophiolite on Mt Okhi north-east of Karystos.

9

Thessaly and the Northern Sporades

Thessaly is a land of wide plains and high mountains: Mts Olympos, Ossa and Pelion to the east; Mt Othris to the south and the Pindos range to the west (Fig. 9.1). It is drained by the river Peneios, which rises in the Pindos range and runs south and then east and through the Vale of Tempe between Mts Ossa and Olympos, and into the Thermaikos Gulf. The climate is somewhat continental, and the rich soil supports cattle and sheep in addition to its horses, and produces excellent crops of cereals.

Thanks to its remarkable fertility, the Thessalian Plain was settled as early as the Neolithic period, about 5000 BC. Archaeology and legend agree in placing its greatest days in the Mycenaean period, 1600-1100 BC. Here, the story goes, lived Achilles and his Myrmidons. Here, at Iolkos (modern Volos) Jason was believed to have built the good ship Argo to capture the Golden Fleece. Here archaeologists have found rich Mycenaean tombs and a royal palace. After this, Thessaly was always prosperous, but never again as important.

Most of the older rocks of this region are from the Pelagonian, Sub-Pelagonian and Pindos zones. The Pelagonian zone is now exposed in the northern and eastern parts of the region, from the Gulf of Pagasae (Paragasitikos) north-westward past Mt Olympos (Fig. 9.1). This continental fragment was a ridge or shallow sea for much of its history, hence there was relatively little sedimentation, and the rocks that formed were mostly limestones. However, the older metamorphic core of this ridge is now widely exposed, and is composed of marbles, gneisses and schists (see below). The Sub-Pelagonian zone lies parallel to the Pelagonian zone from Mt Orthris to north of Kalambaka. It is the remains of an ancient continental margin comprising deep-water limestones and the underlying igneous rocks of the adjacent oceanic crust, now altered and slightly metamorphosed. The Pindos zone underlies the south-western part of the region, including Mt Pindos. It started as a deep ocean basin, where limestones accumulated. Later, during the Alpine regional compression, it was filled with flysch sediments shed from the adjacent rising mountain chains. These compressions continued and finally thrust the Pelagonian and Sub-Pelagonian zones south-west onto the Pindos zone in the late Eocene period.

Slightly later, during the Oligocene and Miocene periods, compression changed to extension, with two effects:[240] the sedimentary rocks were stripped off the continent along flat-lying normal faults, exposing the core of metamorphic rocks, principally schists and marbles, beneath. Secondly, a trough formed within the mountain chain from Thessaly to Albania. Once formed, the trough immediately started to fill up with sediments shed from the adjacent mountains.[190] Much ended up in the deep water along the centre of the trough. However, some were also deposited at the edges of the trough in alluvial fans and deltas. The speed of erosion, and the short distance of transport of the sediments did not give many opportunities for reduction in size of the sediments, hence conglomerates are especially common. Such sedimentary rocks are called molasse, and up to 5 km accumulated in this region. It is these rocks that crop out in the Kalambaka region (see below). A somewhat similar situation is now present in the Gulf of Corinth.

Neogene stretching affected this region, as elsewhere in the Aegean. North-east/south-

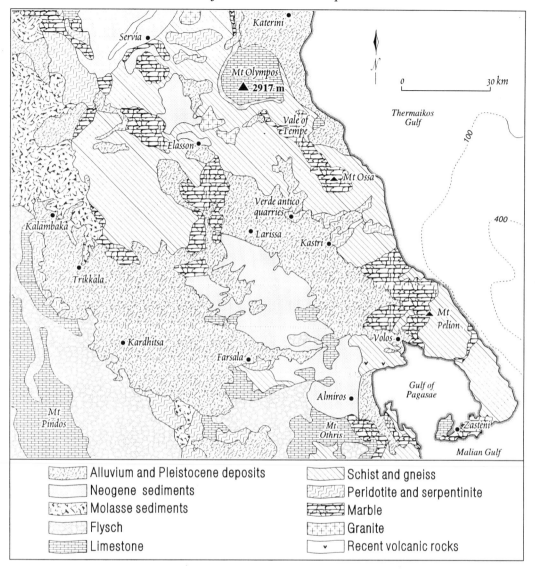

Fig. 9.1. Thessaly.

west tension produced a series of horsts and grabens parallel to the earlier isopic zone boundaries. A high horst from Mt Olympos to Mt Pelion and a lower horst from Almiros to Kalambaka separate two broad interior grabens and the Thermaikos Gulf graben. The fertility of these valleys reflects the rich alluvium shed from the surrounding mountains and the abundant, perennial water supply.

Kalambaka and the Meteora

The Meteora form one of the most remarkable sights in Greece. The word means 'suspended in mid-air', and refers to the lofty pinnacles rising up from a remote corner of the Thessalian Plain to a height of 450 m, topped in many cases by monasteries. The earliest were built in the fourteenth century by monks who

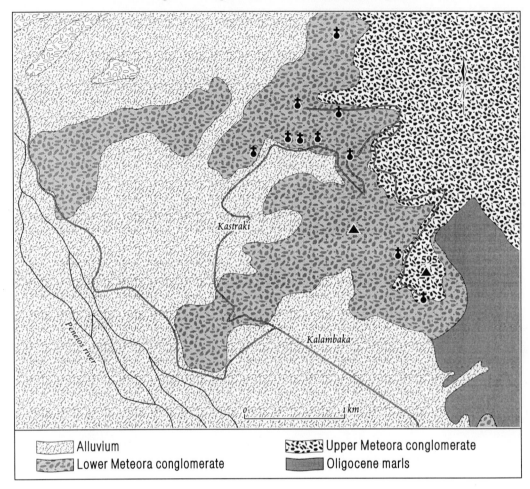

Fig. 9.2. Kalambaka and the Meteora.

wished to worship God and mortify their flesh, far from the world below. In their heyday there were 24 monasteries, perched on their almost inaccessible pinnacles and reached by means of rickety ladders or in baskets suspended from ropes. Today only five are occupied, and these can now be reached by steps cut in the rock.

The valley of the Peneios river, south of the Meteora cliffs, is an asymmetrical graben, formed during the Neogene stretching of the Aegean region (Fig. 9.1). The south-western side of the graben is a fault, but much of the movement on the other side has been accommodated by bending of the rocks.

The great cliffs and stacks of the Meteora are made of Oligocene-Miocene conglomerate with layers of sandstone and shale (Fig. 9.2, Plates 9A, 9B).[190] The steepest parts of the cliffs are dominated by conglomerate of the Lower Meteora formation. Many different rock types are represented in the pebbles of this rock, including limestone, marble, serpentinite and metamorphic rocks, all set in a hard greenish matrix. These rocks are spectacularly cross-bedded, typically descending at an angle of 15-20° to the south-west.

Some of the highest parts of the cliffs, together with the area covered with vegetation to the north-east, are made of a slightly different type of conglomerate, together with layers of sandstone and marl, called the Upper Meteora formation. These rocks were deposited on top of the Lower Meteora formation following a short period of erosion. They are more easily eroded, which is why they form better soils, and have been removed from most of the rocks near the escarpment. They are also well-bedded, but the beds are almost horizontal or descend in the other direction from the Lower Meteora conglomerates, towards the north-east.

These conglomerates formed from sediments deposited in the deltas of streams flowing south-westward from the mountains. As the delta built up, southward-flowing streams cut down into the existing deltaic sediments, forming wide channels, that were later also filled with sediments. The combination of these processes has created the pattern of beds that we see today.

The rocks of the Meteora have acquired their striking shapes through weathering, along almost horizontal and vertical planes, and erosion.[293] Although the conglomerate resists weathering, the gently sloping layers of sandstone and marl are easily altered. These tend to erode, ultimately isolating blocks of rock at the top of cliffs and creating rounded boulders that appear to have been carefully balanced on the underlying pinnacles. Less extreme erosion of these layers on cliffs produces overhangs or caves.

Weathering also occurs along almost vertical joints in the rocks, creating the pinnacles and steep cliffs. The grandeur of the scenery is partly due to the wide spacing of the joints, up to 100 m, which has defined large, resistant blocks of rock. The paucity of joints in these rocks is because they have never been deeply buried. There are two intersecting sets of joints, oriented north-west/south-east and north-east/south-west. Weathering along these joints, and erosional removal of the material by streams and torrents has formed the jagged landscape of the Meteora.

Mt Olympos, Mt Ossa and Mt Pelion

The mountain ranges of Olympos, Ossa and Pelion run in an almost continuous chain along the western shore of the Thermaikos Gulf (Fig. 9.1). Mt Olympos (2,917 m), in the north is the grandest and highest mountain in Greece. There were many other mountains of this name in Greece and Asia Minor, but this was by far the most famous. It was revered by many as the home of Olympian Zeus and the other gods and goddesses. Others believed that they lived in the sky above Olympos; a belief which gave rise to the legend that the Giants tried to storm Heaven by piling Ossa on Olympos and Pelion on Ossa, an idea without geological support. Olympos was also associated with the Muses. Ossa (1,978 m) was venerated as the home of the Nymphs and from its western slopes the Romans and Byzantines obtained the ornamental green stone known today as Verde Antico (see below). Pelion (1,651 m) is the most fertile of the three mountains, and was believed to be the home of the mythical man-horse hybrids, the Centaurs.

The Olympos-Ossa-Pelion range is a Neogene horst between the Larissa graben to the west and the huge Thermaikos graben to the east (Fig. 9.1). Much of the latter lies under the waters of the Thermaikos Gulf, but continues to the north-west into the Plain of Thessaloniki.

The massif of Mt Olympos is a tectonic window, or hole in the Pelagonian zone, through which we can see the rocks of the underlying Parnassos zone. The surrounding Pelagonian zone rocks consist of a series of thin nappes of ophiolites, gneiss, schist and less metamorphosed sedimentary and volcanic rocks, that continue southwards to the Pelion peninsula. Ascending the mountain, we actually descend the geological succession and pass over a thrust fault into the Parnassos zone. The massif is dominated by a series of Upper Triassic to Eocene limestones in the north-east that pass eventually, in the west and south, into Eocene flysch. The remarkable relief of Mt Olympos is partly due to recent uplift, and partly due to the more resistant nature of its bedrock, limestone, as compared to that of the surrounding

91

gneisses. Mt Olympos, together with Mt Ida on Crete, are the only parts of Greece that were glaciated.

The summit of Mt Ossa is made of marble, but the lower slopes are dominated by schist (Fig. 9.1). Serpentinite (see below) only occurs in the low lands to the south of the mountain. Although the northern part of Mt Pelion is also made of erosion-resistant marble, the peninsula is dominated by schist, which yields a much more fertile soil than marble. In addition, here water does not disappear into the ground but runs along the surface where it can be more readily exploited.

Verde Antico quarries

Verde Antico ('Ancient Green') is the name given by Italian masons, from the Renaissance onwards, to a green rock that was first used in the first century AD, but was most popular in the fifth/sixth centuries, after the Imperial Porphyry quarries in Egypt closed (about AD 450). Its ancient name was Marmor Thessalicum or Lapis Atracius. It is still quarried today. The quarries lie on a small hill beneath the western slopes of Mt Ossa, just north of the village of Chasambali (Fig. 9.1).

Verde Antico is a conglomerate composed of rounded serpentinite and marble blocks set in a fine-grained matrix of similar composition (Fig. 9.3).[132, 162] The rock is layered, with contrasting sizes and compositions of clasts in the different beds. The blocks were transported by water, but could not have travelled far as serpentinite is a very soft rock. This rock therefore probably formed very rapidly in a broad river valley surrounded by high mountains of serpentinite, part of an ophiolite complex. This rock was not formed recently, but probably during the Tertiary period and is a variant of the molasse seen in the Meteora. The geological term for this rock is ophicalcite, a confusing name as the main mineral is not calcite, but serpentinite and the amphibole actinolite.

Roman, Byzantine and modern quarries all lie in the same region, on the southern slopes of the hill. The age of the quarries can be determined from the method used to extract the rock: hammers, chisels and wedges were

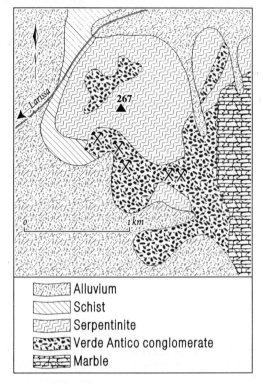

Fig. 9.3. Verde Antico quarries (after 132).

used in antiquity, producing uneven, 'pecked' surfaces. However, in recent quarries wire-saws have been used, producing large, flat surfaces. In such quarries the structure of the rock is beautifully exposed.

Marble quarries

There are ancient marble quarries near the village of Kastri, 25 km east of Larissa (Fig. 9.1, Plate 10A). The quarries lie in a small block within a large area of serpentinite. They produced a medium-grained marble ranging in colour from white to blue-grey, which was used in Byzantine times. Ancient marble quarries near the bay of Zasteni, on the north slope of Mt Tissaion south-east of Volos, produced a better quality of marble, paler and finer-grained. These quarries were exploited in Classical and Byzantine times.[52]

Vale of Tempe

The Vale of Tempe is a deep, narrow valley through which the Peneios river leaves the Plain of Larissa for the sea (Fig. 9.1). The steepest part, to the north-east, cuts through marble, whereas the gentler slopes further south-west are made of schist. The valley follows a north-east/south-west fault, which was probably recently active. This fault runs parallel to the major strike-slip North Aegean Fault zone to the south (see Chapter 12), which terminates against the mainland, and the Vale of Tempe fault may receive part of this movement (see Volos below). It is possible that the route of the river predates the formation of the Olympos-Ossa range, and that erosion by the river has kept pace with the rising mountains, to give this deep valley.

Volos

The city of Volos is located near the southern end of a graben that extends parallel to the coast, from Larissa in the north, to the Gulf of Pagasae in the south (Fig. 9.1). An earthquake zone extends from the gulf westwards towards Trikkala. This zone partly takes up movements on the North Aegean Fault zone which terminates in the sea to the east.

Near Volos the floor of the graben has been lifted up, so that soft Neogene sediments are less common and older metamorphic rocks dominate the surrounding hills. These basement rocks consist of Triassic-Jurassic marbles, together with schists and gneisses, probably of similar age. Initial metamorphism was in the greenschist facies, followed by high-pressure blueschist facies. There are small deposits of bauxite within the marbles.

There are a number of young, small cones and flows of andesite and latite in this region, dated between 3.4 and 0.5 million years. They are considered to be the northernmost part of the South Aegean volcanic arc, but on a local scale they are probably related to the graben which extends east-west from the strait between Euboea and the Pelion peninsula to the Malian Gulf and beyond into mainland Greece. The deep faults of this graben cut the crust and

provided an access route for magmas generated deep within the mantle by partial melting of the subducted plate.

Northern Sporades

Skiathos, Skopelos and the smaller islands to the east are the uppermost parts of a horst extending eastwards from the Pelion peninsula (Fig. 9.4). The overall tectonic situation is rather confused here: the major North Aegean Fault zone comes down from the north-east and terminates against these islands and the mainland. The strike-slip movement of this fault is transferred in a complex way to a number of less important faults that cut across the mainland to the trench on the other side of the Ionian islands. This horst is probably related to the redistribution of these movements. The tectonic setting of Skyros is different from that other the other Northern Sporades, but it is not easy to relate to any large-scale geological features.

Skiathos and Skopelos continue the geology of the Pelion peninsula to the west: Skiathos is made of schists and gneiss whereas Skopelos is dominated by marble. Later on flysch was deposited on the metamorphic basement of these islands. Cretaceous limestone occurs in eastern Skopelos and becomes the dominant rock in the smaller islands to the east.

Skyros

Skyros is the largest and most easterly of the Northern Sporades. It is divided by a narrow isthmus into a fertile northern half and a more mountainous southern half (Fig. 9.5). A Mycenaean presence between 1600 and 1100 BC is attested archaeologically and confirmed by legend. Here Achilles is said to have hid, disguised as a woman, to avoid the Trojan war; and here Theseus was murdered. Skyros must have been rich in the early Bronze Age, as much gold jewellery has been found in tombs of 1000-700 BC. But the chief attraction today is the tomb of the poet Rupert Brooke, who died and was buried here in 1915.

Skyros lies on an isolated underwater plateau, separated from the other Northern

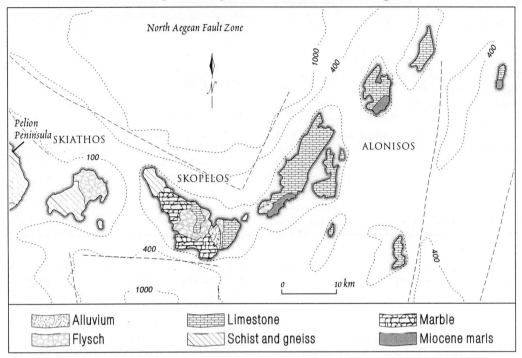

Fig. 9.4. The Northern Sporades.

Sporades by a series of north/south submarine grabens. To the south is one of the northeast/south-west shear zones that cut up the central part of the Aegean plate. The island itself is almost completely bisected by two faults parallel to this shear zone, which lie under alluvium in the 'waist' of the island.

The lowest exposed rocks are Middle Triassic-Early Jurassic marbles and schists of the Pelagonian zone.[126] The marbles are resistant to erosion and make up the hill of Marmari, north-west of Linaria, and Mt Kokhilas (782 m) on the southern part of the island. Schists underlie the lower hills between Skyros and Linaria. Over these rocks has been thrust a slice of metamorphosed ancient oceanic crust, both ophiolite and the overlying sediments. Finally Late Cretaceous limestones were thrust over the whole package.

Andesite lava domes and flows were erupted about 15 million years ago in the north-central part of the island.[91] At about the same time the north-east part of the island dropped down below sea-level and sediments were deposited there. Later this region was lifted up forming the fertile plains on the north-east coast. Skyros town lies partly on beach deposits and partly on a small basin of alluvium on a plateau of schist. Behind the town rise hills of serpentine and marble.

The variegated marble of Sykros was popular in Roman times. It is a breccia, with blocks of white, beige and red marble and limestone in a fine-grained red matrix. The rock was re-metamorphosed and slightly deformed after formation of the breccia. The ancient quarries lie on the southern part of the island, near the bays of Tris Boukes and Renes, and on the adjacent island of Valaksa.[52] Today this marble is extracted from a quarry between Tris Boukes and Renes.

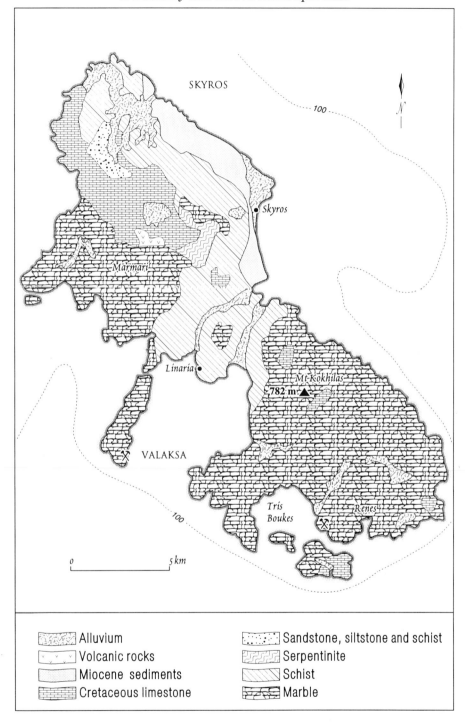

Fig. 9.5. Skyros. Only the modern quarries have been indicated.

10

North-west Greece and the Ionian Islands

Epeirus comprises the bulk of the mainland of north-west Greece. It is a land of precipitous mountains, large rivers, and a few maritime plains and lagoons. The mountains are rich in pasture and timber; cereals and olives are grown in the plains. The name Epeirus, which goes back to antiquity, means 'The Mainland', as seen from the island of Kerkira (Corfu). There is good evidence for occupation in the Neolithic and Bronze Ages, 6000-1100 BC, and from 1600 BC Epeirus was gradually penetrated from the coast by Mycenaean Greeks. In historic times the Epeirotes were regarded by the Greeks as barbarians, because of their Illyrian heritage. They did, however, possess two famous oracles, much patronised by the Greeks: the Oracle of Zeus at Dodona and the Oracle of the Dead at the mouth of the river Acheron, east of Paxos.

The Epeirotes do not appear on the stage of history until the fourth century BC, when they benefited from the victories of Philip II of Macedon. But in 167 BC Rome took control of the country after a bloody victory. Emperor Augustus founded the town of Nikopolis ('Victoryville') to commemorate his victory over Antony and Cleopatra at the Battle of Actium in 31 BC. Afterwards the importance of Epeirus declined rapidly, until the rule of the notorious Ali Pasha in the nineteenth century AD. It did not become Greek territory until 1913.

The Ionian Islands (alternatively the Eptanesa, or 'Seven Islands') are situated for the most part in the Adriatic Sea, along the west coast of Greece. The name is comparatively recent, but is taken from an ancient name for the Adriatic, 'The Ionian Sea' (not to be confused with the district of Ionia in western Turkey). The principal islands are, from north to south (Fig. 10.1): Kerkira (Corfu), Paxos, Levkas, Kephallinia, Ithaca and Zakinthos (Zante). The seventh, Kythera, from its situation south of Laconia, is commonly excluded, and we will follow this example.

The islands, with three times the average rainfall of the Aegean, are by far the greenest and most fertile of the Greek islands, though they are also for the most part mountainous. Their early history will be considered below, under the individual islands. They gradually came under the control of Venice in the fifteenth century, and so remained until captured by Napoleon in 1797, who considered them 'more important than the whole of Italy'. After various vicissitudes, in 1815 the Seven Islands became a protectorate of Great Britain and in 1864 they were ceded to Greece.

North-west Greece contains all the westerly elements of the Hellenic collision zone, now stacked upon each other by thrust faults. However, before the compression, which still continues now, the rocks were stretched out over a much greater distance and made up a continent, its margin and the adjacent ocean basin.

The remains of the ocean basin are seen today in the chert, limestone and ophiolite suite rocks of the Pindos zone, cropping out in the eastern part of the region, from the Pindos mountains past Naupaktos into the Peloponnese. This basin formed by spreading along a mid-ocean ridge during the Triassic period. Shortly afterwards, during the Jurassic, regional compression started and the basin closed. The ophiolites of the Pindos zone were thrust eastwards over the Pelagonian zone. They soon rose above sea-level and shed sediments onto the adjacent areas.

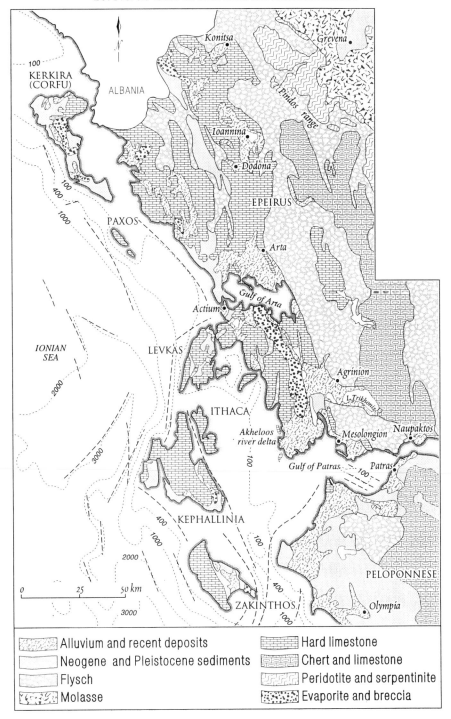

Fig. 10.1. North-west Greece and the Ionian islands.

97

The Gavrovo zone was originally part of the continental shelf. It now crops out in a narrow belt west of the Pindos zone. The oldest rocks are limestones, rocks typical of shallow seas, far from mountains. This situation changed later when stacking of thrust sheets of rock produced mountains in the Pindos zone to the east. The weight of these mountains bowed down the crust and formed a basin in front. Sediments shed from the mountains accumulated in the basin as flysch.[40] Further west still the Ionian zone was a deep-water trough, but not a true ocean basin. It crops out throughout much of the western part of this region and is dominated by deep-water limestones. Finally, rocks of these zones were thrust westwards onto the continent during Early Miocene and Pliocene times.[268]

The remains of the stable continental platform are seen today as the Pre-Apulian zone, which crops out on the western parts of the Kephallinia, Levkas and Zakinthos. This zone is almost part of Italy: continental crust continues north-west from the Ionian islands to the south-eastern peninsula of Italy, Apulia. Deformation associated with regional compression in Greece is slowly spreading west, and has now started, in a rather limited way, in this zone.[268]

The interior parts of this region were stretched in a north-north-east direction during the Neogene, as elsewhere in most of the Aegean region, forming a series of basins.[35] One such basin contains Lake Trikhonis, and may be a western extension of the Gulf of Corinth, with which it is co-linear. The Gulfs of Patras and Arta (Amvrakikos) are other basins oriented in a similar direction. These gulfs are linked by a north-north-west strike-slip fault with leftward movement.[40] Undulations in the fault direction have produced a series of small basins, now filled by lakes.

The high incidence of earthquakes in the central and southern parts of the region testifies to the presence of a plate boundary just to the west: the Apulian plate is descending to the east below the Aegean plate. Some of these earthquakes have caused rapid changes in the height of the land. For instance, the peninsulas north and south of the mouth of the Gulf of Arta were produced recently by such uplift: hence, the battle of Actium may have been fought on what is now dry land.

Ioannina

Ioannina was founded in around the eleventh century AD, and took its name from a nearby monastery of St John. Its importance dates from 1205, when it received refugees from Constantinople and the Peloponnese. In 1431 it fell to the Turks. In the early nineteenth century it was the capital of the notorious Ali Pasha, an Albanian adventurer who made himself master of nearly all Greece. Today it is the principal town of Epeirus.

The Ioannina area is a large arch-like fold, dominated by Late Jurassic to Eocene limestones (Figs. 10.1, 10.2). The city of Ioannina lies on the shores of Lake Pamvotis which occupies the core of this fold where erosion has been deepest. It partly fed from karstic springs, discharging from fissures and cave systems in the surrounding hills. The presence of such springs is revealed by the density of vegetation along the north-east shore. One spring discharges into the lake on the shore opposite Nisi island. In the nineteenth century the lake extended more than 10 km the north and to Kastritsa in the south, where it drained into sink-holes.[43] The construction of a storm drain and tunnel to the Thiami basin to the north, in 1944, changed the extent of the lake. At present it is up to 10 m deep and partly drains through sink-holes in its bed.

Three blocks of Late Cretaceous limestone poke through the valley floor: the peninsula of the Kastro of Ioannina, the island of Nisi in Lake Pamvotis and Mt Goritsa, beside Perama. The abundance of limestone breccia in this unit has increased its permeability for groundwater, and made it particularly susceptible to the development of caves. A cave below part of the Kastro (currently the local museum) was first used by Ali Pasha for the storage of ammunition. Some caves and fissures are also present on the island of Nisi. However, the best cave in the region, the Perama Cave, was developed beneath Mt Goritsa.

The Perama cave was discovered in the

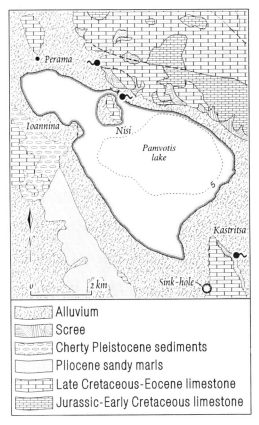

Fig. 10.2. Ioannina and Lake Pamvotis.

naean Greeks. The Oracle was probably functioning at this time, if not earlier. Legend has it that Odysseus consulted the Oracle, situated in an oak tree, on his return from the Trojan War. By the sixth century BC Dodona had been overtaken by its more accessible rival at Delphi, but it continued to exist until the closing of the pagan sanctuaries in AD 393 by the Christian Emperor Theodosius I. It was finally destroyed by the invasion of the Goths, followed by a terrible earthquake.

The site is at the bottom of a narrow valley, enclosed on almost all sides (Fig. 10.1). There is no river at the bottom of this valley at this point as the drainage from the surrounding hills disappears into sink-holes. Mt Tomeros rises over the site to the south-west and is made of Jurassic limestone. Small valleys on the upper slopes have shed huge, steep cones of scree, that now cover much of the lower slopes.

The acropolis was constructed on a platform of Palaeocene-Eocene limestone, which crops out below the theatre. This rock was itself used to constructed many of the buildings, including the theatre. This limestone contains veins of chert, typically 1 cm thick, which were used on the upper surfaces of the seats, either for decoration or because they withstood wear much better than the limestone.

Mesolongion

Although an ancient site, the town of Mesolongion does not really enter history till the Greek War of Independence (1821-32), when Prince Mavrogordato made it his headquarters. Here in 1824 the philhellene Lord Byron died of fever while organizing the Greek resistance.

Mesolongion is situated on the northern shore of a large lagoon, part of the delta of the Evinos river, north of the Gulf of Patras (Fig. 10.1). West of Mesolongion, across the bay, is another large delta, that of the Akheloos river. Both these rivers drain large areas of Tertiary flysch sediments to the north and east, seen as the hills behind Mesolongion. As in many deltas in the Aegean region, deposition of sediments has been extremely rapid, resulting in similarly rapid changes in geography.[219]

1940s and is open to the public.[216] It was part of an underground river system that formed about 1.5 million years ago and is very rich in different types of cave formations, including stalagmites, stalactites, flowstone, curtains and pool-rims. Very little new material is forming now as climatic change has drastically reduced the flow of water into the cave. Unfortunately, high levels of artificial lighting have caused the growth of much algae on the formations.

Dodona

Dodona was celebrated in antiquity for the Oracle of Zeus, which was regarded as the oldest in Greece. There was a sanctuary here, probably in honour of a fertility goddess, as early as 2200 BC. About 1400 BC the Sanctuary, by now sacred to Zeus, was visited by Myce-

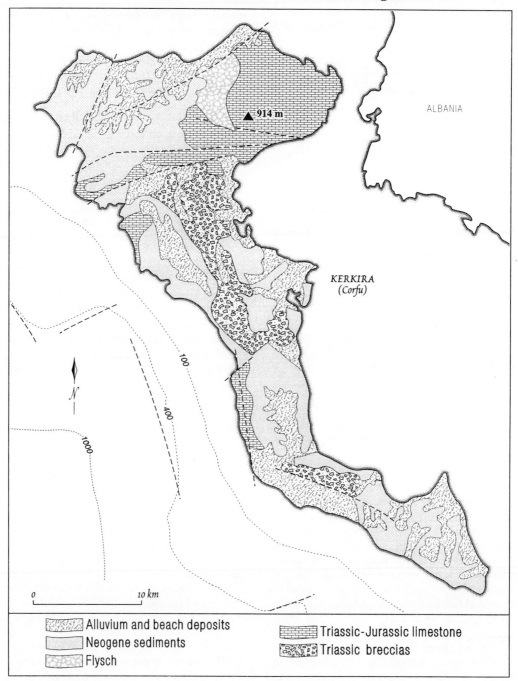

ALBANIA

914 m

KERKIRA
(Corfu)

100

400

1000

N

0   10 km

	Alluvium and beach deposits		Triassic-Jurassic limestone
	Neogene sediments		Triassic breccias
	Flysch		

Fig. 10.3. Kerkira (Corfu).

Kerkira (Corfu)

The island of Kerkira (formerly Corcyra), commonly known today by its Venetian name of Corfu, is the most fertile of the Ionian Islands. It was first inhabited about 50,000 years ago, during the Palaeolithic Age. Surprisingly, the Mycenaean Greeks never settled here. Nevertheless, the Classical Greeks claimed this island as Homer's Scheria, land of the Phaeacians, where Odysseus was washed ashore, met the Princess Nausicaa, and was entertained by her father King Alcinous. In fact, the city of Kerkira was founded by Greek colonists from Euboea about 760 BC, but soon passed to the Corinthians, who used the city as a staging point on the way to their colonies in South Italy and Sicily. In 1204 Corcyra passed to the Venetians who ruled it for most of the next 500 years as a vast olive plantation.

Kerkira lies on the shallow continental shelf west of Epeirus and Albania (Fig. 10.1). The channel between Kerkira, the mainland and islands to north was a land bridge prior to 6000 BC.[250] Much of the steep western coast of the island follows a fault, along which the island has been uplifted recently. This sharp relief continues to the west of the island, where the sea-floor drops rapidly to a depth over 1,000 m along a series of normal faults. This region has a low incidence of earthquakes, especially compared to the Ionian islands to the south.

The island lies entirely in the Ionian zone, a former deep basin in the continental margin (Fig. 10.3). The oldest rocks on the island are Triassic-Jurassic limestones which are exposed on Mt Pantokrator (914 m) in the north. The southern margin of this massif is a major east-west left-moving strike-slip fault. Further south there is a series of Triassic breccias formed by the dissolution of gypsum and the collapse of the overlying rocks into the holes. Much of the rest of the island is covered with Pliocene-Miocene marine sediments, including gypsum. A two-metre thick bed of hard shelly limestone (coquina or 'panchina') rests on the Pliocene sediments in the western part of the island. In former times it was quarried extensively for construction. The coquina and other recent marine sediments are commonly cov-

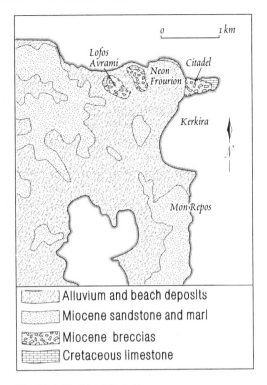

Fig. 10.4. Kerkira (Corfu) town.

ered by terra rossa soils, up to 30 m thick. Many Palaeolithic implements have been found within this soil, suggesting that it continued to form until recently.[250]

The town of Kerkira lies in the east, on alluvium and low hills of Miocene sandstone and marl (Fig. 10.4). Within the town lie three low hills, the Citadel, Neon Frourion and Lofos Avrami, which are made of pale Late Cretaceous limestone, covered with Miocene breccias. The low hill to the south, under the ancient acropolis and Mon Repos, is made of Miocene sandstone.

Levkas

The island of Levkas was first inhabited from Early Neolithic times (6000 BC) and there was a particularly rich settlement there toward the end of the Early Bronze Age, 2500-2200 BC. It was colonised by the Corinthians in 640 BC.

Most of the island is in the Ionian zone and

comprises Triassic to Cretaceous limestones (Fig. 10.1). The south-western peninsula is made of rocks of the Pre-Apulian zone, including the 60-metre high white cliff of Cretaceous limestone after which the island is named. It is almost joined to the mainland by a spit of sand that encloses a shallow lagoon around the modern town of Levkas.

Kephallinia (Cephalonia)

Kephallinia (or Cephalonia), the largest of the Ionian Islands, is rugged and mountainous, culminating in Mt Aenos (1,628 m), the highest point in the Ionian Islands. The mountains are clothed with the Kephallinian pine; in the valleys and on the plains are grown olives, citrus, currants and cotton. The island was inhabited from about 3000 BC, and was very prosperous in later Mycenaean times, from 1300 to 1100 BC. From here the Mycenaeans set out for Sicily and South Italy. Kephallinia and Ithaca are among the few remaining habitats of the Mediterranean monk seal.

Kephallinia is situated on the edge of the continental margin, but is surrounded by deeper water than Kerkira or Levkas (Fig. 10.1). Thrust faults on either side, and within, the island are related to regional compression and subduction of crust beneath the sea just south-west of the island (Fig. 10.5). Kephallinia is close to the northern end of the Hellenic subduction zone, and it is offset by north-east/south-west strike-slip faults to the north. The combined effect of these two active fault systems ensures that the island is regularly rocked by earthquakes, one of the most destructive in recent times being in 1953. During that earthquake the central part of the island was raised 30 to 70 cm.[257] Such events must be geologically relatively frequent: a sea-level stand 1.2 m above present sea-level around the central part of the island must have been produced by movements associated with one or more earthquakes during the fourth to sixth centuries AD.

The island is dominated by limestone (Fig. 10.5). The oldest rocks are exposed in the east as a series of Triassic to Cretaceous limestones of the Ionian zone. These have been thrust westwards along the Ionian Fault and other faults onto Cretaceous limestones and minor Tertiary limestones and sediments of the Pre-Apulian zone that make up most of the island. The western margin of the zone of Alpine compression has moved progressively westward, and thrusting has occurred recently in the previously stable western parts of the island.[188]

The strong relief of the island is partly due to the resistance to erosion of the limestone, and partly to the recent thickening of the sedimentary sequence by thrust faulting.

Katavothres of Argostoli

Near Argostoli there is a very unusual karstic phenomenon (Fig. 10.5): the sea drains into sink-holes (katavothres) in the land with sufficient flow (0.3 cubic metres per second) that it was once used to generate electricity.[216] This water appears, mixed with freshwater, 14 km away on the other side of the island in springs near Sami at Karavomilos, Frydi and the cave-lake of Melissani, and at Ayia Euphenia 4 km to the north.[68]

This strange phenomenon is largely driven by the energy derived from the dilution of the seawater by freshwater. The caves or fissures that connect the sink-holes with the outlets descend below sea-level, and were formed when the sea was far below its present level. The dense seawater descends into the cave, where it mixes with lighter fresh water. The brackish water is lighter than the seawater and, therefore, floats at a higher level, finally discharging about one metre above sea-level.[68] In total there are about 40 springs around the coast of Kephallinia, many of which discharge brackish water. The other sink-holes that feed these springs must be in the sea-bed.

Ithaca

Ithaca has been inhabited from about 6000 BC, and was believed by the ancients to have been the home of the Homeric hero Odysseus (Ulysses to the Romans). His date, insofar as he was

Fig. 10.5. Kephallinia (Cephalonia) and Ithaca.

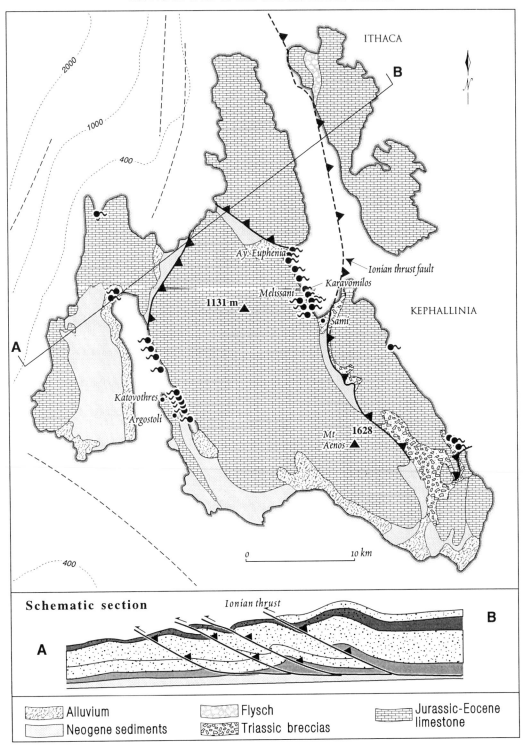

ITHACA

B

2000

1000

400

Ay. Euphenia

Ionian thrust fault

Melissani *Karavomilos*

1131 m

Sami

KEPHALLINIA

Katovothres

Argostoli

Mt Aenos 1628

0   10 km

400

Schematic section   *Ionian thrust*   B

A

	Alluvium		Flysch		Jurassic-Eocene limestone
	Neogene sediments		Triassic breccias		

a historical person, would be about 1200 BC. His palace has not yet been found, but plentiful Mycenaean remains, of the right date, have come to light on the Isthmus, at Aetos, and in the north, at Pelikata, so there is still hope that it might be located.

In contrast to Kephallinia, Ithaca is almost completely within the Ionian zone (Figs. 10.1, 10.5). The island largely consists of a series of folded Jurassic to Eocene limestones. The strong relief of the island is probably related to relatively recent uplift on the Ionian thrust fault, which lies just to the west, under the Straits of Ithaca. As on Kephallinia, the dominance of limestone has led to a lack of surface water, and this, coupled with the scarcity of flat land, has made the island agriculturally very unproductive.

Zakinthos

The island of Zakinthos (alternatively Zante), the southernmost of the four central Ionian Islands, lies off the coast of the Peloponnese west of Olympia. The eastern half is low-lying and fertile, growing currants and olives, whereas the western half is mountainous and barren. There was a small Mycenaean presence here between 1600 and 1100 BC, but the island was not properly settled until about the seventh century BC, by Greeks from Achaea in the Peloponnese. The island is celebrated for its springtime flora (hence its other name 'Di Fliori de Levant'), for the loggerhead sea turtles which nest here, and for its springs of bitumen at Limni Keri (see below).

Zakinthos is separated from the Peloponnese by a channel up to 600 m deep (Fig. 10.1). To the south-west the sea-floor drops rapidly into the Hellenic trough. The general tectonic setting is similar to that of Kephallinia: beside the Hellenic subduction zone and in a zone of regional compression. Also, like Kephallinia, this island is situated in a zone of high seismic risk. Most of the local earthquakes occur along faults east of Zakinthos town and in the bay of Lagana.

The bedrock geology of Zakinthos also much resembles that of Kephallinia (Fig. 10.6): Mt Yiri (756 m) and the ridge in the western part

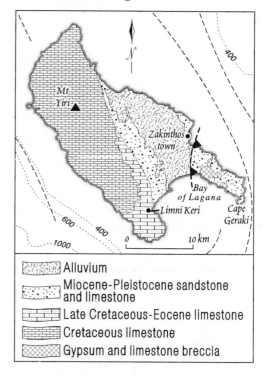

Fig. 10.6. Zakinthos (Zante).

of the island are made of Late Cretaceous to Eocene limestones. Oligocene-Pliocene sandstones and other sediments underlie the central lowlands.[267] Layers of gypsum in these rocks were formed when the Mediterranean dried out during the 'Messinian Salinity Crisis'. Deposits occurring south of the town of Zakinthos have been extensively quarried.[267]

The south-eastern peninsula contains older rocks, Triassic in age, which have been thrust over the younger rocks to the west. Gypsum also occurs here, as well as extensive breccias produced by collapse of the overlying rocks into the caves developed by solution of the gypsum.[267] Such rocks make up the summit of Mt Skopos (485 m). Pliocene sandstones have been quarried near Cape Geraki.

The town of Zakinthos is constructed on Pliocene-Pleistocene marls and sandstones (Fig. 10.7). The flat-topped castle hill is capped by a layer of Pleistocene conglomerate, which is harder than the underlying Pliocene rocks

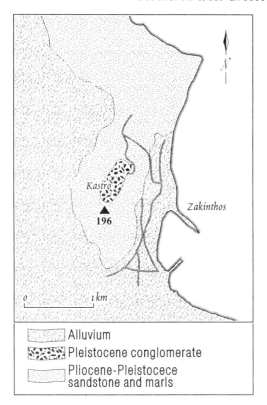

Fig. 10.7. Zakinthos town.

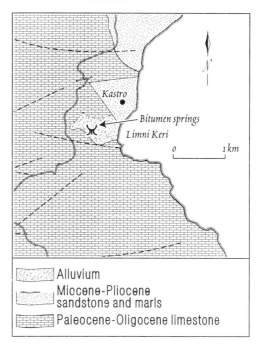

Fig. 10.8. Limni Keri (after 267 and other sources).

and has protected them from erosion.

In the southern part of the island, near Limni Keri, there are natural springs and pools of bitumen (pitch), mentioned by Herodotus (Fig. 10.8). Bitumen was used in antiquity in the Aegean for caulking ships and making wine-jars waterproof.[267, 281] It was applied as a protective coating on metals and for magical purposes. It was thought to have great medical qualities and was prescribed for anything from coughs and diarrhoea to lumbago. Bitumen is the residue left where petroleum has seeped up to the surface and the lighter, more volatile components (similar to paraffin/kerosene and petrol/gasoline) have been lost by evaporation. The bedrock here is Palaeocene-Oligocene limestone, but the petroleum is probably derived from deeper rocks, perhaps the Cretaceous limestones seen elsewhere in the island. In such sedimentary rocks petroleum forms from plant remains by the action of heat in the absence of oxygen. It is lighter than water and hence tends to migrate upwards through permeable rocks or along faults, unless trapped. Despite the presence of bitumen, economic reserves of oil have not yet been found in the region.

11

Greek Macedonia

The Greek province of Macedonia is bounded on the south by Mt Olympos and the Cambunian mountains; on the west by the Pindos range; on the east, for our purposes, by the river Strymon (formerly Struma), which separates it from Thrace; and on the north by a mountain barrier, broken only by the Axios (Vardar) and Strymon rivers. The climate is more continental than Mediterranean.

Macedonia is divided geographically into two parts: Western Macedonia is composed of mountains and high plateaux and is largely pastoral; Lower Macedonia, on the east, comprises the coastal plain, where the Axios and Aliakmon rivers flow into the Thermaikos Gulf. It is a fertile district, producing cereals, fruit (other than olives and figs), livestock and timber. Macedonia was also blessed with rich sources of gold.

Parts of Macedonia were inhabited from Early Neolithic times (about 6000 BC), but little is known of it before the seventh century BC. At this time the inhabitants were of mixed origin, Greek, Illyrian and Thracian. The first recorded king was a Greek, Perdiccas I, who reigned about 640 BC and ruled Lower Macedonia from his capital at Aegae, on the site of the modern Vergina on the Macedonian Plain. About 400 BC the capital was transferred to Pella, some 30 km north-east.

Macedonia was of little political importance until about 350 BC, when Philip II incorporated western Macedonia and Chalkidiki in his kingdom, exploited the newly-acquired gold mines of Mt Pangaion and created the most powerful state in Greece. His son, Alexander the Great, who succeeded him in 336 BC, used the Macedonian kingdom as a springboard for his world-wide conquests. On his death in 323 BC

Macedonia passed, often violently, from ruler to ruler until the Roman conquest of 146 BC. Under the Roman Empire Macedonia regained much of its former importance. Christianity came early, thanks to the efforts of St Paul; but Byzantine Macedonia was constantly harried by barbarians. In 1375 it fell to the Turks, and did not become part of the modern state of Greece until 1912.

Macedonia encompasses a wide range of different rocks from many different isopic zones and massifs (Fig. 11.1). The core is the mountainous Serbo-Macedonian massif; to the east, across the Strymon river in Thrace, lies the rather similar Rhodope massif; to the west the Circum-Rhodope belt is separated from the mountains of the Vardar (Axios) and Pelagonian zones by Neogene sediments in the broad valley of the Axios and Aliakmon rivers.

The Serbo-Macedonian massif is a band of ancient metamorphic and igneous rocks southwest of the Rhodope massif, which extends down into the Athos peninsula (Figs. 11.1, 12.1). The western part is dominated by schists, amphibolites and marbles, whereas the eastern part is composed of gneiss and marble. These rocks have been metamorphosed and deformed many times, finally during the Alpine orogeny, when they were thrust over the Rhodope massif to the east and the Circum-Rhodope belt to the west.[63]

The Circum-Rhodope belt is a band of Mesozoic metamorphosed sedimentary rocks and ophiolites that lies between the Serbo-Macedonian massif and the Vardar zone, with which they are sometimes included. The chain of ophiolites along its south-western edge indicates that an ocean originally lay there which was consumed during the Alpine compres-

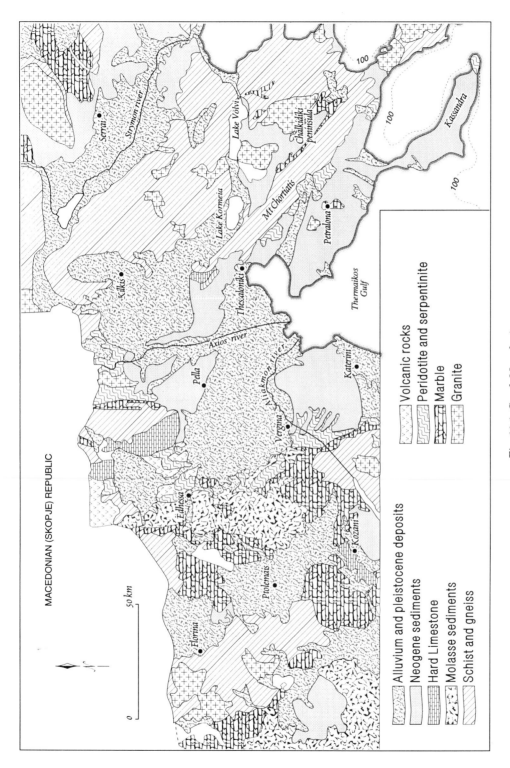

MACEDONIAN (SKOPJE) REPUBLIC

50 km

0

Strymon river

Serrai

Lake Volvi

Lake Kormeia

Chalkidiki peninsula

Mt Chortiatis

Petralona

Kilkis

Thessaloniki

Thermaikos Gulf

Kassandra

100

100

100

Axios river

Pella

Aliakmon river

Katerini

Vergna

Edhessa

Kozani

Ptolemais

Florina

Alluvium and pleistocene deposits

Neogene sediments

Hard Limestone

Molasse sediments

Schist and gneiss

Volcanic rocks

Peridotite and serpentinite

Marble

Granite

Fig. 11.1. Greek Macedonia.

107

sions. The Sithonia peninsula is part of this belt, but is dominated by younger granite plutons (see Fig. 12.1).

The metamorphic rocks of the Serbo-Macedonian massif and Circum-Rhodope belt may have been lifted up rapidly during a period of crustal extension: by this mechanism overlying rocks were removed by movements along flat-lying normal faults rather than by erosion. A similar process has been proposed for the occurrence of metamorphic rocks in Thessaly and the Cyclades.[163]

The Vardar (Axios) zone is the central root of the former Tethys ocean from which the main compressional events were driven. It is almost completely concealed by the sediments of the Thermaikos graben, but is exposed to the north-west, where Triassic-Jurassic limestones and ophiolites are overlain by Cretaceous limestones and Eocene molasse sediments. Although the hills to the south of Thessaloniki and the Cassandra peninsula are undoubtedly also underlain by these rocks, most of what are seen on the surface are Miocene and Pliocene sedimentary rocks.

Granite plutons occur throughout this area. In the Vardar zone they are Jurassic in age and related to subduction of oceanic crust. Those on the Sithonia peninsula are Eocene, again related to subduction, but are not probably related to the widespread Miocene volcanism further east and south.

Western Macedonia is underlain by rocks of the Pelagonian zone. The characteristic Triassic-Jurassic limestones and marbles, seen so commonly further south, are here accompanied by gneiss, the basement (foundation) on which these rocks were originally deposited.

Volcanism occurred during the Pliocene, 5-1.8 million years ago, in the north-western part of the Thermaikos graben, north-east of Edhessa and on into former Yugoslavia.[92] This volcanism is unusual in that it is much younger than that in Thrace, western Turkey and the eastern Aegean islands and is contemporary with that of the South Aegean volcanic belt.

Neogene crustal extension produced a series of north-west/south-east grabens. The largest of these is the broad Thermiakos graben, which extends from the Thermaikos Gulf up the valley of the Axios river. Further west, the position of the Strymon graben has been partly controlled by the important thrust fault that divides the Serbo-Macedonian and Rhodope massifs. This graben appears to have hinged down from a line parallel to the thrust, so that subsidence is much greater in the south-east. The Drama-Philippi graben is another of these Neogene grabens (Fig. 12.1). It is diamond-shaped and completely enclosed within the Rhodope massif. Yet another series of Neogene grabens occur within the Pelagonian zone of western Macedonia. Most of these basins are partly filled with locally derived sedimentary rocks, including seams of lignite, some of which is mined for electricity generation.[87] Lakes Koroneia (Langada) and Volvi occupy the east-west Mygdonian graben, location of a number of earthquakes, including a major one in 1978. This graben is probably younger than the Thermaikos graben and has opened up in response to very recent north/south stretching of the crust.[109]

Gold has been mined in Macedonia and neighbouring Thrace for about 5,000 years. The primary gold deposits are in the metamorphic rocks of the Rhodope and Serbo-Macedonian massifs. Gold occurs in quartz veins as well as associated with iron and copper sulphides.[166] Weathering of these primary deposits liberates the gold, which is transported in the rivers as tiny grains of metallic gold. These sink to the bottom of the stream and form placer deposits. Gold placer deposits may be 'fossilised' if the river migrates elsewhere and may be reworked by a new river at a later time, further increasing the concentration of gold. Almost all the rivers in this area had some placer deposits, but most were exhausted in antiquity. About 300 tonnes of gold were extracted in this region, and in neighbouring Thrace, from 1200 BC to AD 50,[172] much of it during the reign of Philip II (359-336 BC). In recent times the major Axios river and the smaller Gallikos river (Fig. 11.2), to the north of Thessaloniki, have yielded the most gold.

Thessaloniki and the plains

In 316 BC the Macedonian king Cassander founded a city at the head of the Thermaikos Gulf, by enlarging the unimportant town of Therma and filling it with the inhabitants of 25 other towns; he named it Thessaloniki, after his wife. Its growth was assured by its position at the head of the Gulf. In 146 BC, when Macedonia became a Roman province, it became the capital and later the eastern terminus of the Via Egnatia, the road which connected the Adriatic sea with Byzantium (Istanbul). Under the Byzantines it became the second city of the Eastern Empire, and resisted many attacks by the barbarians who overran most of Macedonia. It fell to the Franks in 1204 and to the Turks in 1430, and in 1912 it was ceded to Greece. Today, known also as Salonika, it is the capital of northern Greece and the second city of the country.

The plains of Thessaloniki are the floor of a graben extending from the Thermaikos Gulf to the south, north-westwards into former Yugoslavia (Fig. 11.1). The Pieria mountains to the west of the graben are dominated by ophiolite suite rocks and Cretaceous limestones. Similar rocks occur to the north. To the east rocks of the Circum-Rhodope zone lie in front of the gneisses of the Serbo-Macedonian massif. The low hills within the graben, including the western part of Chalkidiki and Kassandra peninsulas, are made of Miocene-Pliocene marine and terrestrial sedimentary rocks.

At the peak of the last glaciation, some 20,000 years ago, the sea-level was about 120 m lower and the coastline was about 80 km to the south, almost due west of the tip of the Kassandra peninsula.[151] Initially, rising sea-levels produced a major marine embayment, up to 40 km inland from the present coast. Since then sediments deposited by the major rivers that flow into this gulf, particularly the Axios and Aliakmon, have partly filled in the estuary and forced the coastline to the south (Fig. 11.2). Most sediments were deposited in

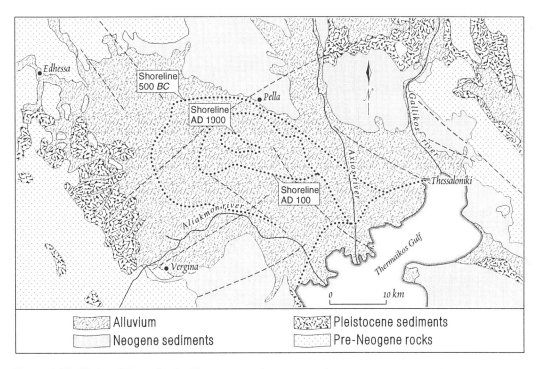

Fig. 11.2. The Plains of Thessaloniki. The positions of ancient coastlines are approximate (after 151 and other sources).

the northern and southern parts of the bay, eventually isolating part of the sea to form a lagoon and finally a lake (see below). This was drained in 1936, and now almost all the plains are under cultivation.

The comparative paucity of earthquakes in the Thermaikos graben indicates that, unlike the Corinth graben, the floor of this graben is no longer sinking at a significant rate. However, there is significant seismic activity within the active Mygdonian graben (containing lakes Kormeia and Volvi) 20 km north-east of Thessaloniki, and these earthquakes have caused much destruction in the region.[109]

Thessaloniki

The city of Thessaloniki lies on the eastern edge of the plains, just within the graben, and extends towards the north-east onto the foothills of Mt Choriatis (Fig. 11.1). Most of the city was constructed on recent alluvium and Miocene-Pliocene sandstones, marls and clays (Fig. 11.3). The eastern suburbs lie on a low hill of gneiss, part of the Serbo-Macedonian massif, which continues in the north-east. To the north, across the north-west/south-east graben fault, lie Triassic-Jurassic sedimentary rocks and gabbro, parts of an ophiolite suite.

Thessaloniki has continued as a port since antiquity because the Axios and Aliakmon rivers debouche in the western part of the gulf, hence little sediment has accumulated in the east. However, the Axios river delta continues to advance and will eventually cut Thessaloniki off from the sea.

Pella

Pella is presently situated in the centre of the Thermaikos graben (Figs. 11.1, 11.2). To the south lie the alluvial plains of the Axios and Aliakmon rivers; to the north lie low hills of Miocene-Pliocene sedimentary rocks deposited long ago in the graben by predecessors of the present rivers. These have been lifted up tectonically and then eroded by the present rivers.

The geographical situation of the site in antiquity was rather different; from Neolithic to Early Roman times Pella was on the coast of

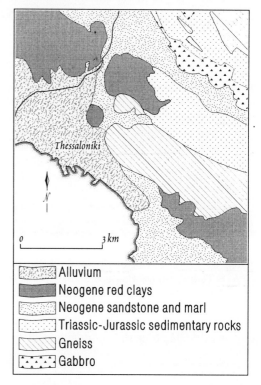

Fig. 11.3. Thessaloniki.

the Thermaikos Gulf, and latterly a port. The low hills to the north provided a site for an acropolis and its position commanded access to the plains. A low island, Phakos, existed just south of the acropolis. A major spring, now known as the Baths of Alexander, issues from the base of the hills, 2 km west of the acropolis, near Nea Pella.

Since antiquity river-transported sediments have filled in the estuary, and forced the coastline to the south: by Late Roman times the city stood on a shallow, but navigable lagoon, Lake Loudias, that was connected to the sea. Later on this lagoon became a lake, isolated from the sea, and was recently drained.

Vergina

The ancient site of Vergina is situated on the south-western side of the Thermaikos graben, at the foot of the Pieria mountains (Figs. 11.1,

The legend for the figure:

Alluvium
Neogene red clays
Neogene sandstone and marl
Triassic-Jurassic sedimentary rocks
Gneiss
Gabbro

11.2). To the west is the valley of the Aliakmon river, and to the south-east the coastal plain narrows southwards between Mt Olympos and the Thermaikos Gulf. The location was important strategically, but Vergina was never a port.

The Pieria mountains are dominated by ophiolites, and descend via Cretaceous limestones and flysch to the plains. The ancient city was constructed on the lower slopes of the hills and the palace stood on the edge of the plain. The tombs were excavated out of the alluvium – here red clays with boulders of serpentinite.

Edhessa

The town of Edhessa is situated on the top of a steep bluff, facing south-east, over which the River Vodas (Edhesseos) falls 24 m to the Plain of Thessaloniki (Figs. 11.1, 11.4). The surrounding hills to the north and west are made of Jurassic to Cretaceous sedimentary rocks, with many fragments of volcanic materials. Elsewhere serpentinite and marble are parts of an ancient sea-floor (ophiolite), now much disrupted and metamorphosed, but essentially similar in age. Much younger Pliocene volcanic rocks, latite and trachyte tuffs, crop out 3 km east of the town, but volcanic activity ceased 2.5 million years ago. The town was constructed on alluvium that has accumulated behind a natural dam of travertine.

The travertine is a freshwater limestone that forms by direct crystallisation of calcite from the river water as it passes over the falls. The travertine started to form in the early Pleistocene and deposition continues today. It is not connected with the nearby volcanism.

The calcite of the travertine probably originates in the marble hills to the west: rainwater dissolves the marble and the groundwater becomes saturated in calcite. The water appears at springs and feeds the Vodas river. As the water passes over the waterfalls in the city, it looses carbon dioxide and calcite crystallises out. The resulting limestone is commonly full of holes and fossilised plant material. It may be dissolved again to form caves and reprecipitated to make stalactites. There must have been a waterfall hereabouts to start the whole

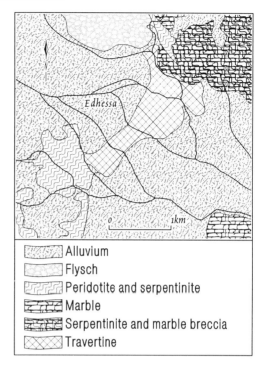

Fig. 11.4. Edhessa.

process – perhaps a scarp of one of the faults that define the Thessaloniki graben. There are travertine terraces 4 km upstream on the Vodas river, and at Flamouria 6 km to the south-west, which probably originated in the same way.

Chalkidiki peninsula

The Chalkidiki peninsula juts out into the Aegean from Macedonia proper (Figs. 11.1, 12.1). In the south-west, near Petralona, is a cave with stalactites, where the skull of a Neanderthal woman was found; she must have lived some 75,000 years ago. From the southern end of Chalkidiki three spurs of land project. From west to east, they are Kassandra (ancient Pallene), Sithonia and Mt Athos. The original inhabitants of this peninsula were not Greeks, but the coastline was thickly colonised by Greeks from the eighth century BC onwards.

The three prongs that terminate the Chalkidiki peninsula each have contrasting geology: Kassandra is largely made up of Neogene sedimentary rocks, Sithonia is several large granite plutons and Mt Athos contains both granites and metamorphic rocks (Figs. 11.1, 12.1). The form of these peninsulas is controlled by north-west/south-east faulting during the Neogene, but these directions follow older directions of weakness that are parallel to the isopic zones. The ends of the three peninsulas are aligned: they have been cut off by relatively recent movements along the North Aegean Fault zone (see Chapter 12). As a result, the sea-floor plunges rapidly to the south-east of the end of the peninsulas into the North Aegean Trough, a south-east extension of the North Anatolian strike-slip fault which dominates Turkish geology. Although movements along the North Aegean Fault zone are mostly strike-slip, it does have an important component of tension, forming a graben.

An important modern mineral commodity of the Chalkidiki peninsula is magnesite. It is extracted from a series of mines in the serpentinite masses that lie in a line south-east of Thessaloniki, especially near the villages of Vardos and Gerakini.[172] It was formed during the metamorphism of ophiolites, when peridotite was converted into serpentinite. Circulating hot water dissolved magnesium from the rocks and redeposited it as magnesite in veins. Magnesite is used in the manufacture of refractory bricks. Copper is also mined in the region.

Mt Athos

The most famous of the spurs of Chalkidiki is the peninsula of Mt Athos (or Ayion Oros, the Holy Mountain), known in antiquity as Akte. This semi-autonomous theocratic republic is covered with mediaeval monasteries, some dating from the tenth century AD. The area is forbidden to women; consequently the monasteries are seldom visited by tourists, and are usually viewed from the sea.

The Mt Athos peninsula is part of the Serbo-Macedonian massif and is dominated by igneous and metamorphic rocks (Figs. 11.5, 12.1). The schist and gneiss of the central part of the peninsula contain bands and masses of

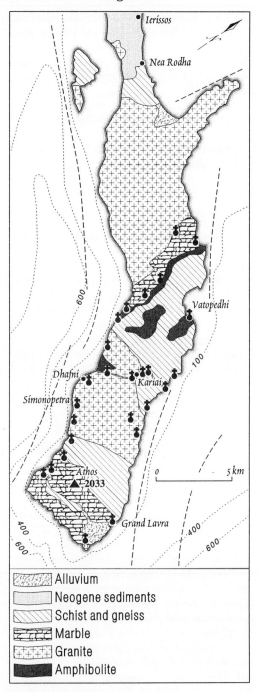

Fig. 11.5. Mt Athos peninsula.

112

dark-coloured amphibolites. Schist also occurs in the south, but the summit of Mt Athos (2,033 m) itself is made of pale marble. Two granite plutons were emplaced into these metamorphic rocks; one is about 5 km in diameter and is exposed on the south-west coast just south of Dhafni. The cliff to the north of Simonopetra is made up of this granite. The other pluton comprises most of the plateau in the north-west part of the peninsula and is almost devoid of monasteries.

To the north-west the peninsula narrows to an isthmus 2.5 km wide made of soft Neogene sediments. It was here in 480 BC that Xerxes ordered a canal to be cut across the peninsula, to avoid the perils of the Mt Athos promontory. Little now remains as sediments have been deposited in the canal and the land has risen since that time by some 14 m (see below), but it is believed to have been just west of Nea Rodha (Fig. 11.5).

Evidence of ancient sea-level stands can be clearly seen from the water around the peninsula: These generally consist of notches or ledges about 1 to 3 m above present sea-level; old sea-caves, excavated by storms, can be seen above these ledges. These sea-level stands are frequently very discontinuous; sometimes we can see many, and sometimes very few. Their height varies enormously also, in some cases across a valley. The peninsula is divided up by faults into blocks, each of which has a separate history of movement, and some of these faults run along the river valleys. The rapidity of uplift and the greater overall altitudes of the land towards the south of the peninsula are probably related to its tectonic position: the graben of the North Aegean Trough lies immediately to the south, and frequently the subsidence of the floor of such grabens is balanced by uplift of the land adjacent to the graben.

12

Thrace, the Dardanelles and Adjacent Islands

To the ancient Greeks the boundaries of Thrace were largely undefined, but it was seen as lying north and east of Macedonia and reaching as far as the Danube and the Black Sea. It thus included what is today north-east Greece, Turkey-in-Europe, and Bulgaria. Much of the western part is wild and mountainous, but is rich in minerals, especially gold, and also timber, cereals and vines. The original people were distinct from the Greeks; they were largely peasants and hunters, and worshipped different gods.

For long the Greeks never penetrated the hinterland, although they planted a few colonies along the coast, whence they bought timber, hired mercenaries and conducted slave-raids. In addition, the people of Thasos exploited the mines of gold and silver under Mt Pangaion at the western end of Thrace. In 342 BC the land was conquered, with difficulty, by Philip II of Macedon, who had his eye on the gold mines. In less than a century it was again independent, until incorporated in the Roman Empire in AD 46. But even the Romans never succeeded in taming the wild Thracians.

Western and central Thrace are dominated by the Rhodope mountains, which rise to 2,278 m and extend into Bulgaria (Fig. 12.1). To the east lie the lowlands of eastern Thrace in Turkey. The Strymon river follows a broad valley, but the other rivers flow in narrow valleys that only open out towards the sea, where the Nestos river has built a considerable delta.

The core of the Rhodope mountains is made up of the Rhodope massif, a series of sedimentary and igneous rocks formed during the Mesozoic or Palaeozoic periods and metamorphosed at high temperatures into amphibolites,

gneisses and marbles. They are divided from the essentially similar rocks of the Serbo-Macedonian massif to the west by the Strymon thrust fault, which runs along the eastern side of the Strymon basin. The age of the initial metamorphism is not clear, but it certainly took place well before the Alpine compressions. The isopic zones of the Hellenides which now make up the Greek peninsula (e.g. Pelagonian, Vardar, etc.) originally lay to the south-west of the massifs as a series of low islands, ridges and ocean floor. The Alpine compressions forced these blocks against the Rhodope and Serbo-Macedonian massifs, which were a more rigid block. Metamorphosed sedimentary and igneous rocks of the Circum-Rhodope zone extend from east of the Serbo-Macedonian massif southwards to the islands of Samothrace and Lemnos, and then north-eastwards to the eastern part of Greek Thrace.

The Eocene period brought a number of changes to this area. When the Alpine compressions ceased the crust was too thick to support its own weight and 'collapsed' along faults to produce overall extension of the crust. This may have been enhanced by the presence of a subduction zone to the south. This extension produced a number of basins, particularly in the east. Initially these basins accumulated only sediments, but soon magmatic activity began. Some of these magmas reached the surface as lavas but others solidified at depths of a few km to produce granites.[124, 129] The largest volcanic field is near Koityli, and extends for 1,500 square km, mostly on the Bulgarian side of the border. Here most of the rocks erupted as hot volcanic ashes, which welded themselves together to form ignim-

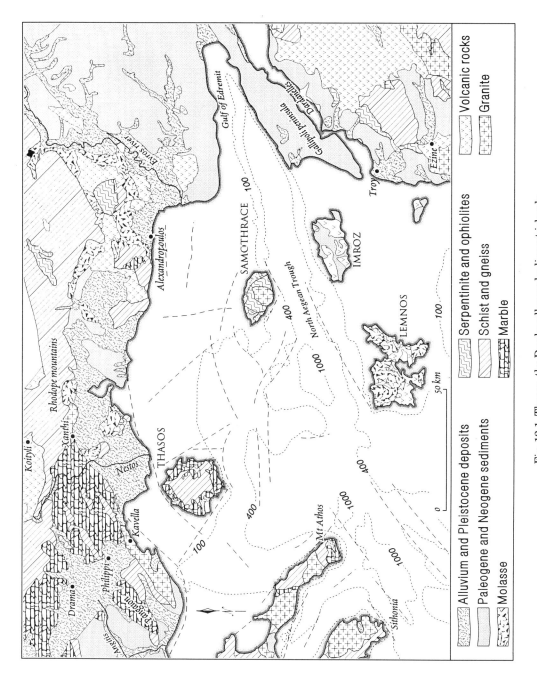

Fig. 12.1. Thrace, the Dardanelles and adjacent islands.

115

brites. Another similar basin 20 km to the east also extends across the border. Extensive volcanism also occurred at the same time in the area north of Alexandroupolis. By the Miocene period volcanism had migrated to the south (see Chapter 13).

Here, as elsewhere in the Aegean, Neogene crustal extension was an important factor in the shaping of the land. In the west the broad valleys of the Strymon and the Angitis rivers are grabens, oriented north-west/south-east, parallel to those of mainland Greece and the Peloponnese. The Prinou basin, to the north of Thasos, seems to run at right-angles to this trend. The northern part of this basin contains the great delta of the Nestos river, but it extends offshore to the south-west, where petroleum has been found. The basin to the east in Turkey is, in essence, a wide graben, but it appears to be slightly older than most in this region as it contains Oligocene sedimentary rocks.

There are many deposits of gold in the rocks of the Rhodope massif, but most of these are too small, or too low grade to be worth mining (but see Mt Pangaion below). However, some gold ore has been eroded and transported, and the gold concentrated by the action of streams and rivers to produce placer deposits. Most of the rivers of northern Greece once had placer gold, but these deposits were easy to extract and were worked out very early (see Chapter 11).

The major, recent tectonic element of this area is the North Anatolian – North Aegean Fault zone. This feature starts near Kariliova, in eastern Turkey, and extends westwards for some 1,200 km.[212] The western part of the fault now traverses the Aegean as the North Aegean Trough, and terminates near Skiathos. This fault is a plate boundary and now takes up rightward horizontal motion between the Anatolian and Black Sea plates. It originated during the Miocene as a result of the collision between Arabia and Eurasia. Initially the fault had three branches: through the Sea of Marmara, to the north and to the south. The northern branch further splayed out and created a broad region of subsidence, the Thrace basin of north-west Turkey. This branch later became inactive, along with the southern branch, and activity was concentrated on the central fault. Since inception there has been at least 85 km of rather irregular movement along the fault zone: periods of intense seismic activity, with frequent 6-7 magnitude earthquakes, are separated by quiet periods of about 150 years.[245] The last seismic period started in 1939 and continues to the present day.

The Gorge of Stena Petras

The Angitis river (ancient Angista) drains the Drama (Philippi) basin and flows through a spectacular gorge to the Serres basin, where it joins the Strymon river (Fig. 12.1). This region is a horst, formed by the subsidence of the basins on either side. It is made of Rhodope massif marbles, overlain by Neogene marls and other sedimentary rocks. Rapid uplift has caused the bed of the river to cut downwards, incising original meanders into the soft Neogene sediments in the west. However, the eastern part of the gorge, the Stena Petras, cuts through marbles and another mechanism has been proposed: the river originally ran parallel to its present course, but a few hundred metres to the south-east, through Neogene sediments, where it had carved a broad meander.[17] At the same time the river water seeped through fissures in the Rhodope limestone to the north-west. This route was more direct, and hence steeper. With time the fissures developed into caves which finally diverted all the river water, a process termed 'stream auto-piracy'. The roof of the cave became thinned by further erosion and eventually collapsed, leaving the steep-sided gorge we see today. All that remains now of this cave system is the gorge and a natural bridge.

Philippi

Philippi lies about 15 km inland from Kavalla, in the fertile plain of Datos (Fig. 12.1). Here a Greek settlement ('Krenides') was founded by colonists from Thasos about 360 BC to exploit the newly-discovered gold mines of Mt Pangaion nearby. Four years later Philip II of Macedon captured the city, fortified it, and renamed it Philippi after himself. The gold mines were intensively exploited and gave Philip a vast income, but were exhausted when the Romans got here in the second century BC. However, Philippi retained its importance as a station on the Via Egnatia, the new Roman road to Byzantium (now Istanbul); it guarded the narrow gap where the road passed between the hill and a marsh.

To the north of Philippi lie mountains of Mesozoic metamorphic rocks, largely marble with minor mica-schists, of the Circum-Rhodope zone: to the south and east opens the wide valley of the Angitis river (Fig. 12.1). This box-like graben was formed by the intersection of north-west and north-east trending faults. It is cut off from the Aegean by a ridge of granite, on which stands the city of Kavalla. The floor of the graben is subsiding at approximately the same rate as it is filling up with sediment, hence much of the valley was marshy until it was recently drained. The partly decayed vegetation accumulated to form deposits of peat covering about 700 square km. Deep down, at the base of these deposits, heat, pressure and time have transformed the peat into lignite, a form of low-grade coal.

The acropolis and other parts of the ancient city were constructed on a small spur of marble, 311 m high, projecting out from the mountains to the north (Fig. 12.2). Most of the actual city was built on a cone of alluvium shed from the valley to the east. This valley was produced by preferential erosion of softer schists.

The water that rises in the springs, from which the original settlement of Krenides took its name, originally fell on the marble hills to the north. The water descended below the surface into fractures and caves and flowed downwards to the valley. Here it is forced to the surface by less permeable mica-schists or by the shallow water-table, and appears as springs.

Mt Pangaion

Mt Pangaion (1,958 m) was famous in antiquity for its oracle of Dionysos and for the gold and silver mines in its neighbourhood, whose production peaked in the reign of Philip II. The

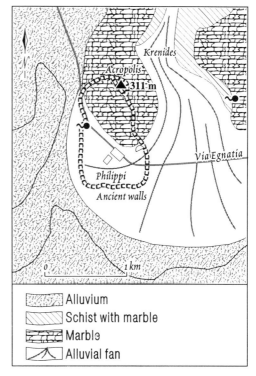

Fig. 12.2. Philippi.

mountain is part of the Rhodope massif, and the Pangaion block has been isolated from the rest of the massif by Neogene faulting, which produced the grabens of the Strymon and Angitis rivers (Fig. 12.1). It is a horst of marbles and gneisses, intruded by a series of granites, with the upper parts dominated by white marble. The gold and silver ores are in quartz veins, together with pyrite and arsenopyrite, in the gneiss.[172] Hot water, probably associated with the metamorphism or the intrusion of the granites, circulated deep into the earth and extracted a number of minerals, including gold and silver, from the surrounding rocks. These minerals were redeposited in veins as the waters cooled. Some gold was also extracted from placer deposits in the surrounding streams and rivers.

Thasos

Thasos, the northernmost of the Aegean islands, is exceptional in its plentiful water supply and consequent luxuriant vegetation, and in its delightful climate. A range of mountains, rising to over 1,200 m, runs across the island from north-east to south-west. From antiquity it has produced metals, marble, timber, wine and olive oil and today grows tobacco.

The earliest inhabitants were Thracians, and it was not till about 700 BC that there was a Greek presence, in the form of colonists from Paros. The colonists grew rich from the gold mines on the island (which, however, were soon exhausted) and on the mainland opposite, under Mt Pangaion. They also produced marble, silver, lead, iron and copper. In 340 BC the island was captured by Philip II of Macedon and remained in Macedonian hands until taken by the Romans in 196 BC. In the Middle Ages it was under Genoese rule, before falling to the Turks in 1455.

The island of Thasos is separated from the mainland by a channel 8 km wide and less than 100 m deep, and is surrounded by a broad, shallow shelf of the sea-floor that continues south to the North Aegean Trough (Fig. 12.1).

Thasos is almost completely made up gneiss, schist and marble of the Rhodope massif, as on the adjacent mainland to the north (Fig. 12.3).[279] These metamorphic rocks started out as a series of sedimentary rocks, such as limestone, dolomite, sandstone and clays together with some volcanic rocks. They have been metamorphosed and deformed several times. The age of the earliest, and most important, metamorphism is not known, but was probably several hundred million years ago. The last metamorphism was associated with the Alpine mountain-building event about 60-35 million years ago.

Faulting about 15 million years ago during the great Neogene extension of the Aegean region dropped down the south-west corner of the island, west of Limenaria, to produce a small basin. Here conglomerates accumulated, formed by the erosion of rocks towards the island's interior. Since then the only sedimen-

tation has been in the lower parts of the river valleys.

The town of Thasos (Limen)

The Greek colonists built a number of cities on the island, of which the principal, also known as Thasos, was on the north-east coast; it possessed two good harbours and a distinctive acropolis with three peaks. It is still the capital and is known either as Thasos or Limen ('The Harbour').

The modern town of Thasos was built on the site of the ancient city, on the western side of a peninsula of gneiss and marble (Fig. 12.4). Gneiss forms the outcrops near the sanctuary in the northern part of the site as well as the slopes of the southern and eastern parts of the city. The western part of the city is built on alluvium deposited by a river that drains the interior of the island.

The acropolis is made of marble, which is slightly more resistant to erosion than the gneiss and hence forms the higher land. The oldest marble quarries on the island are on the westernmost of the three peaks, which form the acropolis.[112] These quarries furnished marble for the walls and buildings of the acropolis.

There is an ancient gold mine under the south-west peak of the acropolis, with entrances about 100 m east of Parmenon Gate and near the Sanctuary of Pan.[185] The ore is in veins close to the contact between the marble and gneiss (see above) and includes quartz, pyrite, limonite and chalcopyrite. At the time of Herodotus it was only second in importance to the mines at Kinyra.

Silver, gold and iron mines

A number of deposits of gold, silver and iron as well as antimony and zinc occur in the western part of the island, along a line from Cape Salonikos to Cape Prinou (Fig. 12.3). These deposits are generally found in intensely fractured dolomite marbles. The ore minerals crystallised from weak, watery solutions that formed during the metamorphism.

Metamorphism tends to produce dryer rocks and the water in the original rocks must

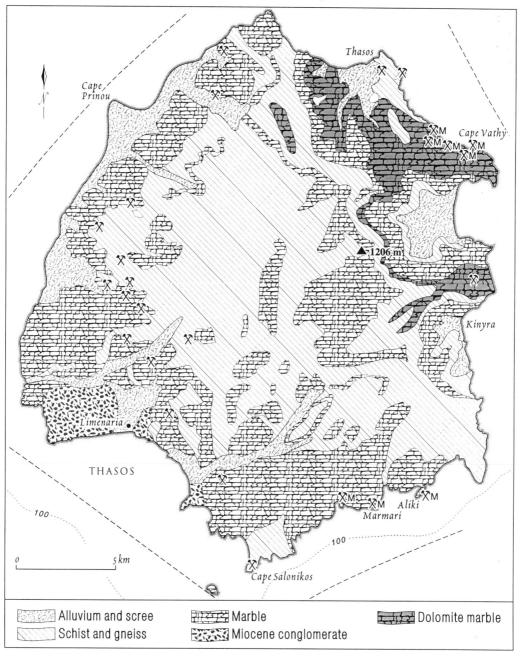

Fig. 12.3. Thasos. Marble quarries are indicated with an 'M'.

escape. The water tends to use any existing channels, such as faults, to escape upwards. In Thasos the major alignment of deposits suggests that there is a major fault that cuts the island and guided the fluids. This water contains many metals in solution, such as lead, zinc, copper and gold. As the fluid rises upwards it cools and minerals start to crystallise. Different minerals will crystallise at different temperatures, giving a series of different mineral deposits. Changes in the chemistry of the host rocks may also cause precipitation of minerals. All the mineral deposits of Thasos were deposited from such watery solutions. The metallic 'flavour' of the deposit depends on the temperature of crystallisation and the chemistry of the rocks. However, almost all deposits tend to be close to faults and also close to changes in the rock composition, such as gneiss-marble.

The ancient miners tended to exploit the upper parts of the mineral deposits where oxidation by the air and water changed the original mineralogy, and increased the concentration of metals in the ore. Thus at Thasos the mineral cerussite was mined for lead.[75, 214, 274]

The gold mines near Kinyra, visited by Herodotus in the fifth century BC, were considered the most important, although there were others.[48] Much of the gold occurs in veins and layers rich in iron and copper sulphides, but modern investigations have found the highest concentrations in sediments filling cavities in the marble.[273, 285] These cavities form by solution of the carbonate minerals in percolating rainwater, exactly as caves form in limestones. Streams that run through these passages wash in gold-bearing sediments. This process is very similar to that which forms placer gold deposits.

The iron deposits of Thasos have a long history of exploitation: in Palaeolithic times red ochre (hydrated iron oxide) was extracted for cult purposes.[284] Its underground exploitation produced one of the largest Palaeolithic mines in Europe. From the ninth century BC onwards extraction of iron ore for the production of metal became important. Sources were limonite/haematite ores, associated with other sulphide ores (see above) and beach sands rich in magnetite and ilmenite (iron-titanium oxide).

Many of the ancient mines were reopened during the nineteenth century for the exploitation of zinc and antimony, elements little used in antiquity.

Marble quarries

Thasos was well-known in antiquity for its white marble, known to the Romans as Marmor Thasium and to modern Italian masons as Marmo Greco Livido. Typically coarse-grained and translucent, it was quarried at many places on the east coast (see below). In Greek times it was used for architecture and sculpture, and in the seventh and sixth centuries BC Thasos maintained a flourishing school of sculpture. In the third and second centuries BC Thasian marble was extensively used for new buildings in the Sanctuary at Samothrace. In Roman times it was particularly in demand for sarcophagi.

The earliest marble quarries are a series of small shallow pits on the westernmost peak of the acropolis of Thasos town (Fig. 12.4).[112, 147] Quarries at Cape Phanari, immediately to the east, are much larger, with faces up to 50 m long. The floors of these quarries, and many others along the coast, are presently under-

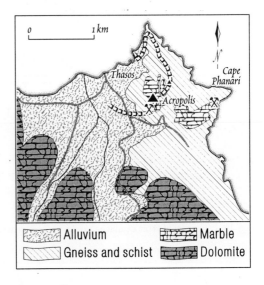

Fig. 12.4. Thasos town.

water, indicating that sea-level has risen since ancient times. The marble here is made of very large crystals of calcite, with minor graphite colouring the grey marbles. Other ancient quarries north-west of Cape Vathy have been partly destroyed by modern exploitation. However, some ancient quarries can be seen, partly submerged, along the coast, containing many unfinished pieces of sculpture. The marble is made of relatively fine-grained dolomite rather than the coarse calcite seen in the other quarries. This is to be expected as dolomite normally tends to be more fine-grained than calcite after metamorphism under the same conditions. This is the only place in the Eastern Mediterranean where dolomitic marble was exploited in antiquity.[112]

The largest ancient quarries on the island, and indeed some of the largest exploited in antiquity, were on the south-eastern coast at Aliki (Fig. 12.3). They were first operated in the sixth century BC when the temples on Thasos were constructed. By Roman times Aliki marble was one of the most popular in the empire. A rise in sea-level in the seventh century AD drowned some quarries, but production continued until Ottoman times. Here the marble is in beds up to 300 m thick and is faintly banded.[112] The layers slope at about 15° towards the sea, facilitating extraction of the blocks of marble. The marble here is made of calcite, with traces of graphite in the greyish bands, as well as quartz and mica.

Samothrace

The island of Samothrace, a strange and lovely place, was a religious and commercial centre from very early times. Its importance was largely due to its situation on the sea-lane between Greece and the Bosphorus and thence to the Black Sea. It has one small harbour, Kamariotissa, on the western tip; but it is well-watered and produces much fruit and (as it always has) the best onions in Greece. In the centre Mt Phengari ('The Mountain of the Moon') rises steeply to a height of 1,664 m. From the summit, according to Homer, the god Poseidon watched the battle raging on the Plain of Troy. Samothrace was first inhabited

by Thracians from the mainland, who were joined by Greeks in about 700 BC from the island of Lesbos. It rapidly grew rich from its situation and its fertile soil, and from the Mystery Religion of the Great Gods, which was celebrated at Palaeopolis.

Samothrace is set on the southern edge of a broad shelf, less than 100 m deep, which extends all the way to Thrace (Fig. 12.1). The steep slopes of the south-eastern coast continue underwater to depths of about 1,000 m in the North Aegean Trough, an extension of the North Anatolian Fault zone which divides the European tectonic plate from the Turkish and Aegean plate to the south. This fault is very active, accounting for the many earthquakes in this region. The island itself is a horst, probably related to movements along the North Aegean Trough.

The oldest rocks exposed on Samothrace are a series of Late Jurassic ophiolite suite rocks, mostly metamorphosed gabbros and slate, with minor Late Jurassic-Cretaceous limestones and marbles (Fig. 12.5).[54, 265] These rocks are part of the Circum-Rhodope belt, a series of sedimentary and metamorphic rocks thrust over the Rhodope massif, which continues into eastern Thrace. Mt Phengari, the highest point of the island, is dominated by metamorphosed gabbro.

Two granite intrusions in the central and southern parts of the island are about 28 million years old. Volcanic rocks are widespread and were erupted in two episodes, before and after the granites. In Late Eocene times (42-35 million years ago) volcanic ashes were erupted. This magmatism was related to extension of the crust following thickening during the Alpine compressions.[129] These rocks are now deeply weathered and/or altered by fumaroles. Volcanism restarted about 20 million years ago with the eruption of andesites, rhyodacite and trachyte lava flows and domes. Again, the volcanism may have been related to crustal extension or possibly to subduction of oceanic crust to the south.

Pliocene to recent marine deposits at lower elevations complete the map.[54] A hot spring on the north coast near Loutra is related to one of the deep horst-faults that have elevated the

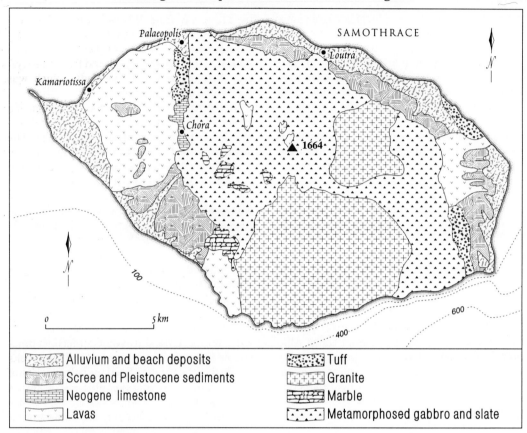

Fig. 12.5. Samothrace (after 54).

island above the surrounding sea-floor. This spring is said to have medicinal properties and has been frequented at least since Byzantine times.

Palaeopolis

The first settlement on Samothrace was located at Palaeopolis because of the presence of springs and a small cove. However, it is better known for the ruins of the Sanctuary of the Mysteries. The Mysteries were available to all, men and women, slave and free; they offered to the initiate good fortune in this life, especially when braving the dangers of the sea, and life and happiness after death. The Sanctuary was specially honoured and beautified by Alexander the Great, his successors and finally the Romans. In AD 200 it was badly damaged by an earthquake but was soon restored. Nevertheless, decline set in soon afterwards, and towards AD 400 the Sanctuary was closed on the official adoption of Christianity.

The lower parts of steep hill west of the Sanctuary are underlain by grey-green slates, formed by the metamorphism of clay-rich sediments (Fig. 12.6). Further east are a series of metamorphosed basalts and gabbros. Both rocks are part of the ophiolite complex. Breccias formed from the metamorphosed basalts, now cemented by red chalcedony and green chlorite, occur sporadically and are probably associated with a major north/south fault that defines the western edge of the ophiolite massif in the central part of the island. The springs are probably also related to this fault.

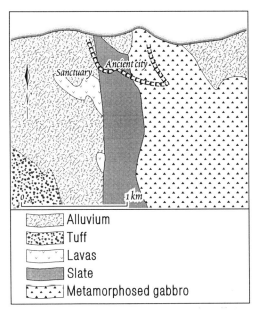

Fig. 12.6. Palaeopolis.

Much of the Sanctuary is underlain by an Eocene volcanic rock, rhyodacite porphyry, which also crops out sporadically all over the western part of the island. This rock contains large crystals of white sanidine, pink orthoclase, as well as plagioclase, biotite and hornblende. The overall colour varies from grey to green-grey and red-grey, depending on the amount and character of the alteration. It was used for the construction of buildings as well as altars. Other construction materials include local yellow limestone and white marble from Thasos.

Lemnos

The island of Lemnos, situated in the centre of the north Aegean, is almost bisected by two large bays. The western half, which is hilly rather than mountainous, is barren; the eastern half, lower-lying and more fertile, grows a certain amount of corn and vines. But the chief product of Lemnos, from antiquity onwards, was Lemnian Earth (see below).

There are many legends associated with Lemnos: the god Hephaestus (Vulcan) set up his forge here when thrown out of Olympos; Jason and the Argonauts were welcomed by the Lemnian women, who had recently murdered their husbands and were looking for male company.

To turn to history, the prehistoric site of Poliochni (its ancient name is not known) was of great importance. This city closely resembled the First and Second Cities of Troy (3000-2300 BC), and was even more magnificent. Later, Lemnos seems to have been inhabited by Thracians, then in the fifth century BC by people apparently related to the Etruscans of central Italy. Their capital, Hephaestia to the Athenians, was on the Bay of Pournia. Finally, it was from Mudros that the British Expeditionary Force set out for the disastrous Gallipoli campaign in 1915.

Lemnos stands on a shallow underwater plateau, an extension of the Turkish coast 60 km to the east (Fig. 12.1). Indeed, 20,000 years ago, when sea-level was much lower than it is now, Lemnos was not an island but a peninsula of the Turkish coast. This underwater plateau descends steeply to the north-west to the North Aegean Trough (see below). To the south and south-west the sea-floor shelves gently away.

Lemnos is unusual amongst the Aegean islands in that the oldest rocks exposed are Eocene to Oligocene sandstone and marl (Fig. 12.7). These rocks, known as molasse, were deposited on land, or in shallow lakes, adjacent to a rising mountain range.[53] Rocks with a similar origin are found in central Macedonia and crop out at the Meteora.

Although the blacksmith god Hephaestus is associated with the island there is no evidence of recent volcanic activity. However, about one third of the island is now covered with volcanic rocks, which started to erupt during the Early Miocene, about 20 million years ago. This volcanism continued for about 2 million years, and was roughly contemporary with widespread volcanism on Lesbos, other islands and, most importantly, western Turkey.[90] Most of the volcanic rocks are andesites and dacites. Lava domes and flows predominate in the west, especially near the port of Myrina. Tuffs are more common in the central and eastern parts of the island.

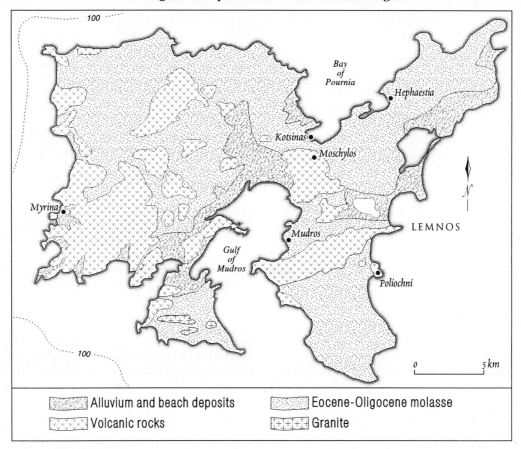

Fig. 12.7. Lemnos (after 53).

The port of Myrina (formerly Kastro) is completely surrounded by ancient volcanos: the small headlands to the north and south are both lava domes, and there are flows towards the interior. The ancient site of Poliochni was also constructed on a small headland of volcanic rocks, in this case tuffs and not lavas.

The bays of Mudros and Pournia are not volcanic in origin, but are probably tectonic features produced by north-east/south-west faults, probably splays of the North Aegean Trough. Similarly the hot springs on this island are not related to the volcanism as this ceased much too long ago. Instead they are produced by the deep circulation of water in faults.

Although few earthquakes are centred directly beneath Lemnos, the North Aegean Trough to the north is an active transform fault and produces many earthquakes, some of them strongly felt on Lemnos.

Lemnian Earth

Lemnian Earth is a red loose sediment, which occurs at Moschylos near the Bay of Pournia (Fig. 12.7). It was widely exported from antiquity down to the nineteenth century for its medicinal properties, and is still used locally. It was known to the Romans as Terra Sigillata or 'stamped earth', as it was made into little cakes, stamped with the head of Artemis.

Lemnian Earth is a form of ochre, a material rich in hydrated iron oxides, deposited from former springs. Rainwater falling on the nearby volcanic tuffs soaked into the rock and broke down the minerals. Iron was liberated and dissolved in the water. Where the springs debouched the iron was oxidised by the air and precipitated as ochre. Similar ochre springs have been culturally important in many parts of the world.

The Dardanelles and the Sea of Marmara

The recent geological history of north-west Turkey has been dominated by the effects of movements along the North Anatolian Fault, which now runs under the Sea of Marmara and north of the Dardanelles (Figs. 12.1, 12.8). This fault divides the European plate to the north from the Anatolian plate, which comprises most of Turkey, to the south. It has dominantly horizontal motion (strike-slip), but where it crosses the Sea of Marmara a change in direction of the fault has produced extension. This has produced a rapidly subsiding graben (basin) in the northern part of the sea, with a maximum depth of 1,000 m, which has accumulated some 3-4 km of sediments during the

Neogene period.[79] Islands in the southern part of the sea (including Marmara) are made of granite and metamorphic rocks, including marble, hence the name of the sea.

The main branch of the North Anatolian Fault zone does not go through the Dardanelles, as might be expected, but instead passes to the north, across the neck of the Gallipoli peninsula and into the Gulf of Edremit (Saros). The Dardanelles probably follow another old, inactive splay of the fault.

During the last glacial period, when sea-level was more than 100 m below the present level, the Black Sea and the Sea of Marmara were freshwater lakes, and the Dardanelles were a valley down which flowed a great river that drained these lakes. This changed about 10,000 years ago when rising sea-levels turned the Dardanelles into the open marine channel that we see today. However, several major rivers flow into the Black Sea and there is a swift current down the Dardanelles into the Mediterranean Sea.

The hills on either side of the Dardanelles are made of Late Tertiary sediments, deposited when this area was below sea-level. The

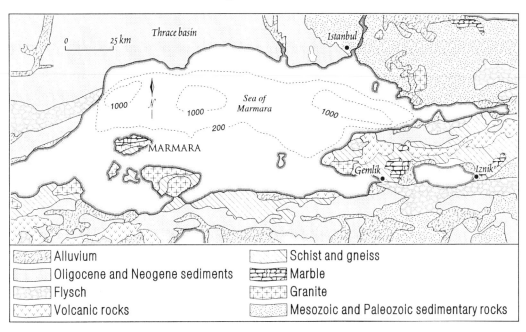

Alluvium

Oligocene and Neogene sediments

Flysch

Volcanic rocks

Schist and gneiss

Marble

Granite

Mesozoic and Paleozoic sedimentary rocks

Fig. 12.8. The Sea of Marmara.

shapes of these hills are the results of erosion produced during the great fluctuations in sea-level throughout the last few million years.

The generally low-lying northern margins of the Sea of Marmara are made of Oligocene and Neogene sedimentary rocks deposited in the Thrace basin. The steeper relief to the south is underlain by schists, gneisses, marbles and granites. Miocene volcanic rocks are also abundant here.

Marmara island

The city of Proconnesus (now Marmara), in the south-west of Marmara island, was founded from Miletus about 700 BC and continued into the Middle Ages, thanks to abundant supplies of excellent marble on the island (Figs. 12.8, 12.9). The quarries, mostly on the north-east coast near Saraylar,[16] were exploited from the sixth century BC, but not intensively until the foundation of Constantinople in AD 330 and for the next three centuries.

The marble was known to the Romans as Marmor Proconnesium or Cyzicenum, from the city of Cyzicus on the adjacent mainland. It was very popular in antiquity as it has widely-spaced joints and hence could be extracted in large blocks. The most common type, used for architecture and sarcophagi, is coarse-grained

and greyish-white, with parallel bands of blue or grey. A plain bluish-white variety was used for sculpture. A third variety, pure white and fine-grained, was suitable only for mosaics, as it is always badly cracked. The age and origin of the marble deposits are unknown.

Troy

The ancient city of Troy, or Ilion, was situated at a strategic point on the Dardanelles, known in antiquity as the Hellespont (Fig. 12.1). It is represented today by a low mound, known as Hissarlik or Truva, on a plateau bounded by the Kara Menderes river (ancient Scamander) and the Dümrek stream (ancient Simois). The mound constituted the entire Bronze Age city, but was only the acropolis of the Greek and Roman cities.

The most important legend is that of the Trojan War, as narrated by Homer in the *Iliad*: King Priam lived here with his queen and fifty sons. His son Paris brought the fair Helen here after abducting her from her husband Menelaus in Sparta. The ensuing war, fought for her recovery, lasted ten years and was won by the Greeks by means of the stratagem of the wooden horse.

The site has been occupied for a long time: the first city dates from about 3000 BC. This city was destroyed in 2500 BC and replaced by another, which was much more magnificent. The vast amount of gold plate and jewellery found there has led to the belief that there were local sources of gold, but they have not yet been identified. The next important stage was the sixth city, which was built about 1800 BC and destroyed, perhaps by an earthquake, around 1250 BC. It was a grand place, with well-built walls, wide streets and strong towers, and probably corresponds, in part at least, to Homer's Troy. Alexander the Great captured the city in 334 BC, and it achieved a degree of greatness that lasted under the Romans till at least the sixth century AD.

The site of ancient Troy lies 30 m above sea-level on a bluff of Neogene sediments between the Kara Menderes river and Dümrek stream (Fig. 12.10). These rivers rise in the hills of Paleozoic and Mesozoic metamorphic

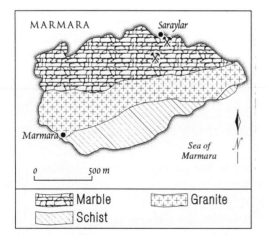

Fig. 12.9. Marmara.

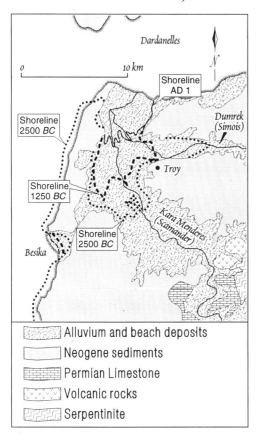

Fig. 12.10. Troy (after 154 and other sources).

down the Dardanelles to the Aegean Sea. The beds of these tributaries were deeply incised into the plain.[154, 229]

The waning of the Ice Age produced rapidly rising sea-levels, and by 8000 BC the Dardanelles had become marine. At this time the valley of the Kara Menderes river was a broad, low-lying plain. Further rises in sea-level caused the sea to encroach up the river valleys, reaching a maximum around 5000 BC. At this time the lower 15 km of the Kara Menderes was a shallow muddy and sandy estuary. From then on sea-level, now almost stable, could not keep pace with the rising of the floor of the valley produced by deposition of sediments from the rivers: the river delta began to recover lost ground and advanced towards the Dardanelles.

At the end of the first settlement, about 2500 BC, the city was surrounded on three sides by a broad sandy and muddy estuary which abounded in fish and shellfish. At the time of the Trojan War (if it actually occurred), about 1250 BC, the delta had advanced towards Troy and lay to the south-west. It is possible that there were low-lying swamps around the base of Troy at this time. If the Trojan War did take place, the battles must have been fought south and west of the city, on the plain of the river delta. By Strabo's time (first century BC/AD) Troy was about 3 km inland, but there remained a sandy estuary to the north. Since then the delta has advanced further to the north, until prevented from further advance by the erosive effects of the currents that flow along the Dardanelles. The long history of deposition of sediments in the valleys, as the delta advanced, means that any ancient settlements on the flood plain will have been deeply buried by at least 10 m of sediment.

The story of infilling of a bay was repeated at Besika, 10 km south-west of Troy (Fig. 12.10).[155] In antiquity the bay here may have been sufficiently deep to provide an alternative access to Troy, and may have been used by the Greeks in the Trojan war.

rocks and ophiolites, and Tertiary volcanic and plutonic rocks towards the interior. They flow out onto a low plateau, commonly 60 to 125 m above sea-level, composed of Neogene sediments deposited in an earlier graben parallel to the present Dardanelles. A recent intensive drainage programme to stabilise the bed of the Kara Menderes has almost eliminated the floods that regularly turned this valley into a lake. However, this has also made it more difficult to understand the role and importance of sediments deposited by the river.

At the peak of the last glaciation, 20,000 years ago, when sea-level was about 120 m below the present level, these rivers were tributaries of a great river that drained the ancestral Black Sea, then a lake, and flowed

A Geological Companion to Greece and the Aegean

Istanbul and the Bosphorus

The city strategically placed on the borders of Europe and Asia and at the junction of the Sea of Marmara and the Bosphorus, was known successively as Byzantium, Constantinople and Istanbul (Figs. 12.8, 12.11). Roughly triangular in shape, it is bounded on the west by Thrace, on the south by the Sea of Marmara, and on the north-east by the superb deep-water harbour known as the Golden Horn.

Under the name of Byzantium, it was founded as a colony of the Greek city of Megara about 650 BC and grew rich from agriculture and the plentiful fish of the Bosphorus. It endured Persian occupation in the sixth century BC, and was incorporated in the Roman Empire in AD 73. In AD 330 the Emperor Constantine the Great rebuilt and fortified the city as eastern capital of his newly-Christianised Roman Empire, and it soon acquired the name of Constantinople, after its founder. It remained the capital of the Eastern Roman (Byzantine) Empire until the Turkish conquest of 1483. Thereafter, until 1923, it was the capital of the Turkish Empire.

The Bosphorus is 0.5-3 km wide and 50-120 m deep. It is an ancient river valley, probably formed during the Pleistocene, when sea-level was much lower. At that time the Black Sea was a lake which drained, along the Bosphorus, into the Sea of Marmara lake. The Golden Horn was a tributary valley. Rising sea-levels drowned these valleys and they probably became marine around 8000 BC.

Istanbul is largely built on Devonian sediments, including dark grey and black limestones, which continue to the north on either side of the Bosphorus, almost to the Black Sea (Fig. 12.11). Here Late Cretaceous volcanic rocks crop out on either side for about 3 km. Palaeozoic sedimentary rocks also continue to the east, where they are cut by two granite intrusions. To the west of Istanbul the Palaeozoic rocks descend below Tertiary sedimentary rocks which are a peripheral part of the Thrace basin.

The main construction material for Istanbul during Roman and Ottoman times was the

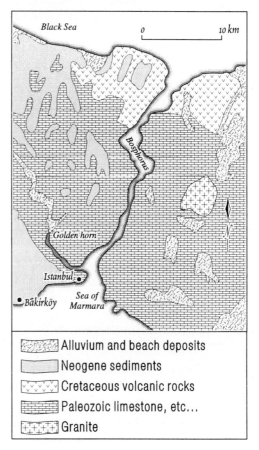

Fig. 12.11. Istanbul and the Bosphorus.

Legend:
- Alluvium and beach deposits
- Neogene sediments
- Cretaceous volcanic rocks
- Paleozoic limestone, etc...
- Granite

Bakirköy limestone. This grey, fossiliferous limestone of Miocene age was extracted from extensive quarries about 10 km west of the city centre, now buried under urban developments.[80] Marble from Marmara island was also used extensively, as well as decorative conglomerates from Hereke (Herakleia) and Karacabey, and red fossiliferous limestone from Gebze, south-east of Istanbul.

The Black Sea is a remnant of an oceanic basin that formed in Cretaceous time between a continental land-mass to the north and an island arc to the south, rather like the Japan Sea today. Alpine compressions destroyed part of the basin, and turned the island arc into the Pontide mountains south of the Black Sea. Since the formation of the

128

Black Sea Basin about 15 km of sediments have been deposited here.[104] The Black Sea receives much more water from its rivers than is lost from evaporation. The excess flows down the Bosphorus to the Sea of Marmara, creating an important current.

The Eastern Sporades and the Ionian Shore

This chapter covers the Greek islands of Lesbos (Mytilene), Chios and Samos, and the adjacent Turkish mainland (Fig. 13.1, Plate 11). The ancient Greek cities, on the western Turkish coast, which will be considered in conjunction with these islands are Pergamon, beside Lesbos; Izmir (formerly Smyrna), Teos and Sardis beside Chios; and Ephesus, Priene and Miletus, beside Samos.

Apart from a few Mycenaean settlements between 1400 and 1100 BC, the Greek presence in this region really starts about 1000 BC, when bands of refugees from the troubles in mainland Greece made their way eastwards across the Aegean. Some stopped off in the islands, while others moved on to the Asiatic coast. Thanks to the fertile soil, excellent climate, and excellent harbours, these settlements grew rich, but were never strong enough to withstand any powerful neighbour who might have designs on them. Consequently, between 550 and 525 BC, they fell to the Persians. Although freed by Athens after about fifty years, they were soon back under Persian control, and it was left to Alexander the Great to liberate them again in 333 BC. Henceforward they prospered. Rich in Hellenistic times, they were even richer under the Roman and Byzantine empires. The end came in the seventh century AD, caused by the silting up of the harbours, the onset of malaria, and attacks by pirates.

The bedrock of this region is divided into two parts: the Izmir-Ankara zone roughly to the north of the Gediz river and the Menderes massif to the south (Fig. 13.1). The Izmir-Ankara zone is made up of flysch sediments, limestones, volcanic rocks and serpentinite, mostly of Early Triassic to Late Cretaceous age.[78] The rocks of this zone have a chaotic structure, with blocks of limestone up to 20 km long, set in a matrix of smaller blocks and flysch sediments. This structure was produced by tectonic movements during deposition of the flysch: the limestones were originally part of a shallow continental shelf that was broken up and slid into deeper water where the flysch was being deposited, during the Late Cretaceous. The whole unit was further disrupted when it was thrust southwards partly onto the Menderes massif, and perhaps beyond. The Izmir-Ankara zone may be equivalent to parts of the Pelagonian zone in Greece.

The Menderes massif is an area of older metamorphic and igneous rocks similar to the Attic-Cycladic metamorphic belt to the west, although the exact relationship between the two is not clear. The Menderes massif has a concentric structure, roughly decreasing in age and degree of metamorphism from core to edge. The core is made of gneisses metamorphosed during Late Precambrian to Cambrian time (more than 600 to 500 million years ago). Metamorphic rocks of this age are common throughout Africa (the Pan-African event) which suggests that this part of Turkey was originally part of that continent.[246] The core is enveloped by a series of mica-schists and marbles, some with emery deposits of Palaeozoic age. Finally there is a series of Triassic to Early Tertiary marbles. The metamorphism that produced these rocks was probably related to the Alpine orogeny in Early Tertiary time. The three series of rocks of the massif were originally placed on top of each other by the Alpine compressions, but the core of the massif has suffered more erosion to reveal the underlying older rocks.

The geological history of western Turkey

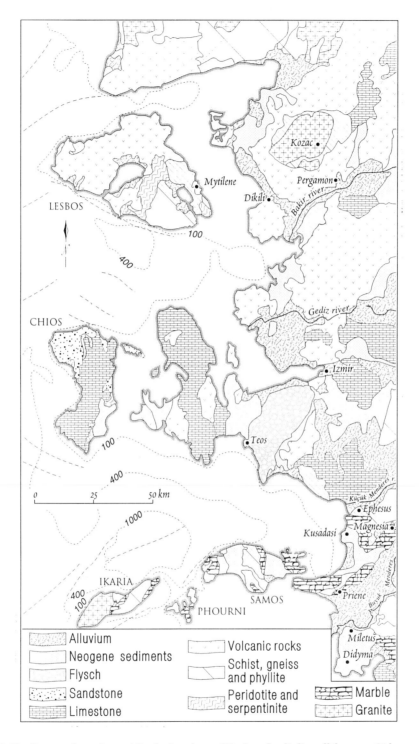

Fig. 13.1. The Eastern Sporades and the Ionian shore of Turkey. Sardis lies off the map, 94 km east of Izmir.

131

during the Neogene has been dominated by north/south stretching of the crust. This is part of the overall plate tectonic evolution of the Aegean region. The east/west faults produced by this extension have strongly controlled the topography of the region: almost all the major rivers in this area, the Bakir ('Copper river'), Gediz, Büyük Menderes and Küçük Menderes, flow along grabens. The floors of these valleys are still dropping today, which maintains the relief against the levelling effect of erosion. The rugged topography also leads to high rates of erosion and the resulting sediment is transported by the rivers to the sea, where it forms large deltas. One such graben is the valley of the Küçük Menderes river, which flows past the ancient city of Ephesus (Fig. 13.1). This graben continues underwater to the west as the gulf between the islands of Chios to the north and Samos and Ikaria to the south.

Neogene sediments have been deposited in many of these grabens. Of particular importance are now the deposits of lignite around Soma, about 100 km north-east of Izmir.[121] These rocks were formed from decayed vegetation in swamps during the Miocene period. Seams up to 20 m thick are mostly exploited for the generation of electricity.

Since the peak of the last glaciation about 20,000 years ago, sea-level has risen rapidly at least 100 m, greatly changing the topography. At the time of lower sea-level the valleys and their rivers extended further out to sea. Rivers drop their load of sediment (mud, silt and sand) when they meet the sea and slow down. In the past, therefore, the sediments of these rivers was deposited far out to sea. Initially, sea-level rose faster than the retreating valleys could be filled with sediments, and produced bays that cut deep into the continent. However, the large amount of sediments transported by the rivers quickly filled up these bays and today the process is almost complete.

Overall, this region has a low number of earthquakes, compared to the Aegean as a whole.[36] The Aegean Sea west of the islands is particularly low in earthquake activity, but this is compensated for by a higher activity near the channels east of the islands, especially Samos, and on the mainland.

Lesbos

Lesbos (or Mytilene), one of the largest of the Greek islands, lies close to the Turkish coast (Figs. 13.1, 13.2). The easternmost of the two large inlets, the Gulf of Geras, forms an excellent harbour. Behind the coastal plain is a mountainous interior, barren on the west side, but planted on the east with luxuriant olive trees and vines.

Lesbos was settled from nearby Asia Minor about 4000 BC (Late Neolithic). From 3000 to 2300 BC it enjoyed a flourishing civilization, revealed at Thermi on the east coast, which bears a striking resemblance to the first and second cities of Troy. Later the Mycenaean Greeks came; an event perhaps recorded by Homer's story that Agamemnon conquered the island during the Trojan War. Around 1000 BC Aeolian Greeks came from the Greek mainland and founded six cities, of which Mytilene and Mithimna were the most important. Thanks to the fertile soil and their excellent harbour, the Lesbians grew rich. Terpander, the father of Greek music, lived here as well as the poets Sappho and Alcaeus; the ruler, Pittacus, was counted one of the Seven Wise Men. We hear little of Lesbos in Roman and Byzantine times; but there was a revival in AD 1354 when the Genoese Francisco Gattilusio acquired the island and built the castle at Mytilene.

Lesbos is situated on a shallow shelf extending from the Turkish coast (Fig. 13.1). The channel between the island and the mainland would have been dry 20,000 years ago when sea-level was depressed by the Ice Age. To the south the sea-floor drops off rapidly into an underwater graben, an extension of the Bakir graben on the mainland. The graben originated about 10 million years ago during the Neogene stretching of the Aegean region.

The oldest rocks are exposed on Mt Olympos (1,055 m) and the surrounding plateau in the south-east part of the island, and in several small areas in the west (Fig. 13.2). These are a series of metamorphosed sediments of Carboniferous to Triassic age that were formed before the Alpine mountain-building event. This group of rocks includes schists, sandstones and conglomerates around the Gulf of Geras and

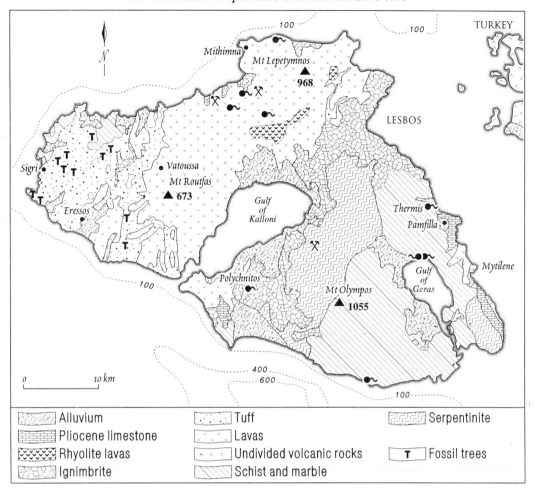

Fig. 13.2. Lesbos.

limestones north-west of the town of Mytilene. In some areas they are covered by Jurassic basalts, gabbros and peridotites, now commonly altered to serpentinite, which are members of the ophiolite suite. These rocks were originally part of the floor of an ocean to the north, which closed during the Alpine compressions, thrusting parts of the sea-floor onto the land along almost horizontal faults. Deposits of magnesite in the serpentinite have been exploited recently on the east side of the Gulf of Kalloni.

Volcanic rocks cover more than half of Lesbos and were emplaced over a short period of time, mostly within 2 million years, synchronously with volcanism on the adjacent parts of Turkey.[209] Volcanism started 22 million years ago with the eruption of lavas, now exposed in a small area east of Eressos. There was then a hiatus until 18 million years ago when the main volcanic episode started. Initially, basalt and andesite lavas were erupted around Vatoussa and south of Mithimna. Then followed a phase of more silica-rich, explosive volcanism. Volcanic ash (tuff) was deposited to the west, partly burying a forest (see below). In the east the ash was sufficiently hot that it welded together after it fell to form a sheet of ignimbrite. The source of the ash may have been a caldera near Vatoussa. Domes and flows of rhyolite and dacite were emplaced north of the Gulf of Kalloni. Some of these rocks have been exploited for the manufacture of perlite (see Melos). The last major volcanic phase was the eruption of basalt, andesite and dacite lavas in the central part of the island. Great thicknesses of lavas accumulated to the north-east and south-west forming stratovolcanos whose eroded remains are Mt Routfas and Mt Lepetymnos. Volcanism continued in a very minor way in the east, near Mytilene, with the eruption of minor basalt and andesite lavas. All volcanism on Lesbos ceased 16 million years ago.

Minor faulting and subsidence of the land followed this period of volcanism and allowed sedimentary rocks to be deposited along the coast and around the gulfs of Kalloni and Geras. These movements may be a part of the overall Neogene stretching of the region.

Lesbos has many hot springs: most are rich in common salt and many debouche near or under the sea. The water in these springs is a mixture of rainwater and seawater. The most important spring issues from volcanic rocks about 1,500 m south-east of Polychnitos and feeds the Almiropotamos stream. It is the largest and hottest spring (87°C) on the island and one of the hottest in Europe. The composition of the dissolved minerals indicates that the water is not from the sea but is dominantly recycled rainwater. During its passage through the earth this water has dissolved calcite, which has been redeposited around the exit of the spring as travertine. Although this spring rises through volcanic rocks they are much too old to be the source of heat.

The town of Mytilene

Along the south-east coast of Lesbos there are a series of lowlands, underlain by Miocene lavas and tuffs, Pliocene freshwater limestones and Pleistocene sediments (Fig. 13.3). These rocks formed in a graben, isolated from the sea, whose eastern half has dropped down beneath sea-level in geologically recent time. The magmas that fed the volcanism rose up

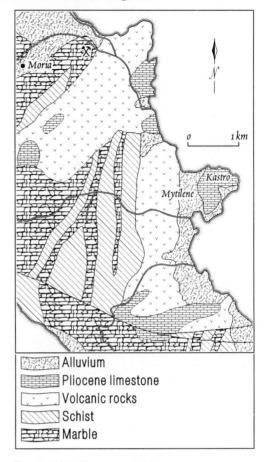

Fig. 13.3. Mytilene town, Lesbos.

from deeper chambers along the graben faults.

The town of Mytilene is built on one of these lowlands. The lowest part of the town is underlain by Pleistocene sediments and alluvium, but the low hills to the west are made of volcanic rocks. Behind rise the hills of Permian-Triassic marbles and schists that comprise the backbone of the peninsula. To the north-east of the town the peninsula of the Kastro is made of Pliocene freshwater limestone, isolated from the mainland by lowlands that conceal a north-south fault.

Marble was extracted from a large quarry near the coast, 1 km east of Moria and 3 km north of Mytilene (Fig. 13.3). This pale grey marble was formed by metamorphism of Triassic limestones. It was considered to be of lower quality than that extracted from quarries further north, near Thermis, which are still exploited. Volcanic cones also occur as small isolated hills around Pamfilla, 8 km to the north of Mytilene.

The ancient site of Thermi, 12 km north of Mytilene near (Loutra) Thermis, has been occupied from the Early Bronze Age, almost 5,000 years ago. The ancient attraction was the hot spring, which issues at 40°C. The saline nature of the water indicates that it is recycled seawater. The spring is associated with an important normal fault, running north-west/south-east, delineating a horst, which continues southward as the Mytilene Peninsula, and a graben to the north, now partly filled with volcanic rocks.

The 'petrified forest'

There are the remnants of a petrified forest in the far west of the island, mostly within 5 km of Sigri (Fig. 13.2). Over 200 fossilised sequoia trunks, together with roots and cones, and occasionally also palm trees, have been found at over 35 locations on land and underwater. The trunks, some of which are in their original growth positions, range up to 5 m long and 2.5 m in diameter. The Petrified Forest has been declared a Protected National Monument and the fossils should in no circumstances be removed. These trees were engulfed by ash from volcanic vents to the east about 18 million years ago. Rainwater circulating through the ash dissolved the finer particles and these dilute solutions then soaked into the tree trunks. The different chemical environment within the wood caused minute crystals of silica, pyrite and iron oxides to be deposited within the cells, replacing the wood and fossilising it.

Pergamon

Situated on the Turkish mainland some 30 km from the sea, the lofty site of Pergamon was for long too far inland to interest the Greeks, who seldom ventured far from the coasts (Fig. 13.1). It was, however, inhabited from about 700 BC by local Asiatics. It soon became part of the Persian Empire, to be conquered in 330 BC by Alexander the Great. On his death the empire disintegrated: the fortress of Pergamon and its gold treasure passed to Philetairos who built a remarkable city, running down the hillside in a riot of Baroque town-planning. It was renowned, amongst other things, for a health-centre, the Asklepieion, in the lower ground south-west of the acropolis, where there were sacred springs. The Romans inherited the city in 133 BC and continued to beautify the city in the same flamboyant way. The Asklepieion was now reckoned the equal of Kos and Epidauros. Pergamon flourished for about a thousand years, but it had long been deserted when the Turks arrived in the fourteenth century AD and built their town Bergama, at the foot of the old acropolis.

The acropolis of Pergamon is situated on the northern edge of the Bakir valley (ancient Caicus), which stretches for 5 km to the south, and runs down to the sea at Dikili (Fig. 13.1). This valley is a graben, produced during Neogene north/south crustal stretching. A very large amount of volcanic rocks were produced

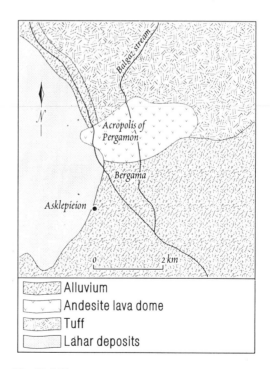

Fig. 13.4. Pergamon.

in Western Turkey at about the same time as the extension and were probably related to it. In this area these rocks are 18-16 million years old and they mostly consist of andesites and dacites. The hills to the north of Pergamon are made of such volcanic rocks. On the southern side of the graben the hills are also made of andesite with Permian limestones to the south-east and south-west.

The acropolis itself was constructed on a steep-sided hill that rises to about 450 m (Fig. 13.4). It is cut off to the south by the Bakir graben, and the east and west sides of the hill are defined by the valleys of the Selinus and Balgaz (ancient Cetius) streams, small tributaries that flow into the graben to join the Bakir river. Somewhat unusually for a classical site, the bedrock here is andesite, which contains phenocrysts of dark biotite and pale plagioclase up to 3 mm long. The acropolis hill is a lava dome, subsequently modified by erosion.[4, 76] Similar domes occur along the graben towards Dikili. The magma probably rose up the graben faults. The hills on either side are made of volcanic ash and lahar (volcanic landslide) deposits.

The Asklepieion is situated in the river valley below the acropolis. The springs are produced where the shallow water-table in the valley reaches the surface. The water originally fell on the surrounding hills.

Granite quarries

Although little used by the Greeks, granite (in the broad sense) was an important material for the Romans and was traded widely. There were two major sources of granite in the Aegean region: Marmo Misio (or Granito Bigio) from near Kozac, 15 km north-west of Bergama (Fig. 13.1) and Marmo Troadense (or Granito Violetto) from Mt Cigri, 10 km south-west of Ezine (Fig. 12.1).[99] Both rocks are grey, fine-grained and principally composed of quartz, feldspar and biotite. Marmo Misio is a true granite, but rather richer in quartz than most granites. Marmo Troadense is not quite a true granite as it has too much plagioclase feldspar in it, and it is more correctly termed a quartz-monzonite. Both intrusions are about the same

age as the volcanic rocks in the region, i.e. 18-16 million years old.

Chios

The large island of Chios lies close to the Turkish coast (Fig. 13.1). Its fertile plains are sheltered by a mountain range running from north to south which culminates in Mt Pelinaion. It produces the tree resin mastic (a Chian specialty); fruit, especially figs; and wine, for which it was famous in antiquity.

Chios has a long history, starting in the Neolithic (about 6000 BC). Mycenaean Greeks arrived here around 1400 and stayed until 1100 BC, when their settlements were destroyed. Then, shortly after 1000 BC, Ionian Greeks from Euboea settled at several places on the island and made their capital on the site of the present Chios town. The seventh and sixth centuries BC were the great days for Chios. Her citizens were famous as sculptors, bronze-workers and potters; even Homer was believed by some to have been a Chian. Thanks to their fertile soil, their mercantile skills and their productive marble quarries the Chians grew rich in Roman and Byzantine times. The once glorious monastery of Nea Moni is witness to their prosperity in the eleventh century AD. Then came Venetians, Genoese and Turks. The latter perpetrated a ghastly massacre in 1822, from which Chios never recovered, and a terrible earthquake in 1881 made a bad situation even worse.

Chios is geologically and geomorphologically an extension of the Aegean coast of Turkey, linked by a channel 8 km wide and only 75 m deep (Fig. 13.1). In all other directions the sea-floor slopes off gently, descending eventually to 800 m in a broad basin between Chios and the Cyclades, and to 1,000 m north of Ikaria.

The oldest rocks are Palaeozoic flysch sediments, predominantly sandstones and shales, and volcanic rocks, that crop out in the north-western part of the island and to the north of Chios town (Fig. 13.5).[29, 197] Magmatic rocks of the same age are widespread in the Karakaya belt of north-west Turkey.[208] The central part of the island, including the highest point Mt Peli-

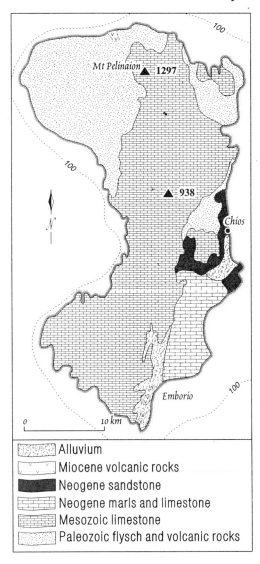

Fig. 13.5. Chios.

Minor, but widespread, volcanism occurred on Chios 17-14 million years ago.[210] Tuffs were deposited in the Neogene sedimentary rocks south of Chios town. Near the southern tip of the island magma reached the surface quiescently along the graben faults and formed a series of four plugs, domes and flows. The outcrop north of Emborio, Profitis Elias, is a rhyolite plug whereas that to the south is made of a series of columnar-jointed andesite flows.[210] There is also a small rhyolite dome on the north coast and many other smaller domes, flows and tuffs elsewhere on the island.

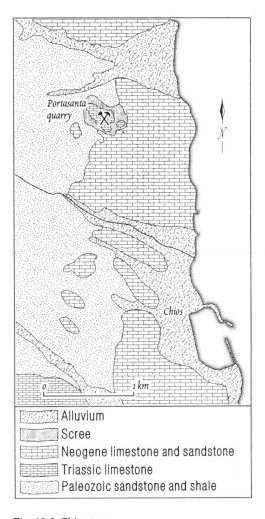

Fig. 13.6. Chios town.

naion (1297 m), is made of Triassic and Jurassic limestones. Sedimentary rocks now exposed in the south-east part of the island were deposited in a graben from rivers and shallow lakes during the Miocene and Pliocene. Sandstones are more common in the north, around Chios town, but to the south marls and limestones predominate. These Neogene sediments, especially the marls, yield fertile soils.

137

Portasanta quarries

Chios also produced a salmon-pink marble known to the Romans as Marmo Chium and to the Italians as Portasanta from its use on church doors in Rome. It was particularly popular in Rome from the time of Augustus (late first century BC) to the fourth century, and was used for columns, wall panels and floor-decorations. It became popular again in the sixteenth century in the form of re-used stones from Roman buildings.

The Portasanta quarries are 2 km north of Chios town (Fig. 13.6). The rock is a recrystallised limestone, half-way to becoming a marble. It is commonly a breccia; mostly salmon-pink, with red and white inclusions, but the base is occasionally cream or grey. The pink colours reflect the abundance of iron, particularly haematite, in the rock. This block of rock is Triassic in age and similar to that of the hills to the north-west. It is probably part of a sheet of rock thrust over the surrounding Palaeozoic and Neogene sediments.

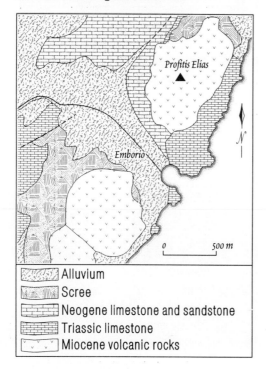

Alluvium
Scree
Neogene limestone and sandstone
Triassic limestone
Miocene volcanic rocks

Fig. 13.7. Emborio, Chios.

Emborio

The village of Emborio lies on alluvial plains between two volcanic domes, both of Miocene age (Fig. 13.7). Along the coast there is a strip of Triassic limestones, which forms the headlands on either side of the bay, and has protected the volcanic rocks from erosion by the sea. The ancient settlement on Mt Profitis Elias, north of the village, was built on the rhyolite plug of Miocene age.

Izmir

The city of Izmir (formerly Smyrna) lies at the eastern end of the 24 km long Gulf of Izmir, near the mouth of the river Gediz (ancient Hermus; Figs. 13.1, 13.8). Spacious, sheltered and accessible, this has always been one of the best ports in the Mediterranean. In addition to possessing a very fertile soil, from earliest times Izmir has been the centre of export of the products, agricultural and mineral, of the interior, via the valley of the Gediz river.

The earliest settlement, dated at about 3000 BC, was on the low hill of Tepekula, near Bayrakli, about 5 km north of the present centre of Izmir. The acropolis was on a hill about 2 km to the north-west. The first Greeks arrived about 1000 BC, and the city rose in prominence until destroyed by the Lydians in 627 BC. About 330 BC it was refounded by Alexander the Great on the slopes of Mt Kadifekale (ancient Mt Pagus) and soon grew very rich as a mercantile and artistic centre. In AD 178 it was completely destroyed by an earthquake, but was soon rebuilt. In the seventh century AD Arab raids devastated the city, which was already impoverished by the silting up of the harbour; and in the fourteenth century, when the Knights of Rhodes came here to build a castle, they found it a ruin. Captured shortly afterwards by the Turks, it became a trading centre for European merchants in the seventeenth century. The old city was burnt down during the hostilities in 1922, and has been completely rebuilt.

Izmir lies at the head of a convoluted bay, part of the rather untidy Gediz river graben, which penetrates eastwards deep into the con-

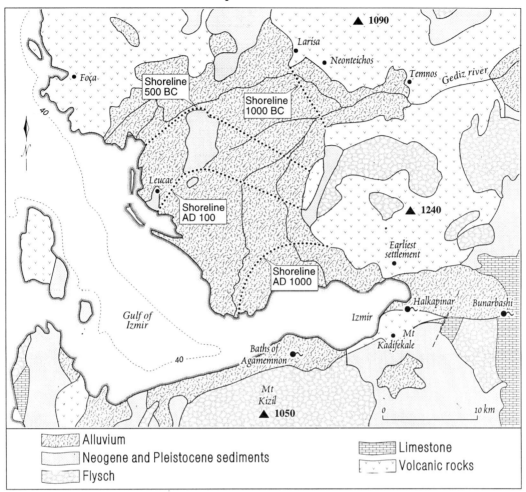

Fig. 13.8. The Gulf of Izmir (after 3, 139 and other sources).

tinent (Figs. 13.1, 13.8). To the north of the city the hills are dominated by Miocene andesite lavas and tuffs. The hills to the south-east and south-west (Mt Kizil) are made of Cretaceous limestone and flysch respectively.

Both the earlier acropolis, north of the present city centre, and the later city, on Mt Kadifekale ('Velvet castle') were constructed on hills of andesite lavas, breccias and tuffs.[122,][139] To the south of the city the volcanic rocks were covered by younger marls. Until recently andesite lava was extensively quarried for construction, both in Izmir and on the north side of the valley.[139] However, now Tertiary lime-

stones are used as aggregate in the concrete that has taken its place.

The Gediz is a major perennial river that drains a large area and transports 3-6 million tonnes of sediment each year, most of which is deposited in Izmir Bay.[3] At the end of the last glacial period sea-level rose rapidly and the coastline retreated inland, covering at its maximum the whole of the current Gediz delta (Fig. 13.8). However, soon the deposition of sediments transported by the river began to fill in the bay and force the coastline back out. The ancient former ports of Temnos, Neonteichos and Larisa were isolated from the sea by 1000

BC. By 350 BC the island on which the port of Leucae stood was transformed into a headland. The delta front continued to advance southwards, threatening to cut off the port of Izmir. In AD 1886 the Gediz river was diverted into the northernmost channel, almost completely cutting off flow in the southern branches, and the advance of the delta southwards was stopped.

The coastline at the far eastern end of the Gulf of Izmir has also advanced since ancient times. A number of small streams have transported sediment from the surrounding hills and dumped it into the bay. The advance is quite modest, a maximum of about 1 km, but sufficient to have turned the ancient site of Tepekule from a peninsula into a low hill.

A cool perennial spring, Halkapinar ('Diana's Bath') wells up near the present city centre, in the grounds of the municipal water company. This spring feeds a short stream that may be the river Meles of antiquity. Another important cool spring issues 10 km east of the city at Bunarbashi, fed by water that falls on the surrounding hills.[37]

Warm, sulphurous springs known as the Baths of Agamemnon well up 10 km west of the city. The springs range up to 54°C and were well known in antiquity. However, nothing of any great age remains. These springs are related to the deep faults of the graben.

Sardis

The ancient city of Sardis (near the modern village of Sart) was built on the southern edge of the fertile plain of the Gediz river (ancient Hermus), 94 km east of Izmir. Here the Sart torrent (ancient Pactolus), rising on the Mt Boz range (ancient Tmolus) to the south, flows through the centre of Sardis on its way to join the Gediz river.

The site was inhabited continuously from at least 3000 BC, but is not known to history until about 700 BC, when it was the capital of Lydia, a kingdom situated inland from the Ionian coast. For some 250 years Sardis flourished, thanks chiefly to the plentiful gold and silver obtained from the Pactolus river. Herodotus relates that the precious metal was trapped on sheepskins suspended in the river, a technique which gave rise no doubt to the legend of the Golden Fleece. Under such kings as Gyges and Croesus the Lydians were renowned as the inventors of coinage (about 600 BC), and as bankers, traders, horsemen and musicians. In 545 BC Sardis was taken by the Persians, following ambiguous advice from the Delphic oracle, and subsequently ruled from Pergamon and Rome. In AD 14 it was rebuilt after a terrible earthquake, and flourished until destroyed by the Sassanians in AD 616. Rebuilt, it was finally destroyed by Tamerlaine in 1401.

The valley of the Gediz river, north of Sardis, is a major geographical feature of the region. It follows an east/west graben which penetrates deep into the continent, bisecting the Menderes massif in this region (see above). The Mt Boz range rises to the south reaching 2,159 m and is dominated by metamorphic rocks such as marble, schist and gneiss. To the north the hills are made of gneiss and Neogene sedimentary rocks.

The Gediz graben originated during early Neogene regional extension in a north/south direction. The earliest sediments in the graben are sandstones, conglomerates and freshwater limestones formed by the river and in lakes. These are most commonly seen near the edge of the graben, and around Sardis form a band about 3 km wide, south of the main highway (Fig. 13.9). In places large boulders, or patches of more resistant rock have protected the underlying conglomerates, giving steep-sided, conical hills, such as those that underlie the acropolis and necropolis. Part of the valley of the Sart torrent, between the two hills, follows a north/south fault, which has weakened the rock and allowed more rapid erosion.

The ancient city of Sardis covered the northern slopes of the acropolis hill and was built on alluvium and old landslide deposits. The imposing acropolis hill is made of weakly cemented conglomerates and sandstones. In antiquity at least 130 m of tunnels were excavated in the upper parts of the acropolis hill. They appear to have been excavated from below, near the base of the hill, and may have been constructed to augment the water supply of the city. Elsewhere on the site the water-

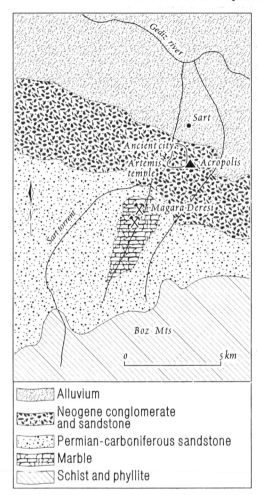

Fig. 13.9. Sardis.

After it was abandoned the city was buried, commonly to a depth of 10 m, by sediments transported by the Sart torrent, and by landslides from the acropolis hill. Landslides are common here due a combination of weak, porous rocks, heavy winter rainfall and frequent earthquakes.

Ancient gold and silver deposits

At its zenith the wealth of Sardis was due to the placer gold deposits of the Pactolus river. The gold of these deposits started out in the metamorphic rocks of the Menderes massif to the south. During metamorphism high temperature water dissolved a number of elements from the rocks through which they passed, including gold. As the fluids ascended and cooled these elements were precipitated as new minerals in veins. One type of vein is dominated by quartz, but can contain small amounts of gold, in the form of the metal. Such veins are quite common, but only rarely attain sufficient size and richness for a mine.

The gold of the Pactolus was concentrated from the metamorphic rocks and their primary deposits by two cycles of weathering and erosion.[262] Initially the metamorphic rocks were broken down by weathering, liberating the gold particles. These sediments, including the gold, were transported by rivers and deposited in the Gediz graben. Gold is heavier and more resistant to weathering than the other minerals, and hence is concentrated by the action of the rivers. Subsequently these sediments were cemented to form the Neogene conglomerates and sandstones, such as those seen on the acropolis hill. These rocks were in turn weathered and the gold further concentrated in placer deposits in the river gravels of the Pactolus torrent.

In all probability all the rivers in this area provided small amounts of placer gold, but the Pactolus was richer that the others because the concentration process was repeated twice. The very nature of placer deposits makes it impossible to determine exactly where the gold came from after extraction. Even in antiquity placer gold mining was extremely easy and the Pactolus was exhausted by Strabo's time (first

table is low, necessitating the construction of wells up to 20 m deep.

The city was constructed of local Neogene sandstone and limestone, and a pale-grey to white coarse-grained marble. The latter was extracted from quarries at Magara Deresi, 4 km south of the city, on either side of a torrent flowing north into the Pactolus.[181] These outcrops of marble are part of the Menderes massif to the south, and protrude through the overlying younger sediments. This lower level of erosion is due to the presence of weakened rock adjacent to a north/south fault, which continues northwards in the lower part of the Pactolus valley.

century BC to first century AD).

The metal extracted from the rivers of this region always contains a proportion of silver, making the natural alloy called electrum. Initially, coinage was made directly from this alloy, but the variation in silver content from 36 to 53%, some of which was undoubtedly natural, may have shaken public confidence in the currency. Hence, during the reign of Croesus the metals were separated to produce pure gold and silver coins. Silver was also produced, together with lead, in the Balya mine, Balikesir region.[108]

Teos

Teos was a Greek city, whose ruins are situated 40 km south-west of Izmir, and 2 km south of the village of Sigacik (Fig. 13.1). It was settled by Ionians about 1000 BC. Thanks to its two good harbours it did well and founded colonies of its own. In 133 BC Teos fell to the rising power of Rome and almost passed out of history, but not entirely, as it supplied the Roman market with a desirable coloured marble.

This marble is a breccia with a dark, fine-grained matrix and inclusions of pink, yellow, blue-grey and white marble. It was known to the Romans as Marmo Luculleum; to the Italians it is Marmo Africano, apparently because the matrix is dark like the skin of an African. It was much used in Roman architecture in the first and second centuries AD, especially in Italy and North Africa. Its subsequent use in the churches and palaces of Rome consists of the recycling of Classical Roman material. The quarries are east of Sigacik, on the road to Seferihissar. The most important, which was worked out before AD 200, is now a lake known as Kara Gol. An unbrecciated, blue-grey marble is part of the same unit, and was also quarried in Roman times for decorating buildings. These marbles are a small block of the Menderes massif that protrudes through flysch and Neogene sedimentary rocks.

Ephesus

The city of Ephesus was founded about 1000 BC by Ionian Greeks, probably from Athens, at the mouth of the Cayster river (now Küçük Menderes: Fig. 13.1). On the northern slopes of Mt Pion (now Mt Panayir) they found Carians and other native people living round a sanctuary of the Asiatic nature-goddess Cybele. They came to an arrangement with these people and established a joint city which was to last for over 400 years. They became very rich, thanks to their harbour at the mouth of the Cayster, which provided easy passage to the interior, to their Sanctuary of Artemis, and to the fertile flood-plain of the river. In 334 BC the city was conquered by Alexander the Great. Forty years later, badly affected by silting, the city was moved again to the spot where the ruins now stand, between Mt Panayir and Mt Bulbul (ancient Mt Koressos). Here it flourished for many centuries until replaced about AD 1000 by the town of Selçuk (formerly Ayasoluk).

The Temple of Artemis (Artemesion) was rebuilt many times over a period of 1,400 years and the last version, the largest in the Greek world, was numbered among the Seven Wonders of the Ancient World. It was the first monumental building to be constructed entirely of marble. It lasted intact until it was sacked by the Goths in AD 263. Partially rebuilt, it continued until the end of the fourth century when it was closed by the Christians. The marble was re-used to a large extent for building churches, and the remaining ruins were gradually covered by the silt of the Küçük Menderes river.

The wealth of the ancient city of Ephesus was controlled by the geography of its situation: at the head of a fertile valley that penetrates deep into the hinterland and on a deep bay that provided a good harbour (Fig. 13.1). The position and orientation of this valley, together with valleys to the north (see Pergamon and Izmir) and south (see Priene and Miletus) were controlled by the tectonics of the area during the last 20 million years. The deep bays, once so common on this coast, were related to the rapid rise of sea-level following the last glaciation. The loss of this bay, which figures so prominently in the demise of this city, was merely the correction of a temporary situation following the rise in sea-level.

The geography in antiquity was rather dif-

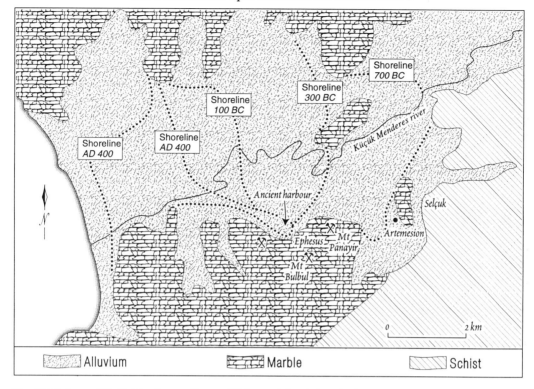

Fig. 13.10. Lower Küçük Menderes valley and Ephesus (after 152 and other sources).

ferent from that today (Fig. 13.10).[152] During Hellenistic times the coast was about 10 km inland from its present position. The sea lapped up close to the Temple of Artemis, and Ephesus was constructed on a promontory of the south shore of the bay. The deep bay would have provided a safe harbour. By early Roman times the shoreline had advanced until it was opposite the city and started to engulf the harbour. Despite the efforts made to keep the harbour open by dredging, the shoreline advanced so rapidly that by late Roman times the harbour was lost and with it the prosperity of the city.

The effects of the advancing coastline are evident in the history of the Artemesion. The first major temple was constructed in 550 BC above the flood level of the river. By 356 BC the level of the land, and also the water-table, had risen so much that the new temple had to be constructed on foundations three metres higher than those of the earlier temple. Now

even the foundations of this temple are often underwater.

The bedrock of this region is made of metamorphosed sedimentary rocks of the Menderes massif. The oldest rocks are schists and gneisses but marbles become more important in the upper parts of the series and eventually completely dominate. The steep slopes around Ephesus are made of this marble, which is at least 200 m thick. The marble of lower parts of the unit occurs in thick beds, and was extensively exploited in antiquity.

Ancient quarries can be seen on the northern and eastern slopes of Mt Panayir and on the slopes above the ancient harbour and channel (Fig. 13.10).[275] Higher quality marble (paler and more uniform) for the great Temple of Artemis was quarried at Belevi, 15 km to the north-east. The column drums were shaped on site and rolled to Ephesus by inserting pivots in the ends, an unusual technique devised by the architect Chersiphron. Other blocks were transported by water, as the estuary extended up to here in ancient times.[7] In addition marble from Aliki on Thasos was used in the fourth century.

One of the cult images of the Artemesion may have been a meteorite, as St Paul, in the Acts of the Apostles, states that it fell from Jupiter. However, he may have been confusing it with a meteorite cult-image of Cybele at Pessinus, 400 km to the north-east. Cybele, the Anatolian mother goddess, was closely associated with and assimilated into Artemis. The attribution of the origin to Jupiter is fortuitously correct, as we now know that most meteorites come from the asteroid belt between the orbits of Mars and Jupiter.

Ikaria

The island of Ikaria is a horst between underwater grabens that are part of a system of faults that runs from the Küçük Menderes graben (see Ephesus) to Melos and originated about 10 million years ago (Fig. 13.1). The

eastern part of the island is made of gneisses and schists with minor marbles along the southern coast (Fig. 13.11). The western part of the island is almost entirely composed of Miocene granite.[111] Hot springs (33-58°C) on the south coast are produced by circulation of water deep into the crust along the horst faults.

Samos

The island of Samos is only 3 km from the Turkish coast, to which it is geologically and geographically related (Figs. 13.1, 13.12). A range of mountains, rising to a height of nearly 1,500 m, runs east to west, and continues the line of the Mt Samsun peninsula (ancient Mt Mykale) in western Turkey. Throughout its history this beautiful, fertile island has produced timber, olive oil and wine. Today it also grows oranges and tobacco.

In antiquity Samos was one of the most famous of all the Greek islands. Carians arrived in about 3000 BC and were followed by Mycenaeans, who settled in small numbers

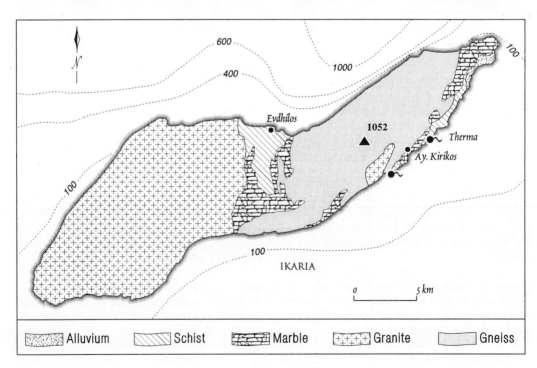

Fig. 13.11. Ikaria.

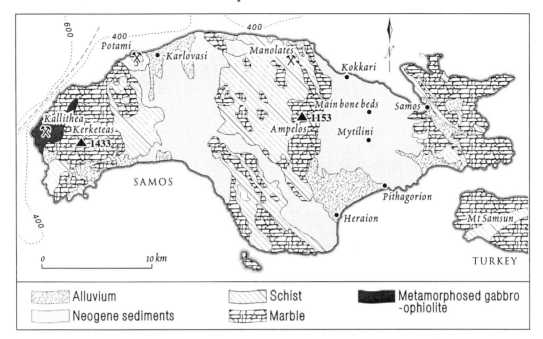

Fig. 13.12. Samos.

about 1400 BC. The first proper settlement by Greeks was about 1000 BC, when a body of Ionians arrived from Athens. They made their capital, also known as Samos, on the southeast coast, near modern Pythagorion. They prospered, thanks to the fertile soil, the excellent harbour, and their seamanship. They were also famous for their artists, who pioneered in Greece bronze-casting techniques learned in Egypt. In 538 BC Polycrates made himself ruler and established a brilliant court round him. Herodotus attributes to him the three greatest works of engineering in the Greek world: a 1,000 m long tunnel through the mountain; a 480 m long harbour mole at Pithagorion sunk up to 40 m into the water and the large Temple of Hera. Polycrates' rule, and Samos' greatness, were terminated by the Persian invasion of 522 BC.

Samos lies on a shallow plateau extending from the Mt Samsun peninsula (Fig. 13.1). The channel is less than 100 m deep, and the island was connected to the mainland during the Pliocene and much of the Pleistocene. The high cliffs and steep slopes of much of the north coast of the island continue offshore where the sea-floor drops off rapidly. This area is probably an extension of the Küçük Menderes graben on the mainland (see Ephesus above). To the south the sea is relatively shallow, but similarly, it is probably an extension of the broad Büyük Menderes graben on the mainland (see Priene below). Hence the island of Samos is a horst, like Ikaria to the west.

The basement of the island of Samos is made of metamorphic rocks of the Attic-Cycladic metamorphic belt, or possibly the Menderes massif, which stick up through the younger rocks as three high massifs, in the west, centre and east of the island (Fig. 13.12). The basement has been divided into four nappes, piled on top of each other during the Alpine compressions. Marbles, schists and phyllites dominate, except for one nappe of metamorphosed basaltic volcanic rocks. Many of these rocks have been metamorphosed at high pressures to produce blueschists, but sometimes these have been converted to the lower pressure greenschists.[189] Both types of rock, easily distinguished by their colours, can sometimes be seen in a single block of rock. Finally a thin nappe of unmetamorphosed Triassic-Jurassic ophiolites and limestones, exposed around Kallithea, was thrust over the metamorphic rocks. During the Late Miocene to Pliocene periods erosion and faulting produced two basins that were filled with lake and river sediments, including limestones and clays as well as volcanic ash. These rocks were folded and lifted up towards the end of the Neogene.

Between Mytilini and Kokkari, in eastern Samos, a rich collection of well-preserved fossil mammal bones has been found in limestones and marls deposited in lakes during the Late Miocene (8.5 to 7 million years ago).[286] The fauna includes lions, mastodons, monkeys, rhinoceroses, early gazelles and an ancestral giraffe unique to Samos called a *Samotherium*. At that time Samos was connected to the mainland, and the animals migrated over a land-bridge. The animals lived around the lakes and their bones were washed there after death, to be preserved in the lake sediments. There is a collection of these fossils in the museum at Mytilini.

As usual the marbles are much more resistant to erosion that the other rocks and form the high peaks of Kerketeas and Ampelos, and the hills east of Samos town. These peaks are almost barren as marble does not produce good soil. Erosion of the schists has produced the lower hills and better soils. But the lowest topography and most fertile soils are in the areas of Neogene sediments.

Samos town

Samos town lies at the head of a deep inlet, Varthi Bay (Fig. 13.12). This bay is a small graben that continues inland almost across the island. To the north and south of Samos town are marbles and schists, but the south shore of the bay is made of Neogene sedimentary rocks.

Pithagorion and ancient Samos

North-west of the modern town of Pithagorion lies the acropolis of ancient Samos, which was built on a low hill of beige, moderately hard, Miocene limestones (Fig. 13.13). The valley to

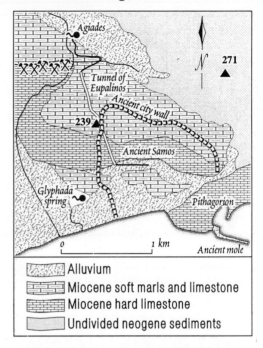

Fig. 13.13. Pithagorion and ancient Samos.

the north is underlain by Miocene marls and soft limestones, which have been eroded more deeply. The walls of the city, and many of the buildings, were constructed of the harder limestone, mostly from cave-like quarries on the south-east side of Agaides hill, 1,000 m to the north-west.[253] Two types of limestone were extracted here: a porous, bitumen-bearing limestone that was easy to cut, and a silica-rich hard limestone that was more resistant to erosion.

The famous Tunnel of Eupalinos was cut through this hill of Miocene limestone and marl, to a valley behind the acropolis. What makes this achievement even more impressive is that it was excavated from both ends, the two operations meeting near the middle. Much of the tunnel is unreinforced, but faulting and cave formation led to the creation of weak breccias, so that parts of the tunnel were lined with masonry. Recent removal of an ancient rock-fall, and metal reinforcement of the roof have now made it possible to go right through the tunnel.

The tunnel has two levels; an upper one for the movement of people, and a lower level for water. A spring near the chapels of Agiades (opposite the hill of the same name) fed a reservoir, and was then conducted via clay pipes in a narrow trench and tunnel along the contours to the entrance of the tunnel, 850 m away. Some water was also tapped within the tunnel, and these percolating waters have now formed stalagmites and flowstone up to 15 cm thick. At the other end of the tunnel, the water left the hill downhill from the main entrance, and was conducted to the east by clay pipes.

At the base of the hill there are two lagoons, fed by springs of water that fell on the acropolis hill and was forced to the surface by the high water-table of the alluvial plain.

The remains of the ancient harbour mole lie just south of the present breakwater in 3-4 m of water. Most of this submergence is due to erosion, but the level of some surviving harbour installations indicates that the level of the land has sunk about by about 50 cm during the last 2,500 years.[183]

The Heraion

This place, located on one of the few coastal plains on Samos, was scared for the Mycenaeans from 1400 BC, and when the Ionians arrived in about 1000 BC they continued the tradition by the worship of Hera.

The first temple was constructed between 575 and 560 BC and was made of a mixture of local Neogene sedimentary rocks, some of which were very poorly cemented and readily eroded. It is not clear why construction stopped so suddenly, but it may have been when the builders realised the unsuitability of the rock or it may have followed an earthquake that partly destroyed the building and caused the land to sink – the area is now swampy and there is evidence at Pithagorion of subsidence of about 50 cm.[183]

A new temple was started in 530 BC, at a level 1-5 m higher than the earlier temple. It was one of the largest in the Greek world, and was built in the Ionic style. It used columns and facings of more durable local streaky-white marble. This marble, and other construction

materials, were extracted from quarries at Poundes near Kallithea, Manolates and Potami (Fig. 13.12), and on the island of Phourni 5 km south-west of Samos (Fig. 13.1). The temple was never finished but lasted until AD 262, when it was badly damaged by an earthquake. It was subsequently sacked by the Goths and has now practically vanished from sight, except for one surviving column.

Priene

The Ionian Greek city of Priene was founded about 1000 BC, probably from Athens, somewhat to the east of the ruins which we see today. The exact site is lost, but it must have been on or near the mouth at the time of the river Meander (now Büyük Menderes). About 350 BC, thanks probably to the silting up of the river mouth, the city was moved to its present location on the south slope of Mt Samsun (ancient Mt Mykale), looking southwards over the former Latmian Gulf to the ancient city of Miletus. The constant silting of the river mouth has pushed the sea back some 30 km, and the Latmian Gulf is now the delta of the Büyük Menderes river.

Although on a steep slope, the new city was built on the gridiron plan associated with Hippodamus of Miletus. Priene proves one of the best examples of a small Greek city of some 5,000 inhabitants, with all the usual amenities. Alexander the Great freed Priene from the Persian yoke in 334 BC and paid for the completion of the Temple of Athena. Priene passed to the Romans in 133 BC who neglected it and it gradually sank into obscurity.

The bedrock geology of Priene is very similar to that of Ephesus; both lie in the belt of marbles that forms the outermost part of the Menderes massif (Fig. 13.14). These rocks crop out in the cliff behind the site and in the ancient streets, but they are most clearly seen in columns and building blocks. The original rock was a rather heterogeneous limestone with layers of purer material and breccias. Such breccias are common in limestones and form when caves collapse. Metamorphism, probably during the Alpine event, converted the limestone to a marble, closed up the holes in the

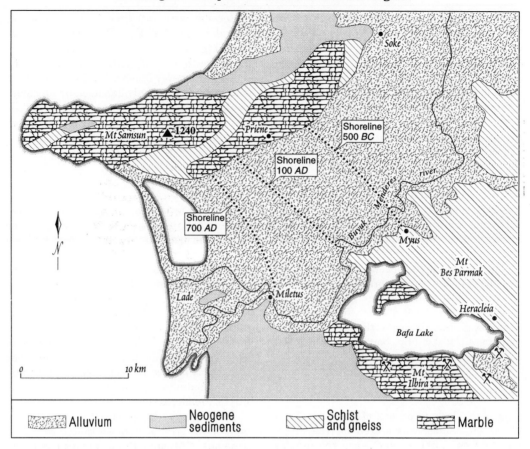

Fig. 13.14. The lower Büyük Menderes valley, Priene and Miletus (after 152 and other sources).

rocks and deformed the rock. Original structures in the limestone were not eliminated, but remain as colour differences, and the original blocks of the breccias can be seen clearly. The various shades of grey in the marble are due to variable amounts of graphite. The marble used to construct the city was obtained from quarries nearby.[181] Metamorphism also produced a number of silver deposits in the hills 10 to 20 km north-east of Priene, some of which may have been exploited in ancient times.[55]

Priene lies on the northern slopes of the valley of the Büyük Menderes river (ancient Meander). The river formerly wound its way across a broad valley and has given its name to this feature in other rivers. It has now been canalized in its lower reaches. This valley, like

that of the Küçük Menderes to the north (see Ephesus above), is a graben formed by tectonic stretching of the crust during the last 20 million years. It penetrates about 250 km eastward into the continent and brings down huge quantities of sediments. The northern fault of the graben passes close to Priene, and continual movement on this fault to this day maintains the steep relief against the levelling effects of erosion.

Rising sea-levels associated with the melting of ice at the end of the last glacial period caused the sea to penetrate deep into the continent, perhaps reaching the position of Magnesia, 12 km north-west of Soke (Figs. 13.1, 13.14). In Hellenistic times the coastline was about 35 km inland from its present position and Priene stood on a broad bay that stretched to Miletus, 15 km to the south.[152] Since then the coast has advanced at an average of about 15 m each year, isolating Priene from the sea in late Roman times.

Miletus

Miletus was founded by Minoans from Milatos in east Crete in around 1700 BC on what was then the southern shore of the Latmian Gulf (Fig. 13.14). Originally bounded by the sea on three sides, it is now completely landlocked as a result of the silting up of the mouth of the Meander, and is a sad, desolate site. The Mycenaeans arrived in about 1400 BC and were followed 400 years later by Ionian Greeks, who made it the largest and the most important of their cities of the Turkish coast. Destroyed by the Persians in 500 BC, the city was rebuilt soon afterwards by Hippodamus on the grid plan to which he gave his name; but it never regained its former stature. Nevertheless, in Hellenistic and Roman times it was again rich. But early in Byzantine times, from the eighth century AD, the silting up of the harbour and Arab raids greatly weakened the city. After many changes it was finally deserted in the fifteenth century.

Miletus lies on the southern side of the Büyük Menderes valley, opposite Priene, at the foot of low hills that make up the Milet sedimentary basin (Fig. 13.14). This block of crust was part of the ancestral Büyük Menderes graben, when the southern fault passed south of Didyma. In Miocene times limestones were deposited in shallow lakes, followed by a series of marls, sandstones and conglomerates.[243] The youngest rocks are again freshwater limestones, the Milet limestone, deposited during the Early Pliocene. Next, the graben fault jumped to the northern side of this block, just to the north of Miletus. Simultaneous uplift and tilting of the basin formed a plateau rising up to 300 m in the north. Pleistocene erosion isolated blocks of the Milet limestone, and earthquakes triggered landslides. Blocks of limestone up to 2 km long slid up to 2 km into the valleys. Quaternary sea-level rises turned this region into a peninsula, with Miletus on a broad bay.

The limestones are more resistant to erosion and tend to form hills. They are also much more permeable than the underlying marls, hence water that falls on the limestone tends to appear along the base of the hills as springs. These springs partly controlled the location of the ancient settlements of Miletus and Didyma.

The city of Miletus was built on two low limestone hills and a spur of land jutting out from the hills to the south and east (Fig. 13.15). On the skyline to the north the highest part of the Milet basin is visible as a plateau at 300 m. In antiquity the flat alluvial plains to the north would have been a broad estuary. There has been little change in sea-level since antiquity here; the change in geography is entirely due to deposition of sediments by the river.

The city was constructed from a variety of different rocks. The local limestone was used, but for the most part it is too soft. There is a

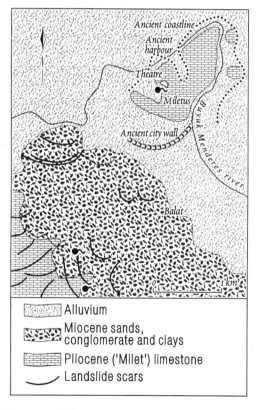

Fig. 13.15. Miletus and environs (after 243).

small quarry north of the Theatre, but most must have come from further inland. White and pale grey marble was used very extensively. It came from three areas of quarries, all along the southern shore of lake Bafa (Fig. 13.14), on the lower slopes of Mt Ilbira (formerly Mt Grion).[215] In antiquity lake Bafa was a bay of the sea, reducing transportation problems to Ephesus. A green-grey schist, with veins of quartz, was also used in some buildings. This rock occurs with the marble in some areas.

Didyma

Didyma is the site of one the great monuments of antiquity, the Temple of Apollo (Fig. 13.1). An oracle and sacred well were established here before the arrival of the Ionian Greeks.

They adopted the existing cult and completed the first temple in about 560 BC. The present building was started in 300 BC after Alexander the Great passed through the region. Construction continued for 500 years, but the temple was incomplete in AD 385 when the cult was abolished by the Christians.

Didyma, like Miletus, stands on a low hill of Milet limestone. The sacred spring or well is located where the limestone meets the underlying, less-permeable marls. The foundations of the temple were made of local soft limestone, but all exterior surfaces were made of white and grey marble. This marble was supplied from the same areas of quarries used by Miletus as well as another area was further east, near modern Bucak, which also supplied the ancient city of Herakleia to the northwest.[215]

14

The Dodecanese and the Carian Shore

The Dodecanese ('Twelve Islands') are situated off the south-west coast of Turkey (Fig. 14.1). The term Dodecanese is of recent origin (1908): there are in fact fourteen major islands and numerous smaller ones. Most are dry and barren, but two of the largest, Rhodes and Kos, together with Leros, are exceptional for their fertility.

The islands have a long history. A limited Minoan presence on Rhodes and elsewhere from about 1700 BC was followed by substantial Mycenaean settlement from 1450 to 1150 BC. Around 1000 BC there was a general occupation by Dorian Greeks from the Argolid. For the next 1,500 years the islands flourished, following the fortunes of Rhodes, which for much of this period was one of the leading maritime states of Greece. A period of stagnation started in the sixth century AD and lasted till 1309, when the islands were occupied by the Knights of St John (the Hospitallers), whose domination lasted till 1522. There ensued nearly 400 years of Turkish rule, followed by Italian occupation from 1912 until 1947 when the Dodecanese were united with Greece. In the hinterland, now part of western Turkey, the history of Knidos, Bodrum (ancient Halicarnassus) and Iasos runs in general parallel to that of the Dodecanese.

The region covers a wide variety of different geological environments. In the north metamorphic rocks of the Menderes massif crop out on the mainland and probably continue further south and west as the Palaeozoic metamorphic basement of Patmos, Leros, Kalymnos and Kos. Over these rocks have been thrust shallow water limestones and ophiolite fragments during the Alpine compressions. These rocks are fragments of continental crust and adjacent

sea-floor. On the Greek side of the border these nappes are considered to be part of the Pelagonian and Sub-Pelagonian zones, but on the Turkish side they are called the Lycian nappes.[28] Further south, Rhodes contains rocks of the Ionian and Gavrovo zones that have been further stacked up onto the pile of nappes.

Subduction of the African plate beneath the Aegean plate and broadly synchronous crustal stretching during the Neogene had an important role in shaping the landscape we see today. In the north it produced a series of east-west grabens than start deep in the mainland to the east and continue westwards into the Aegean Sea. Sediments have accumulated in many of the Neogene grabens and basins in this region, including the low-quality coal called lignite. Lignite was formed by the action of pressure, temperature and time on decayed vegetation accumulated in swamps. Seams up to 20 m thick are present in many of the basins 40 to 80 km east of Bodrum.[121]

Further south crustal stretching took a slightly different role: extension north of the ancestral arc stretched it out, and broke it up into the four main islands of the non-volcanic Hellenic arc, Crete, Karpathos, Kasos and Rhodes. In the west of the arc the crust goes down the subduction zone into the mantle, but further east the story changes: here, changes in the direction of movement of the plates since the inception of the arc have resulted in movements of the African plate, with respect to the Aegean plate, which are parallel to the arc. Hence there is no subduction and the plates move horizontally along several major strike-slip faults.

Some of the smaller islands, together with the Bodrum peninsula, are dominated by caps

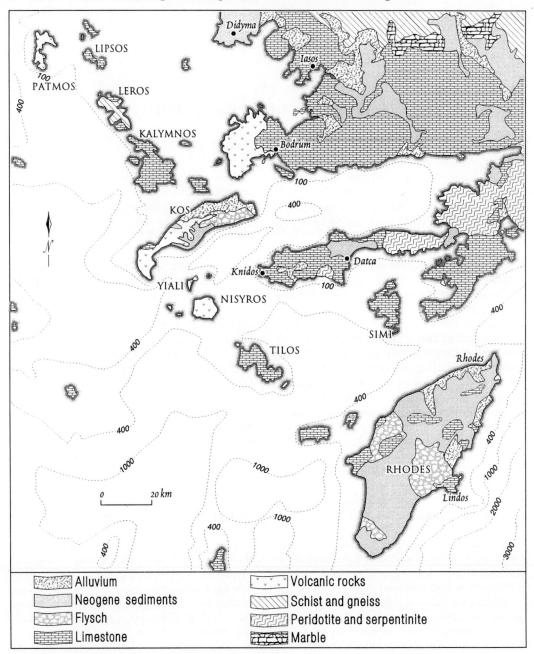

Fig. 14.1. The Dodecanese and the Carian shore of Turkey.

of volcanic rocks related to subduction of the ocean floor during the last 12 million years. All these volcanos were built on existing continental rocks.

Rhodes

Rhodes is by far the largest island of the Dodecanese and is dominated lengthwise by a mountain range which culminates in Mt Ataviros (1,215 m; Fig. 14.2). The climate is excellent and the soil extremely fertile. The poet Pindar in his Olympian odes relates the myth that this island arose from the sea to become the domain of the Sun God Helios, who was indeed the patron deity of Rhodes in Classical times.

The first settlers were Minoan colonists, who arrived from Crete about 1700 BC, and lived in the north of the island. They were followed by Mycenaean Greeks, in about 1450 BC, and Dorians around 1000 BC. The latter divided the island into three parts ruled from Ialysos, Lindos and Kamiros. They soon grew rich and joined Kos, Knidos and Halicarnassus in a commercial and political league. In 408 BC, faced with shrinking markets, the three city-states amalgamated and built a federal capital on the north tip which they named Rhodes, after the island. With five harbours and a fertile hinterland the new city soon became the capital of a great maritime state. In 305 BC Demetrius of Macedon attacked Rhodes and was defeated. The proceeds of the sale of his siege equipment was used to construct a bronze statue of the sun god Helios, over 30 m tall. Considered one of the Seven Wonders of the Ancient World, the Colossos of Rhodes stood until 226 BC, when it was knocked down by an earthquake. The island continued to flourish until the sixth century AD. In 1309 the Knights of St John conquered the island and held it until expelled by the Turks in 1522. The restored fortifications which we see today are those of the Knights.

Rhodes is separated from Turkey by a channel almost 400 m deep (Fig. 14.1). A deep trough to the south-west, between Rhodes and Karpathos, resulted from the Neogene stretching of the Hellenic arc. To the south-east the sea-floor drops off rapidly to a depth of over

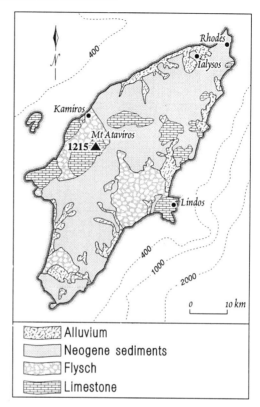

Fig. 14.2. Rhodes (after 186).

3,000 m in the Rhodes basin, a block of crust dropped down between two of the major strike-slip faults that are here the boundary between the African and Aegean plates. The proximity of Rhodes to these faults has made for frequent earthquakes.

The earlier geological history of Rhodes resembles that of Crete, much of the Peloponnese and western Greece.[186] The oldest rocks still close to their original place of deposition are Jurassic to Cretaceous deep-water cherty limestones of Mt Ataviros (1,215 m) and the peninsula to the south-west (Fig. 14.2). The relief of Mt Ataviros and the headland to the south-west reflects the resistance to erosion of these rocks. During the Oligocene period sedimentation changed and flysch was deposited, indicating the presence of land nearby, raised up by Alpine compressions. This flysch crops out throughout the southern part of the island.

Over these rocks have been thrust Triassic to Early Tertiary limestones, which underlie all the other important hills on the island, including the Lindos peninsula.

Major compression and mountain-building ceased during the Pliocene. Erosion of the mountains produced sediments, such as sands, conglomerates and brown marls, which were deposited initially in basins on land. As the land subsided incursions of the sea increased until much of the area was below sea-level, except for the limestone hills. The rocks formed at that time today yield the most fertile soils, especially the marls. It was also at this time that Rhodes was severed from the Turkish coast to become an island.

The top of the Neogene series of rocks is marked by a thin limestone locally called 'panchina', which is very important from a geomorphological and cultural point of view. The panchina is a 2 m thick layer of limestone made up of broken shells, typically 2-3 mm long (similar to 'coquina' elsewhere). The shells grew in a vast expanse of shallow water that stretched as far south as Lindos during the Early Pleistocene. Some of the piles of shell fragments were lithified in place, but some were blown by the wind into sand dunes, and then cemented. This rock is much more resistant to erosion than the underlying sediments and where it has been removed there is rapid erosion. It covers much of the surface in the northern part of the island and was an important construction material (see City of Rhodes below).

Finally, much of the interior is covered with a soft limestone, usually without shelly fossils, locally known as 'poros'. This rock is a type of caliche, an impure, porous limestone which forms in the soils of arid regions from the evaporation of mineral-laden groundwater below the surface. It was formed during the Pleistocene and is presently being eroded.

There have been large and rapid changes in the height of the land, with respect to sea-level, in this region probably because of the proximity to the edge of the Aegean tectonic plate. Such changes during the last 10,000 years are recorded in up to eight different ancient sea-levels which can be seen in wave-cut notches in sea-cliffs and ancient beaches above the present sea-level.[221] The ancient sea-levels are very variable throughout the island, indicating that large blocks of the island, each up to 20 km long, have moved independently. Relative movements between blocks were accommodated by movements along faults and accompanied by earthquakes (see City of Rhodes below). Large earthquakes have also been produced south of the island on the strike-slip faults that form the boundary between the African and Aegean plates.

The city of Rhodes and the acropolis

The northern tip of the island of Rhodes has emerged from the sea during geologically recent times (Fig. 14.3). This area is underlain by soft, largely weakly cemented sediments that were deposited on land from rivers about between 3 and 1 million years ago. At the end of this period the area was submerged below sea-level and the panchina was laid down. Subsequent uplift, faulting and erosion have created the present landscape.

The most important construction material

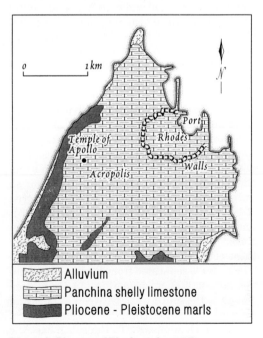

Fig. 14.3. The city of Rhodes (after 186).

of the ancient city of Rhodes, the Castle of the Knights and the ancient acropolis was panchina. This rock was available close by and was easily cut as it is so porous. However, the less well-cemented parts of the unit are readily eroded, though more resistant than the underlying sedimentary rocks. It was extracted from a number of quarries around the city and also from a series of quarries along the east coast, 2-8 km to the south of the city.[221]

The ancient acropolis of Rhodes is situated on a low hill (Ayios Stephanos) west of the centre of the modern city, formed by geologically recent uplift and tilting. The extent of the movement can be estimated from the altitude of the panchina rocks, which were close to sea-level during the early Pleistocene, but are now at altitudes up to 110 m. These gentle slopes terminate to the north-west in steep cliffs, formed as a result of offshore faulting parallel to the coast. This recent uplift reached its maximum, 270 m, on Mt Philerimos, which can be seen to the west.

The acropolis was originally completely covered with panchina, but this was extensively quarried for construction, and the foundations of the major buildings were laid on the underlying Pliocene sedimentary rocks. A particularly good section can be seen in the Temple of Pythian Apollo (Plate 13). The underlying rocks are less permeable than the panchina, hence wells were dug through this unit to the aquifer.

The coast of northern Rhodes has recorded many ancient changes in sea-level.[221] Many of the coastal quarries, thought to be Roman, have been submerged to a depth of 40 cm, indicating that the land has gone down since that time. However, there is a prominent sea-level notch in the cliffs at a height of 3.4 m, dated at 300 BC. The land must therefore have risen about 3.8 m between 300 BC and Roman times. The mostly likely cause was the earthquake of 222 BC, which toppled the Colossos of Rhodes and was the largest earth movement in the region during the last 10,000 years.

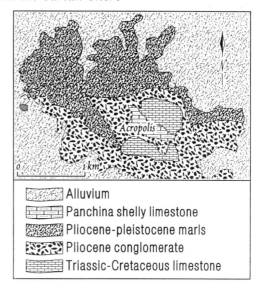

Fig. 14.4. Ialysos (after 186).

Ialysos and Mt Philerimos

About 15 km south-west of the city of Rhodes, Mt Philerimos rises sharply from the surrounding plains to a height of 270 m. The summit of this hill is occupied by the monastery of Philerimos and the acropolis of the ancient city of Ialysos (Fig. 14.4). This hill is a horst surrounded by down-dropped blocks. Much of the upper part of the hill is made up of Late Triassic limestone with bands of chert, which is more resistant to weathering than the surrounding rocks. Panchina and poros also occur here, indicating considerable uplift in geologically recent times.

Lindos

Lindos was the chief of the three cities of the island before the foundation of Rhodes. The site was occupied in the third millennium BC, but major construction on the acropolis did not start until the tenth century BC with the Temple of Athena and other buildings. Those visible today were mostly built after the fire of 348 BC. Later on the acropolis was converted into a fortress by the Knights of St John.

As approached from the north, the whole peninsula of Lindos stands up dramatically from the plains. The peninsula is dominated by grey Cretaceous crystalline limestone which is harder than the surrounding rocks and consequently tends to form headlands (Fig. 14.5). During the Neogene the limestones of the peninsula have been broken up by vertical faults into large blocks, forming a series of horsts and grabens. At times of high sea-level the horsts were islands and sediments were deposited in the grabens.

The acropolis of Lindos town was built on a block of hard, grey Cretaceous limestone that rises 120 m from the sea. It is part of a discontinuous horst that extends north-eastwards across the bay to the next headland, and south-westward for 1 km. A small graben, about 500 m wide, runs north-east/south-west and contains the town of Lindos and the big harbour.

During the Neogene sedimentary rocks were deposited in this graben. They can now be

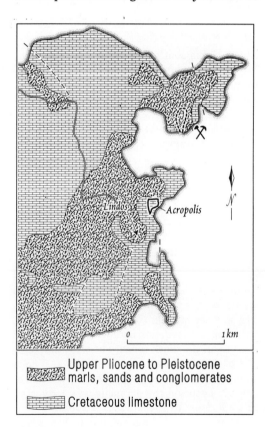

Fig. 14.5. Lindos (after 186).

Upper Pliocene to Pleistocene marls, sands and conglomerates

Cretaceous limestone

seen as two ledges, resembling bath-tub rings, one at about 50 m, which carries the road, and a lower one at 20 m, which covers much of the low land of the peninsula to the north. The rocks of the upper ledge are also seen on the top of the acropolis as a layer about 5 m thick. This rock is pale-brown silty marl, similar to the poros that covers much of the interior of the island. The lower ledge is made of panchina, the shelly limestone so common around the city of Rhodes. This rock does not crop out on the acropolis.

Neither the grey limestone nor the poros were much used in the construction of the monuments and buildings on the acropolis. Instead the builders commonly used panchina, from quarries that can be seen across the bay to the north. They used this material because it has few joints and is very easy to cut. However, it is not always very well cemented, and some blocks can weather very easily. A grey marble, cut by white calcite veins, was also used in the construction of some of the buildings.

Iasos

Iasos occupied a small peninsula on the coast of Asia Minor, between Didyma and Bodrum (Fig. 14.1). Its excellent harbours and rich fishing attracted Carian settlers as early as 3000 BC. In about 2000 BC Minoans arrived from Crete; they were replaced by Mycenaeans from the Argolid around 1400 BC. About 1000 BC, after the fall of Mycenae, more Greeks arrived and henceforth their fortunes were tied to those of Rhodes.

Iasos had another asset, which was exploited in Roman and later times: its marble quarries. Some of these were located outside the city in the direction of the modern village of Abkuk. They yielded two sorts of marble: one was fine-grained, red with white bands, the other white. The red marble was used by the Romans in the third century AD and became very popular in Byzantine times. Known as Marmor Carium or Iassense to the Romans, and Cipollino Rosso or Africanone to the Italians, it closely resembles the Rosso Antico of the Mani Peninsula.[160] The white marble was also used in Classical antiquity. It has actually been identified among the marbles used to decorate the Mausoleum at Halicarnassus. These marbles are part of the Menderes massif, and are probably of Palaeozoic or Mesozoic age.

Patmos

The small island of Patmos is the northernmost of the Dodecanese (Fig. 14.1). It is also the holiest to Christians, and one of the driest. Little is known of its early history, but it seems to have been inhabited from Mycenaean times. In Classical Greek times a temple of Artemis is recorded where the monastery now stands, and a temple of Apollo by the harbour. The Romans used Patmos for deporting political exiles, such as St John the Divine who arrived here in AD 95. During his exile he is said to have composed the Book of Revelation in a cave on the hill below the present monastery. Churches were built on the island from the fourth to the sixth century; but in the seventh century Patmos was deserted as a result of the unceasing assaults of the Arabs. This changed in 1088 when Christodoulos built a monastery in honour of St John on the high ground above the cave.

Patmos is an irregularly shaped island made up almost exclusively of volcanic rocks, but the island is not now volcanically active. The rounded hills of weathered volcanic rocks contrast strongly with those of the metamorphic islands to the north and west and the young volcanic islands to the south. The island is situated on the edge of a shallow shelf projecting from the Turkish coast (Fig. 14.1). There do not appear to be any major active faults in the area and there are relatively few earthquakes.

The overall structure of Patmos is that of a graben: faults running north-west/south-east have cut the island into vertical slices and the central slice has dropped down (Fig. 14.6). The result is that the oldest rocks are exposed at the extremities and the youngest in the middle.[232, 291]

The only non-volcanic rock exposed on Patmos is a patch of marble in the south-west, which is probably part of the Attic-Cycladic

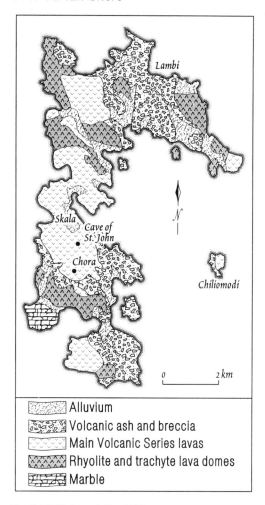

Fig. 14.6. Patmos (after 232).

metamorphic belt. However, this patch is isolated from the rest of the island by a fault and it is therefore uncertain whether these marbles are part of the basement on which this volcanic island was constructed.

The volcanism on Patmos is ultimately related to the subduction of the African plate, portions of which are currently about 300 km beneath Patmos.[193] The earliest volcanic rocks are a series of rhyolite and trachyte domes, now seen in the northern and southern parts of the island.[232] They were followed by basalt, trachyandesite and trachyte lavas of the Main Volcanic Series. These rocks were erupted

157

about 7-5 million years ago from several different volcanic vents. The last volcanic activity occurred about four million years ago and produced sodium-rich basalt and phonolite lavas which are exposed on the small island of Chiliomodi, east of Patmos. It is not known which eruption(s) produced the volcanic ash and breccias that cover much of the island.

Skala and Chora

The town of Skala is built on sediments recently shed from the surrounding volcanic hills. The different colours of the rocks in the hills largely reflect their history following crystallisation. Where rainwater, heated by the volcanism, has circulated through the rocks they may be oxidised to pink and red, or finally reduced to clay. Black and brown iron oxides can also be deposited from these circulating waters.

The path from Skala towards Chora leads past the 'Cave of St Anne', where St John is said to have written the Book of Revelation. The cave is a natural overhang, produced by the erosion of weaker underlying rock, which has been artificially enlarged. The bedrock is part of a thick flow or dome of trachyandesite lava containing large crystals of plagioclase and biotite. The clefts attributed to the voice of God appear to be joints in the rock produced either by contraction during cooling or by reduction of pressure following the erosion of overlying rocks.

The town of Chora lies round a monastery 152 m above sea-level. This hill is the remains of the volcano that produced the surrounding trachyandesite lavas of the Main Volcanic Series. Erosion has reshaped the volcano and in some places may have removed large amounts of rock. The buildings of Chora are largely constructed of the lavas which form the bulk of the hill.

Lipsos, Leros and Kalymnos

Although these three islands lie between the largely volcanic islands of Patmos to the north and Kos to the south they contain no volcanic rocks (Fig. 14.1). Instead they are dominated by Triassic to Jurassic limestones of the Pelagonian zone. The basement on which these limestones were deposited is exposed on Leros, where these schists make up most of the interior of the island.[134] These rocks weather more readily than the limestones and produce a better soil, which accounts for the fertility of Leros.

Kos

The island of Kos is second in importance after Rhodes in the Dodecanese. It is the best watered of all the islands. Along the north side is a fertile coastal plain, which grows cereals, fruit and vegetables. Further south, a mountain range runs the length of the island. It was famous in antiquity for its springs, which were used for medicinal purposes even before the time of the great Hippocrates, the father of Greek medicine (*c.* 460-357 BC).

The early history of Kos parallels that of Rhodes. There was prehistoric occupation on the site of present-day Kos town, where there is an excellent harbour; but when the Dorians arrived around 1000 BC, they made their capital far to the south, near the present village of Kephalos. Here Hippocrates would have lived and worked. In 366 BC the capital was transferred to the site of modern Kos town. With its excellent harbour it soon became a great maritime power, and the island also became famous for its wines and silks. However, the great feature of Kos was the Asklepieion, or Sanctuary of Asklepios, the Greek God of Healing.

Kos is separated from Kalymnos and the Bodrum peninsula by a shallow underwater shelf (Fig. 14.1). To the south-east of the island the sea-floor descends rapidly into a small basin, which is part of an important graben stretching from the Cretan Sea via the gulf that separates the Bodrum and Datca peninsulas in Turkey. The frequency of earthquakes and the presence of hot springs, as well as the recent volcanism, attest to the presence of active faults in the area.

The central highlands of the island, including Mt Dicheos (Mt Oromedon; 847 m), are dominated by schist and marble, probably part of the Menderes massif of the Turkish main-

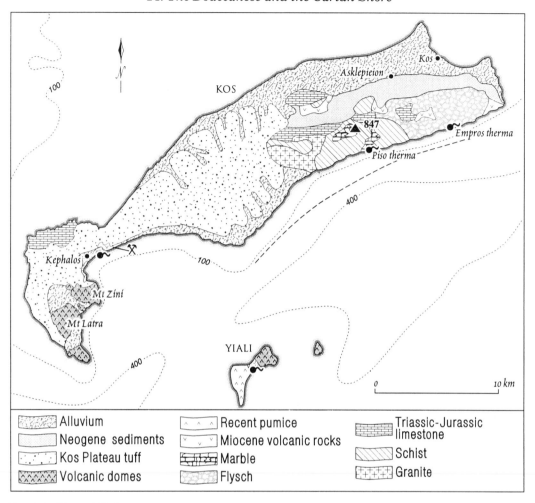

Fig. 14.7. Kos and Yiali.

land (Fig. 14.7). Triassic to Jurassic limestones and flysch lie on top of the metamorphic rocks and are exposed in the central and north-western parts of the island. They are covered in turn with a series of Neogene sediments, exposed on the northern slopes of the Dicheos range and beneath recent volcanic rocks on the plateau to the west.

Volcanic activity started on Kos about 10 million years ago during the Miocene period,[27] as part of a widespread zone concentrated in the north-western part of Turkey. The volcanism is probably related to subduction of oceanic crust further south, with the magmas guided to the surface by the faults of the Neogene grabens that figure so importantly in the history of the Aegean.

The earliest product was a thick, widespread ignimbrite (welded tuff) which is exposed sporadically over the whole island. This rock was quarried extensively near Kephalos bay for construction of the substratum of Hellenistic temples and parts of the Asklepieion.[39] Some magma never reached the surface but crystallised as monzonite, a granite-like rock, exposed today south of Pyli.[6] Erosion then reduced much of the western part of Kos to a plain close to sea-level, but pre-

159

served highlands in the east and west. This plain was then lifted up, along with the rest of the island, at some time before the eruption of the Kos Plateau tuff (see below).

The most recent phase of volcanism, and the most important, began about three million years ago with the eruption of two large domes of rhyolite on the Kephalos peninsula at the south of the island.[204] These domes are still relatively uneroded today, with the peak of Mt Latra at 428 m. Volcanic activity continued with the eruption of pumice from a vent in the bay of Kamares 550,000 years ago.[51] This eruption ended when the magma chamber was empty and the overlying, now unsupported, crust collapsed into the cavity along a circular fracture to produce a caldera (see Thera below in Chapter 15). During the final phase rhyolitic magma oozed up the southern part of this fracture to produce the Mt Zini dome.

The most recent eruption occurred 145,000 years ago and was one of the most powerful eruptions in the eastern Mediterranean in recent times: 35-55 cubic km of volcanic ash was erupted covering an area of 5,000 square km.[50] This enormous amount of material did much to shape the landscape of Kos, as its products (the Kos Plateau tuff) blanket most of the western part of the island. Pumice from this eruption also covers the islands of Kalymnos, Tilos and Chalki, as well as parts of western Turkey. The vent has not been located, but is thought to lie in the sea between Kos and Yiali, though at the time of the eruption there must have been land here.

The eruption had several phases: the first was plinian (see Thera) and produced a layer of fine pumice about 30 cm thick. This was followed by another explosive phase which produced a series of well-bedded pumice deposits about 3 m thick. These rocks were deposited from surges of hot, dust-charged gas moving at great speed from the volcanic vent. Finally, the eruption developed its full fury and produced a deposit of volcanic ash up to 30 m thick. This phase initially produced relatively fine pumice from hot gas and dust-charged flows. The increasing size of blocks of pumice (up to 40 cm) and rock (up to 3 m) torn from the sides of the volcanic conduit and ejected with the pumice in

the later deposits indicates that the violence of the eruption reached a maximum towards the final stages. This mighty eruption culminated in the production of a caldera 5-12 km in diameter between Kos and Yiali, which was invaded by the sea.

Kos has been well known since ancient times for its springs. The hottest (45°C) are on the south-east coast at Piso Therma (Ayios Irene) and Empros Therma (Ayia Phokas). They are unrelated to the recent volcanic activity in the west, and are channelled up a major fault running parallel to the coast. Cool sulphurous springs, gas vents and hydrothermally altered, sulphur-rich rocks occur on the western part of the island near Volcania, north-west of Kephalos.[22] Gas vents also occur in the sea nearby at 'Paradise Bubble Beach'. These features may be related to the presence of a shallow magma chamber and there may be potential for geothermal energy in this area.

The city of Kos is built on recent alluvial sediments shed off the hills to the south. The Knights' Castle was constructed from a wide variety of materials mostly recycled from the ancient town. Two types of rock, a green tuff and a pink, big-feldspar trachyandesite, were probably obtained from the Mausoleum at Bodrum on the opposite coast.

The Asklepieion

The Asklepieion was started about 350 BC, soon after the inauguration of the new capital, on the site of a sacred spring 5 km south-west of the city. The sanctuary took a long time to complete; in its final form it occupied three terraces with a dramatic vista over the sea. It was in fact a sort of health centre, where the precepts of Hippocrates were followed. Although various religious practices were also observed, the Asklepieion was a much more scientific institution than Epidauros. The sanctuary continued into the fourth century AD. When it was destroyed by a terrible earthquake in AD 554, the Temple of Asklepios had already been converted to a church.

The Asklepieion was built on a series of terraces at the foot of Mt Dicheos. Most of the upper parts of this mountain are made of Triassic-Jurassic flysch and limestone, but lower down, south of the Asklepieion, the bedrock is Neogene sediments, including conglomerates, sandstones and limestones, all of which crop out at the site. The Dicheos range has been recently uplifted along a fault that runs east-west, along the base of the mountains, near the site of the Asklepieion. The famous medicinal springs may have been forced to the surface along this fault.

The cold springs debouche towards the lower part of the site and have coated the ancient fountains in travertine. The original springs must have formed travertine terraces on these slopes, most of which were quarried for construction materials in antiquity. Some of the travertine blocks in the walls have abundant plant fossils. The springs are now dry, except in the winter, but were perennial in antiquity. These changes probably reflect deforestation of the slopes of Dicheos, which has increased run-off and hence reduced the amount of water that can soak into the rocks.

The sanctuary was largely constructed of local travertine and limestone, partly quarried from above the site, and a pink tuff, also used for the reconstruction. The tuff is a Miocene ignimbrite that covers much of the island. It was extracted from quarries in western Kos, on the coast immediately east of the Bay of Kephalos.[39]

Yiali

The volcanic island of Yiali lies between Kos and Nisyros, but it is a separate volcano (Fig. 14.7).[62] Although undoubtedly built on a non-volcanic basement, no pre-volcanic rocks are exposed. The island is composed of two volcanic units joined at a narrow waist.

The north-eastern part of the island consists of a lava dome 24,000 years old, with a core of obsidian and a rind of perlite. The obsidian is quite distinctive: black with white spots. The spots are spherulites, areas of the glassy obsidian which have started to crystallise: The tiny crystals all point outwards from the original point of crystallisation, giving a radial structure. They reflect more light than the surrounding glass and hence appear paler. This rock was occasionally used by Minoan craftsmen for stone vases. However, unlike the extensively used black obsidian of Melos, it was not suitable for making blades.

The south-western part of the island is composed of sedimentary rocks and pumice. The presence of these sediments at elevations up to 140 m above sea-level indicate that the island has been strongly uplifted by tectonic forces. The pumice has not been dated but must be very young as it covers soils containing Neolithic implements.[136] The pumice is mined in large quantities for lightweight concrete aggregates and other uses, such as 'stone-washing' jeans. Warm springs (14-33°C) issue underwater, just off Yiali bay, around the pumice loading terminal.[272] Iron oxides are being deposited from these waters, a phenomenon similar to that seen around the Kameni islands (see Thera below in Chapter 15).

Bodrum peninsula

The ancient city of Halicarnassus (now Bodrum) was founded by Dorian Greeks at around 1000 BC. They integrated with the local Carians and produced a mixed population, which was eventually absorbed by the Ionians from further north. In about 550 BC they were conquered by the Persians and, apart from a brief interval in the fifth century BC, were part of the Persian Empire until liberated by Alexander the Great in 334 BC.

One of the great Halicarnassians was Herodotus and another was Mausolus, a Carian and Governor of the Persian province of Caria in the fourth century BC. A great admirer of things Greek, in 377 BC he transferred his capital from Mylasa to the Greek city of Halicarnassus. He rebuilt the city on a much larger scale, including a palace (which no longer survives) of brick with facings of Proconnesian marble. And he built for himself a tomb, known later as the Mausoleum, so magnificent that it was classed as one of the Seven Wonders of the Ancient World.

The Bodrum peninsula lies on the northern edge of an east-west graben that extends deep

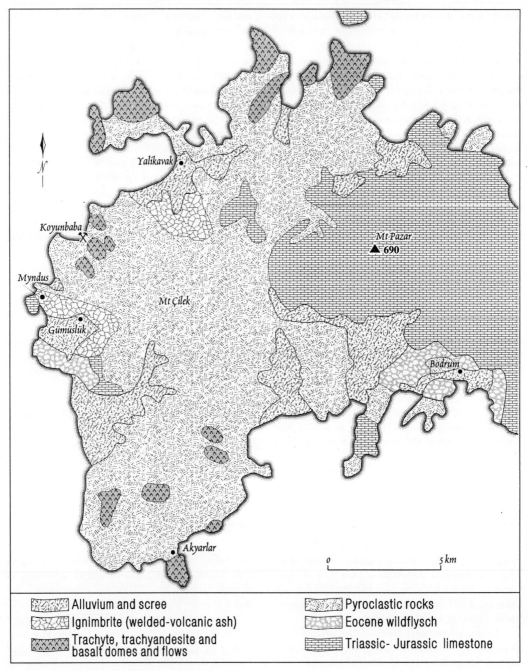

Fig. 14.8. Bodrum peninsula (after 233).

14. The Dodecanese and the Carian Shore

into the continent (Fig. 14.1). In the east the main graben fault lies to the south of the peninsula, but further west it passes south of Kos. The sea to the north is shallow, less than 100 m, and is part of the continental shelf.

The exposed basement of the Bodrum peninsula is dominated by limestones (Fig. 14.8). The oldest are a series of pale, massive, shallow-water limestones of Late Triassic to Jurassic age. Later on the water deepened and yellow to grey limestones with layers rich in chert were deposited. Finally, during the Late Cretaceous, a rock with the delightful name of wildflysch was formed. This is a series of shales and sandstones with included blocks of limestone up to 500 m long. Active faults produced underwater cliffs of this older limestone. Underwater landslides then broke off blocks and transported them to deeper water where the shales were accumulating. These limestone blocks are important from a geomorphological viewpoint as they are harder than the shales and strongly shape the topography (see below). None of these rocks is thought to be in its original position, but to have been thrust onto the older rocks of the Menderes massif during the Eocene compression of the region.

These older series of rocks are covered by Miocene volcanic rocks, a southern extension of a broad swathe of Miocene volcanism that extended from the eastern Aegean to western Turkey (see Kos above). Bodrum is the only one of these Miocene volcanic centres that has conserved its volcanic structure against the forces of erosion.[233] This volcano is made up of about 500 m of pyroclastic rocks, mostly block and ash flows, together with some lavas. Most of these rocks were intensely altered by circulating hot water, probably soon after their emplacement. Alteration is most intense north and west of Mt Cilgri, beneath the original volcanic centre. The volcanic rocks range in composition from basalts to rhyolites, but were dominated by trachyandesites. The main phase of volcanism appears to have been rather short, about 10-9 million years ago.[233] In places erosion has revealed plutonic rocks that originally crystallised underneath the volcano. Since then the region has not been volcanically active, although parts of the peninsula are

covered by ash from the eruption of Kos 145,000 years ago.

The city of Bodrum

The bedrock geology has controlled the local topography around the city of Bodrum (Fig. 14.9). The hills to the north and east of Bodrum are made of Jurassic limestone which is resistant to erosion. This same rock can been seen in the slabs used to pave some of the streets of Bodrum. Many surfaces are covered with fossil animal tracks, probably from worms, some in the form of rosettes. The basin in which the city lies is underlain by soft, easily eroded Late Cretaceous shale. Within these shales are blocks of Jurassic limestone up to 500 m long. These blocks are again more resistant to erosion than the shales and stand up as small hills, one such hill making up the peninsula on which the castle stands. The harbour has formed by erosion of shale between this block and another that makes up the adjacent headland.

The peninsula to the south-west is made of

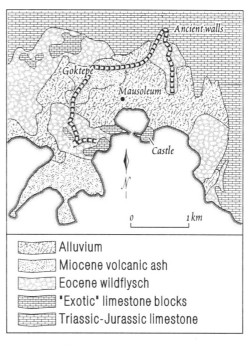

Fig. 14.9. Bodrum town.

163

younger volcanic rocks, mostly block and ash flows, as is the hill of Goktepe to the north-west. These beds of ash are nearly horizontal, suggesting that they are the erosional rem-nants of a much larger volcanic pile. Numerous tombs have been cut into the upper parts of the hill of Goktepe, because the ash is so easily excavated and the resulting caves are dry.

Near the western point of the harbour there was a spring, reputed in antiquity to induce effeminacy (a view doubled by Strabo). It is difficult to test this quality as rising sea-levels have drowned this spring and it now bubbles up in the sea adjacent to the lighthouse fenced off in the military reserve. Perhaps the mili-tary still believes in its effects!

The Mausoleum

The Mausoleum was started by King Mausolus in 355 BC and completed by his wife and other relatives. It probably measured about 32 m square and 55 m high, but most reconstruc-tions are very conjectural. It survived more or less intact until the thirteenth century AD, but was reduced to ruins by an earthquake some time before the arrival of the Knights of St John in 1402. They used the ruin as a quarry to build their castle at Bodrum (as Halicarnassus was now called). A certain amount of fragmen-tary sculptural and architectural decoration has been recovered from the castle and used, together with ancient descriptions, to make numerous reconstructions of the monument.

The bedrock in the area of the Mausoleum is a white poorly-welded tuff either from the eruption 145,000 years ago between Kos and Yiali (see Kos above) or from the Bodrum vol-cano. This rock was occasionally used as ashlar blocks. In places the builders of the Mausoleum excavated down through this rock into the un-derlying ancient soil and the Bodrum shale. Good sections can be seen in the pre-Mausolus tomb chamber.

The foundations and the core of the plat-form on which it stood were of a Miocene green tuff extracted from quarries near the modern Koyunbaba, on the western coast of the Bo-drum peninsula north of Gümüslük. These quarries were developed down to sea-level, but

subsidence of the land has since partially drowned them. This rock contains many frag-ments of older volcanic rocks, set in a poorly sorted fine-grained green matrix. It is moder-ately well welded, but is easy to cut. It made a good material for the interior of the building, but weathers easily when exposed to the ele-ments, as can be seen at the castle.

The upper parts of the building were sheathed in marble and decorated with marble sculptures from a wide variety of different sources: Penteli, Paros, Iasos, Phrygia (central Turkey) and probably other nearer sources. The lower parts of the building were covered in a local grey limestone from quarries in the surrounding hills.

The peribos wall was partly constructed from a coarse-grained pink trachyandesite, with large feldspars up to 4 cm long. This rock occurs in rounded hills in the south-west of the peninsula and small rocky islets towards Kos (Fig. 14.8). These hills are lava domes or sub-volcanic intrusions. No quarries have yet been located, and it may have been extracted from surface boulders.

The Castle of St Peter

The Castle of St Peter is built on a block of Late Cretaceous limestone, transitional to marble. The contact with the Bodrum shales, within which this block 'floats', can be seen on the east side of the peninsula. The castle was con-structed of a variety of materials, but a dominant rock is the green tuff that originally comprised the core of the Mausoleum. The Knights also used blocks of pink trachyan-desite, grey limestone and marble, mostly also from the Mausoleum.

Knidos and the Datca peninsula

About 1000 BC Dorian Greeks established a city on the tip of the Datca peninsula, which they named Knidos (Fig. 14.1). With two excel-lent harbours, the city grew rich from colonisation and commerce and was generous in support of the Sanctuary at Delphi. By the end of the fourth century BC, Knidos was fa-mous for its medical school, its astronomical observatory, its Temple of Aphrodite with the famous cult-statue by Praxiteles, and its wine.

The Datca peninsula is separated from the Bodrum peninsula to the north by a deep gulf (Fig. 14.1). This gulf, together with the lowlands further inland, is a graben similar to those that form some of the valleys to the north (see Pergamon, Ephesus and Priene above in Chapter 13). It was formed as a result of the stretching of western Turkey in a north/south direction during the Neogene period. There is probably another graben to the south, making the Datca peninsula a horst.

The Datca peninsula divides into two parts, both geologically and topographically. The highlands of the western part of the peninsula, including the ancient port of Knidos, are made of sedimentary rocks, dominantly limestones, of Late Triassic to Eocene age. The eastern part of the peninsula is dominated by peridotites and their metamorphosed equivalents serpentinites, which are part of an ophiolite complex.

Explosive volcanic eruptions on Nisyros, 18 km to the west, showered the peninsula with up to 40 m of ash.[77] Much of this was rapidly eroded, but some has remained in valleys, particularly around ancient Knidos and the village of Cesmekoy, 10 km to the east. Pumice also fell in the sea and was floated onto the beaches of the peninsula, where it forms deposits up to 1 m thick, with blocks as large as 50 cm in diameter.

Nisyros

The small, almost circular, island of Nisyros lies off the Turkish coast, opposite Knidos (Fig. 14.1). The land rises steeply from the shore to the rim of a huge volcanic crater, 4 km in diameter, filled with smaller craters and a high volcanic cone and smelling strongly of sulphur. Nisyros was celebrated in antiquity for its hot springs, its millstones, and its excellent wine. It is also noted today for the almond trees which cover the hillsides.

The early history of Nisyros is not known, but it is mentioned by Homer as taking part in the Trojan War. In the fourth century BC the city possessed a fine circuit wall with square towers and gateways, much of which has been preserved. In the Middle Ages the Knights of Rhodes built a castle here, which still survives, though ruined. The subsequent history of the island is that of the Dodecanese in general.

Nisyros is the easternmost active volcano of the South Aegean volcanic arc, with much potential for further explosive eruptions in the future.[252] It has the classic form of a stratovolcano with a large central caldera, almost half the size of the island (Fig. 14.10). The last eruptions were phreatic (steam) explosions in AD 1887.

Older sedimentary and metamorphic rocks are not exposed on the island, but their presence as xenoliths in the lavas and at a depth of 700 m in a drill-hole indicates that the island was built on continental crust like the other islands of the South Aegean volcanic arc. The basement is probably a horst extending out from the Datca peninsula to the east.

Volcanic activity probably started on Nisyros about 200,000 years ago with the eruption of lavas underwater.[62, 280, 292] These rather untidy rocks are exposed immediately to the west of the village of Mandraki: rounded, pillow-like blocks of black andesite float in a matrix of smaller blocks and fine-grained yellowish material. The pillows in this rock indicate that it formed by an underwater eruption. The matrix is devitrified and altered volcanic glass. The next eruptions had exactly the same chemical composition, but were erupted on land, and hence had a very different physical appearance. They can be seen as a few relatively thin flows above the pillow lavas.

Most of the island is covered with lava and tuff deposited by a number of explosive eruptions 66,000-10,000 years ago. They range in composition from andesite to dacite and contain crystals of plagioclase (pale), pyroxenes (brown to black) and other minerals. These eruptions created an island about 7 km in diameter and 1,000 m high. This phase finished with a major eruption: loss of magma from a magma chamber beneath the volcano was followed by collapse of the central part of the island into the chamber and the formation of the caldera seen today. We do not know when this occurred, but it must have been quite

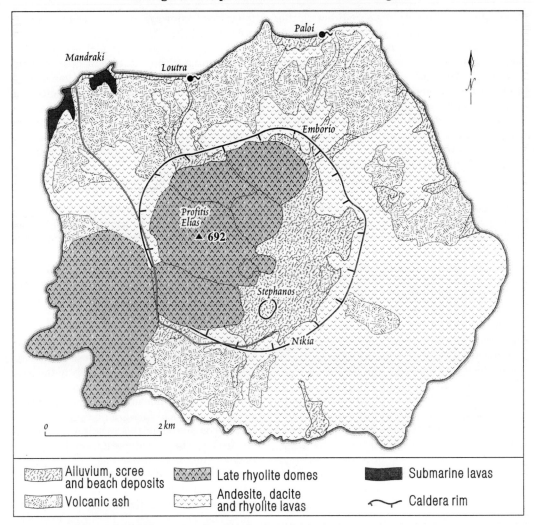

Fig. 14.10. Nisyros (after 280).

recently, possibly 10,000 years ago.

Since the formation of the caldera several very large dacite lava domes have erupted and flowed both away from the caldera and into the caldera, half filling it. These domes are really very short, thick lava flows (1 to 3 km by 500 m) and can form very quickly – within a few months or years. A similar dome has formed in the crater of Mt St Helens, USA, since the catastrophic eruption of 1980. No volcanic ashes have been found, so it likely that these eruptions were relatively quiet. The rocks are very rich in crystals of plagioclase (pale) together with minor pyroxene (dark). The steep slopes of the domes, the presence of volcanic spines up to 7 m high and the lack of soil all indicate that these domes are very young, possibly as little as 1,000 years old.

The most recent activity is the formation of small craters on the floor of the caldera by phreatic (steam) explosions. Some of these craters are only a little over 100 years old (see below) and formed in the following way. The process started when rainwater seeped into the loose sediments of the caldera floor. As the water descended it was heated by the hot rocks surrounding the magma chamber until it turned to steam. The force of the steam pushed up and removed some of the overlying rocks and hence lowered the pressure at depth. The reduced pressure then lowered the boiling point of the water, which had been increased by the pressure, and turned it instantly to steam. Geysers, as seen in Iceland and elsewhere, are produced by exactly the same agency, which is similar to opening a pressure-cooker without first reducing the pressure.

There are many fumaroles on the caldera floor and on some of the lava domes. These emit superheated steam (hotter than 100°C) together with other gases, including hydrogen sulphide ('rotten-egg gas'). When these gases meet the atmosphere the hydrogen sulphide is oxidised and forms needles of sulphur, which crystallise around the vents and in the rocks. Nisyros was an important source of sulphur, both in antiquity and during the eighteenth century.

Several warm, saline springs occur along the northern and southern coasts. The source of water for the springs is the sea, which descends along faults, is heated by residual volcanic heat or the normal increase in temperature with depth, and rises up other faults.[65] Two springs on the north coast, at Loutra (47°C) and Paloi (40°C), have both been exploited recently by spas, now defunct, and there is currently no access to the springs. Hot, humid air vents from the ground just below Emborio, to the north, forming a natural Turkish bath.

Mandraki and environs

The oldest rocks on the island crop out to the west of Mandraki and underlie the Kastro (Fig. 14.11). These rocks weather readily and the cliff under the Kastro has been reinforced with brown cement painted with yellow lines, just to confuse the unwary. The other side of this promontory shows many ancient sea-level stands, indicating recent uplift. The most obvious is a wave-cut platform at 2 m, but there are notches at up to 15 m. This is the only part of

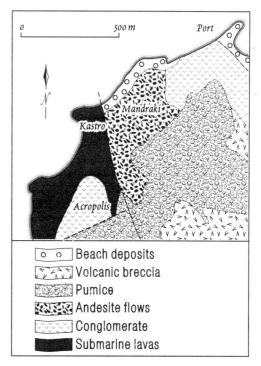

Fig. 14.11. Mandraki (after 280).

the island where there is such evidence of uplift.

The Kastro itself was constructed from a variety of different volcanic rocks, but the favoured material was a beige welded pumice tuff, presumably because it was so easy to cut. However, like many weak materials, it is also easily eroded. As elsewhere, the Knights did not build for posterity, but considered speed of construction more important.

The ancient acropolis lies on Palaeokastro hill, above and to the south of Mandraki (Fig. 14.11). The hill is made of erosion-resistant andesite lavas that cover the submarine volcanic rocks of the Kastro. The walls of the acropolis were beautifully constructed from these lavas, quarried on the site itself. Blocks of marble from the acropolis must have been imported, probably from the mainland.

The track to the caldera

A very interesting walking track leaves from near the acropolis for the caldera (Fig. 14.10).

The first kilometre goes over pumice, block and ash flows, and small lava flows. At a point where the track turns sharply from a westward direction to the south there are three lava tubes, just upslope. The first is about 2 m wide and 5 m deep, and preserves all its original features, the second has been converted into a cistern and the third, although intact, is very small. This ridge is formed by a series of andesite lava flows. Such lavas tend to flow in tubes, which are commonly drained as the flow of lava diminishes.

The track climbs over the caldera rim to a pass between the post-caldera lava domes, actually within the caldera. The volcanic spines visible on the domes are produced when molten lava is squeezed out like toothpaste from between solid blocks on the exterior of the dome. Such spines topple easily, so their presence indicates that the domes are very young.

As the track leaves the pass the scenery changes: the steep slopes of the domes are replaced by more gentle slopes of lava and volcanic ash formed before the caldera. Finally the track recrosses the caldera wall and the floor of the caldera, with its phreatic explosion craters, is visible.

The caldera and craters

Much of the floor of the caldera not filled by the domes is a gently sloping plain, covered by sediments washed from the walls (Fig. 14.10). But in the south there are many phreatic explosion craters, both in the floor and the walls of the caldera and in the volcanic domes (Fig. 14.12).[170] The floor of the craters is generally flat, covered with sediments washed in since the explosion. The state of erosion of the sides gives an indication of the relative age of the craters.

The largest of the phreatic craters, Stephanos, is about 300 m in diameter and 25 m deep (Plate 12B), but it is not the youngest as the more recent craters lie about 700 m to the north, at the base of the main lava domes. Here several smaller lava domes have been partly destroyed by many phreatic explosions. The walls of the largest crater here reveal a long history of repeated phreatic explosions in

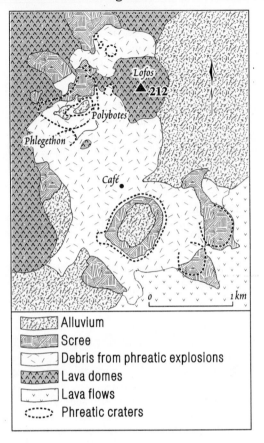

Fig. 14.12. Nisyros caldera (after 170).

this area, and there is no reason why this will not continue in the future.

The phreatic eruptions of the nineteenth century have been well described.[170] In late 1871 a violent earthquake took place, followed by phreatic explosions. Two small craters opened up: Polybotes, in the Polybotes Megalos depression, and another on the southern side of the Lofos dome, Phlegethon (Fig. 14.13). Activity recommenced in 1873 again with an earthquake. Initially rocks were ejected and hot brine flowed from the crater. Soon, however, this was replaced by dark mud, which flowed from both craters onto the plain for three days. The area of this flow is known today as Ramos, 'burnt area', as the high sulphur content of the material, and lack of soil, restrict plant growth. Another explosion occurred in

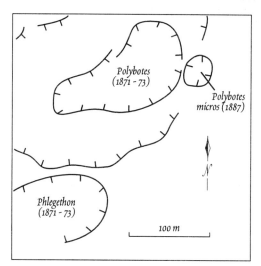

Fig. 14.13. The craters Polybotes, Phlegethon and Polybotes micros in Nisyros caldera.

1887, in the eastern part of the crater area. This produced a small crater, Polybotes Micros, about 20 m in diameter.

There are fumaroles in almost all the craters, but there are also steam vents in the centre of Stephanos, which do not deposit sulphur. In the winter rainwater flows into this crater as it is the lowest point in the caldera. The water is heated by the gases from the fumaroles and boils, producing the steam vents.

Two wells were drilled near the craters to depths of 1.5 and 1.8 km during the 1980s to determine the potential for the generation of electricity from geothermal energy. Although the holes tapped very hot water in suitable quantities (up to 210°C), environmental and political considerations have prevented the exploitation of this resource.

15

The Cyclades

The islands of the Cyclades were so called by the ancient Greeks, who saw them as a wheel, or cycle, placed round the sacred isle of Delos (Fig. 15.1). On the map they look more like stepping-stones between Europe and Asia, and that has been their role many times in history. They number about 30 islands, large and small; some twelve are important. They are for the most part dry, rocky and picturesque, dotted with dazzling white buildings. They are mountainous and largely barren, but many have useful minerals, and all inhabited islands have at least one good harbour. The larger islands produce olives, vines, and a little barley, but the main industry of most is now tourism.

They were first properly settled about 3000 BC by prospectors for metals and other minerals, who brought with them the Bronze Age culture of their home in western Turkey. They quickly grew rich from metal-working and trading. Their great days were the Early Bronze Age, 3000-2000 BC, during which they produced those exquisite marble figurines known as Cycladic idols and superb silver jewellery. About 2000 BC Minoans from Crete took over the islands and to a large extent transformed their culture. This mixed culture was further diluted around 1600 BC, when the influence of Mycenaean Greece was increasingly felt. This is especially noticeable in the destruction layers on Thera, which will be considered below. The curtain falls on the Cyclades about 1100 BC and (as elsewhere in the Greek world) a Dark Age of some three centuries ensued. It would, however, appear that around 1000 BC Mainland Greeks, fleeing from troubles in their homeland, settled in these islands. The Ionians occupied most of the islands, but it was

the Dorians who chose Milos and Thera.

The fortunes of the individual islands will be considered below. Suffice it to say here that the Cyclades were very prosperous in the seventh and sixth centuries BC, but then their luck turned. Overrun by the Persians in 490 BC, they voluntarily entered into the Delian League, which eventually developed into the Athenian Empire. In due course they passed to the Romans and then the Byzantines, who abandoned them to the raids of Goths, Saracens and Slavs. After the fourth Crusade in AD 1204 the islands were given to various Venetian adventurers, who held them until the fall of Constantinople to the Turks in 1453.

The Cyclades are part of a band of dominantly metamorphic rocks, the Attic-Cycladic metamorphic belt, which continues north to Attica and southern Euboea. To the east it abuts similar metamorphic rocks of the Menderes massif exposed on the northern Dodecanese islands and the Turkish mainland (Fig. 15.1). The oldest rocks are part of the Hercynian belt, a chain of mountains formed during the Late Proterozoic by collision of continents (like the Alps and Himalayas), but soon eroded down to their roots. This chain extended to southern Britain. Sedimentary and volcanic rocks were deposited on this basement during the Mesozoic period. Compressions associated with the Alpine orogeny reached this area during the Eocene and parts of the ocean floor descended a subduction zone beneath the Pindos basin (zone). When this ocean had been completely consumed the edge of the Pelagonian micro-continent was dragged down the subduction zone to a depth of about 50 km, before subduction ceased. The rocks were metamorphosed at high pressures and rela-

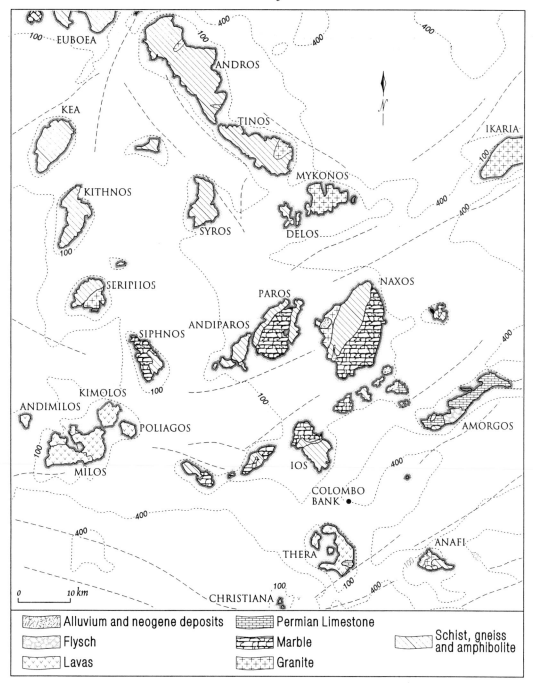

Fig. 15.1. The Cyclades.

171

tively low temperatures to become blueschists and related rocks.[241]

By Oligocene or Miocene times the overall tectonic force had turned from compression to tension. Movement along shallow normal faults (unlike the steep graben faults that followed in the Neogene) resulted in the rapid uplift of the blueschist rocks, and their juxtaposition against rocks that had never descended very far into the earth.[19, 163] Metamorphism at lower pressure produced greenschists and other rocks. Hot crustal rocks were brought towards the surface by these faults where they melted to form the widespread granite plutons that were emplaced after the faulting ceased. The final result of the extension was that the crust was rather thinner than normal, and hence 'floated' rather lower on the mantle.

Finally, subduction of the eastern Mediterranean sea-floor beneath the Aegean began to produce volcanism about 5 million years ago along the South Aegean volcanic arc from Corinthia to the Dodecanese. In the Cyclades volcanism started on Andiparos and continues now on Milos and Thera.

The Cyclades now lie on a broad underwater plateau, generally less than 200 m deep. This plateau is mostly underwater as the crust is somewhat thinner here than elsewhere in the Aegean region. The widespread Neogene stretching of the crust probably occurred here also, but has not been so significant as elsewhere. Hence the Neogene grabens that are so fertile on the mainland are here underwater.

Syros

Syros was inhabited in the Bronze Age, but otherwise little is known of the history of this rocky island. However, it may have been the source of jade in antiquity (see below). It is now an industrial island with an active port.

The bedrock of Syros is dominated by marbles, schists and quartzites (Fig. 15.2).[168] These rocks were originally deposited during the Mesozoic period as limestones, shales and sandstones. Basalts, peridotites and granites, probably parts of an ophiolite, were then thrust on these sedimentary rocks. The whole pack-

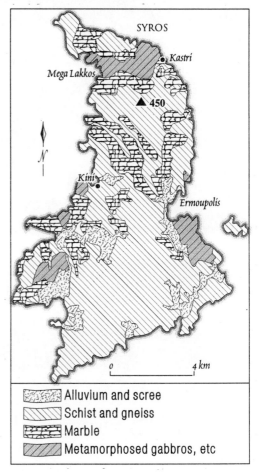

Fig. 15.2. Syros.

age was metamorphosed at great depths, in the blueschist metamorphic facies, about 45 million years ago, and subsequently at lower pressures. The high pressure metamorphism produced a number of interesting minerals, including the blue amphibole glaucophane and the green pyroxene jadeite.

Jadeite is the main mineral of one form of jade, a hard, dense and tough rock much valued in antiquity for the manufacture of axe-heads and other objects. Although the mineral jadeite is fairly common, it is rare to find it comprising the bulk of a rock. However, such material occurs as blocks in a band of serpentinite between Kastri and Mega Lakkos in the northern part of the island.[64] It is not known if jade was exploited here in antiquity, but jade axes have been found in Greece and elsewhere, and the provenance of the stone is not known.[238]

Mykonos

Although the island of Mykonos is now a major holiday resort, in antiquity it was unimportant: Strabo notes only that baldness was prevalent here. In recent times the island has produced a little manganese and baryte, as well as wine and tomatoes.

Mykonos is almost completely made up of a single mass of hornblende-biotite granite which was emplaced into the metamorphic rocks of the Attic-Cycladic metamorphic belt about 11 million years ago (Fig. 15.1).[111] The granite is well exposed around Mykonos town and consists of orthoclase phenocrysts up to 5 cm long, set in a matrix of quartz, orthoclase and biotite. Sedimentary and metamorphic rocks exposed around Panormos bay and on the north-eastern coast were emplaced tectonically on the granite, possibly during the last stages of solidification. Indeed, the granite may have risen up this fault from greater depths during regional stretching of the crust.[163]

Pliocene volcanic ashes, now well lithified, crop out in a small area in the north-east, near Mavro Vourno and Profitis Elias, and on the adjacent island of Tragonissi. Fluids probably associated with this volcanism crystallised in north-west-directed faults as 1-3 m wide veins of baryte, with minor amounts of lead, silver, zinc and iron sulphides, now strongly oxidised to depths of up to 200 m. Iron, lead and silver were mined in the nineteenth century, but recently only baryte has been produced.[18, 158]

Delos

Although in its day the most significant of the Cyclades, the barren island of Delos is one of the smallest. It owed its importance in antiquity to its being regarded as the birthplace of the god Apollo and his twin sister Artemis, born to Leto under a palm tree near the Sacred Lake. There was a flourishing Mycenaean presence between 1600 and 1150 BC and Delos may actually have been a sanctuary at that early date. About 700 BC the historical sanctuary of Apollo was founded by the Naxians and Delos became the religious centre for all Ionian Greeks. The sanctuary was beautified with statues made by Naxian artists of their marble, among them a colossal statue of Apollo and an avenue of lions. About 550 BC the Athenians replaced the Naxians and from 314 BC Delos became increasingly a commercial rather than a religious centre, a process which was accelerated when in 166 BC the Romans turned the city into a free port. The houses and public buildings which we see belong chiefly to this era, which came to an end in 88 BC when Delos was destroyed.

The island of Delos is dominated by schist and granite (Fig. 15.3). The oldest rocks are mica schists, transitional to gneiss, with minor blocks and layers of marble.[38] These rocks are especially common on the northern part of the island and on the adjacent island of Rheneia. A granite intrusion was emplaced into these rocks about 11 million years ago.[111] This intrusion dominates the southern parts of the island, and is an extension of a larger granite body on Mykonos. In places the granite flowed during crystallisation and orthoclase crystals up to 3 cm long were aligned. The large size of these crystals serves to distinguish this rock from the schist.

Although marble is very sparse on the island it was quarried in antiquity at a number of locations for local use. Layers of white marble about 1 m thick above the theatre were exploited, but numerous other occurrences in the ravine of the Inopos were too small. Both white and grey marble were extracted from small quarries on the hill of Ghlastropi, southeast of the theatre. The grey was used on the Patico of Philip.[269] The largest mass of marble is situated on the coast south-east of Mt Kynthos. This unusual white marble contains very large, branching crystals of calcite, up to 25 cm long. It was used from the Archaic period onwards, and can be seen in the steps of the Great Temple of Apollo.

Most of the ancient city is underlain by granite, with outcrops of schist principally

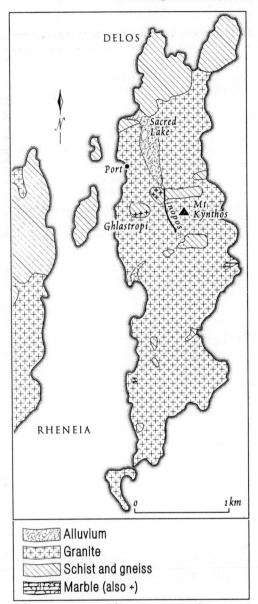

Fig. 15.3. Delos (after 38).

struction material for the houses. Public buildings had foundations of granite or schist, but commonly with superstructures of marble, generally from Naxos or Delos itself.

The island has no streams, except in winter when the small Inopos torrent drains into the bay of Skardhana. The ancient Sacred Lake in the centre of Delos was formed by artificial enlargement of swamps in the lower part of the torrent. Water supply for the ancient town was from countless wells, and many houses had their own rainwater cisterns.

Seriphos

Seriphos was an important source of iron in antiquity. Iron replaced bronze very slowly partly because of the higher temperatures necessary for smelting. It came into general use at about 1000 BC. Despite the importance to the ancient world of the iron of Seriphos, the island home of the evil King Polydekes of the Perseus legend was only mentioned with contempt in antiquity because of its poverty.

The northern part of Seriphos is made up of blueschists similar to those elsewhere in the Cyclades (Fig. 15.4). There are layers of calcite and dolomite marble within these schists, especially in the central part of the island.[239] A granite pluton was emplaced about 9 million years ago into the southern part of the island.[111]

Hot, watery solutions were released during the crystallisation of the granite and circulated into the adjacent rocks. These solutions contained iron and other elements, which were precipitated during cooling and reaction with calcite or dolomite in the marble, forming a rock called skarn. Skarns formed near the contact, in the central part of the island, were deposited at high temperatures (500-600°C) and are rich in magnetite. These deposits were mined at Playa between AD 1850 and 1930. The limonite iron deposits of Mega Livadi were formed at lower temperatures away from the granite.[64] Reaction with the host marbles also produced many large, fine crystals of green quartz, hedenburgite amphibole, andradite garnet and the unusual calcium and iron silicate mineral ilvaite.[100] A total of about 7 million tonnes of iron have been produced on Seriphos

around the Sanctuaries of Foreign Gods. Mt Kynthos (113 m) is dominated by granite, massive in its upper parts but with well-aligned orthoclase crystals at the base of the steps. The streets and squares were paved with local schist, which was also the most important con-

174

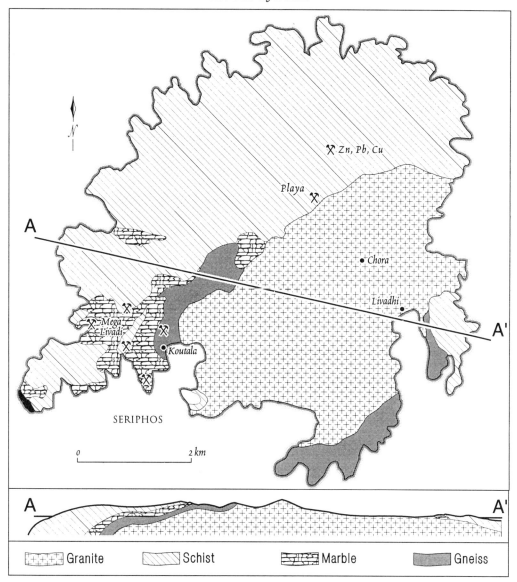

Fig. 15.4. Seriphos (after 239 and other sources).

since antiquity.

A cave opens off one of the iron mines near the bay of Koutala.[216] It is a typical karstic cave, developed in the marble host-rock long after the mineralisation. It was a sanctuary in antiquity as ancient objects were discovered cemented into stalagmites.

Siphnos

Siphnos is a fertile, well-watered island with a mountainous interior. Until recently it lived by fruit-growing, grazing, and the production of excellent pottery, but in antiquity things were a little different: Herodotus writes that, thanks to their gold and silver, the Siphnians

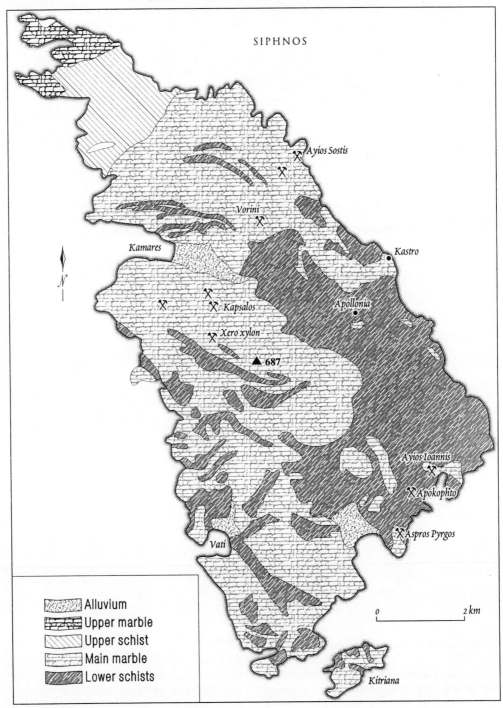

Fig. 15.5. Siphnos.

were the richest of the islanders, and this is borne out by the opulence of their Treasury at Delphi, which they built about 530 BC of Siphnian, Naxian and Parian marble. But 600 years later Pausanias mentions that their gold mines were flooded out, perhaps in the fifth century BC, because they denied to Apollo at Delphi the promised tithe of their wealth.

Much silver jewellery and plate and many lead objects belonging to the Early Bronze Age (3000-2000 BC) have been found in the Cyclades. The principal sources of these metals were the island of Siphnos and Lavrion in Attica.[95] Gold appears not to have been produced at that time. During the sixth and fifth centuries BC silver, lead and gold were produced in large quantities, but the mines were soon exhausted, and from then on Siphnos was poor and unimportant. In the late nineteenth century many of the ancient mines were reopened for iron and zinc.

The geology of Siphnos resembles that of many of the other Cycladic islands and consists of a series of layers of schists and marbles about 2,500 m thick (Fig. 15.5). The lower schist was metamorphosed in the greenschist facies and is mostly exposed in the east. This is overlain by the main marble unit, about 800 m thick, that covers much of the island. The highest units crop out in the north, and comprise an upper schist 400 m thick made of blueschist, and an upper marble unit.

Ancient mines

The ore deposits of the island cluster in the middle and south-eastern parts of the island, mostly within the main marble unit (Fig. 15.5). The five main deposits in the centre line along a rough line, oriented north-east, perhaps reflecting a deeper major fault. All these deposits contain lead and silver, as well as iron minerals. The deposits in the south-east also contain gold.[283]

The deposits were formed from fluids associated with the metamorphism, or with a granitic pluton not exposed on the surface, in the same way as those in Siphnos. The lead deposits, which contain silver and gold as by-products, formed at lower temperatures, probably from fluids that had already precipitated iron elsewhere.

Most of the ancient mines on Siphnos were worked for silver and lead, but antimony is also present in the ore, though not exploited in antiquity. The workings at Ayios Sostis on the east coast mostly date from the Early Bronze Age and the Late Archaic period (520-480 BC). Other ancient workings at Ayios Silvestros, Vorini, Kapsalos, and Xero Xylon are mostly Late Archaic. All the mines seem to have ceased working about the fifth century BC. Only Ayios Sostis is sufficiently low-lying to have been possibly flooded out; perhaps the others were exhausted by the fifth century BC.

There are three localities on the south coast that are believed to be ancient gold mines, probably dating from the sixth or fifth centuries BC. The ore at Apokophto is a quartz-pyrite vein, that at Aspros Pyrgos is rich in copper and the third mine is at Ayios Ioannis.[283]

Naxos

Naxos is the largest of the Cyclades, the greenest and, some say, the most beautiful. It is traversed from north to south by a mountain range, culminating in Mt Zas (Zeus) at 1,004 m. Fruit, olive oil, cheese, corn and wine are produced, and the honey is particularly good. The island is also famous for its white marble. Here, according to legend, the God Dionysus found and loved the Cretan Princess Ariadne, abandoned by Theseus on his return from Knossos after killing the Minotaur.

The prehistory of Naxos is that of all the Cyclades: a brilliant Early Bronze Age (3000-2000 BC), with particularly fine 'idols' and vessels of the local marble, followed by an equally brilliant period of first Minoan, then Mycenaean influence. This world ended about 1100 BC, but a century later Naxos was resettled by Ionian Greeks, who rapidly became leaders of all the Ionians and protectors of the Sanctuary of Delos. Thanks to their plentiful supplies of excellent marble, regarded as second only to Parian, and emery, the Naxians founded a school of sculptors second to none in Greece. In 490 BC Naxos was sacked by the

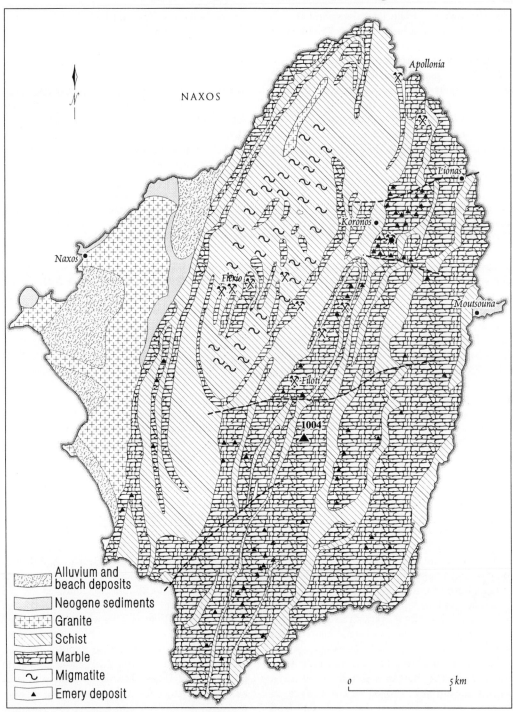

Fig. 15.6. Naxos (after 128 and other sources).

Persians. This was the end of her prosperity until the Venetian occupation in the thirteenth century, which has left many castles and mansions in the Naxian towns and villages.

Much of Naxos is dominated by metamorphic rocks – in the east, marble and dolomite with layers of schist, and in the centre, schist with layers of marble (Fig. 15.6).[128] These rocks were originally limestones and shales, deposited on the Hercynian basement, and were metamorphosed several times, notably 45 and 25 million years ago at depths of 25 to 15 km and temperatures of 400 to 700°C. The temperature of the metamorphism was highest in the centre of the island, where parts of the schists melted. Most of this magma was retained in the original rock, which is called migmatite, but some escaped to form a small granite intrusion.

The original limestones contained layers of bauxite, similar to that found today in central Greece. When the limestone was metamorphosed into marble the bauxite layers were transformed into emery, a rock containing the hard mineral corundum together with magnetite, haematite and margarite mica.[200] In some deposits these minerals have recrystallised to form fissures lined with well-formed crystals of margarite, platy green diaspore, tourmaline, magnetite, rutile and chlorite.

Much of the western part of the island is underlain by a granite which was emplaced about 12 million years ago, long after the end of the metamorphism.[111] This granite contains pale phenocrysts of orthoclase up to 8 cm long, set in a matrix of finer-grained orthoclase, quartz and biotite.

Finally, sedimentary rocks were deposited on parts of both the granite and metamorphic rocks during the Tertiary period. Late, low-angle normal faulting moved these sediments onto the granite.

Naxos town

The town of Naxos is built on the edge of an area of low hills and plains (Fig. 15.7). This whole area is underlain by granite, which easily breaks down in this climate initially to produce a fine gravel and finally a fertile soil.

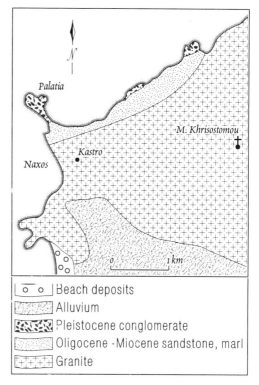

Fig. 15.7. Naxos town and environs.

o o	Beach deposits
	Alluvium
	Pleistocene conglomerate
	Oligocene -Miocene sandstone, marl
+++	Granite

Weathering of the granite also releases large amounts of quartz, which is reworked by the sea to produce the 'white' sand beaches south of Naxos town.

The Islet of Palatia contrasts with Naxos as it is made of well-cemented Pleistocene conglomerates. Evidence for recent submergence of this area can be seen in a small Roman fish-tank, on the peninsula just north of the isthmus, whose lip now lies about 50 cm below sea-level. The site of the Mycenaean city a few hundred metres north is also partly submerged.

Marble and emery quarries

The white, coarse-grained marble, widespread on the island, is excellent for sculpture and architecture. It was quarried in antiquity from many parts of the island, especially towards the centre, where whiter material was available (Fig. 15.6). This is probably related more to the lower stratigraphic level exposed there, which was purer than higher strata, rather than the higher temperature of metamorphism. Unfinished statues of the sixth century BC survive in the ancient quarries at Flerio (Melanes) and Apollonia – the statue in the latter quarry would have been 10.5 m in height (Plate 14A).

Emery was very important in antiquity as an abrasive to shape marble and other stone. Although it occurs at several other places in the Aegean, rarely does the quality match that of Naxos. In ancient times emery was extracted from a large number of shallow quarries, principally in the eastern part of the island between the villages of Lionas, Koronos and Moutsouna.[200] More recently it was extracted from underground mines and transported by aerial tramways to the coast.

Paros

Paros is the second largest of the Cyclades after Naxos. The interior is almost entirely occupied by Mt Profitis Elias (771 m), which is dominated by the white marble for which Paros was renowned in antiquity. It slopes down to a maritime plain which completely rings the island. Paros is fertile by Cycladic standards, if not as fertile or as well wooded as Naxos.

The earliest settlement was on Saliagos, an islet between Paros and Andiparos, which was settled in Late Neolithic times (5000-4500 BC), a very rare occurrence in the Cyclades. The brilliant Bronze Age civilisation echoes that of Naxos, particularly in the production of 'idols' and vessels in the translucent Parian marble. Around 1000 BC the Ionians arrived, and Paros grew rich. The superb statuary marble of Paros came into its own about 700 BC and for a thousand years there was a famous school of sculptors here.

Like most of the Cycladic islands Paros is dominated by marble and schist (Fig. 15.8). The central, high part of the island is underlain by marble, which better resists erosion, with layers of schist and amphibolite.[198] The lower relief to the east and west reflects the abundance of more readily eroded schist. The original limestones and shales were probably

of Permian to Cretaceous age. Three small granite bodies were emplaced into metamorphic rocks around, and possibly beneath, the alluvial plain to the west of Naoussa.

Weakly metamorphosed serpentinite, probably the remains of an ophiolite, and conglomerates of Cretaceous to Miocene age crop out in the north-east and south-east parts of the island. They have been emplaced by low-angle normal faults over the strongly metamorphosed rocks. Finally, these rocks have been partly overlain by Pliocene limestone.

The island was sliced up by faults during the Neogene and a graben. now partly filled with alluvium, stretches almost all the way from Paroikia to Naoussa. The lowlands near the north-east coast were probably formed by erosion of the soft serpentinites, limestones and conglomerates. The relative fertility of Paros is due to the presence of these plains.

Ancient marble quarries

Parian marble was famous throughout the Greek world. Some of the ancient quarries still exist, in the form of tunnels running deep into the mountainside, following the best veins; that is why Parian marble was known as Lychnites, because it was quarried by the light of a lamp (*lychnos*).

Marble was mined in several different areas in antiquity, but the most important was the Lychnites mine near Marathi (Fig. 15.8). This mine exploited a seam of medium-grained, pure white marble 3-4 metres thick. The purity and crystallinity are such that it is translucent. This marble could be extracted in large blocks as it has few joints, cracks or karstic voids.

The mine extends underground at an angle of 35° for about 200 metres. The chisel marks of the ancient workers can be clearly seen on the ceiling and walls. Stalagmites and stalactites have started to develop in the mine, some since it was reopened in the nineteenth century.

Above and below this seam the marble is not so pure and is coloured grey by the presence of graphite. The banding of the marble is related to original layering in the limestone, but the

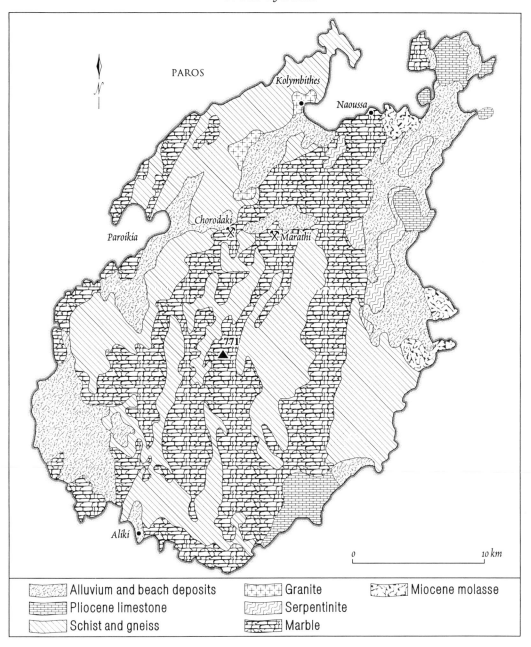

Fig. 15.8. Paros (after 198 and other sources).

181

orientation has been changed by deformation during metamorphism.

Naoussa

The beach at Kolymbithes, just across the bay from Naoussa, is well-known for the strange shapes of the rocks (Fig. 15.8). The bedrock here, and on the hills behind the beach, is a grey granite, which is slightly foliated and is comprised of quartz, feldspar and muscovite. Distant from the beach the rock erodes along joints to produce a blocky, barren landscape, but at low elevations the erosional style is quite different. Here, erosion by the sea has produced dimples, basins and lace work. The process starts with the adsorption of seawater into the rock surface. Crystallisation of the salts on drying expands the rock and small amounts flake off. Once the process has started it continues in the same place, like rust, and hollows out the rock beneath the surface.

Andiparos and adjacent islands

Andiparos and the two islands to the south-west are dominated by gneiss, schist and marble of the Attic-Cycladic belt (Fig. 15.1).[8] The earliest volcanism of the South Aegean volcanic belt started about 5 million years ago with the eruption of a series of lava domes in the southern part of Andiparos and the two smaller islands to the south.[123] Magmas formed at depth within or above the subduction zone reached the surface via a major zone of faulting which stretches from Ikaria to Milos (see Chapter 2).

All the volcanic rocks here are rhyolites and most are glassy. However, this obsidian was little used in ancient times as it was not available in large enough blocks. Instead the better quality material from the adjacent island of Milos was used.

Andiparos is well-known for the cave on the side of Mt Ayios Ioannis where the Marquis de Nointel celebrated Christmas in 1673. This is a large cave developed in fine-grained marble, following joint planes that dip at about 35° into the side of the hill. The cave probably formed when the topography was very different from its present form. The well-developed formations in the cave date from a time when the climate was much moister as little new material is now being deposited.

Milos

Milos is one of the two dominantly volcanic islands of the Cyclades. It is almost bisected by an enormous bay with an entrance on the north (Fig. 15.9). The east side of the island is largely low-lying, while the west side is dominated by Mt Profitis Elias (751 m). Apart from some warm springs, Milos lacks surface water and produces little agriculturally but olives and vines. However, it is rich in economic minerals and rocks, used both now and in antiquity.

The natural volcanic glass obsidian was a rare and important commodity in antiquity: it was used for the manufacture of tools and weapons as it gave a much better edge than chert (flint). Melian obsidian has been found in the lower excavated levels of the Franchthi Cave (Peloponnese), and so must have been taken from Milos before 8000 BC, perhaps as early as 11,000 BC. However, there were no settlements on Milos anything like as early as that, and it would appear that for long the obsidian was collected by visiting sailors.

Milos was first settled about 3000 BC at Phylakopi on the north-east coast, presumably with the object of exploiting the obsidian. A royal palace built about 2300 BC lasted till 1100 BC, when the town was deserted. A century later Dorian Greeks from Laconia established a new settlement near Plaka, which has been the capital of the island ever since. Again Milos grew rich, thanks to the thermal springs and the economic minerals. But in 416 BC tragedy struck: the Melians wanted to remain neutral but the Athenians invaded the island, slaughtered the men and enslaved the women and children. Milos never recovered.

Although most of Milos is covered with volcanic rocks, the basement of the island is exposed in a small area in the south-east (Fig. 15.9). It consists of greenschists, minor marbles and relics of blueschists similar to other parts of the Attic-Cycladic metamorphic belt.[142, 247] About 100 metres of yellow conglom-

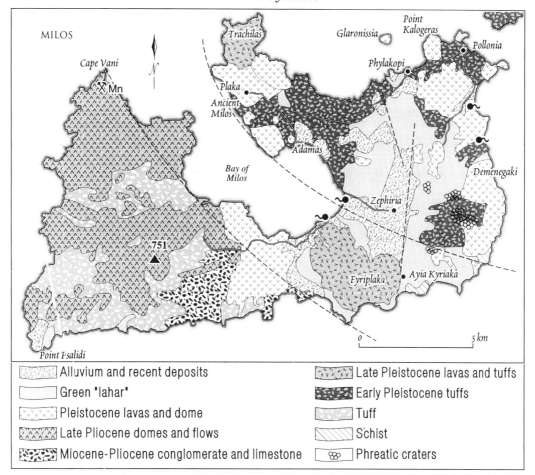

Fig. 15.9. Milos (after 93 and other sources).

erate and limestone were deposited on these metamorphic rocks during the Upper Miocene and Lower Pliocene. Their original extent is unknown, but they now crop out in the south-central part of the island.

Volcanism started on Milos about 3.5 million years ago with the eruption of a series of volcanic ashes in the south-west.[93] Milos must have been submerged at this time as these rocks were erupted underwater. This series of rocks finished with the eruption of andesite pillow-lavas. The next phase of volcanic activity occurred about 2.5 million years ago. It was sub-aerial and was confined to the western part of the island. Andesite and dacite domes

and flows, together with the volcanic ashes produced during the eruptions, almost completely covered the earlier volcanic rocks. Volcanic activity then switched to the east, with the eruption of rhyolite domes and submarine andesite lavas and pyroclastic rocks around 1.7 million years ago. These rocks are commonly highly altered and brecciated and may be the source of bentonite and kaolin (see below). This phase of activity finished with the eruption of rhyolitic domes and flows in the central part of the island one million years ago. Activity resumed about 400,000 years ago at Trachilas, north of Plaka. This eruption started with explosive production of pyroclastic rocks, which formed a broad tuff-ring. The violence of the eruption decreased with time until finally lavas were erupted that flowed towards the north. A similar eruption occurred further south at Fyriplaka 140,000 to 90,000 years ago (or possibly more recently, see below). Explosive eruptions of ashes produced a small cone and finally gave way to lavas. This was followed by extensive phreatic eruptions, which deposited rocks made up of pulverised metamorphic basement, the 'Green Lahar'. Following a pause sufficiently long for the development of a soil, volcanism restarted with explosive eruptions and the production of a tuff-ring 1,500 m in diameter. Smaller cones were formed within the larger cone, and lavas flowed from these cones north-eastward to the Bay of Milos.

More recently Milos has again been affected by strong phreatic activity: craters from these explosions are widespread in the easternmost parts of the island. In one area repeated explosions have reworked earlier debris, to give a mass of interlocking craters.

Debris from a phreatic explosion on the south coast, south of Ayia Kyriaka, has buried ancient walls, staircases and unbroken amphorae, indicating that the explosion destroyed an ancient town. This event has been dated at between AD 80 and AD 205, making it the most recent activity on Milos. The volcanic ashes of the Fyriplaka tuff-ring lie under the debris of the explosion, with little sign of erosion, suggesting that the Fyriplaka eruption may have been much more recent than initially estimated.[263]

The two grabens that cross Milos have had an important effect on the geology and topography. The largest comprises most of Milos bay, and continues to the south-east under the Fyriplaka volcanic field (Fig. 15.9).[199] This graben is still very active, as testified by the hot-springs and a significant earthquake in 1992. Most of the damage was restricted to the graben. Another graben runs north-south around the village of Zephiria. The graben fault is well defined on the eastern side by a steep scarp, indicating that it is still active, but the west side may be a hinge.

The heavily indented coastline of Milos and the absence of raised sea-level stands (see Chapter 2), except for a small area around Point Psalidi, shows that the island is subsiding. Other evidence includes drowned beach-rock and ancient structures. Initial work suggests subsidence of up to 7 m since antiquity. This subsidence may be related to the cessation of major volcanism on Milos about 90,000 years ago – since then the crust has cooled and contracted. Or it may reflect crustal tension in this region, as the non-volcanic Naxos is also subsiding.

The earliest settlements in Milos were in the areas with the richest soils. Most of Milos is covered with volcanic ash or scree. This material is transported before there is sufficient time for weathering (chemical breakdown) of the igneous minerals into the clays and other minerals of soils. However, there are parts of the island where streams, and their sediments, have no outlet or restricted access to the sea. In these areas there is sufficient time for weathering and fertile soils can form. One such area is the plain around Zephiria, which is a graben formed by tension in the crust during recent times.

There is no evidence that volcanism has completely ceased on Milos. It is only 90,000 years or less since the last eruption, and pauses of this duration are common. Significant thermal sources at shallow depth (see below) suggest that magma is present beneath the island. However, resumption of volcanic activity would undoubted be preceded by increased hydrothermal activity, such as fumaroles.

Plaka and ancient Milos

The village of Plaka is built on a series of andesite and dacite domes and short, thick flows about 1 million years old (Fig. 15.10). The Kastro hill is the youngest of these domes and towers above the rest. The end of another flow underlies the small hill of Profitis Elias and has been isolated from the main flow under Plaka by faulting. Material from these flows was used to construct the ancient city of Milos. The steep, straight coastline here follows one of the graben faults.

The Christian catacombs were cut into pale-

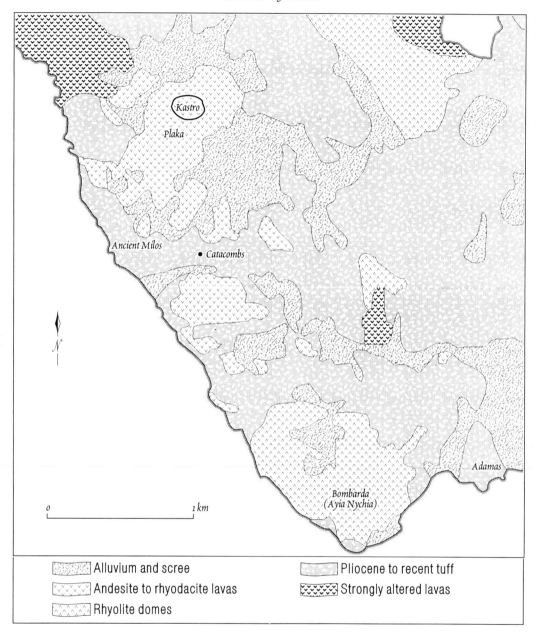

Fig. 15.10. Plaka and Ancient Milos.

grey volcanic tuffs of Late Pliocene-Pleistocene age.[11] This rock is easily excavated as it is light, being mostly made of pumice fragments, and loosely-cemented. It is very porous, so that accumulation of water is not a problem.

Obsidian quarries

Obsidian was extensively exploited in Palaeolithic to Neolithic times, but was not completely displaced by the arrival of bronze in

3000 BC, as it was cheaper and gave sharper blades. Only the coming of iron in about 1000 BC finally supplanted obsidian for blades, but its use continued for ornaments and mirrors.

Obsidian was extracted at two different locations in antiquity.[230] The most important was in the east at Demenegaki where it occurs in the external parts of a 1.8 million-year-old rhyolite dome (Fig. 15.9). Obsidian was also extracted from similar rocks in the Bombarda dome (Ayia Nychia) west of Adamas (Fig. 15.10). In both areas obsidian occurs near the external parts of the domes, where cooling was most rapid. Obsidian is not stable once erupted and eventually crystallises to fine-grained, pale-coloured rhyolite. Layers with bubbles devitrify first and then the crystallisation proceeds along cracks into the bubble-free layers. The result is layers of rounded blobs of fresh obsidian set in fine-grained rhyolite (Plate 15A).

The Glaronissia islands and Point Kalogeros

Thick andesite flows near Cape Kalogeros and on the Glaronissia islands have well developed columnar joints (Fig. 15.9, Plate 14B). These joints form after solidification of the lava during cooling and contraction. They propagate inwards from the outer surfaces of the flow, even when they are fan-like. The joints in the lavas at Cape Kalogeros converge towards the centre, showing the original convex shape of the flow. Hexagonal prismatic blocks of andesite from these flows were used in construction at the ancient site of Phylakopi. Caves along the south-west coast have been excavated relatively recently by the sea into old tuffs of the earliest volcanic cycle.

Hot springs and geothermal energy

The largest hot spring on the island bubbles up into the Bay of Milos, a few metres offshore near Kanava. A small fumarole issues from a cave beneath caliche adjacent to the salt pans. There is also a small fumarole at Atmoloutra in the lavas of Fyriplaka volcano that has been converted into a Turkish bath but its thermal output is variable, depending on the direction of the wind. Geothermal wells drilled near Zephiria, on the eastern fault of the graben, have located interesting thermal anomalies, although currently there is no thermal activity on the surface. The exploitation of this resource has been prevented for technical and political reasons. The heat source on Milos is probably a cooling body of magma at a depth of several kilometres. Surface water heated by these rocks circulates towards the surface along the graben faults.

Bentonite, kaolin and other products

The volcanic products of both Trachilas and Fyriplaka volcanos are rhyolites with unusually high water contents. After extraction the rock is heated, which boils the internal water, and the expanded material, 'perlite', is used as a lightweight aggregate and insulator.

Bentonite and kaolin are rocks rich in clay formed by the alteration of volcanic rocks by circulating hot water.[61] The initial rocks were rhyolite pumice and submarine andesite lavas and breccias. Long after the eruption of these rocks the heat from renewed volcanism circulated water at temperatures of 160 to 230°C. The rhyolite was converted to kaolin and the andesite to bentonite (a rock rich in montmorillonite). These rocks now occur as veins, pipes and irregular masses, and have frequently been eroded and redeposited in depressions. Both are white when pure, but may be coloured red by iron oxides, green by chlorite or yellow by sulphur. Both bentonite and kaolin are extracted from many quarries in the north-east of the island.

The 'alumen' of antiquity was probably bentonite. It had many uses: as a deodorant, as a salve when mixed with honey and as an emetic with copper salts. It was also used in dyeing, soldering and cloth finishing.

Circulating hot waters not only altered the rocks, but also deposited the yellow mineral sulphur, which was mined here in Hellenistic and Roman times. Sulphur was burnt as a disinfectant and for religious purification. It was also applied externally as a medicament and used to whiten and soften wool.

Baryte occurs on Milos as veins and irregular masses associated with the volcanic rocks.[288] It was deposited from circulating hot waters and generally contains other hydrothermal minerals such as sulphides. Some of the veins on Milos are associated with important amounts of silver which was also mined in antiquity.

Extensive deposits of the manganese minerals pyrolusite and cryptomelane occur in the north-west part of the island, near Vani. These minerals have a curious botryoidal form and were probably deposited from large mineral springs during the last few 100,000 years. These deposits have been heavily exploited during the last 150 years.[288]

Andimilos, Kimolos and Poliagos

The islands of Andimilos, Kimolos and Poliagos are covered with volcanic rocks that are roughly contemporary, and similar in composition to those of Milos (Fig. 15.1). Andimilos is the top of a complex volcano dominated by lavas. Activity ceased here about 320,000 years ago.

The island of Kimolos is dominated by pyroclastic rocks.[89] The Kastro ignimbrite was erupted from a vent west of Kimolos about 3 million years ago and originally covered the whole Milos group, but is today mostly exposed in the north-western half of the island. A complex series of younger pyroclastic rocks, with some lavas, covers the south-eastern side of the island. A number of hot springs debouche near the coast, especially in the north-west. Early fumarolic activity altered the pyroclastic rocks to give important deposits of the clay bentonite. Bentonite is mined on Kimolos and minor deposits of lead and silver have been exploited.

Poliagos is also dominated by pyroclastic rocks.[89] It was covered with tuff by a major eruption about 2 million years ago, which also covered much of the Milos group. These rocks are exposed in the north-west part of the island, but have been buried by more recent lava domes and flows in the south-east.

Thera (Santorini) island group

Sailing into the 10 km diameter multiple caldera at Thera (Santorini), one experiences one of the most impressive geological sights in the Aegean. Three hundred metre high cliffs show a magnificent section of the geological history of the island and the 700 m deep caldera gives an idea of the explosive force required to excavate such a hole. The eruption that produced part of the present caldera, probably the largest in recent times, buried a town near the modern village of Akrotiri, and created a Bronze Age Pompeii.

The early history of Thera, from Late Neolithic (about 4000 BC) down to about 1600 BC, runs parallel to other Cycladic islands. Then between 1600 and 1500 BC (to use the chronology preferred by most archaeologists, but see below) there flourished a brilliant civilisation, excavated at Akrotiri and elsewhere, which was closely linked to Minoan Crete. In about 1500 BC a terrible earthquake forced the inhabitants to leave the island. In due course they returned and set about repairing the damage, but were soon interrupted by a cataclysmic volcanic eruption that changed the landscape dramatically. For about 150 years afterwards Thera was uninhabited. There followed a limited re-occupation by Mycenaean Greeks at Monolithos until about 1100 BC. We next hear of Thera about 800 BC, when Dorian Greeks from Sparta established a new city at Mesa Vouno, on the south-east coast. Ancient Thera (as it is known today) prospered from the start, and continued into Roman and Early Byzantine times. When the Venetians took control in the thirteenth century they created a new capital on the west coast called Santorini (today Fira) after Saint Irene. The next important event was the partial rediscovery of Bronze Age buildings in the 1860s in ash and pumice quarries on Thera and Therasia. These discoveries were not followed up until 1967 when the fabulous remains at Akrotiri were unearthed (see below).

One last point – is there any foundation for the suggestion that the story of Atlantis is based on the events at Thera? Most archaeologists feel that there is not: many aspects of the

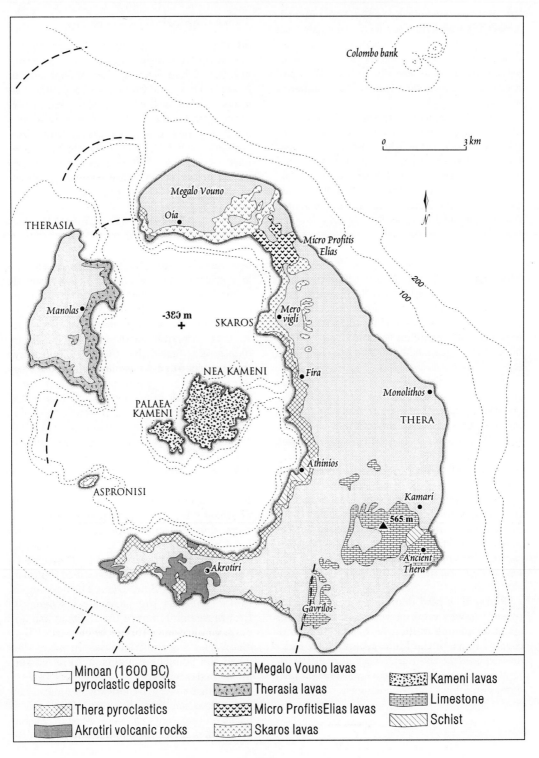

Minoan (1600 BC) pyroclastic deposits

Thera pyroclastics

Akrotiri volcanic rocks

Megalo Vouno lavas

Therasia lavas

Micro ProfitisElias lavas

Skaros lavas

Kameni lavas

Limestone

Schist

story just do not fit with what happened at Thera and most scholars would agree that the Atlantis story was no legend, but the invention of Plato in the fourth century BC in his books *Timaeus* and *Critias*. As his famous pupil Aristotle said: 'The man who dreamed it up made it vanish.'

Although Thera and the adjacent islands are now mostly covered with volcanic rocks, the volcano was built on a base of non-volcanic rocks (Fig. 15.11). The highest hills of the main island, Mt Profitis Elias (565 m), Mesa Vouno (Ancient Thera) and Gavrilos, are dominated by Triassic crystalline limestone transitional to marble. The underlying rocks are also exposed in the lower parts of the caldera walls near the port of Athinios. Here a series of schists and other metamorphic rocks are cut by minor granite intrusions. Fluids associated with the granite reacted with the host rocks to produce a small deposit of lead and silver.

Volcanism started about 1.5 million years ago in this region, and was related to subduction of the African plate beneath the Aegean plate. Volcanic features on the island of Nea Kameni and in the northern part of Thera are oriented north-east/south-west, a direction reflected in the location of the Colombo Bank underwater volcano 10 km to the north-east (Fig. 15.11; see below) and the volcanic Christiana islands 18 km to the south-west (Fig. 15.1).[227] The prevalence of this direction suggests that magmas probably rose up steep north-east/south-west faults, produced during Neogene regional tension in the crust.

The volcanic history of Thera is complex and about seven different volcanic centres (more or less independent volcanos) have been active. The earliest volcanic rocks are exposed on the Akrotiri peninsula: small amounts of andesite and dacite lavas and ashes were erupted intermittently from 1.5 to 0.6 million years ago.

Volcanism restarted about 200,000 years ago and has continued to the present day.[70] The most active volcanic centre was situated near the town of Fira, in the presently flooded cal-

Fig. 15.11. The Thera island group and the Colombo bank (after 218 and other sources).

deras, or beneath the recent Kameni islands. There have been at least twelve major eruptions from this centre, particularly 100, 79, 54, 37, 18 and 3.5 thousand years ago. Many eruptions started with a fall of pumice and culminated in pyroclastic flows. In several eruptions the magma chamber was partly emptied and the roof fell in to produce a caldera. The last major eruption, the Minoan, 3,500 years ago, resembled many of the previous eruptions (see below). The volcanic centres in the north of the island, Therasia, Megalo Vouno, Micro Profitis Elias and Skaros, were also active during this period. They produced lava as well as pyroclastic rocks.

There has been much research on the exact geography of the islands just before the Minoan eruption because of the archaeological implications.[69] The Thera caldera is the product of at least four major eruptions during the last 100,000 years. Just before the Minoan eruption the caldera formed 21,000 years ago had become shallow, but was still flooded by the sea (Fig. 15.12). The coast followed a line close to that of the present caldera, except that Thera, Therasia and Aspronisi were all jointed together to form a single horse-shaped island with a gap to the south-east. At the centre of the bay was a volcano, rather similar to the Kameni islands today, except larger. The bay would have provided an excellent harbour, sheltered from the prevailing winds.

The Minoan eruption

The Minoan eruption was one of the largest in recent times, producing about 36 cubic kilometres of rhyodacite pumice and ash over a period of a few days, and its effects were felt around the world. The eruption occurred between 1650 and 1500 BC, but there is still considerable debate on the exact date (see below). Strangely enough there are no written records of the eruption, although various biblical episodes have been attributed to it. The description given below is based on the study of the rocks produced by the eruption.

The eruption began from a north-east/south-west fissure on an island in the bay

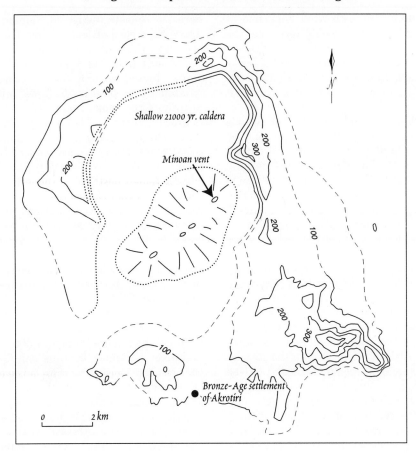

Fig. 15.12. Pre-Minoan eruption geography (after 69). The solid lines indicate the most well-defined coastline; the broken lines show where it is less certain; and the dotted lines are conjectural.

about 1 km south-west of Fira town and was initially of the 'Plinian' type.[110] The magma erupted as a fast-moving jet of hot gas and pumice blocks some of which rose to a height of 36 km in the atmosphere. During the next phase the fissure grew towards the south-east, into the shallow bay. Interaction of the magma with seawater produced steam (phreatomagmatic) explosions which widened the vent and increased the rate of eruption. Some of the fine ash simply fell from the cloud, but most was deposited from surges of dust and gas that moved at great speed horizontally from above the fissure, commonly producing great dunes. The next stage of the eruption is enigmatic:

The pumice and rock blocks of this phase may have been produced by pyroclastic flows, mudflows, or by very large phreatomagmatic explosions, or perhaps a combination. The final phase of the eruption produced thick ash flows that were sometimes sufficiently hot to weld themselves together to produce a hard, dense rock called ignimbrite. Fig. 15.13 is a schematic section through the products of this eruption.

Most of the pumice and ash fell close to the volcano, covering much of Thera and the surrounding sea-bed to a depth of several metres. However, substantial quantities of ash also fell on the islands of the western Aegean and on

190

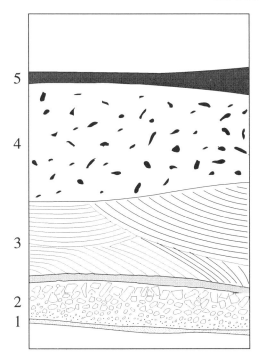

Fig. 15.13. Generalised stratigraphy of the Minoan deposits (after 110). 1 = Ash of precursor? eruption, 1-4 cm thick. 2 = Ash of Plinian phase, 10-600 cm thick. 3 = Phreatomagmatic, base-surge deposits, 10-1200 cm thick. 4 = Ash-flow deposits 1-55 m thick. 5 = Ignimbrite 0-40 m thick.

form the channels north and south of Therasia.

The Minoan eruption was almost certainly accompanied by a major tsunami, either produced by the eruption itself, or by associated landslides and earthquakes.[14, 203] Wave-borne pumice has been found in Israel at a height of 7 m, and on the nearby island of Anafi at a maximum height of 40 m. These heights can be extrapolated to give a maximum wave height at Thera of about 50 m and about 12 m on the north coast of Crete. Such waves would have been extremely destructive, though it is debatable whether they caused the final destruction of the Minoan palaces.

The exact age of this eruption has been much debated, with many archaeologists favouring 1500 BC and much geological evidence supporting 1650 BC.[107, 169] Archaeological evidence is based largely on the styles of pottery and other artifacts found at Akrotiri, and this assumes that the town was abandoned immediately before the eruption. This chronology was calibrated by reference to Egyptian king lists and an astronomical fix. The most direct geological evidence of the date of the eruption comes from carbon-14 dating of vegetation killed shortly before or by the eruption. Most recent analyses give ages in the range 1700-1600 BC.

Major eruptions can also be dated indirectly by their global effects, although the identification of the volcano responsible is not always clear. One such effect was produced by injection of sulphuric acid into the upper atmosphere during the eruption. Layers of ice deposited in Greenland at about 1645 BC were especially rich in sulphuric acid, but there is no significant anomaly at 1500 BC. Injection of ash into the upper atmosphere produced climatic effects: widths of tree-rings in Californian bristlecone pines indicate that there was extensive frost damage in the winters of 1628 to 1626 BC, which could be ascribed to a large volcanic eruption. Chinese records indicate that at the end of the reign of King Chieh (about 1600 BC) the sun was dimmed and there was a yellow fog. Floods followed by severe drought led to massive crop failures. We cannot be sure that all these effects were not caused by an eruption of another volcano in the northern hemisphere

western Turkey. Thin layers have also been found 800 km away in the Nile delta,[255] lending credence to the descriptions of the veiling of the sun in Egyptian papyrus records and the book of Exodus in the Bible: 'There may be darkness over the land of Egypt, even darkness which may be felt.'

Draining of magma from the chamber beneath the island during the eruption created an unsupported roof, which collapsed to produce much of the caldera that we see today. This started in the west, along what is now the eastern shore of Therasia, and unzipped towards the east along a circular fracture. The original vent area and fissure were destroyed and the new caldera had a floor about 400 m below sea-level or about 700 m below the summits of the shield volcanos. The sides of this hole were unstable and huge blocks 1-2 km wide slipped into the caldera. These areas now of similar magnitude, slightly earlier than the eruption of Thera, but there is no evidence for this.

If the geologically established age is shown to be correct, the archaeological chronology must be adjusted. A possible source of error in the archaeological chronology may be in the Egyptian king lists used for calibration.

The caldera wall

A wonderful 250-metre section of the caldera wall can be seen from the cable car and the zig-zag steps up to Fira (Fig. 15.14). Almost all the rocks seen are tuffs (hardened volcanic ashes) of variable composition, in contrast with the predominance of lavas on the Kameni islands with a limited range of composition (see below). The lowest part of the section is probably about 100,000 years old and is made up of tuffs formed during the large eruption that produced the southern part of the present caldera. This was followed by a 35,000-year-old sequence of tuffs. Finally at the top there are silica-rich lava flows and domes, and a thick section of tuff produced during the Minoan eruption on which the town is built (Plate 15B).

The colour of the rocks in the caldera wall reflects both variations in original composition as well as oxidation and alteration of the rocks since their crystallisation. The steepness of the cliff is related to the hardness of the rock. Ashes that were still at high temperatures when they were deposited welded themselves together as they settled to give a very durable rock (ignimbrite). Those ashes that were cool when they fell gave a weaker rock (tuff) that can be crumbled in the hand. Some of the vertical wall-like structures seen in the rock-face are dykes, cracks that have been filled with magma. Some of these dykes may have been the 'plumbing' system, up which magma flowed to produce lavas or ashes. These dykes tend to be harder than the surrounding rocks and hence stand out after erosion. Some of the vertical structures lack a core of solidified magma and hence are not dykes. They too started as cracks, but only hot watery fluids passed up them to form fumaroles on the surface. Crystallisation of minerals from these hot fluids in the walls of the crack made these rocks slightly harder than those surrounding them, and hence they have better resisted erosion and now stand out.

Palaea Kameni and Nea Kameni islands

The names of these islands, Palaea Kameni, 'Old burnt island' and Nea Kameni, 'New burnt island', reflect their present, inhospitable appearance. Although now almost uninhabited, the islands, such as they were, supported a small fishing community during the Middle Ages.

The Kameni islands are the summits of a volcano that rises 400 m from the floor of the caldera (Fig. 15.15). Volcanic activity may have restarted soon after the Minoan eruption, but nothing broke the surface until 197 BC when a new island called Lera was formed. It was located near the old Minoan fissure but was rapidly eroded to below sea-level. The oldest rocks now seen date from AD 46 and make up most of the island of Palaea Kameni.[23] A further eruption occurred near the same spot in

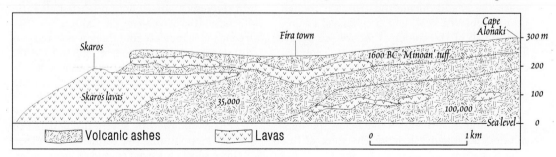

Fig. 15.14. The caldera wall near Fira town (after 118).

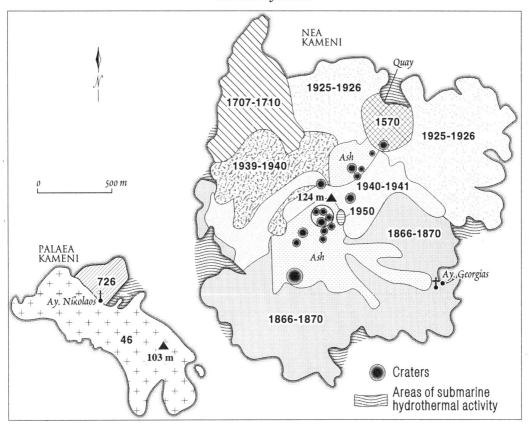

Fig. 15.15. Kameni islands (after 23, 280 and other sources). The age of each series of flows is indicated. The ash comes from many different eruptions.

AD 726, but since then activity has shifted to the north-east to form Nea Kameni. The last eruption was in AD 1950. Most of the eruptions have been relatively quiet, except those of 197 BC and AD 726. The latter was sufficiently spectacular, and produced so much floating pumice, that it was noted by the Emperor Leo III in Constantinople. He interpreted it as a sign of divine displeasure, and imposed the Iconoclasm.

In contrast to the preponderance of ash on the main islands, both Kameni islands are dominated by lava. The composition of the rocks erupted on these islands has not changed substantially since AD 46 and is a dacite, with phenocrysts of pale plagioclase and minor green olivine.

The boat from Thera passes the lava flows

of the AD 1925-6 eruption before docking in a small cove between two lobes of these lavas. Here the AD 1570 lavas and ashes are exposed. These are more strongly weathered than the recent flows and hence provide a better landing point. From here a path follows a line of ash cones produced from AD 1570 to 1950. The line is approximately north-east/south-west, and is probably the expression of a deep fault that taps the magma chamber 2-4 km below. About halfway up we see the lavas of the AD 1940-1 eruptions.[101] In general the amount of vegetation is related to the age of the lava flow or ash.

At the summit (148 m) there are many intersecting cones and craters. The youngest was formed in 1950 and is about 100 m south-east of the triangulation point. The eruption which formed this crater started on 10 January 1950 with an explosion. The frequency of the explosions reached a maximum on 17 January and then decreased until 2 February, when the eruption ceased.[102] Eruption of lava started around 17 January and produced a small dome, about 10 m thick and 40 m in diameter. This eruption was much less important than the eruption of 1939-41.

There are many fumaroles in the walls of the craters near the summit, and their activity changes from year to year. These are vents where gases, largely water vapour, escape from the earth. These gases alter the surrounding rocks to produce clays, silica and red iron oxides. Small amounts of hydrogen sulphide in the gases are oxidised by the air to sulphur which crystallises as yellow needles around the vents. These gases originated as seawater from the bay which seeped into the rocks at the base of the islands and was warmed by heat from the magma chamber below. This hot water then rose up below the island, all the time interacting with rocks on the walls of the cracks and dissolving sulphur, iron and other elements. Therefore, although the water in the fumaroles comes from the sea, the heat and the sulphur come from the volcanic rocks.

Much of the water that circulates at depth does not emerge in the fumaroles, but as hot springs in the bays around the islands. Iron dissolved in these waters is precipitated as they interact with the cool seawater. The fine particles of iron hydroxide colour the waters brown and green, and form a brown deposit on the surrounding rocks and the floors of the bays. One such spring is on Palaea Kameni, beneath the chapel of Ayios Nikolaos.[272]

Ancient Akrotiri

South-east of the modern village of Akrotiri lies a Bronze Age town buried by the Minoan eruption (Figs. 15.11, 15.16). The remains were discovered after ancient walls were exposed in a gully cut into the Minoan tuff deposits. The town (now also known as Akrotiri) will be described below, but what of the geological environment at the time of the eruption? To the west of the town lay low hills of much older dacite lavas and andesite ash cones, such as at

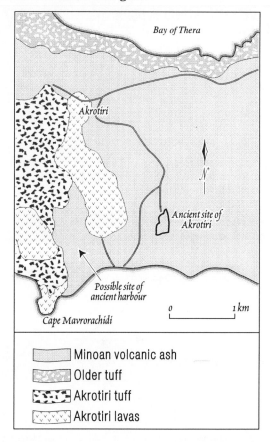

Fig. 15.16. Ancient and modern Akrotiri (after 218).

Cape Mavrorachidi.[218] These rocks were partly covered by tuff from eruptions 100,000, 35,000, and 13,000 years ago. Weathered tuff from the last eruption formed an ancient soil on which the town was constructed.[225] There may have been a harbour to the west, beneath the hills (Fig. 15.16).

And now for the human situation, as revealed by the recent excavations. The community at Akrotiri inhabited a prosperous city with cobbled streets and small squares. The houses, of stone and clay with timber reinforcements, had up to four storeys; staircases were usually of stone, doors and windows of wood. The best houses were decorated with lively frescoes on the walls, many like those of the Minoan palaces, but often with a strong local flavour. There were domestic toilets connected with sewers which ran beneath the streets.

Walls in the ancient town were commonly constructed of black to brown tuff, with occasional glassy lenses, derived from eruptions about 35,000 years ago.[73] A lava with the same composition (which can be distinguished from the tuff by the presence of gas bubbles) is harder and was used for cornerstones, stairs, etc. Harder blocks were carved into vases. Another construction material was a fine-grained white to greenish rock, formed from one-million-year-old andesitic tuffs by the action of hot water. The colour is due to clays and quartz. This rock is exposed about 100 m west of the site.

The Minoan eruption was probably preceded by a major earthquake that severely damaged the town. The inhabitants had started to clear the debris and begin reconstruction when the main eruption occurred. The lack of human skeletons and valuables suggests that the inhabitants had warning of the eruption, either by a minor precursor eruption, represented here by a 1 to 4 cm thick layer of fine-grained, light grey to orange ash (Fig. 15.13), or by a continuous shaking of the ground, called harmonic tremor, which commonly precedes major eruptions.

The first phase of the main eruption produced a rain of white pumice blocks about one metre thick. Subsequent phases produced bedded and massive ash deposits, each also about one metre thick. The eruption finished with an ignimbrite. All these layers can be seen in the Akrotiri region but each section is not neces-

sarily complete.[225] Since 1600 BC the only geological process in the area has been erosion, which has occurred very rapidly in these soft volcanic sediments.

Ancient Thera

The acropolis of the city of Ancient Thera was built on a fault-bounded block of the non-volcanic roots of the island which towers 300 m above the surrounding plains (Fig. 15.11). The saddle and valleys to the west are underlain by metamorphosed sandstones and conglomerates, which are softer than the grey crystalline limestones under the city and hence have been eroded away. Mt Profitis Elias (565 m), to the west, is made of similar, resistant grey limestone.

The Colombo Bank volcano

There is a recently active volcano 10 km northeast of Thera, the Colombo Bank volcano, but it is little known as it lies underwater (Fig. 15.11). This small volcano rises up from the sea-floor at a depth of 280 m to a height of about 20 m below sea-level.[88] It started to erupt on 29 September AD 1650 and continued for three months. Calm extrusion of lava, punctuated by periodic explosions, built a island several metres above sea-level. The volcano also emitted large quantities of sulphur dioxide gas, which killed many people and animals on Thera. The eruption was also accompanied by a tsunami. After the end of the eruption the volcano was rapidly eroded to below sea-level.

16

Crete

Crete is the largest of the Greek islands. It is dominated by a mountainous spine comprising the White Mountains (Lefka Ori) in the west, Ida (Psiloritis) in the centre, Dikte in the east, and the Sitea Range in the far east. On much of the north side of the island the mountains slope gently down to the sea, whereas the south coast is steeply precipitous, except for the Mesara valley. In the mountains are a number of upland plains.

In antiquity the climate may have been slightly wetter than it is now, as Crete was one of the granaries of the Roman Empire. Today the principal crops are the olive and the vine, with (in suitable places) citrus and other fruits. Plastic greenhouses are especially common. Similarly, the mountain slopes were once rich with timber; but now they are clothed in scrub (phrygana, maquis). However, a recent reduction in subsistence agriculture, and hence in grazing, has started to change the vegetation once again: trees and other wild plants have increased, together with the risk of fires.[228] In fact, since the original fauna is extinct, Crete may now be less grazed than it has been for millions of years.

Effectively blocking the southern end of the Aegean, Crete has always looked east to Asia Minor and south to Libya and Egypt (Plate 16A). From its proximity to these more advanced cultures, around 6000 BC, it became the home of the earliest European civilisation. The first settlers were farmers and stock-breeders from western Turkey. They lived in well-built houses and used tools and weapons of polished stone; soon they were making pottery. About 3000 BC the Bronze Age was brought to Crete by new settlers from the same region. Bronze now replaced stone for tools and weapons, and

there were other major advances. This brilliant civilisation, which lasted till about 1100 BC, was named Minoan by Arthur Evans, the excavator of Knossos, after the legendary King Minos. At about 2000 BC, palaces were built at Knossos and other centres. They were destroyed by an earthquake or a series of earthquakes around 1700 BC and replaced by grander palaces, whose ruins we see today at Knossos, Phaistos, Mallia, Zakros and Chania (Kydonia). This is the period to which we should ascribe the later Greek legends associated with Knossos. Around 1450 BC all these palaces, except Knossos, were destroyed by fire, and it is generally believed that Knossos was captured by invaders from Mycenae, who ruled all Crete from there, having destroyed the other palaces to stifle any resistance. The palace of Knossos was itself destroyed by fire some time later, but the Minoan civilisation continued at a lower level until 1100 BC, to be followed by a Dark Age. There was a revival about 900 BC, which did not last. From 500 BC and throughout the Roman and Byzantine periods Crete was a political and cultural backwater. The last period of comparative greatness was when it was occupied by the Venetians between AD 1204 and 1669. Many of the sites included here are illustrated, together with brief geomorphological descriptions, in *The Aerial Atlas of Ancient Crete*.[187]

Crete is part of the Hellenic arc, a series of islands and shallow waters which stretches from the Peloponnese to Turkey. This arc formed in response to the subduction of the African plate beneath the Aegean (see below). Thus the channel to the west of Crete is only 600 m deep and that to the east scarcely deeper at 1,000 m. To the north of Crete, beneath the

Cretan sea, the sea-floor slopes gently down into a broad basin with depths up to 2,200 m. This basin is a young feature, formed by back-arc spreading as the subduction zone rolled back towards the south. However, it is not floored by true deep ocean crust, as is found, for example, behind the Japanese islands, but by thin continental crust. North of the basin lie the Cyclades, including the volcanic islands of Thera and Milos. South of Crete the sea-floor descends steeply, over a distance of 5-10 km, along a series of east-west normal faults, into water mostly more than 2,000 m deep. The north-south asymmetry of the topography of the sea-floor mirrors that of the intervening land (see below). Further south is a series of three deep trenches that mark the location of strike-slip faults. Further south still lies the broad Mediterranean Ridge, which is a compressive feature formed in front of the subduction zone. Finally we reach Africa, 300 km south of Crete.

The basement of Crete consists of a stack of nappes representing rocks from several different environments (Fig. 16.1). They were originally distributed over a horizontal distance of several hundred kilometres, but were stacked into a pile about 6 km thick during the Alpine compression.[141] The 'Plattenkalk' series of rocks, probably part of the Ionian zone, is the lowest unit and may be in, or close to, its original location. It comprises limestones and dolomites, with minor phyllites, and is of Triassic to Oligocene age. The characteristic rock is Plattenkalk, a platy limestone with abundant layers and nodules of chert, which formed in the deep waters of an open ocean. The overlying nappe, the 'Phyllite', is dominated by phyllites and quartzites, with minor limestones, marbles and other rocks and is of Permian to Triassic age. These rocks formed near a continent in shallow water. The nappe was broken up during emplacement so that it is now a melange, or chaotic mixture of blocks ranging in size from centimetres to hundreds of metres, set in fine-grained sediments or phyllites. Towards the base of the nappe temperatures were sufficient for metamorphism to produce marbles. The next nappe, the Tripolitza, comprises Jurassic to Eocene shal-low-water limestones, overlain by flysch sediments. It is part of the Gavrovo zone. These rocks remained as a rigid block during deformation. The next nappe, the Pindos, is comprised of similar rocks, except that the limestones formed in deep waters. The uppermost nappe is dominated by ophiolite-suite rocks and represents one or several disrupted sections of ocean floor and their overlying sediments thrust up onto the continental crust.

The rocks of these nappes were originally deposited to the north of Crete. Compressional movements started in the Late Jurassic with the emplacement of the uppermost nappes. The pile migrated to the south as it acquired the lower nappes, finally reaching Crete during the Oligocene.[26]

The fragmentation of Crete into fault-bounded blocks started during the Miocene, about 12 million years ago, when roll-back of the subduction zone towards the south commenced (see Chapter 2). This led to a broad zone of extension behind the arc, where the crust was stretched by up to a factor of two.[176] This extension produced a series of grabens and horsts which give the island its rugged topography.

Most of the grabens occur in the northern part of the island, forming the lowlands south of the principal cities of Crete. It is only in central and eastern Crete that the grabens extend through to the south coast. The rest of this shore is bordered by the horsts, which plunge steeply into the sea. At this time the horsts were islands and the grabens were shallow seas where sedimentary rocks, such as conglomerates, impure sandstones, shales and marly limestones, accumulated. By the Mid-Pliocene most of Crete was lifted up and became dry land.

During much of the Pleistocene sea-levels were much lower than at present (see below) and wide beaches were exposed. Winds passing over these beaches picked up shell fragments and transported them inland to produce dunes of calcareous sand.[196,282] Percolating water then cemented the sand with calcite into a porous, soft, eolian, calcareous sandstone locally called ammoudha. This rock was extensively used for construction as it is easily cut, though not

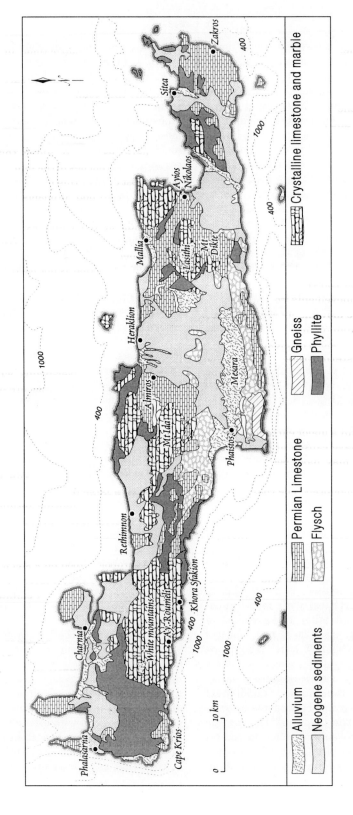

Fig. 16.1. Crete.

Alluvium

Neogene sediments

Permian Limestone

Flysch

Gneiss

Phyllite

Crystalline limestone and marble

always very durable.

To turn to the Pleistocene fauna, the island was inhabited by deer, elephant and dwarf hippopotamus. These animals may have been exterminated by the earliest human inhabitants of the island and replaced with domestic grazing animals.

Crete, like the rest of the Aegean region, shows much evidence of earlier sea-levels different from the present level.[222, 223] This variation records movements of the height of the land with respect to the sea. In many areas and on short time scales such movements are dominated by tectonic forces. The shoreline of the western part of Crete records one of the most important of these sea-level changes.[222] There, a block about 200 km long subsided in a series of about ten movements from about 2000 BC to AD 200. These movements were reversed by a major, rapid uplift of up to 10 m sometime between AD 430 and 580. The maximum uplift was in south-western Crete around Cape Krios. It has been suggested that similar uplifts as far away as Israel were part of the same event. It is interesting to note that there are no historical records of this event in the area of maximum uplift, but a major earthquake in AD 551 is known to have caused drastic damage further east, and may have been associated with the uplift. Elsewhere in Crete movements have been less pronounced. The coasts of central and eastern Crete appear to have subsided by 1-2 m since antiquity, except on the southeast coast where sea-level has not changed significantly.[223]

The relationship between the huge Late Bronze Age eruption of Thera and the widespread and roughly contemporary destruction of the palaces on Crete has been hotly debated. Volcanic ash, presumably from the Minoan eruption on Thera, has been found on Crete, but not in well-defined layers.[278] Hence it is impossible to correlate these ash falls with archaeological data. Archaeomagnetic dating of mud walls fired during the burning of the Minoan palaces and of the volcanic ash of the 'Minoan' eruption on Santorini suggests that this destruction was synchronous with the eruption,[67] but evidence from pottery suggests that there was a significant time difference.

However, these destructions may not have been directly related to the volcanic effects of the eruption, but only to the earthquakes and tsunamis that commonly precede and accompany major eruptions.

The proximity of a plate margin to the south means that earthquakes are relatively common here, especially along the strike-slip faults in the trenches to the south of Crete. One of the most devastating historical earthquakes occurred in AD 365, probably to the south of Crete. The ensuing tsunami caused the loss of thousands of lives and extensive damage throughout the eastern Mediterranean.[201]

Weathering of the limestones produces a thin terra rossa that is not particularly fertile, and has commonly been eroded from the steep slopes of the hills. In contrast the Neogene sediments, particularly the marls, produce a brown fertile soil (rendzina) that was also favoured elsewhere in Greece during the Bronze Age. This soil was particularly important in this region as the river-plains, which are normally the most fertile areas, are not extensive on Crete.

Phalasarna

The ancient port of Phalasarna was constructed at the base of the Gramvousa peninsula, a large block of Jurassic limestone (Fig. 16.1). The peninsula terminates to the south in a series of low hills, mostly composed of Miocene limestone and marl, part of an ancient graben.

The acropolis stood on a steep-sided hill of Jurassic massive grey limestone, which is a fault-bounded block of rock similar to that of the peninsula to the north (Fig. 16.2). The hills immediately to the east are a complex mixture of limestone, marble and schist. A narrow strip along the coast is covered by Pleistocene 'fossil' sand dunes. This sandstone, locally called ammoudha, was used extensively for the construction of the ancient town and harbour as it was much more easily cut than the grey limestone. The ancient quarries can be seen to the south-west and south-east of the ancient port (Plate 16B).

This area was uplifted in the fifth or sixth

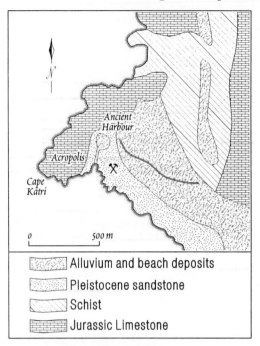

Fig. 16.2. Phalasarna.

century AD by about 7 m, possibly during a single earthquake (see above). Evidence for this uplift can be seen in the harbour, which is now dry and far above sea-level; in the floor of the ancient quarries to the south of the town, which must have originally been close to sea-level; and in well-developed notches in the cliffs and raised wave-cut platforms around Cape Katri. Another old sea-level stand can be seen at an altitude of about 15 m.

The White Mountains and Samaria Gorge

The White Mountains are a horst, dominated by limestones (Fig. 16.1). The lowest rocks are a series of Jurassic-Eocene platy limestones of the 'Plattenkalk' series which are exposed in the centre of the mountains, on either side of the Samaria Gorge. Triassic-Jurassic limestones have been thrust over the top of these rocks, and are exposed in the east and west.

A number of gorges cut through the White Mountains to the Libyan sea, the most famous

of which is Samaria Gorge (Fig. 16.3). The commonly held view is that these gorges originated as faults which were enlarged by flowing water. There is, however, no evidence of major faulting in the Samaria Gorge and it is more likely that the gorges are related to the rapid uplift of the White Mountains. Small streams, formed at an early stage, would have cut deeply into the mountains as they rose up, to keep pace with the uplift. There is abundant evidence in the area for this rapid uplift, such as raised sea-level stands and dissected river gravels (see below).

The Samaria Gorge trail starts at a saddle above the Omalos Plain, a polje or small basin draining internally into sinkholes. Such basins may provide much of the water for karst springs in the valleys below. The saddle is made of Jurassic-Eocene (?) platy limestones, which are relatively resistant to erosion. The trail descends the rear wall of a steep amphitheatre which has been excavated out of Permian-Triassic (?) phyllites, with minor limestones and sandstones which are generally softer than the limestones to the north.

Just above the chapel of Ayios Nikolaos a spring-fed stream joins the valley from the left. These waters are depositing yellow travertine which has sealed the bed against infiltration. Calcite is also being deposited on leaves in the stream, starting the process of fossilisation. Further down the stream disappears at the point where all the travertine has been deposited and hence the bed is not sealed against infiltration.

The bed of the valley near the former village of Samaria is filled with river gravels cemented together to give a conglomerate similar in appearance to concrete. These rocks were transported by the river and cemented by minerals precipitated from groundwater as it rose up and evaporated below the surface during a period of greater rainfall. They have been dissected by the present river, showing that there has been recent uplift of the area.

Just below Samaria the trail re-enters the 'Plattenkalk' cherty limestones first encountered in the saddle at the trailhead. This rock is resistant to erosion, which accounts for the change from the wide valley above Samaria to

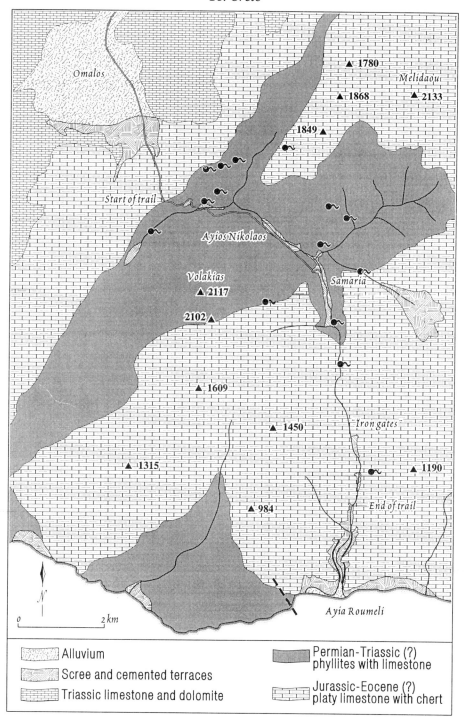

Fig. 16.3. Samaria Gorge.

the steep-sided main gorge below. These limestones contain abundant chert and have been
slightly metamorphosed and complexly folded.
If the valley follows a fault, then it is here that
we would expect to see the evidence, in the
form of closely-spaced joints parallel to the
valley. But these are not present, and hence it
is not likely that there is a fault here.

The coast from Ayia Roumeli eastwards to
Khora Sfakion shows much evidence for recent
uplift, with well-developed sea-level stands at
about 5, 10, 20 and 40 m. The highest is at a
break in the slope above a series of cliffs. The
stand at 5 m is related to the major uplift event
in the fifth-sixth centuries AD which raised up
the harbour of Phalasarna (Plate 1A).

Chania

Modern Chania occupies the site of ancient
Kydonia (Fig. 16.1). There was a strong Minoan presence here from 4000 BC until 1100 BC
and there may have been a palace, probably
where the Venetian Kastelli now stands. Under the Venetians, as La Canea, it regained
something of its earlier importance and between 1898 and 1971 it was the capital of
Crete.

Chania lies in a small, asymmetrical graben
between the White Mountains to the south and
the hills of the peninsula of Akrotiri to the
north-east. Both these uplands are dominated
by Triassic-Cretaceous limestones. The graben
itself is lined with Miocene marls and limestones, commonly covered with a thin veneer of
Quaternary terra rossa soils. The city itself is
constructed on Miocene marls and Pleistocene
alluvial deposits. To the west of Chania lies
Souda bay, which is a small graben.

The Spring of Almiros

An important spring at Almiros, 8 km west of
Heraklion, has been known since Minoan
times (Fig. 16.1). It is the largest spring in
Crete (4,000-30,000 litres per second) and
feeds a river for its 5 km passage to the sea.[177]
A peculiarity of this spring is its variation in
salinity with discharge: at times of maximum
flow it is almost fresh, but when the discharge

is reduced its salt content can approach half
that of seawater.

The spring discharges from the base of a
hill, along the trace of the western fault of the
Heraklion graben. The water comes from two
sources: rainwater and seawater. This volume
of freshwater requires a catchment area of at
least 300 square km, in the limestone hills to
the west and south-west. This enormous mass
of limestone extends offshore to the north and
is riddled with caves and fissures. Seawater
drains into the limestone through fissures in
the sea-floor.

The driving force for the circulation of the
rainwater is clear: water descends under gravity from the mountains until its passage is
blocked by the high water-table of the Neogene
graben sediments and it appears from the
ground as a spring. For the seawater the case
is a little more complex: seawater is more
dense that freshwater, hence if two columns of
water are at the same pressure at a depth of
several hundred metres and are interconnected, the seawater column would be several
metres lower than the column of freshwater. If
the freshwater column has an outlet below this
height, then the seawater will flow 'uphill' to
dilute the fresh water and issue from the
spring. A similar effect occurs on the island of
Kephallinia.

Knossos

Knossos is situated 5 km south of Heraklion, on
the Kairatos stream (Figs. 16.1, 16.4). The palace is the largest and most famous of the
Minoan palaces. Minos was, according to legend, the King of Knossos. It was his Queen who
gave birth to the monstrous Minotaur, killed
by Theseus with the aid of the Princess
Ariadne. Minos' architect, Daedalus, having
incurred his master's displeasure, flew out of
Knossos with his son Icarus on home-made
wings.

About 6000 BC Neolithic settlers arrived
from western Turkey and founded what was
arguably the oldest town in Europe. Three
thousand years later another wave of Asiatic
immigrants introduced a Bronze Age civilisation now called Minoan. The first palace was

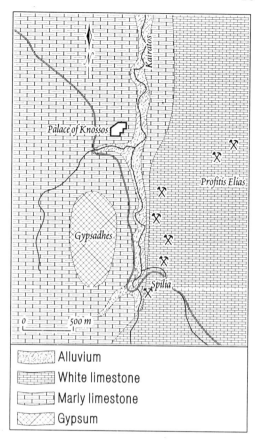

Fig. 16.4. Knossos (after 195, 234). Cretaceous lime-stone is exposed on the northern slopes of Profitis Elias, just off the north-east corner of the map.

Legend:
- Alluvium
- White limestone
- Marly limestone
- Gypsum

---

built in about 2000 BC on the ruins of the older settlements and Knossos became a sort of royal capital. When this palace was destroyed by an earthquake in 1700 BC, a new and even more magnificent one arose on its ruins, the remains of which we see today. This is the setting for the legend. It was known as the Labyrinth ('The House of the Double-axe'), a name that came to mean a maze. About 1450 BC Knossos was apparently captured by Mycenaean Greeks from the mainland who ruled all Crete from here. Some time later, perhaps about 1300 BC, their palace was burned down and was never rebuilt.

The site of Knossos lies in the fertile low-lands of a small stream, the Kairatos, within the broad Heraklion graben (Fig. 16.1). The valley of the Kairatos is itself a half-graben within the larger graben. The eastern side, which follows the course of the Kairatos, is a fault and the land to the west has hinged downwards like a trap-door. The Kairatos rises from springs near Arkhanes to the south and was probably perennial in antiquity. The proximity of this river, together with local springs and a high water-table, make this area well-watered by the rather dry Cretan standards.

A grey to dark grey Cretaceous limestone crops out to the north-east of Knosssos, on the northern slopes of Mt Profitis Elias (250 m). This rock is strong, as it has few holes, and a similar rock was used extensively by the Minoan masons elsewhere. However, at Knossos it was less important for construction than other rocks.[195, 234]

The rest of the region around Knossos is underlain by Neogene sedimentary rocks. To the west of the Kairatos they comprise soft marly limestones locally known as 'kousk-ouras'. Most of Mt Profitis Elias is underlain by white, sometimes shelly limestones, locally known as 'poros'. These rocks were quarried extensively from pits and underground workings for the construction of the palace. Such workings can still be seen in the Spilia area to the south of Knossos, where they are now·used as storehouses.[195] As at many other Minoan sites, eolian sandstone was also used, but its source is unclear.

The hill of Gypsadhes to the south of Knossos is partly made up of gypsum, which formed when the Mediterranean dried up about 6 million years ago. Bands in the rock formed during deposition and were folded later by tectonic forces. The presence of calcite or dolomite impurities in some samples increases their strength and resistance to erosion. Gypsum was used extensively in the construction of the palace, but only where it was not exposed to the rain, as it is soluble in water. The finer-grained varieties of gypsum were used for facing stones and for some floor slabs, whereas the coarse-grained varieties were used in some columns. Gypsum blocks uncovered by the excavators and left open to the weather have lost over one centimetre of material in 30 years. The ancient gypsum quarries on Gypsadhes were visible at the time of the excavations, but have now been refilled. Gypsum from these quarries, or possibly other Cretan quarries, was also used at Akrotiri in Thera.[98] The clay used by the Minoans of Knossos probably came from the Kairatos valley, 2 km south of the palace.[130]

Mt Ida

Mt Ida (or Psiloritis, 'the high one') is the highest mountain in Crete at 2,456 m (Fig. 16.1). High up are two large caves which were used in antiquity for religious purposes. The Idaean cave on the east side at 1,540 m was sacred in Minoan times and later became the most famous of all the Cretan caves (Fig. 16.5). Zeus was believed to have been brought up here, having been removed from the Dictaean cave (see Psykhro cave below) as a baby to

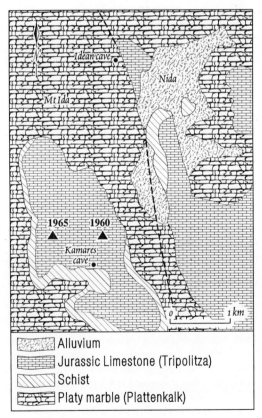

Fig. 16.5. Mt Ida and the Kamares and Idaean caves.

ensure his safety. Worship seems to have been continuous from the fifteenth to the sixth centuries BC. The cave consists of an enormous grotto 30 m wide and 10 m high, with a smaller grotto leading out of it.[82] The Kamares cave is on the south slope of Ida at 1,524 m (Fig. 16.5). It was a sacred place for the rulers of Phaistos, who could see its enormous mouth from the palace. It was in use from 2000 to 1700 BC, and was then deserted. Possibly the entrance was blocked by the earthquake which destroyed the palace. The offerings recovered were mostly the beautiful polychrome pottery of the first palace, the so-called Kamares ware.

Mt Ida is a horst bounded to the south by the Mesara graben and to the east by the Heraklion graben (Fig. 16.1). The block has been tilted as the highest land is in the south and it slopes gently towards the north. The mountain is largely composed of limestone from two different nappes. The western parts, including the summit, are dominated by Plattenkalk marble-limestone (Jurassic-Eocene). To the east Tripolitza limestones (Jurassic-Eocene) have been thrust over the Plattenkalk.

This mountain is the only part of the Aegean islands with sufficient relief to have been glaciated.[81] Features typical of valley glaciers, such as sharp mountain peaks, cirques and U-shaped valleys, can be seen on at elevations above 2,200 metres. The glaciation happened during the coldest part of the last glacial interval, about 20,000 years ago.

The road to the Idaean cave passes across the plain of Nida, a polje with an altitude of about 1,400 m (Fig. 16.5).[81] The cave itself is 140 m above the plain, close to a thrust fault that separates the overlying Jurassic Tripolitza limestones from the underlying Plattenkalk marble. The normal fault that defines the western edge of the polje also passes close to the cave. Groundwater circulating along these faults, or adjacent parallel joints, dissolved the limestone and enlarged the passages to produce the cave.

The Kamares cave, although only 4 km south of the Idaean cave, is situated on the southern face of the mountain (Fig. 16.5). The geological environment is similar to that of the Idaean cave; the same thrust fault separates outliers of Tripolitza limestone from the under-lying Plattenkalk schist and marble. Similarly, this fault has been enlarged to form the cave.

The Mesara plain, Phaistos and Ayia Triada

The Mesara Plain is a long strip running east from the Gulf of Mesara, between Mt Ida, to the north, and the Asterousia Mountains to the south (Fig. 16.1). Watered by the Geropotamos river, it is probably the most fertile area in Crete: olives, fruit and vegetables are grown.

Thanks to its rich soil, this plain was settled very early, possibly about 4000 BC, and these earliest settlers have left once-rich communal tombs for us to see. When, about 2000 BC, the first palace was built at Phaistos, this became the capital of the Mesara. Although less celebrated in legend, this palace was quite as grand as that at Knossos. Destroyed by an earthquake about 1700 BC, it was rebuilt on an even grander scale. Destroyed again about 1450 BC, this is the palace which we see today, slightly restored by the excavators.

Associated in some way with the second palace was the royal villa at Ayia Triada, 3 km to the west. Later, Gortyn became the principal city of the Mesara, and in 68 BC the Romans made it the capital of their new province of Crete and Cyrene.

The Mesara plain is a graben, the only major one on Crete that runs east-west, and the only one that breaches the south coast (Fig. 16.1). It is floored by with low hills of Miocene to Pleistocene sedimentary rocks mostly deposited by the rivers that drain the mountain horsts to the north and south. Periodically, sea-level changes or subsidence have caused inundations by the sea. One such inundation occurred at the end of the Miocene when the Mediterranean was below present sea-level and largely a desert. Evaporation of the sea-water produced thin deposits of gypsum.

The ancient site of Gortyn is situated on the northern edge of the graben, close to the fault. The acropolis hill, and Mt Profitis Elias to the east, are made of Cretaceous-Oligocene sandstone-flysch, partly covered by Pleistocene conglomerate. The hills to the north and west, beneath Mt Ida, are underlain by Miocene marls and other sediments, including gypsum.

The Cave of Gortyn (or Labyrinth), about 3 km west of the site, is a Minoan gypsum mine, possibly enlarged from a natural cave. About 2.5 km of tunnels, mostly 2.5-4 metres high, were excavated, and many of the surfaces were sculpted with columns, seats and altars.[58] The underground source ensured a supply of unaltered gypsum. The gypsum here is well

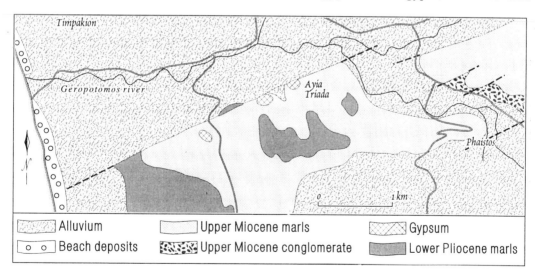

Fig. 16.6. Phaistos and Ayia Triada. The ancient port near Kommos lay 2 km to the south of the map edge.

laminated, fine-grained and contains calcite, making it much harder than pure gypsum rock. The cave is now sealed off to visitors.

Both Phaistos and Ayia Triada were constructed on opposite ends of a low hill of Late Miocene and Pliocene marls and limestones, originally deposited on the floor of the graben and subsequently uplifted and eroded (Fig. 16.6). Gypsum occurs as layers and conglomerates within the marls. That used in the palace was extracted from quarries south-west of Phaistos and near Ayia Triada. Some of this material may have been exported to Mycenae.[98]

The steep slopes south of Phaistos and north of Ayia Triada are fault scarps, formed by recent movements of east-west faults parallel to the sides of the graben. The faults partly accommodate the continuing subsidence of the graben. The Geropotamos river cuts diagonally across this fault block and has produced the steep slopes to the north of Phaistos.

Part of the site is covered with caliche. This layer is hard and not very permeable, so that groundwater is conserved underneath it. Wells still visible on the site have been cut through the caliche to tap the underlying groundwater.

Although the ancient geography of the Geropotamos valley has not been investigated, the sea probably reached the fault-scarp that runs just to the north of Ayia Triada at some time since the last glaciation. However, this was almost certainly before human occupation of this region.

The Minoan site of Kommos, a few kilometres south of the mouth of the Geropotamos river, was the port of Phaistos and Ayia Triada. It was built on a low ridge of Neogene marls, protected from erosion by a layer of fossiliferous limestone. At first glance the exposed site, beside a sandy beach, seems totally unsuitable for a harbour, but in antiquity the geography was a little different.[183] Submerged notches indicate that in antiquity sea-level was 3-4 metres lower than at present. The coast lay 80 m to the west and a small reef, now 300 m offshore, was an islet 130 m long. The protection from the prevailing winds that this reef afforded the harbour may have been augmented by a sand-spit. By Roman times the

land had sunk, so that the sea was only 1.2 m below its present level, with a corresponding retreat of the coast and shrinking of the islet.

Skoteino cave

One of the most impressive caves in Crete is located near Gouves, between Mallia and Heraklion. The Cave of Skoteino descends from a small hollow in a low plateau south of the main highway (Fig. 16.1). The bedrock here is Cretaceous grey limestones of the Tripolitza zone. The striking location of the cave, on a almost flat surface, shows that it started as a doline on the plain and subsequently developed into a sink-hole. The main chamber of the cave is large and extends for at least 160 m downwards at four different levels. The cave was one of the most important sanctuaries in Crete and huge quantities of broken pottery can still be seen there.

Mallia

The palace of Mallia lies on alluvium close to the coast beneath the Late Triassic to Cretaceous limestone of the Dikte Mountains (Figs. 16.1, 16.7). Along the coast to the north a low ridge of Cretaceous limestones underlies the necropolis of Khrysolakkos, and forms the sea-cliffs. Pleistocene fossil sand-dunes (ammoudha) cover parts of this ridge, as well as the coast to the west.

The palace was largely built of ammoudha from the fossil dunes. The quarries lay beside the beach, to the west of the palace for about 2.5 km.[282] One of the larger quarries was at Mill Point, 800 m north-west of the palace.

Mallia today lies on an open bay, without protection for small vessels, but in antiquity the geography may have been a little different. The floors of some of the ammoudha quarries are submerged about one metre indicating a rise in sea-level. In addition, it is possible that the swampy area 500 m north-west of the palace was once a harbour, now filled in by alluvium.[187]

The hard limestones of Khrysolakkos initially seem to be a poor choice for a necropolis. However, these rocks have prominent vertical

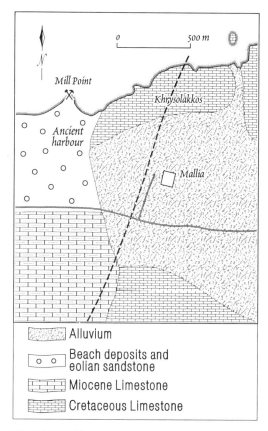

Fig. 16.7. Mallia.

joints that have been deeply weathered. Communal burials were made in these natural trenches during Minoan times.[187]

Mt Dikte

Mt Dikte, like the other major mountain ranges of Crete, is comprised of a lower series of Plattenkalk limestones, over which has been thrust a series of Jurassic-Eocene Tripolitza limestones (Fig. 16.1). The detailed structure of the mountains is very complex as they are much faulted.

The Lasithi plain

Lasithi is a polje, or internally draining plain with an altitude of about 850 m, within the northern slopes of Mt Dikte (Fig. 16.1). The plain is extremely productive thanks to the fertility of the soils and the shallowness of the water-table.

The plain is a small graben produced during the Neogene extension of the island. The surrounding hills are made of a lower nappe of schist, phyllite and quartz, over which have been thrust Triassic-Jurassic limestones and dolomites.

Sediments washed down from the surrounding mountains accumulated in a shallow, seasonal lake that formerly occupied this valley. The lake was drained by a large swallow-hole near the western end. Accumulation of the sediments eventually filled in the lake to a level above that of the swallow-hole, but springtime flooding was a problem until the construction of drainage ditches in the seventeenth century. The sink-hole is readily visible beneath the hill of Kato Metokhi, but its entrance is choked with large boulders. Without doubt there is an extensive cave system beneath here.

Psykhro cave

The Psykhro cave, overlooking the Lasithi plain, was possibly the famous Dictaean cave of Classical times where, according to legend, Zeus was born. It seems to have come into use about 1700 BC, when the Kamares cave was deserted, and to have continued without a break down to the sixth century BC, with a brief revival in the Roman period. It was re-discovered in 1883. It is composed of an upper and a lower grotto. In the latter were found some 500 offerings in gold, bronze and other materials, many of them wedged in crevices in the stalactites which fill the grotto.

The cave opens from a broad arch half-way up the hillside south of the village of Psykhro and follows close to the thrust fault that divides the underlying phyllites and the overlying limestones. The cave originated when groundwater, descending in the limestone, encountered the less permeable phyllites and was channelled horizontally towards the surface. This flow slowly dissolved the limestone and excavated the cave. It was aided by periodic collapses of the roof.

The cave descends steeply to pools about 65 m below the entrance. The cave is richly decorated with stalagmites and stalactites, but many of these were formed in an earlier, wetter period, perhaps before the ice age, and little new material is now forming. Activity was probably much greater in antiquity as many cult objects were found encased in stalagmites.

Ayios Nikolaos

The town of Ayios Nikolaos is largely built on late Triassic to Late Jurassic limestones and dolomites (Fig. 16.1). These rocks were overlain by marls in Pliocene times and subsequently faulted. The 'bottomless' Lake Voulismeni is funnel-shaped and descends to a depth of 64 m. It is an ancient sink-hole formed in the limestone when sea-level was much lower than at present, during either the Late Miocene or glacial periods. It developed by the action of groundwater descending a fault that bounds a block of Pliocene marls to the south of the lake.

An important brackish spring, named Almyros, flows about 1 km south of Ayios Nikolaos.[178] The water of this spring comes from both the rain and the sea, which are mixed in caves beneath the peninsula, similar to the Spring of Almiros near Heraklion.

Rods of Digenis quarry

There are few exploitable deposits of good quality marble on Crete. The only ancient marble quarry found so far lies 3 km north of the village of Chamezi and 7 km west of Sitea.[71] The quarry is known as the Rods of Digenis, from the presence of several unfinished columns at the site. The outcrop is rather small, a lens-shaped mass 60 by 30 m, and the marble varies from a breccia at the margins through a red-veined variety to pure white at the centre. The host rock is a green to reddish phyllite, of the Phyllite nappe. The quarry was exploited in Greek, rather than Roman times, for blocks and columns of both white and red-veined marble, but their destination is unknown.

Zakros

The palace known today as Zakros (in antiquity Dikta or Dikte) lies at the eastern end of Crete in a harsh and barren landscape, whose only redeeming feature is an excellent harbour, Kato Zakros (Fig. 16.1). Above the palace is the substantial village of Ano or Eparo (Upper) Zakro, where there are good springs, possibly piped to the palace in antiquity. The two villages are joined by a deep and picturesque 'Gorge of the Dead', named after the Minoan burial caves in the cliffs.

The site was probably settled about 3000 BC. A palace was built about 2000 BC; like other Cretan palaces it was destroyed by an earthquake about 1700 BC and replaced by a grander version. The excellent harbour and its proximity to Egypt and Western Asia brought great prosperity. This palace in its turn, was burnt down in about 1450 BC and never reoccupied.

The village of Ano Zakro, 5 km east of the palace at Kato Zakro, is set in a north/south valley, probably a graben formed by the east/west extension that has affected most of Crete. It is floored by Miocene conglomerates and other sediments. To the east the range of hills parallel to the coast is dominated by Triassic-Eocene dark limestones, which pass up into Eocene flysch sediments (sandstone, conglomerate, marl and shale). A syncline near the palace has brought the flysch sediments down to sea-level, where they have been partly eroded by the sea to form the bay (Fig. 16.8).

The sinuous form of the Gorge of the Dead was formed as follows: initially a stream meandered across an almost flat plain and rapid uplift of this area caused the stream to cut downwards, rather than sideways, incising the meanders into the block of rock as the gorge.

The palace of Zakros was constructed at the foot of a low ridge of sandstone and marl (flysch). In front is a small, fertile alluvial plain, between the bay and the exit of the gorge. Abundant springs near the site are probably fed from waters flowing underground down the gorge. The builders of the palace used several different types of local hard and soft limestone, but the most important material was ammoudha. This Pleistocene sandstone

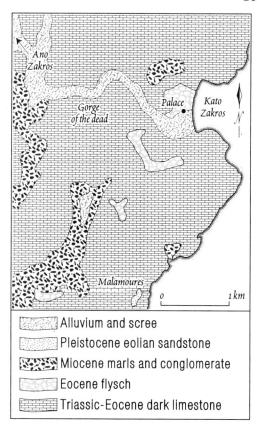

Fig. 16.8. Kato Zakros and the Minoan Palace. Ano Zakros lies about 3 km west of the edge of the map.

Alluvium and scree
Pleistocene eolian sandstone
Miocene marls and conglomerate
Eocene flysch
Triassic-Eocene dark limestone

was extracted from coastal quarries near Pelekita, 3 km to the north, and Malamoures, 2 km to the south. Another major quarry at Ta Skaria, 10 km to the north, provided building material for the Minoan town of Roussolakkos, near Palaeokastro.[196]

This region has subsided by at least 1 m, and possibly 2-3 m, since antiquity. Hence the site is now commonly waterlogged, and the ancient fields may be up to 2 m below the present surface. With the sea-level 2-3 metres lower the stream that leaves the gorge may have flowed within well-defined banks, and hence been less prone to catastrophic floods.[187]

17

Future Geological Hazards

Most of geology, like archaeology, is concerned with the interpretation of past events. There is, however, a branch of geology concerned with the prediction of geological events in the future: Geological Hazard Assessment tries to use geological information to predict the location, timing and size of future geological events that could affect people. It is essential to be precise in these predictions as they cannot otherwise be used constructively.

The term geological hazard is here taken to include both geological events whose occurrence is little influenced by human activities, such as earthquakes, and those commonly provoked by humans, such as landslides. In both cases the effects of these phenomena are strongly influenced by human activities. Earthquakes do not generally kill people directly, but they frequently cause buildings to collapse or catch fire. Some of these hazards have already been discussed briefly in earlier chapters.

Volcanic eruptions

Volcanic activity can produce many different geological hazards, including lava flows, explosions, ash falls, ash flows and lahars (mud flows). Some earthquakes and tsunamis are associated with volcanic eruptions; they will be discussed separately below.

Non-explosive eruptions of lava can cause considerable destruction of forests, fields and buildings, but they are not usually dangerous to people as most lavas move slowly. Flows of andesite, the most common lava composition in the Aegean, will typically move only a few tens of metres each day.

Explosive eruptions, however, can cause considerable destruction, especially when accompanied by hot volcanic ashes. A particularly dangerous form of ash-flow is the *nuée ardente*: clouds of hot, sometimes glowing, ash and gases roll down the sides of the volcano at speeds of up to several hundred kilometres per hour engulfing and incinerating anything in their path. They can even cross the sea.

Another dangerous type of flow is a lahar or mud-flow, which forms when ash on the sides of the volcano is combined with rainwater, lakewater or melting snow, to from a thick, commonly hot, mud. Lahars can flow rapidly down valleys, destroying anything in their path and burying the landscape where they settle. The resulting rock can be very hard and difficult to distinguish from ash-flow deposits.

An important volcanic hazard is the gas produced by eruptions: the amounts are commonly not related to the quantity of lava or ash produced. The submarine eruption of the Colombo Bank volcano (7 km north-east of Thera) in AD 1650 produced large amounts of gas which killed 50 people and 1,000 animals on Thera.

Volcanic activity in the Aegean region during the last 5,000 years is thought to have been confined to the South Hellenic volcanic arc.[258] On the Thera island group volcanism since the famous Minoan eruption 3,500 years ago has occurred in the centre of the caldera, on the islands of Nea and Palaea Kameni. There has been little loss of life as these islands have been sparsely inhabited or uninhabited. The time interval between eruptions has been decreasing for the last 2,000 years, and we can expect another within the next fifty years, although it is unlikely to be very explosive.[88] Explosions on Nisyros about 100 years ago produced a new crater, but no lava or ash was produced. However, it is believed that Nisyros has potential for major explosive activity in the future.[254]

Earthquakes

The Aegean region has the highest incidence of earthquakes (seismicity) in Europe.[266] Most of these earthquakes are ultimately connected to large-scale tectonic movements, such as the Hellenic subduction zone and the regional crustal extension. There are many ways of expressing potential earthquake risk.[36, 167, 202] The most useful, from a cultural point of view, is the maximum observed earthquake intensity (hereafter maximum intensity; Fig. 17.1), as this expresses the potential destructiveness of an earthquake in that region (see Chapter 1).[120] Unfortunately such data is only available for Greece.

The high maximum intensity of the Ionian islands and south-western Peloponnese is due to the subduction of the ocean floor (albeit thicker than normal) beneath the Aegean sea. The ocean floor must bend to go down the subduction zone, and this movement causes the earthquakes. High maximum intensities on Crete and Rhodes are also related to the same plate motions, but here the direction of movement is almost parallel to the Hellenic arc, and hence the two plates slide past each other along transform faults.

Most of the other zones of high maximum intensity are related to crustal extension north of the Hellenic arc: this has produced a series of approximately east/west grabens. There are still important movements on the Corinthian and Euboean gulf grabens, hence their high maximum intensity. The high intensity of many of the island in the eastern Aegean is probably related to grabens that stretch from the Aegean sea itself deep into the mainland.

Just before many earthquakes there are changes in the environment which have been used to try to predict the timing of the earthquake. The water level in wells changes and springs may dry up as the stress builds up on the fault. The amount of gas in these waters may change also. The general level of ground noise (very small earthquakes) may change

before the earthquake. Lastly, many people have noticed unusual behaviour of animals in the period before an earthquake. This may be related any of the effects listed above or to changing magnetic and electrical fields. As yet there has been little success in the prediction of most earthquakes.

Tsunamis

Tsunamis are extraordinary ocean waves which can become very high close to land. They have been called tidal waves, but this is a misnomer as they have nothing to do with the tides. Each tsunami typically has only a few cycles of rising and falling water, but can be reflected off the coast and hence repeated. In the open sea tsunamis are not very high, typically less than 50 cm, travel fast at speeds up to 200 km per hour and have a very long wavelength, of the order of tens of kilometres: hence they are not noticed generally by people in boats. Near to the coast their character changes dramatically: as the sea becomes shallower the wave slows down and energy is concentrated towards the surface. The height of the wave increases, and may exceed 50 metres. Such waves can be extremely destructive of coastal communities.

Most tsunamis are produced by undersea earthquakes (see above). Earthquakes change the height of parts of the sea-bed. These moving blocks then generate a wave in the overlying water. In the Aegean region tsunamis are mostly produced by shallow (less than 70 km deep) earthquakes with magnitudes greater than 6.5 on the Richter scale.[192] Even then only 25% of the earthquakes in the Aegean region of this type produced tsunamis and of those only 25% were destructive.

Tsunamis produced by volcanic eruptions are commonly rather small, although the submarine Colombo Bank eruption of AD 1650 produced a tsunami up to 20 m high on the coast of Thera. This event may have been caused by collapse of the roof of the volcano. The great Minoan eruption of Thera is though to have been closely associated with a major tsunami that devastated settlements on the northern shore of Crete (see Chapter 15).[14, 203]

211

However, this tsunami must have been produced by a tectonic earthquake at about the same time and not by the eruption itself.

Finally, tsunamis can be produced by underwater landslides. These occur when sediments deposited in the sea adjacent to the mouth of a river become too steep and start to slide. These underwater slides can have an enormous extent. A slide of this type in the western part of the Gulf of Corinth in AD 1963 produced a tsunami 5 m high.

Although the tsunami hazard is generally low in the Aegean region there are coasts more affected by tsunamis (Fig. 17.1). These are areas near earthquake zones where the shallowness of the sea-floor and the shape of the

coastline may augment the height of the tsunamis. Ten such zones have been found, to which must be added those areas affected by volcanism, such as Thera.

Finally, if you are on the beach and the level of the sea suddenly goes down, do not stop to admire the new landscape, but run for your life to higher ground, as a tsunami may be on its way!

Landslides

The term landslide refers to a large number of different geological events, but all involve the movement of solid materials without the participation of large amounts of water, such as in

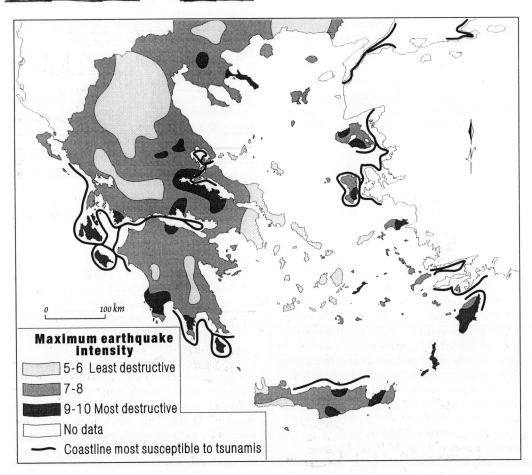

Fig. 17.1. Maximum observed earthquake intensity and coasts most commonly affected by tsunamis (after 120 and 192).

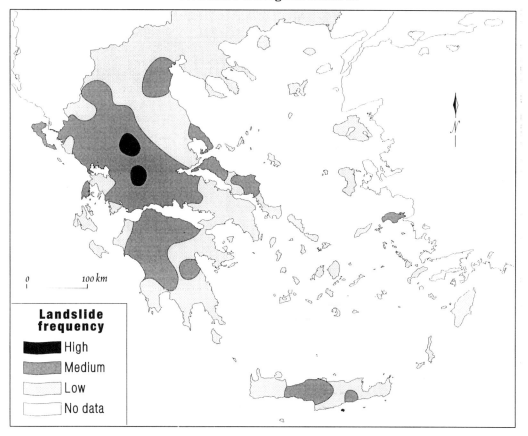

Fig. 17.2. Landslide frequency (after 144).

a river. Movements can be fast, as in the case of a rock-fall or rock avalanche, or slow, as in the downward creep of soil or blocks of rock a few metres a week or year. The movements can disrupt the rock into small pieces or the whole hillside can rotate away as a single block.

Landslides are fairly common in Greece, but most are quite small or surficial.[144, 145] However, about 500 villages have been relocated during the last 30 years as a result of actual or potential landslides, and considerable damage has been done to roads and other structures. The occurrence of landslides is principally controlled by three factors: climate, relief and local geology.

Many landslides are triggered by rainfall, human activities and earthquakes. Saturation of rock masses with water increases their weight and lubricates the potential failure surface. Landslides tend, therefore, to occur in winter when rainfall is highest, and in the regions of greatest precipitation – the mountains of the west and central regions. Formation of ice can expand cracks and wedge off blocks of rock.

Local relief is an important factor: the average elevation of landslides in this region is 500 m, and the average slope is 25°. Relief is strongest in western and central Greece, because this is where active thrust faulting is now occurring. Over 80% of landslides occur in the western and central parts of Greece, because of the combination of relief, rainfall and geological conditions (Fig. 17.2).

The geological environment of landslides is rather different in the western and eastern

213

parts of Greece. Although in the west they occur in rocks of widely different ages, the most dangerous are Late Cretaceous limestones and overlying flysch sediments. The limestones have thin, tightly folded beds and hence are easily fractured. The flysch contains weak rocks such as shale and clay. Another detrimental factor in this region is the common siting of villages close thrust faults, because of the availability of water. The scree slopes that commonly cover such faults can slide easily, especially when there is an earthquake. The situation in the east is quite different: the basement rocks are less folded, and many comprise thick, strong beds. Most of the landslides, therefore, occur in the fine-grained Neogene sediments and the loose Quaternary rocks.

Human activities frequently enhance the possibilities of landslides: tree roots can tie slopes together, and deforestation removes this restraint. Undercutting of slopes for road or house construction increases the apparent slope, and hence the possibility of a landslide. Irrigation and dam construction can load the rocks with water and produce landslides (as well as earthquakes).

Appendix 1

Important marbles and other related stones in Greece and the Aegean

White marble was used extensively by the Greeks, but the Romans also valued coloured marbles.[32, 103, 161] Individual marble quarries are treated separately in the text, but here we will describe some of the general features of marble, and how they form.

Marble is metamorphosed limestone or, more rarely, dolomite: that is, it has been changed by the action of heat and pressure. Quarry workers and archaeologists commonly refer to a number of other softer rocks as marble, such as some lavas and serpentinite, but to a geologist only metamorphosed limestone or dolomite is marble.

The action of heat, commonly several hundred degrees Celsius, promotes the recrystallisation of the rock so that the calcite, or more rarely dolomite, crystals become much larger, commonly big enough to see with the unaided eye. The heat can also lead to the formation of new minerals, and hence change the colour of the rock. The hot rock is much weaker than cold limestone, hence it is commonly deformed without cracking. This can give a new banding to the rock, in addition to the structures already present in the limestone.

The colour of marble reflects the amounts of minor minerals because pure calcite and dolomite are white. Red is produced by the mineral haematite, from iron oxide impurities. Grey and black are commonly due to graphite, produced during the metamorphism from organic matter, such as plant or animal remains. These colours are more rarely produced by magnetite or manganese oxides. Green can be produced by the mineral chlorite (which does not contain chlorine), muscovite mica or serpentine minerals. However, some green marbles are so rich in serpentine minerals that they are termed ophicalcite or serpentinite.

The textures of marble are a combination of those originally present in the limestone and those produced during metamorphism. Both limestone and marble are soluble in rainwater, which is how most caves are formed. Collapse of material from the roof and cementation by circulating waters produces limestone breccias, commonly with a contrast in colour between the matrix and the blocks. Original sedimentary layering in the limestone can also be inherited by marble. These textures can be preserved in the marble or they can be deformed or smeared out. Metamorphism can also produce another texture, veining. During the metamorphism there is a film of water between the crystals that is saturated with calcite in solution. If there is a sudden loss of pressure, or increase in stress, then a crack may open up which may soon be filled with relatively pure, white calcite. These veins are a good way to distinguish marble from limestone.

Colour	Rock type	Origin	Popular name	Roman name	Notes
White	Marble, medium	Mt Penteli	Pentelic	Pentelicum	Used only in Greece
White, blue tint	Marble, fine	Mt Hymettos	Hymettan		Rarely used
White	Marble, coarse	Paros	Parian	Lychnites	Best for sculpture
White	Marble, coarse	Naxos	Naxian	Naxium	Widespread
White	Marble, coarse	Thasos	Greco Livido	Thasium	Extensively used in Roman times
White	Marble	Belevi, nr Ephesus		Artemesion	Used at Ephesus
White	Marble	Doliana, nr Tegea	Doliana		Used at Tegea
White, grey streaks	Marble, coarse	Island of Marmara	Marmara	Proconnesus	Widespread 6C BC to 6C AD
White, yellow & red in grey matrix	Marble breccia	Southern Skyros	Breccia di Sette Basi	Scyrium	Roman
Grey	Granite, fine	Mt Cigri, nr Ezine	Granito Violetto	Marmo Troadense	Widespread in Roman times
Grey	Granite, fine	Kozac, nr Bergama	Granito Bigio	Marmo Misio	Widespread in Roman times
Green, streaky	Marble	Karystos, Euboea	Cipollino	Carystium	Widespread, Roman, splits easily
Green, with black inclusions	Serpentinite breccia	Larisa, Thessaly	Verde Antico	Thessalicum, Lapis Atracius	Roman, especially Byzantine 1C AD to 5-6C AD
Green	Metamorphosed andesite lava	Krokeai, nr Sparta	Spartan porphyry	Lapis Lacedaemonius	More popular in Roman times
Green	Rhyodacite lava	Samothrace	Porphyry		Local use
Red (also green)	Marble	Mani, Laconia	Rosso Antico	Taenarium	Dominantly Roman
Red in black matrix	Marble breccia	Teos	Africano	Luculleum	Roman
Red, white bands	Marble	Iasos	Cipollino Rosso	Carium, Iassense	Roman, also white marble
Red and white	Marble	Crete	Rods of Digenis		Roman
Violet, white in red matrix	Marble breccia	Khalkis, Euboea	Fior di Pesca	Chalcidicum	Roman
Orange-pink	Marble breccia	Chios town	Portasanta	Chium	Roman and Byzantine
Black	Marble	Chios			
Black	Marble	Lesbos			
Black	Marble	Cape Taenarum, Laconia	Nero Antiquo	Lapis Taenarius	

Appendix 2

Glossary of geological terms

The following definitions are, by necessity, simplified and do not include all eventualities. Explanations of many of the terms and concepts can also be found in Chapter 1. Further definitions can also be found in the many glossaries and dictionaries of geology, such as *The Penguin Dictionary of Geology*, by D.G.A. Whitten and J.V.R. Brooks, Penguin Books Ltd, the more complete *Glossary of Geology*, American Geological Institute, or any introductory geology textbook. All glossary terms mentioned in other entries are in italics.

Alabaster See *gypsum*.

Alluvial fan Gently-sloping, fan-shaped accumulations of *alluvium* deposited where the slope of the river bed and hence the speed of the river diminishes rapidly. They are formed where a river leaves the mountains or exits a gorge onto a plain.

Alluvium Loose gravel, sand, silt and clay deposited recently from rivers.

Amphibole A group of minerals with a complex and variable chemical composition, but basically hydrated aluminosilicates. Amphiboles are commonly dark-coloured. An example is *hornblende*.

Andesite A volcanic rock with a silica content intermediate between that of *basalt* and *trachyte*. Usually pale in colour, it may contain phenocrysts of *plagioclase*, *biotite* and *hornblende*. Flows can be thick and magmas can readily form *volcanic ashes*. The *plutonic* rock equivalent in composition is *diorite*.

Aquifer A layer of *rock* that contains abundant quantities of water.

Asbestos Fibrous minerals, usually of the serpentine group. Asbestos commonly crystallises in veins in *serpentinite*, at right-angles to the walls of the vein.

Ash-cone A conical hill of loose *volcanic ash*.

Baryte A mineral with the composition of barium sulphate. It is dense and commonly white.

Basalt A black *volcanic* rock with a relatively low silica content. It may contain *phenocrysts* of *olivine*, *pyroxenes* and *plagioclase*. Molten basalt has a low viscosity (i.e. is runny) and hence gives thin lava flows and, rarely, ashes. A plutonic rock of similar composition is called *gabbro*.

Basement The lowest part of the geological succession of rocks. Commonly made up of *metamorphic* rocks.

Bauxite A red earthy rock made of hydrated aluminium oxide together with iron oxide and other minerals. Bauxite forms by the tropical weathering of *limestones* and other rocks and is the main ore of aluminium.

Beach-rock Beach sands and gravels cemented by *calcite* to give a hard rock. It usually forms close to sea-level.

Biotite A potassium aluminosilicate mineral, belonging to the *mica* group. It occurs as dark brown plates with a single, mirror-like breakage plane.

Blueschist A *metamorphic* rock formed by *metamorphism* of a variety of rocks under conditions of high pressure and low temperature, such as might be found above a *subduction zone*. It commonly contains the blue *amphibole* mineral glaucophane.

Breccia A breccia is made of angular fragments of rock. It has not been transported far and may form at the base of a cliff, as a result of volcanic explosions or in caves (cf. *conglomerate*).

Calcite A pale-coloured mineral with the composition calcium carbonate. It is the main constituent of most *limestones* and *marbles*.

Caliche A bed of impure *limestone* which forms in the soils of arid regions by the evaporation of mineral-laden groundwater below the surface.

Carbon-14 A naturally occurring radioactive isotope of carbon. It is continually produced in the upper atmosphere and is incorporated into all living organisms. After death carbon-14 is no longer replenished and the amount remaining can be used to obtain the time of death.

Chert Nodules of finely-crystalline *quartz* in

limestone. The quartz is derived from the shells and skeletons of some organisms, which are dissolved during *lithification* and precipitated as nodules of chert. Flint is a type of chert that occurs in chalk (a soft *limestone*).

Chlorite A platy mineral akin to *mica*. It commonly gives the green colour to many *metamorphic* rocks, especially those formed at low temperatures.

Clay A rock made up of *clay minerals* together with variable amounts of *quartz* and other minerals. Primary clays are formed by the weathering or alteration of silicate minerals in rocks. Secondary clays form by the redeposition of primary clays.

Clay minerals A group of several different minerals, including montmorillonite, kaolinite and smectite. All are hydrated sodium and potassium aluminosilicates, with a platy structure. New, harder silicate minerals form when clay is fired.

Columnar joints A set of *joints* produced during cooling of lava flows where the rock is broken up into columns, usually with 5 to 7 sides. The joints start at the edges and progress towards the centre.

Conglomerate A *sedimentary* rock made up of rounded pebbles. The rounding indicates that the material has been transported in a stream or on a beach (cf. *breccia*).

Crust The uppermost part of the earth. It is thin (about 8 km) in the oceans but much thicker on the continents (30-80 km). The upper part of the continental crust is dominated by *sedimentary* rocks, but lower down *metamorphic* and *plutonic* rocks become more important. Below the crust is the *mantle*.

Dacite A volcanic rock similar to *andesite*, but commonly containing *quartz*.

Diorite A *plutonic* rock intermediate in silica content between *gabbro* and *granite*. A volcanic rock of similar composition is called *andesite*. It is commonly pale to dark grey.

Dolomite A pale mineral with the composition calcium, magnesium carbonate: the name also refers to a rock made of dolomite. Dolomite is very similar to *calcite* and occurs in some *limestones* and *marbles*.

Dome (lava) Very viscous lavas (such as *dacites* and *rhyolites*) cannot flow easily and tend to form domes rather than flows. They can have very steep sides.

Dyke A tabular body of igneous rock produced when *magma* is injected into a crack in rock and solidifies.

Earthquake Shaking of the ground produced by movements of the rocks on either side of a fault. The rocks typically move a few centimetres to several metres.

Emery A metamorphic rock containing corundum (aluminium oxide) and other minerals such as magnetite. It is formed by the metamorphism of *bauxite* layers in *limestones*. Corundum is very hard and emery was extensively used as an abrasive for working *marble* and other materials.

Eolian A sedimentary rock deposited by wind.

Fault A crack in the earth's crust, usually stretching for many kilometres. Faults are classified by their direction of movement. Normal faults have up-down movement and are a result of stretching in the horizontal direction. Thrust faults are nearly horizontal and are the result of regional horizontal compression. The upper block of a thrust fault can move many tens of kilometres. Strike-slip faults are vertical and have sideways (horizontal) movements. Transform faults are a special case of strike-slip faults that are the edges of *lithospheric (tectonic) plates*. They generally have very large movements, up to hundreds of kilometres.

Fault-scarp A cliff produced by recent vertical movements of a *fault*.

Feldspars See *plagioclase* and *potassium-feldspar*.

Flowstone (dripstone) *Limestone* deposited from freshwater by the loss of carbon dioxide in a cave or on a cliff (cf. *stalagmite, stalactite*).

Flysch A series of sedimentary rocks, including *sandstone*, *conglomerate*, siltstone and *clay*, deposited rapidly in the ocean adjacent to a rising mountain range.

Fumarole Volcanic vent of hot (100-750°C) gases, generally mostly steam, with minor amounts of sulphur dioxide, carbon dioxide and hydrogen sulphide. Fumaroles oxidise and alter the surrounding rocks to red iron oxides, *quartz* and *clay* and deposit *sulphur*.

Gabbro A dark-coloured *plutonic* rock with a low content of silica, comprised of *plagioclase* together with *olivine, pyroxene* and/or *magnetite*. A volcanic rock with similar composition is called *basalt*. It forms by melting of parts of the *mantle*.

Galena A grey, shiny mineral that is the principal ore of lead and silver.

Garnet A widespread silicate mineral formed during metamorphism. It is commonly red and when clear is a semi-precious stone.

Gneiss (pronounced nice) A *metamorphic* rock produced at medium to high temperatures. It is commonly banded from strong deformation during the metamorphism and is comprised of dark *amphiboles*, pale *feldspars* and *quartz*, and *garnet*; unlike *schist* it does not contain much *mica*.

Graben A tectonic valley. A graben is formed when a large (kilometre-scale) block of rock is dropped down between two faults during regional tension of the *crust* (cf. *horst*).

Granite A plutonic rock that contains *quartz*, *potassium feldspar* and *amphibole* and/or *mica*. It generally forms by the melting of older *crust*, such as *sedimentary* or *metamorphic rocks*. A volcanic rock of similar composition is called *rhyolite*.

Graphite A mineral composed entirely of carbon. It is commonly present in *marbles* as small plates and gives a grey colour to the rock.

Greenschist A platy rock formed by the *metamorphism* of a variety of rocks at relatively low temperatures and pressures. The green colour is commonly due to *chlorite*.

Gypsum A mineral with the composition calcium sulphate. A rock made up of randomly oriented crystals of gypsum is called alabaster.

Haematite A red mineral with the composition iron oxide. It is more oxidised than *magnetite*.

Hornblende A dark-coloured *amphibole* mineral that occurs in some *metamorphic* and *igneous* rocks.

Horst A block of rock, generally many kilometres in size, between two *grabens*. It is uplifted with respect to the surrounding areas.

Igneous rocks Rocks that formed by cooling of molten rock (*magma*). *Volcanic* rocks cooled on the surface, *plutonic* rocks cooled at depths of up to 40 km.

Ignimbrite A rock produced when *volcanic ash* is sufficiently hot that it welds itself together as it settles. Ignimbrites are generally very hard and may resemble lavas.

Intrusion See *pluton*.

Isopic zone A series of different rocks with a similar geological history that contrasts with that of the adjacent zones. The boundaries of the zones are *faults*, commonly almost horizontal *thrust faults*. An isopic zone may contain one or more *nappes*. Isopic zones were stacked on top of each other during the Alpine regional compression of the crust.

Joints A set of cracks in a rock with no movement along them (cf. *fault*). They are best seen in outcrops along the shore, in cliffs or roadcuts as sets of parallel planes. There are commonly three or four such sets with different orientations, isolating polygonal blocks of rock. They are produced by contraction during cooling of rocks, or by expansion following release of pressure from the removal by erosion of the overlying rock.

Lahar A mass of mud and blocks of rock that flows like a *lava*. Commonly associated with volcanic eruptions.

Laterite An earthy, red rock rich in iron and occasionally nickel produced by intense tropical weathering (cf. *bauxite*).

Latite A volcanic rock intermediate in composition between *dacite* and *andesite*.

Lignite A form of low-quality coal. It is formed in swamps from decayed plant remains.

Limestone A *sedimentary* rock dominantly made up of *calcite*. It can be deposited from springs (*travertine*), but is usually formed in shallow seas from the accumulation of fragments of calcareous shells or lime-mud. Crystalline limestone has been metamorphosed at very low temperatures, increasing the size of the crystals. It is transitional to *marble*.

Lithification The process by which loose materials, such as *sediments* or *volcanic ash*, become solid rock. Percolating waters dissolve the finer particles or already carry minerals in solution. These minerals are precipitated between the larger grains, cementing them together.

Magma Molten rock, generally containing some crystals and dissolved gas. Temperatures vary from about 700°C for a *granite* to 1100°C for a *basalt*.

Magnesite A mineral with the composition magnesium carbonate. It is used in the manufacture of refractory bricks.

Magnetite A black, magnetic mineral composed of iron oxide. It is not as oxidised as the red iron oxide mineral *haematite*.

Mantle That part of the earth that lies beneath the *crust*. It is dominantly made up of *olivine* and *pyroxene* which form the rock *peridotite*.

Marble Metamorphosed *limestone*. It is comprised of *calcite*, sometimes with *dolomite*, *muscovite*, *graphite* and other minerals. Pure marble is white, other colours are produced by other minerals.

Marl A soft, impure *limestone* containing *clay* and sand.

Massif A region dominated by old *metamorphic* and *igneous* rocks, commonly deformed many times. Massifs (shields) form the core of many continents, around which younger mountain belts are wrapped.

Metamorphic rocks Rocks formed by metamorphism.

Metamorphism The transformation of an igneous or sedimentary rock under the action of heat and pressure. The old minerals may grow larger and some new minerals may form.

Mica A group of platy minerals, including *biotite* and *muscovite*.

Migmatite A rock produced by *metamorphism* at high temperatures such that part of the rock has melted, but these *magmas* have been retained in the rock.

Mineral A naturally occurring material, usually crystalline, with a fixed composition or one that varies within set limits. Examples are *quartz*, *amphibole* and *magnetite*. *Rocks* are made up of aggregates of one or more minerals.

Molasse A series of sedimentary rocks, dominated by *conglomerates* and *sandstones*, deposited on land from rivers and at the bottom of shallow lakes adjacent to a rapidly rising mountain range.

Muscovite A colourless or pale green mineral of the *mica* group. It can form during crystallisation of *granites* or during *metamorphism* of sedimentary rocks. It is commonly present in *marbles* and gives the green hue of cipollino marble.

Nappe A package of rocks limited above and below by thrust *faults*. Nappes have slid almost horizontally for distances of up to hundreds of kilometres during compressional mountain-building events.

Nuée ardente A glowing cloud of hot gas and *volcanic ash* or *pumice* then descends the side of volcano like a dense liquid,

Obsidian A glassy *volcanic* rock produced by the rapid sub-aerial cooling of silica-rich magma, such as *rhyolite*. Obsidian readily recrystallises and loses its glassy texture following contact with water or during metamorphism.

Olivine An olive-green mineral with the composition iron-magnesium silicate (also known as Peridot). *Phenocrysts* of olivine can be seen in some *basalt* lavas.

Ophiolite A series of different rocks that originally made up part of the sea-floor, but now uplifted and exposed on land. An ophiolite ideally comprises, from bottom to top, *peridotite*, *gabbro*, gabbro-dykes, *pillow-lava basalts* and *cherts*, but commonly some parts are missing.

Peridotite An igneous rock primarily made up of *olivine*. Most of the *mantle* is made of peridotite and this can be seen in the sections of the ocean-floor exposed in *ophiolites*. Peridotite is commonly metamorphosed to *serpentinite*.

Phenocrysts Large or prominent crystals in a igneous rock, commonly visible to the unaided eye. *Olivine, pyroxene, amphibole, plagioclase,* *potassium-feldspar, magnetite* and *quartz* commonly occur as phenocrysts.

Phreatic eruptions Volcanic eruptions produced by *phreatic explosions*. The volcanic productions of such eruptions do not necessarily contain any solidified magma, just disrupted older rocks.

Phreatic explosions Explosions produced by the interaction of hot rock and underground water. The water flashes to superheated steam which expands and disrupts the rock with explosive force. Such explosions can be directly related to movement of *magma* and volcanic activity.

Phyllite A metamorphic rock formed from shale at low temperatures, containing fine-grained *chlorite* or *mica*. Metamorphism at higher temperatures produces *schist*.

Pillow lava When lava erupts underwater or flows into water it forms a series of pillow-shaped blobs between one and five metres long. Pillow lavas exposed on land indicate the former presence of a lake, or of a sea whose bed has been uplifted.

Placer Deposits of heavy minerals, such as gold, that form in rivers or on beaches. The winnowing action of running water removes the lighter minerals and leaves behind a concentrate of heavy minerals.

Plagioclase A sodium, calcium aluminosilicate mineral of the feldspar group. Usually pale coloured or even white, it has several good breakage planes some of which show striations.

Phonolite A lava poor in silica.

Plates Lithospheric (commonly tectonic) plates are made up of continental and/or oceanic *crust* together with the uppermost part of the mantle (*lithosphere*). They are about 200 kilometres thick and slide on a basal zone that contains a small amount of *magma*.

Plinian eruption A volcanic eruption in which the *magma* boils in the conduit at some depth below the surface. The resultant *pumice* and *volcanic ash* leave the volcano as a high-speed jet, which may rise to heights of 30-40 km.

Pluton (intrusion) A body of rock that was originally liquid (*igneous*) and was emplaced in the *crust* (cf. lavas). Plutons can vary in size from a few hundred metres to tens of kilometres.

Plutonic Refers to rocks formed when *magma* solidifies below the surface of the earth, in contrast to *volcanic* rocks. Plutonic rocks are typically coarser-grained than volcanic rocks. Examples are *granite, gabbro* and *peridotite*.

Polje A plain or small basin surrounded by mountains that drains internally into *sink-holes*.

Poros A common term in Greece for soft porous *limestone*, sandy limestone or *sandstone*.

Porphyry A term for a characteristic texture of *volcanic* or shallow *plutonic* rocks in which well-developed *phenocrysts* float in a fine matrix. The name also refers to a rock with this texture, usually an *andesite* or *dacite*.

Potassium feldspar A mineral with the composition potassium aluminosilicate. It is an essential mineral in *granites*.

Pumice A light frothy volcanic rock formed when the water in a silica-rich *magma* boils before solidification. There is not sufficient water vapour to completely disrupt the rock and form a *volcanic ash*.

Pyrite A mineral with the composition iron sulphide. It is yellow and shiny and is commonly called 'fool's gold'. Its shiny breakage surface easily distinguishes it from true gold.

Pyroclastic rocks A general term for all solid volcanic products except lava. It includes loose deposits of *volcanic ash* and *pumice* as well as lithified materials such as *tuff* and *ignimbrite*.

Pyroxene A group of minerals with the composition iron-magnesium-(calcium) silicate. *Phenocrysts* of pyroxene can be seen in some lavas.

Quartz A commonly colourless mineral comprised of silicon oxide (silica). It can crystallise from silica-rich magmas deep in the earth in *granites* or in volcanic rocks such as *rhyolites*. It can also crystallise at much lower temperatures (400 – 200°C) from watery liquids to form the quartz veins seen in many *metamorphic* rocks. Finely crystalline varieties include *chert* (flint), chalcedony, cornelian, agate, opal and jasper.

Rhyodacite A volcanic rock intermediate between *rhyolite* and *dacite*.

Rhyolite A volcanic rock rich in silica. It can contain *phenocrysts* of *quartz*, *feldspar* and *amphiboles*. The magma is usually very viscous and forms short, thick flows or lava *domes*, or *volcanic ash*. Rapid cooling of rhyolite can produce glassy rocks termed *obsidian*. A plutonic rock of similar composition is called *granite*.

Rock A rock is an aggregate of one or more *minerals*. Rock names are generally based on the proportions of the minerals, the texture of the minerals and the way the rock was formed.

Sandstone A sedimentary rock formed by the lithification of sand. The most common mineral is *quartz*. The sand may be deposited from the air (Eolian) or, more commonly, from water.

Scree (talus) Steep, loose piles of rock at the base of cliffs. (cf. *alluvial fan*)

Schist A rock rich in *micas* produced by *meta-morphism* of *sedimentary* and *volcanic* rocks at low to medium temperatures. The presence of mica gives the rock an ability to split into slabs. Metamorphism of *limestones* under the same conditions produces *marbles*, hence the two are commonly intimately mixed (cf. *blueschist, greenschist*).

Sea-level stand An ancient sea-level above the present level. The sea-level stayed at this height for sufficient time to develop features such as notches in the cliffs, wave-cut platforms and raised beaches.

Sediments Loose boulders, pebbles, sand, mud, etc., deposited from water or more rarely from the air.

Sedimentary rocks Rocks formed by the lithification of *sediments*. They include those formed from fragments of rocks (clastic), such as *sandstone* and *conglomerate*, and those formed by accumulation of minerals precipitated from water, such as *gypsum*, salt and some kinds of *limestone*.

Serpentine, serpentinite A soft green rock composed of serpentine minerals, which are hydrated magnesium silicates. These minerals form by the low *metamorphism* at low to medium temperatures of *igneous* rocks rich in *pyroxene* or *olivine*. Changes in the volume of the rock during metamorphism lead to extensive brecciation. This rock is the 'lubricant' of many thrust *faults*. Fibrous forms of serpentine are the most important form of *asbestos*.

Shale A soft sedimentary rock, produced by the accumulation of silt and clay.

Sink-hole (swallow-hole, Katavothres) The entrance to a *limestone* cave system where a river or stream disappears into the ground. The water flows through the cave to reappear at the exit or at a spring.

Skarn A rock produced by the reaction between watery solutions released during the crystallisation of *granite* and the surrounding rocks, especially *limestone*. Skarns can be rich in iron, lead, silver, gold and other metals.

Sphalerite A brown and translucent to grey and shiny mineral which is the main ore of zinc and cadmium.

Steatite or soapstone See *talc*.

Subduction zone An ancient part of the ocean floor that has descended into the *mantle* beneath a continent or ocean. Melting associated with the subduction zone produces *magmas* that rise to form plutons and volcanos.

Stalagmite, stalactite *Limestone* formations in caves precipitated from flowing water. Stalactites grow from the roof (they hold on tite), stalag-mites grow on the floor.

Sulphur A yellow mineral that occurs in vol-canic areas and some sedimentary rocks. Sulphur is a component of the minerals *pyrite, sphalerite, galena, baryte* and *gypsum*.

Talc A soft, green mineral formed by the meta-morphism of rocks rich in *olivine* and *pyroxene*. It is a hydrated magnesium silicate and forms under very similar circumstances to the *serpentine* min-erals. The soapy feel of this mineral has led to the term soapstone or steatite for rocks rich in this mineral.

Tectonics Tectonics is the study of earth-building forces. Tectonic forces are due to large-scale movements of blocks of the crust.

Trachyandesite A *volcanic* rock intermedi-ate in composition between *trachyte* and *andesite*.

Trachyte A *volcanic* rock that contains *potas-sium-feldspar*, but not much *quartz*. Usually pale in colour with *phenocrysts* of *feldspar*, and *amphi-bole*. A plutonic rock of similar composition is called syenite.

Travertine A *limestone* produced around hot or cold springs, by the loss of the gas carbon dioxide and the precipitation of *calcite*.

Tsunami A wave, or series of waves, on the ocean produced as a result of an *earthquake*, land-slide or volcanic eruption.

Tufa See *travertine*.

Tuff Lithified *volcanic ash*.

Tuff-ring A hill of *volcanic ash* or *pumice* with the form of a ring or horse-shoe (cf. *ash-cone*).

Volcanic Refers to rocks formed when *magma* pours out onto the surface of the earth and crys-tallises there. These rocks are generally finer-grained than *plutonic* rocks as they have cooled faster. Examples are *basalt, andesite* and *rhyolite*.

Volcanic ash Ashes produced during explo-sive eruptions of volcanos. Boiling of water in the magma produces a foam which is eventually dis-rupted. (cf. *tuff, pumice*)

Zone See *isopic zone*.

References

1. Aesopos, G., 1976, 'Stations hydrominerales de Grèce', *Proceedings of the International Congress on Thermal Waters, Geothermal Energy and Vulcanism of the Mediterranean Area* 2: 619-41.

2. Ager, D.V., 1980, *The Geology of Europe*. McGraw-Hill, London.

3. Aksu, A.E. and Piper, D.J.W., 1983, 'Progradation of the late Quaternary Gediz delta, Turkey', *Marine Geology* 54: 1-25.

4. Akyurek, B. and Soysal, Y., 1981, 'General geological features of the area to the south of the Biga Peninsula' (in Turkish), *Maden Tetkik ve Arama Enstitusu Dergisi* 95/96: 1-12.

5. Allen, H., 1990, 'A postglacial record from the Kopais basin, Greece', in *Man's Role in the Shaping of the Eastern Mediterranean Landscape*, ed. S. Bottema, G. Entjes-Nieborg and W. Van Zeist. Balkema, Rotterdam.

6. Altherr, R. et al., 1988, 'O-Sr isotopic variations in Miocene granitoids from the Aegean: evidence for an origin by combined assimilation and fractional crystallisation', *Contributions to Mineralogy and Petrology* 100: 528-41.

7. Alzinger, W., 1967, 'Ritzeichneungen in der Marmorbruchen von Ephesos', *Oesterreichische Jahreshefte* 48: 61-72.

8. Anastopoulos, J., 1963, 'Geological study of Andiparos island group', *Geological and Geophysical Research*, IGSR 7, 231-375.

9. Andronopoulos, B. and Koukis, G., 1976, 'Engineering geology study in the Acropolis area – Athens', *IGME Engineering Geology Investigations* 1.

10. Andronopoulos, B. and Koukis, G., 1990, 'Engineering problems in the Acropolis of Athens', in *Engineering Geology of Ancient Works, Monuments and Historical Sites*, ed. P.G. Marinos and G.C. Koukis, Balkema, Rotterdam, pp. 1819-31.

11. Andronopoulos, B. and Tzitziras, A., 1988, 'Geotechnical study of the Christian catacombs in Milos island', in *Engineering Geology of Ancient Works, Monuments and Historical Sites*, ed. P.G. Marinos and G.C. Koukis, Balkema, Rotterdam, pp. 309-25.

12. Andronopoulos, B., Koukis, G. and Tzitziras, A., 1976, 'Engineering geology study in the area of the Temple of Apollo Epikourios (Bassai-Phigalia)' *IGME Engineering Geology Investigations* 3. Athens.

13. Angelier, J. et al., 1982, 'The tectonic development of the Hellenic arc and the sea of Crete: a synthesis', *Tectonophysics* 86: 159-96.

14. Antonopoulos, J., 1992, 'The great Minoan eruption of Thera volcano and the ensuing tsunami in the Greek archipelago', *Natural Hazards* 5: 153-68.

15. Armijo, R., Lyon-Caen, H. and Papanastassiou, D., 1991, 'A possible normal-fault rupture for the 464 BC Sparta earthquake', *Nature* 351: 137-9.

16. Asgari, N., 1973, 'Roman and early Byzantine marble quarries of Proconnesus', in *Proceedings of the Tenth International Congress of Classical Archaeology*, Ankara, Izmir.

17. Astaras, Th., 1988, 'A Karst stream subterranean "Autopiracy" of Angitis river flowing in the gorge of Stens Petras, near Alistraty, east Macedonia, Greece: a contribution to the evolution of the epigenetic valley of Angitis river', *Annales Géologiques des Pays Helléniques* 33 (2): 463-73.

18. Avdis, V., 1986, 'Contribution to the geology of Mykonos', *Geology and Geophysical Research*, IGSR Special Issue, 1-4.

19. Avigad, D. and Garfunkel, Z., 1991, 'Uplift and exhumation of high-pressure metamorphic terrains: the example of the Cycladic blueschist belt (Aegean Sea)', *Tectonophysics* 188: 357-72.

20. Baeteman, C., 1985, 'Late Holocene geology of the Marathon plain (Greece)', *Journal of Coastal Research* 1: 173-85.

21. Bakhuizen, S.C., 1976, *Chalcis-in-Euboea, Iron and Chalcidians Abroad*. E.J. Brill, Leiden.

22. Bardintzeff, J.-M., Dalabakis, P., Trianeau, H. and Brousse, R., 1989, 'Recent explosive volcanic episodes on the island of Kos (Greece): associated hydrothermal parageneses and geothermal area of Volcania', *Terra Nova* 1: 75-8.

23. Barton, M. and Huijsmans, J.P.P, 1986, 'Post-caldera dacites from the Santorini volcanic complex, Aegean sea, Greece: an example of the eruption of lavas of near-constant composition over a 2,200 year period', *Contributions to Mineralogy and Petrology* 94: 472-95.

24. Bassiakos, Y.E., 1993, 'Ancient Greek mining and metallurgical activities and relationships to the geosciences (in Greek)', *Bulletin of the Geological Society of Greece* 28/2: 475-91.

25. Bassiakos, Y.E., Michael, C.T. and Chaikalis, D., 1989, 'Ancient metallurgical and mining studies on S.E. Peloponnese (Greece)', in *Archaeometry*, ed. Y. Mariatos. Elsevier, pp. 253-9.

26. Baumann, A., Best, G., Gwosdz, W. and Wachendorf, 1978, 'The eastern Crete nappe pile – a result of gravity tectonics', in *Alps, Appenines and Hellenides*, ed. H. Closs. Schweizerbart, Stuttgart, pp. 445-8.

27. Bellon, H. and Jarrige, J.-J., 1979, 'L'activité magmatique neogene et quaternaire dans l'île de Kos (Grèce)', *Comptes Rendus de l'Academie des Sciences, Paris*, Serie D, 288: 1359-62.

28. Bernoulli, D., De Graciansky, P.C. and Monod, O., 1974, 'The extension of the Lycian nappes (SW Turkey) into the southeastern Aegean islands', *Eclogae Geologicae Helvetiae* 67: 39-90.

29. Besenecker, H. et al., 1968, 'Geologie von Chios (Agais)', *Geologica et Palentologica* 2: 121-50.

30. Bintliff, J.L., 1977, 'Natural environment of human settlement in Prehistoric Greece', *British Archaeological Reports* Supplemental Series 28, Oxford.

31. Blackwell, B.A., and Schwarcz, H.J., 1993, 'Archaeochronometry and scale', in *Effects of Scale on Archeological and Geoscientific Perspectives*, ed J.K. Stein and A.R. Linse, Geological Society of America Special Paper, 283: 39-58.

32. Borghini, G. et al., 1989, *Marmi antichi*, Rome.

33. Bousquet, B., Dufaure, J.J. and Pechoux, P.Y., 1983, 'Temps historique et évolution des paysages égéens', *Méditerranée* 48(2): 3-25.

34. Brinkmann, R., 1976, *Geology of Turkey*. Ferdinand Enke Verlag, Stuttgart.

35. Brooks, M., Clews, J.E., Melis, N.S. and Underhill, J.R., 1988, 'Structural development of Neogene basins in western Greece', *Basin Research* 1: 129-38.

36. Burton, P.W. et al., 1984, 'Seismic risk in Turkey, the Aegean and the eastern Mediterranean: the occurrence of large magnitude earthquakes', *Geophysical Journal of the Royal Astronomical Society* 78: 475-506.

37. Cadoux, C.J., 1938, *Ancient Smyrna*. Blackwell, Oxford.

38. Cayeux, L., 1911, *Exploration archéologique de Délos, Déscription physique*, vol. IV, part I.

39. Chiotis, E. and Papadimitriou, G., 1993, 'Quarrying of dimensional stones in the Hellenic period at Kefalos Bay on Kos island', *ASMOSIA – 1993 Conference*, p. 13.

40. Clews, J.E., 1989, 'Structural controls in basin evolution: Neogene to Quaternary of the Ionian Zone, Western Greece', *Journal of the Geological Society* 146.

41. Collier, R.E. Ll. and Dart, C.J., 1991, 'Neogene to Quaternary rifting, sedimentation and uplift in the Corinth basin, Greece', *Journal of the Geological Society* 148: 1049-65.

42. Compton, R.R., 1984, *Geology in the Field*. John Wiley & Sons.

43. Conispoliatis, N. et al., 1986, 'Geological and sedimentological patterns in the Lake Pamvotis (Ioannina) NW Greece', *Annales Géologiques des Pays Helléniques* 33: 269-85.

44. Conophagos, C.E., 1980, *Le Laurium antique et la téchnique greque de la production de l'argent*. Athènes Ekdotiki Hellados.

45. Cooper, F.A., 1981, 'A source of ancient marble in the Southern Peloponnesos', *American Journal of Archaeology* 85: 190-1.

46. Cooper, F.A., 1985, 'The stones of Bassae', *Annual of the British School at Athens*, 21-34.

47. Cornwall, I.W., 1958, *Soils for the Archaeologist*, Phoenix House, London.

48. Courtils, J., Kozelj, T. and Muller, A., 1982, 'Des mines d'or à Thasos', *Bulletin des Correspondences Helléniques* 106: 409-17.

49. Curtis, E. and Adler, F., 1892, *Olympia: Ergebnisse*, 2, 6. Berlin.

50. Dalabakis, P., 1986, 'Une des plus puissantes éruptions phréatomagmatiques dans la Méditerranée orientale: l'ignimbrite de Kos (Grèce)', *Comptes Rendus de l'Academie des Sciences*, Serie II, no. 6, 505-8.

51. Dalabakis, P. and Vougioukalakis, G., 1993, 'Kefalos tuff ring (W. Kos): depositional mechanisms, position of the vent and model of the evolution of the volcanic activity', *Bulletin of the Geological Society of Greece* 28/2: 259-73.

52. Daremberg, C., 1904, *Dictionnaire des antiquités grecques et romaines*. Hachette, Paris.

53. Davis, E.N., 1959, 'Die Vulkangesteine der

Insel Lemnos', *Annales Géologiques des Pays Helléniques*, 11: 1-82.

54. Davis, E.N., 1962, 'Der geologische Bau der Insel Samothraki', *Annales Géologiques des Pays Helléniques* 14: 133-210.

55. de Jesus, P.S., 1980, 'The development of prehistoric mining and metallurgy in Anatolia', *BAR* international series 74, Oxford, Britain.

56. Dercourt, J. et al., 1986, 'Geological evolution of the Tethys basin from the Atlantic to the Pamirs since the Lias', *Tectonophysics* 123: 241-315.

57. Dermentzopoulos, T. et al., 1990, 'Building stones of ancient monuments in Attica: an outline', in *Engineering Geology of Ancient Works, Monuments and Historical Sites*, ed. P.G. Marinos and G.C. Koukis, Balkema, Rotterdam. pp. 619-29.

58. Dermitzakis, M.D., Tsipoura-Vlachou, M. and Stamatakis, M., 1990, 'Petrological and geological study of the building material from the underground pit of Gortys, Crete island', in *Engineering Geology of Ancient Works, Monuments and Historical Sites*, ed. P.G. Marinos and G.C. Koukis. Balkema, Rotterdam, pp. 2049-56.

59. Dietrich, R.V. and Skinner, B.I., 1979, *Rocks and Rock Minerals*. John Wiley & Sons.

60. Dietrich, V.J. et al., 1993, 'Geological map of Greece, Aegina Island, 1:25000', *Bulletin of the Geological Society of Greece* 28/3: 555-66.

61. Dietrich, V.J., Nuesch, R. and Ballanti, D., 1993, 'The origin of the Milos bentonite deposits', *Bulletin of the Geological Society of Greece* 28/2: 329-40.

62. DiPaola, G.M., 1974, 'Volcanology and petrology of Nisyros island (Dodecanese, Greece)', *Bulletin Volcanologique* 38: 944-87.

63. Dixon, J.E. and Dimitriadis, S., 1984, in *The Geological Evolution of the Eastern Mediterranean*, ed. J.F. Dixon and A.H.F. Robertson, Geological Society of London Special Publication 17.

64. Dixon, J.E. et al., 1987, 'Excursion guide to the field trip on Seriphos, Syros and Naxos', in *Chemical Transport in Metasomatic Processes*, ed. H.C. Helgeson, NATO-ASI Series vol. 218. Reidel, Dordrecht, pp. 468-518.

65. Dotsika, E. and Michelot, J.L., 1993, 'Hydrochemistry, isotope contents and origin of geothermal fluids at Nisyros (Dodecanese)', *Bulletin of the Geological Society of Greece* 28/2: 293-304.

66. Doutsos, T. and Piper, D.J.W., 1990, 'Listric faulting, sedimentation, and morphological evolution of the Quaternary eastern Corinth rift, Greece: first stages of continental rifting', *Geological Society of America Bulletin* 102: 812-29.

67. Downey, W.S. and Tarling, D.H., 1984, 'Archaeomagnetic dating of Santorini volcanic eruptions and fired destruction levels of Late Minoan civilization', *Nature* 309: 519-23.

68. Drogue, C. and Soulios, G., 1988, 'Absorbtion massive d'eau de mer et rejet d'eau saumâtre dans l'île karstique de Cephalonia (Grèce). Nouvelle interpretation du phenomène', *Comptes Rendus de l'Academie des Sciences, Paris*, Serie 2, Sciences de la Terre, 307: 1833-6.

69. Druitt, T.H. and Francaviglia, V., 1992, 'Caldera formation on Santorini and the physiography of the islands in the late Bronze age', *Bulletin Volcanologique* 54: 484-93.

70. Druitt, T.H. et al., 1989, 'Explosive volcanism on Santorini, Greece', *Geological Magazine* 126: 95-126.

71. Durkin, M.K. and Lister, C.J., 1983, 'The rods of Digenis: an ancient marble quarry in eastern Crete', *Annual of the British School at Athens* 78: 69-96.

72. Dworakowska, A., 1975, *Quarries in Ancient Greece*. Polish Academy of Science, Warszawa.

73. Einfalt, H.-C., 1980, 'Stone materials in ancient Akrotiri – a short compilation', in *Thera and the Ancient World II*, ed. C. Doumas, 523-7.

74. Ellis, S.E., Higgins, R.A. and Hope-Simpson, R., 1968, 'The facade of the treasury of Atreus at Mycenae', *Annual of the British School at Athens* 63: 331-6.

75. Epitropou, N. et al., 1983, 'The Marlou Pb-Zn mineralization of Thasos island (Greece)', in *Mineral Deposits of the Alps and of the Alpine Epoch in Europe*, ed. H.J. Schneider. Springer-Verlag, Berlin, pp. 366-74.

76. Ercan, T. et al., 1984, 'Geology of the Dikili-Bergama-Candarli area (western Anatolia) and the petrology of the magmatic rocks' (in Turkish), *Jeoloji Muhendisligi* 20: 47-50.

77. Ercan, T. et al., 1992, Products of recent volcanism transported from Nisyros island to Anatolian peninsula. Pre-Print.

78. Erdogan, B., 1990, 'Tectonic relations between Izmir-Ankara zone and Karaburun belt', *Mineral Research and Exploration Bulletin (MTA)* 110: 1-15.

79. Ergun, M. et al., 1989, 'Structure and evolution of the sea of Marmara', *Terra Abstracts*, 439.

80. Erguvanli, K. et al., 1988, 'The significance of research on old quarries for the restoration of historic buildings with special reference to Marmara region, Turkey', in *Engineering Geology of Ancient Works, Monuments and Historical Sites*, ed. P.G. Marinos and G.C. Koukis. Balkema, Rotterdam, pp. 631-8.

81. Fabre, G. and Maire, R, 1983, 'Néotectonique et morphogénèse insulaire en Grèce: le massif de Mont Ida (Crète)', *Méditerranée* 48(2): 39-49.

82. Faure, P., 1964, *Fonctions des cavernes crétoises*. Ecole française d'Athènes, E. de Boccard, Paris.

83. Finke, E.A.W., 1988, *Landscape evolution of the Argive plain, Greece: palaeoecology, Holocene depositional history, and coastline changes*. PhD thesis, Stanford University, California.

84. FitzPatrick, E.A., 1983, *Soils: Their Formation, Classification and Distribution*. Longman, London.

85. Flemming, N.C. and Woodworth, P.L., 1988, 'Monthly mean sea-levels in Greece during 1969-1983 compared to relative vertical land movements measured over different time scales', *Tectonophysics* 148, 59-72.

86. Ford, D.C. and Williams, P.W., 1989, *Karst Geomorphology and Hydrology*. Unwin Hyman, London.

87. Foscolos, A.E. et al., 1989, 'Reconnaissance study of mineral matter and trace elements in Greek lignites', *Chemical Geology* 76: 107-30.

88. Fytikas, M., Kolios, N. and Vougioukalakis, G., 1990, 'Post-Minoan volcanic activity of the Santorini volcano. Volcanic hazard and risk, forecasting possibilities', in *Thera and the Ancient World III*, ed. D. Hardy, 2: 183-98.

89. Fytikas, M. and Vougioukalakis, G., 1993, 'Volcanic structure and evolution of Kimolos – Polyegos (Milos island group)', *Bulletin of the Geological Society of Greece* 28/2: 221-37.

90. Fytikas, M. et al., 1976, 'Geochronological data on recent magmatism in the Aegean Sea', *Tectonophysics* 31: T29-T34.

91. Fytikas, M. et al., 1979. 'Neogene volcanism in the Northern and Central Aegean region', *Annales Géologiques des Pays Helléniques*, 30: 106-29.

92. Fytikas, M. et al., 1984, 'Tertiary to Quaternary evolution of volcanism in the Aegean region', in *The Geological Evolution of the Eastern Mediterranean*, ed. J.F. Dixon and A.H.F. Robertson, Geological Society of London Special Publication 17: 687-99.

93. Fytikas, M. et al., 1986, 'Volcanology and petrology of volcanic products from the island of Milos and neighbouring islets', *Journal of Volcanology and Geothermal Research*, 28: 297-317.

94. Fytikas, M. et al., 1988, 'The Plio-Quaternary volcanism of Saronicos area (western part of the active Aegean volcanic arc)', *Annales Géologiques des Pays Helléniques* 33: 23-45.

95. Gale, N.H. and Stos-Gale, Z., 1981, 'Lead and silver in the ancient Aegean', *Scientific American*, no. 244, 142.

96. Gale, N.H. and Stos-Gale, Z., 1982, 'Bronze age copper sources in the Mediterranean: a new approach', *Science* 216: 11-19.

97. Gale, N.H., 1980, 'Some aspects of lead and silver mining in the Aegean', in *Thera and the Ancient World II*, ed. C. Doumas, 161-95.

98. Gale, N.H. et al., 1988, 'The sources of Mycenaean gypsum', *Journal of Archaeological Science*, 15: 57-72

99. Galetti, G., Lazzarini, L. and Maggetti, M., 1993, 'A first characterization of the most important granites used in antiquity', in *Ancient Stones: Quarrying, Trade and Provenance*, ed. M. Waelkens, N. Herz, and L. Moens, Leuven University Press, pp. 167-78.

100. Gauthier, G. and Albandakis, N., 1991, 'Minerals of the Seriphos Skarn, Greece', *Mineralogical Record* 22: 303-8.

101. Georgalas, G.C. and Papastamatiou, J., 1953, 'L'éruption du volcan de Santorin en 1939-1941. L'éruption du Dome Fouque', *Bulletin Volcanologique* 13:3-38.

102. Georgalas, G.C., 1953, 'L'éruption du volcan de Santorin en 1950', *Bulletin Volcanologique* 13:39-55.

103. Gnoli, R., 1971, *Marmora romana*. Edizioni dell'Elefante, Rome.

104. Golmshtok, A.Ya. et al., 1992, 'Age, evolution and history of the Black Sea Basin based on heat flow and multichannel reflection data', *Tectonophysics* 210: 273-93.

105. Gorgoni, C. et al., 1992, 'Geochemical and petrographic characterization of "Rosso Antico" and other grey-white marbles of Mani (Greece)', in *Ancient Stones: Quarrying, Trade and Provence*, eds. M. Waelkens, N. Herz and L. Moens. Leuven University Press, 155-66.

106. Hall, R., Audley-Charles, M.G. and Carter, D.J., 1984, 'The significance of Crete for the evolution of the eastern Mediterranean', in *The Geological Evolution of the Eastern Mediterranean*, eds, J.F. Dixon and A.H.F. Robertson, Geological Society of London, Special Publication 17.

107. Hammer, C.U. et al., 1987, 'The Minoan eruption of Santorini in Greece dated at 1645 BC?', *Nature* 328: 517-19.

108. Hanfmann, G.M.A., 1983, *Sardis – From*

Prehistoric to Roman Times. Harvard University Press, Harvard.

109. Hatzidimitriou, P.M. et al., 1991, 'Seismotectonic evidence of an active normal fault beneath Thessaloniki (Greece)', *Terra Nova*, 3: 648-54.

110. Heiken, G. and McCoy, F. jr, 1984, 'Caldera development during the Minoan eruption, Thira, Cyclades, Greece', *Journal of Geophysical Research* 89: 8441-62.

111. Henjes-Kunst, F. et al., 1988, 'Disturbed U-Th-Pb systematics of young zircons and uranothorites: the case of the Miocene Aegean granitoids (Greece)', *Chemical Geology (Isotope Geoscience)* 73: 125-45.

112. Herz, N., 1988, 'Classical marble quarries of Thasos', in G.A. Wagner and G. Weisgerber, *Antike Edel- und Bunt-metallgewinnung auf Thasos.* Deutsches Bergbau-Museum, Bochum.

113. Herz, N., Cooper, F.A. and Wenner, D.B., 1982, 'The Mani quarries: marble source for the Bassai temple in the Peloponnesos', *American Journal of Archaeology* 86: 270.

114. Higgs, B., 1988, 'Syn-sedimentary structural controls on basin formation in the Gulf of Corinth, Greece', *Basin Research*, 1: 155-65.

115. Hohail, H. and Rashed, M., 1992, 'Stable isotopic composition of carbonate-cemented recent beachrock along the Mediterranean and the Red sea coasts of Egypt', *Marine Geology* 106: 141-8.

116. Howard, H., 1982, 'Clay and the archaeologist', in *Current Research in Ceramics: Thin-Section Studies*, ed. I.C. Freestone, C. Johns and T. Potter, British Museum Occasional Papers 32: 145-58.

117. Hsu, K.J., 1983, *The Mediterranean was a Desert: A Voyage of the Glomar Challenger.* Princeton University Press, Princeton.

118. Huijsmans, J.P.P., Barton, M. and Saltes, J. M., 1988, 'Geochemistry and evolution of the calc-alkaline volcanic complex of Santorini, Aegean Sea, Greece', *Journal of Volcanology and Geothermal Research* 34: 283-306.

119. Hurni, L., Dietrich, V.J. and Gaitanakis, P., 1993, 'CAGC (Computer aided geological cartography) – 3-dimensional modelling of the Methana volcanoes', *Bulletin of the Geological Society of Greece* 28/3: 515-18.

120. IGME, 1989, *Seismotectonic Map of Greece.* Institute of Geology and Mineral Exploration, Athens, Greece.

121. Inaner, H. and Nakoman, E., 1993, 'Lignite deposits of the western Turkiye', *Bulletin of the Geological Society of Greece* 28/2: 493-505.

122. Innocenti, F. and Mazzuoli, 1973, 'Petrology of the Izmir-Karaburan volcanic area (West Turkey)', *Bulletin Volcanologique* 36: 83-104.

123. Innocenti, F. et al., 1982, 'Acidic and basic Late Neogene volcanism in the Central Aegean Sea: its nature and geotectonic significance', *Bulletin Volcanologique* 45: 87-97.

124. Innocenti, F. et al., 1984. 'Evolution and geodynamic significance of the Tertiary orogenic volcanism in northeastern Greece', *Bulletin Volcanologique* 47: 25ff.

125. Jackson, J.A. et al., 1982, 'Seismicity, normal faulting, and the geomorphological development of the Gulf of Corinth (Greece): the Corinth earthquakes of February and March 1981', *Earth and Planetary Science Letters* 57: 377-97.

126. Jacobshagen, V. and Wallbrecher, E. 1984. 'Pre-Neogene structure and metamorphism of the North Sporades and the southern Pelion peninsula', in *The Geological Evolution of the Eastern Mediterranean*, ed. J.F. Dixon and A.H.F. Robertson, Geological Society of London, Special Publication 17: 591-602.

127. Jacobshagen, V., 1986, *Geologie von Griechenland.* Gebrüder Borntraeger, Berlin.

128. Jansen, J.B.H., 1977, 'The geology of Naxos', *Geology and Geophysical Research*, IGSR 19.

129. Jones, C.E. et al., 1992, 'Tertiary granitoids of Rhodope, northern Greece: magmatism related to extensional collapse of the Hellenic orogen?', *Tectonophysics* 210: 295-314.

130. Jones, R.E., 1986, *Greek and Cypriot Pottery – A Review of Scientific Studies.* British School at Athens, Athens.

131. Judson, S., 1985, 'The burial of the site of Olympia, western Peloponnese, Greece', Geological Society of America annual meeting, Program with Abstracts, 621.

132. Jung, D., 1961, 'Die geologie des Gebietes von Chasabali (Thessalien)', *Praktika tis Akademias Athenon* 36: 149-56.

133. Kambouroglou, E., Maroukiou, H. and Sampson, A., 1988, 'Coastal evolution and archaeology north and south of Khalkis (Euboea) in the last 5000 years', in *Archaeology of Coastal Changes*, ed. A. Raban, BAR International Series, Oxford, Britain.

134. Karagas, C.G., 1980, 'Metamorphic zones and physical conditions of metamorphism in Leros Island, Greece', *Contributions to Mineralogy and Petrology*, 73: 389-402.

135. Katsikatsos, G., De Bruijn, H. and Van der Meulen, A.J., 1981, 'The Neogene of the island of Euboea (Evia), a review', *Geologie en Mijnbouw* 60: 509-16.

136. Keller, J., 1980, 'Prehistoric pumice tephra on Aegean islands', in *Thera and the Ancient World II*, ed. C. Doumas.

137. Kissel, C. and Laj, C., 1988, 'The Tertiary geodynamical evolution of the Aegean arc: a palaeomagnetic reconstruction', *Tectonophysics* 146: 183-201.

138. Knauss, J., 1987, 'Die Melioration des Kopaisbeckens durch die Minyer im 2. Jt. v. Chr.', *Kopais 2 – Wasserbau und Siedlungsbedingungen in Altertum*. Technische Universität München, Germany.

139. Koca, M.Y. and Turk, N., 1993, 'Engineering geology of selected abandoned andesite quarries in Izmir, Turkey', *Bulletin of the Geological Society of Greece* 28/3: 581-601.

140. Kohlberger, W., 1976, 'Minerals of the Laurium mines, Attica, Greece', *Mineralogical Record*, May-June 1976, 114-25.

141. Kopp, K.-O., 1978, 'Stratigraphic and tectonic sequence of Crete', in *Alps, Appenines and Hellenides*, ed. H. Closs, Schweizerbart, Stuttgart, 439-42

142. Kornprobst, J. et al., 1979, 'The high-pressure assemblages at Milos, Greece', *Contributions to Mineralogy and Petrology* 69: 49-63.

143. Koukis, G. and Floros, K., 1990, 'Ground foundation conditions and erosion problems of the Kalamata Castle (Greece)', in *Engineering Geology of Ancient Works, Monuments and Historical Sites*, ed. P.G. Marinos and G.C. Koukis. Balkema, Rotterdam, pp. 137-46.

144. Koukis, G. and Ziourkas, C., 1992, Slope instability phenomena in Greece: a statistical analysis', *Bulletin of the International Association of Engineering Geology* 43: 47-60.

145. Koukis, G.C., 1988, 'Slope deformation phenomena related to the engineering geological conditions in Greece', in *Landslides*, ed. C. Bonnard. Balkema, Rotterdam, pp. 1187-92.

146. Kourmoulis, N.E., 1979, *Inventory of Karstic Springs of Greece* (in Greek). Athens.

147. Kozelj, T., 1988, 'Les carrières des epoques grecque, romaine et byzantine: techniques et organisation', in *Ancient Marble Quarrying and Trade*, ed. J.C. Fant, BAR International Series 453, London.

148. Kraft, J.C., 1972, 'A reconnaissance of the geology of the sandy coastal areas of eastern Greece and the Peloponnese – with speculations on Middle-Late Helladic palaeogeography (3000-4000 years before present)', *Technical Report* no. 9, Dept. of Geology, University of Delaware.

149. Kraft, J.C. and Aschenbrenner, S.E., 1977, 'Palaeogeographic reconstructions in the Methoni embayment in Greece', *Journal of Field Archaeology* 4: 19-44.

150. Kraft, J.C., Belknap, D.F. and Kagan, I. 1983, 'Potentials of discovery of human occupation sites on the continental shelves and nearshore coastal zone', in *Quaternary Coastlines and Marine Archaeology*, ed. P.M. Masters and N.C. Flemming. Academic Press, London.

151. Kraft, J.C. et al., 1977, 'Palaeogeographic reconstructions of coastal Aegean archaeological sites', *Science*, 195: 941-7.

152. Kraft, J.C., et al., 1985, 'Geological studies of coastal change applied to archaeological settings', in *Archaeological Geology*, ed. G. Rapp jr and J.A. Gifford. Yale University Press.

153. Kraft, J.C. et al., 1987, 'The pass at Thermopylae, Greece', *Journal of Field Archaeology*, 14: 181-97.

154. Kraft, J.C., Kayan, I. and Erol, O., 1980, 'Geomorphic reconstructions in the environs of ancient Troy', *Science* 209: 776-82.

155. Kraft, J.C., Kayan, I. and Erol, O., 1982, 'Geology and palaeogeographic reconstructions of the vicinity of Troy', in *Troy: The Archeological Geology*, ed. G. Rapp jr and J.A. Gifford Supplementary monograph 4, University of Cincinnati, Princeton University Press.

156. Kraft, J.C., Rapp, G. jr. and Aschenbrenner, S.E., 1975, 'Late Holocene palaeogeography of the coastal plain of the Gulf of Messenia, Greece, and its relationship to archaeological setting and coastal changes', *Geological Society of America Bulletin* 86: 1191-208.

157. Kraft, J.C., Rapp, G. jr. and Aschenbrenner, S.E., 1980, 'Late Holocene palaeogeographical reconstructions in the area of the Bay of Navarino: Sandy Pylos', *Journal of Archaeological Sciences* 7: 187-210.

158. Lahli, H.R. and Govett, G.J.S., 1981, 'Primary and secondary halos in weathered and oxidised rocks – an exploration study from Mykonos, Greece', *Journal of Geochemical Exploration* 16: 27-40.

159. Lambraki, A., 1980, 'Le Cipolin de la Karystie. Contribution a l'etude des marbres de la Grèce exploites aux epoques romaine et palaeochretienne', *Revues Archaeologiques* 1: 31-62.

160. Lazzarini, L., 1990, 'Rosso Antiquo and other coloured marbles used in antiquity: a characterisation study', in *Marble, Art Historical and Scientific Perspectives on Ancient Sculpture*, J. Paul Getty Museum.

161. Lepsius, G.R., 1890, *Griechische Mar-*

morstudier. Verlag Königl. Akademie der Wissenschaften, Berlin.

162. Lepsius, G.R., 1893, *Geologie von Attika*, Berlin.

163. Lister, G.S. et al., 1984, 'Metamorphic core complexes of the Cordilleran type in the Cyclades, Aegean Sea, Greece', *Geology*, 12: 221-5.

164. Loy, W.G. and Wright, H.E., 1972, 'The physical setting', in *The Minnesota Messenia Expedition: Constructing a Bronze Age Regional Environment*, ed. W.A. McDonald and G.R. Rapp jr. University of Minnesota Press, Minneapolis.

165. Lyon-Caen, H. et al., 1988, 'The 1986 Kalamata (South Peloponesus) Earthquake: detailed study of a normal fault, evidences for east-west extension in the Hellenic arc', *Journal of Geophysical Research* 93: 14967-15000.

166. Mack, E., 1983, 'Auriferous mineralization in Northern Greece: history, exploration and evaluation', in *Mineral Deposits of the Alps and of the Alpine Epoch in Europe*, ed. H.J. Schneider. Springer-Verlag, Berlin.

167. Makropoulos, K.C. and Burton, P.W., 1981, 'A catalogue of seismicity in Greece and adjacent areas', *Geophysical Journal of the Royal Astronomical Society* 65: 741-62.

168. Maluski, H. et al., 1987, 'Dating the metamorphic events in the Cycladic area: 39Ar/40Ar data from metamorphic rocks of the island of Syros (Greece)', *Bulletin de la Société Géologique de France* 8 (III) 5: 833-42.

169. Manning, S.W., 1990, 'The Thera eruption: The Third Congress and the problem of the date', *Archaeometry* 32: 91-108.

170. Marini, L. et al., 1993, 'Hydrothermal eruptions of Nisyros (Dodecanese, Greece). Past events and present hazard', *Journal of Volcanology and Geothermal Research* 56: 71-94.

171. Marinos, G. and Petrascheck, W.E., 1956, 'Laurium', *Geological and Geophysical Research*, IGME, Athens, IV, 1: 1-247.

172. Marinos, G., 1982, 'Greece', in *The Mineral Deposits of Europe*, ed. S.H.U. Bowie et al., Institute for Mining and Metallurgy, London.

173. Marinos, G. et al., 1973, 'The Athens schist formation II: Stratigraphy and structure', *Annales Géologiques des Pays Helléniques*, 25: 439-44.

174. Mariolakis, I. and Stiros, S.C., 1987, 'Quaternary deformation of the Isthmus and Gulf of Corinthos (Greece)', *Geology* 15: 225-8.

175. Mark., R.K., Pike, R.J. and Stevens, C.P., 1991, 'Digital shaded-relief image of the Mediterranean sea-floor available as continuous-tone photographic prints from a film-recorder nega-

tive', *U.S. Geological Survey Open-file report* 91-428.

176. Meulenkamp, J.E. et al., 1988, 'On the Hellenic subduction zone and the geodynamic evolution of Crete since the late Middle Miocene', *Tectonophysics*, 146: 203-15.

177. Mijatovic, B.F., 1988. 'Système karstique de la source littorale Almiros d'Iraklion', *Proceedings of the 21st International Hydrogeology Congress – Karst hydrogeology and karst environment protection*, Guilin, China, 461-73.

178. Mijatovic, B.F., 1992. 'Conditions hydrogéologiques de quelques aquifères karstiques de la Crète (Grèce)', *International Contributions to Hydrogeology* 13: 249-62.

179 Millot, G., 1970, *Geology of Clays: Weathering, Sedimentology, Geochemistry*. Chapman and Hall, London.

180. Minissale, A. et al., 1989, 'Geochemical characteristics of Greek thermal springs', *Journal of Volcanology and Geothermal Research* 39: 1-16.

181. Monna, D. and Pensabene, P., 1977, *Marmi dell'Asia Minore*. Rome: Consiglio Nazionale delle Ricerche.

182. Morfis, A. and Zojer, H., 1986, 'Karst hydrogeology of the Central and Eastern Peloponnesus', *Steir. Beitr. z. Hydrogeologie* 37-8: 1-301.

183. Mourtzas, N.D., and Marinos, P.G., 1994, 'Upper Holocene sea-level changes: paleogeographic evolution and its impact on coastal archaeological sites and monuments', *Environmental Geology* 23: 1-13.

184. Mouyaris, N., Papastamatiou, D. and Vita-Finzi, C., 1992, 'The Helice fault', *Terra Nova* 4: 124-9.

185. Muller, A., 1979, 'La mine de l'Acropole de Thasos', *Bulletin de Correspondence Hellénique* supplement 5: 315-44.

186. Mutti, E., Orombelli, G. and Pozzi, R., 1970, 'Geological studies on the Dodecanese islands (Aegean sea). IX. Geological map of the island of Rhodes (Greece). Explanatory notes', *Annales Géologiques des Pays Helléniques* 22: 77-226.

187. Myers, J.W., Myers, E.E. and Cadogan, G., 1992, *The Aerial Atlas of Ancient Crete*. University of California Press, Berkeley.

188. Nriagu, J.O., 1983, *Lead and Lead Poisoning in Antiquity*. John Wiley & Sons, New York.

189. Okrusch, M. et al., 1984, 'High-pressure rocks of Samos, Greece', in *The Geological Evolution of the Eastern Mediterranean*, ed. J.F. Dixon and A.H.F. Robertson, Geological Society of London, Special Publication 17.

190. Ori, G.G., and Roveri, M., 1987, 'Geometries of Gilbert-type deltas and large channels in the Meteora Conglomerate, Meso-Hellenic basin (Oligo-Miocene), central Greece', *Sedimentology* 34: 845-60.

191. Paepe, R., 1986, 'Landscape changes in Greece as a result of changing climate during the quaternary', in *Desertification in Europe*, ed. R. Fantechi and N.S. Margaris. D. Reidel Pub. Co.

192. Papadopoulos, G.A. and Chalkis, B.J., 1984, 'Tsunamis observed in Greece and the surrounding area from antiquity up to the present times', *Marine Geology*, 56: 509-17.

193. Papadopoulos, G.A., 1984, 'Seismic properties in the eastern part of the south Aegean volcanic arc', *Bulletin Volcanologique* 47: 143-52.

194. Papageorgakis, J. and Kolaiti, E., 1992, 'The ancient limestone quarries of Profitis Elias near Delfi (Greece)', in *Ancient Stones: Quarrying, Trade and Provenance*, ed. M. Waelkens, N. Herz and L. Moens. Leuven University Press, pp. 43-60.

195. Papageorgakis, J. and Mposkos, E., 1990, 'Building stones of the Palace of Knossos', in *Engineering Geology of Ancient Works, Monuments and Historical Sites*, ed. P.G. Marinos and G.C. Koukis. Balkema, Rotterdam, pp. 649-59.

196. Papageorgakis, J., Mourtzas, N. and Orfanoudaki, 1992, 'Bronze age quarries on the Eastern coastal zone of Crete (Greece)', in *Ancient Stones: Quarrying, Trade and Provenance*, ed. M. Waelkens, N. Herz and L. Moens. Leuven University Press, pp. 21-8.

197. Papanikolaou, D. and Sideris, C., 1983, 'Le paléozoique de l'autochtone de Chios: une formation à blocs de type wildflysche d'âge Permien (Proparte)', *Comptes Rendus de l'Academie des Sciences de Paris*, Serie D 297: 603-6.

198. Papanikolaou, D.J., 1979, 'Contribution to the geology of the Aegean sea: the island of Paros', *Annales Géologiques des Pays Helléniques* 30: 65-96.

199. Papanikolaou, D. et al., 1993, 'Correlation on neotectonic structures with the geodynamic activity in Milos during the earthquakes of March 1992', *Bulletin of the Geological Society of Greece* 28/3: 413-28.

200. Papastamatiou, I.N., 1951, 'The emery of Naxos', in *The Mineral Wealth of Greece*. Athens, 37-69.

201. Papazachos, B.C. and Dimitriou, P.P., 1991. 'Tsunamis in and near Greece and their relation to the earthquake focal mechanisms', *Natural Hazards* 4: 161-70.

202. Papazachos, B.C. et al., 1987, 'Probabilities of occurrence of large earthquakes in the Aegean and surrounding area during the period 1986-2006', *Pageoph* 125: 597-612.

203. Pararas-Carayannis, G., 1992, 'The tsunami generated from the eruption of the volcano of Santorini in the Bronze age', *Natural Hazards* 5: 115-23.

204. Pasteels, P., Kolios, N., Boven, A. and Saliba, E., 1986, 'Applicability of the K-Ar method to whole rock samples of acid lava and pumice: case of the upper Pleistocene domes and pyroclastics on Kos island, Aegean sea, Greece', *Chemical Geology* 57: 145-54.

205. Pe, G.G., 1973, 'Petrology and geochemistry of volcanic rocks of Aegina, Greece', *Bulletin Volcanologique* 37: 491-514.

206. Pe, G.G., 1974, 'Volcanic rocks of Methana, South Aegean Arc, Greece', *Bulletin Volcanologique* 38: 270-90.

207. Pe-Piper, G., 1983, 'The Triassic volcanic rocks of Tyros, Zarouhla, Kalamae and Epidavros, Peloponnese, Greece', *Schw. Mineral. Petrol. Mitt.* 63: 249-66.

208. Pe-Piper, G., and Kotopouli, C.N., 1994, 'Palaeozoic volcanic rocks of Chios, Greece: Record of a Paleotethyan suture', *Neues Jahrbuch für Mineralogie*, Monstshefte 11: 23-39.

209. Pe-Piper, G., and Piper, D.J.W., 1993, 'Revised stratigraphy of the Miocene volcanic rocks of Lesbos, Greece', *Neues Jahrbuch für Geol. Paläont. Mh.* 1993, H.2: 97-110.

210. Pe-Piper, G. et al., 1995, 'Neogene volcanoes of Chios, Greece: the relative importance of subduction and back-arc extension', in *Volcanism Associated with Extension at Consuming Plate Margins*, ed. J.L. Smellie. Geological Society of London Special Publication 81: 213-31.

211. Pe-Piper, G., Panagos, A.G., Piper, D.J.W. and Kotopouli, C.N., 1982, 'The (?) Mid-Triassic volcanic rocks of Laconia, Greece', *Geological Magazine* 119: 77-85.

212. Perinçek, D., 1991, 'Possible strand of the North Anatolian fault in the Thrace Basin, Turkey – an interpretation', *American Association of Petroleum Geologists Bulletin* 75: 241-57.

213. Perissoratis, C., and van Andel, T.H., 1991, 'Sea-level changes and tectonics in the Quaternary extensional basin of the South Evvoikos Gulf, Greece', *Terra Nova*, 3: 294-302.

214. Pernicka, E. et al., 1981, 'Ancient lead and silver production on Thasos, Greece', *Revue d'Archaeometrie*, Supplement 227-37.

215. Peschlow, A., 1981, 'Steinbruche von Milet und Herakleia am Latmos', *Jahrbuch des Deutschen Archäologischen Instituts* 96: 157-235.

References

216. Petrocheilou, A., 1984, *The Greek Caves.* Ekdotike Athenon S.A., Athens.

217. Phillipson, A., 1959, Der Griechischen Landschaften III/1 – Der Peloponnes Vittorio Klosterman, Frankfurt.

218. Pichler, H. and Kussmaul, S., 1980, 'Comments on the geological map of the Santorini islands', in *Thera and the Ancient World II*, ed. C. Doumas. London, pp. 413-27.

219. Piper, D.J.W. and Panagos, A.G., 1981, 'Growth patterns of the Acheloos and Evinos deltas, western Greece', *Sedimentary Geology* 28: 111-32.

220. Piper, D.J.W. et al., 1990, 'Quaternary history of the Gulfs of Patras and Corinth', *Zeitschrift für Geomorphologie* N. F. 34: 451-8.

221. Pirazzoli, P.A. et al., 1989, 'Crustal movements from Holocene shorelines: Rhodes island (Greece)', *Tectonophysics* 170: 89-114.

222. Pirazzoli, P.A., 1986, 'The early Byzantine tectonic paroxysm', *Zeitschrift für Geomorphologie*, Suppl-Bd 62, 31-49.

223. Pirazzoli, P.A., 1988, 'Sea-level changes and crustal movements in the Hellenic arc (Greece). The contribution of archaeological and historical data', in *Cities of the Sea – Past and Present*, ed. A. Raban. BAR International Series 404, 157-84.

224. Pirazzoli, P.A. et al., 1994, 'Episodic uplift deduced from Holocene shorelines in the Perachora Peninsula, Corinth area, Greece', *Tectonophysics* 229: 201-9.

225. Pomel, R.-S., 1983, 'L'évolution paléoclimatique de Santorin (mer Egée) au quaternaire récent: stratigraphie et paléosols intervolcaniques', *Méditerranée* 48(2): 27-37.

226. Pope, K. and van Andel, Tj.H., 1984, 'Late quaternary alluviations and soil formation in the southern Argolid: its history, causes and archaeological implications', *Journal of Archaeological Science* 11: 281-306.

227. Puchelt, H., Mural, E. and Hubberten, H-W., 1977, 'Geochemical and petrological studies of lavas, pyroclastics and associated xenoliths from the Christiana islands, Aegean sea', *Neues Jahrbuch für Mineralogie Abhandlungen* 131: 140-55.

228. Rackham, O., 1990, 'The greening of Myrtos', in *Man's Role in the Shaping of the Eastern Mediterranean Landscape*, ed. S. Bottema et al., Balkema, Rotterdam, pp. 341-8.

229. Rapp, G. jr and Gifford, J.A., 1982, *Troy. The Archeological Geology.* Supplementary monograph 4, University of Cincinnati, Princeton University Press.

230. Renfrew, C. et al., 1965, 'Obsidian in the Aegean', *Annual of the British School at Athens* 60: 225-47.

231. Richler, D. and Mariolakos, I., 1974, 'Stratigraphische untersuchungen an der kreide/tertiar wende im gebiet van Delphi Amfissa Amfiklia', *Annales Géologiques des Pays Helléniques* 26, 417-34.

232. Robert, U., 1973, *Les roches volcaniques de l'île de Patmos (Dodecanese, Grèce).* Thèse troisième cycle Laboratoire de Petrographie, Université Paris-6.

233. Robert, U., 1992, 'The Dodecanese province, SE Aegean: a model for tectonic control on potassic magmatism', *Lithos*, 28: 241-60.

234. Roberts, N., 1979, 'The location and environment of Knossos', *Annual of the British School at Athens* 74: 231-40.

235. Roberts, N., 1989, *The Holocene: An Environmental History.* Basil Blackwell, Oxford.

236. Robertson, A.H.F., 1990, 'Late Cretaceous oceanic crust and Early Tertiary foreland basin development, Euboea, Eastern Greece', *Terra Nova* 2: 333-9.

237. Rossignol-Strick, M., 1993, 'Late quaternary climate in the eastern Mediterranean region', *Paleorient* 19/1: 135-52.

238. Ruff, E., 1963, 'The jade story, Part 21, Jade of Europe (2)', *Lapidary Journal*, June 1963.

239. Salemink, J., 1979, 'On the geology and petrology of Seriphos (Cyclades, Greece)', *Annales Géologiques des Pays Helléniques*, 30: 342-65.

240. Schermer, E.R., 1990, 'Mechanisms of blueschist creation and preservation in an A-type subduction zone, Mount Olympos region, Greece', *Geology* 18: 1130-3.

241. Schliestedt, M., Altherr, R., and Mathews, A., 1988, 'Evolution of the Cycladic crystalline complex: petrology, isotope geochemistry and geochronology', in *Chemical Transport in Metasomatic Processes*, ed. H.C. Helgeson, NATO-ASI Series Reidel, Dordrecht, pp. 389-428.

242. Schoder, R.V., 1974, *Ancient Greece from the Air.* Thames and Hudson, London.

243. Schroder, B. and Yalçin, Ü., 1992, 'Geology of the non-metamorphic formations around Milet (western Turkey)', *Bulletin of the Geological Society of Greece* 28/1: 369.

244. Sengor, A.M.C. and Yilmaz, Y., 1981. 'Tethyan evolution of Turkey – a plate tectonic approach', *Tectonophysics* 75: 181-241.

245. Sengor, A.M.C., 1979, 'The North Anatolian transform fault: its age, offset and tectonic significance', *Journal of the Geological Society*

136: 269-82.

246. Sengor, A.M.C., 1984, 'Timing of tectonic events in the Menderes massif, western Turkey: implications for tectonic evolution and evidence for pan-African basement in Turkey', *Tectonics* 3: 693-707.

247. Shelford, P., 1982, 'The geology of Melos', in *The Archaeology of Exploitation in Melos: An Island Polity*, ed. C. Renfrew and M. Wagstaff. Cambridge University Press, Cambridge.

248. Shipley, G., 1987, *A History of Samos*, 800-188 BC. Clarendon Press, Oxford.

249. Simpson, R.H. and Dickinson, O.T.P.K., 1979, *A Gazetteer of Aegean Civilisation in the Bronze Age*. P. Astrom, Goteburg.

250. Sordinas, A., 1983, 'Quaternary shorelines in the region of Corfu and adjacent islets, western Greece', in *Quaternary Coastlines and Marine Archaeology*, ed. P.M. Masters and N.C. Flemming. Academic Press, London.

251. Spakman, W., Wortel, M.J.R. and Vlaar, N.J., 1988, 'The Hellenic subduction zone: a tomographic image and its geodynamic implications', *Geophysical Research Letters* 15: 60-3.

252. St-Seymour, K. and Vlassopoulos, D., 1989, 'The potential for future explosive volcanism associated with dome growth at Nisyros, Aegean volcanic arc, Greece', *Journal of Volcanology and Geothermal Research*, 37: 351-64.

253. Stamatakis, M.G., 1990, 'Building stones from the ancient quarries of Agiades area, Samos island, Greece', in *Engineering Geology of Ancient Works, Monuments and Historical Sites*, ed. P.G. Marinos and G.C. Koukis. Balkema, Rotterdam, pp. 2043-8.

254. Stamatelopoulou-Seymour, K. and Vlassopoulos, D., 1989, 'The potential for future explosive volcanism associated with dome growth at Nisyros, Aegean volcanic arc, Greece', *Journal of Volcanology and Geothermal Research*, 37: 351-64.

255. Stanley, D.J. and Sheng, H., 1985, 'Discovery of Santorini volcanic ash in the Nile delta: Bearing of the Minoan eruption on biblical exodus events in Egypt', *Geological Society of America Annual Meeting*, Abstracts with program 725.

256. Stiros, S.C., 1988, 'Archaeology – a tool to study active tectonics. The Aegean as a case study', *Eos, Transactions of the American Geophysical Union* 69: 1933-9.

257. Stiros, S.C. et al., 1994, 'The 1953 earthquake in Cephalonia (Western Hellenic Arc): coastal uplift and halotectonic faulting', *Geophysics Journal International* 117: 834-49.

258. Strothers, R.B. and Rampino, M.R., 1983,

'Volcanic eruptions in the Mediterranean before AD 630 from written and archaeological sources', *Journal of Geophysical Research* 88: 6357-71.

259. Symeouoglou, S., 1985, *The Topography of Thebes*. Princeton University Press.

260. Taymaz, T., Jackson, J. and McKenzie, D., 1991, 'Active tectonics of the north and central Aegean Sea', *Geophysics Journal International*, 106: 433-90.

261. Tooley, M.J. and Shennan, I., 1987, *Sea-level Changes*. Basil Blackwell, Oxford.

262. Topkaya, Y.A., 1984, 'Recent evaluation of Sart placer gold deposit', in *Precious Metals; Mining, Extraction and Processing*, ed. V. Kudryk et al., AIME, Los Angeles, USA.

263. Traineau, H. and Dalabakis, P., 1989, 'Mise en evidence d'une éruption phréatique historique sur l'île de Milos (Grèce)', *Comptes Rendus de l'Academie des Sciences, Paris*, Serie II, 308: 247-52.

264. Trikkalinos, L.K., 1977, 'Die Geologie der Akropolis', *Annales Géologiques des Pays Helléniques* 29: 265-83.

265. Tsikouras et al., 1990, 'A new date for an ophiolite on the northeastern margin of the Vardar zone, Samothraki, Greece', *Neues Jahrbuch für Mineralogie*, Monstshefte 11: 521-7.

266. Udias, A., 1985, 'Seismicity of the Mediterranean', in *Geological Evolution of the Mediterranean Basin*, ed. D.J. Stanley and F.C. Wezel. Springer-Verlag, New York.

267. Underhill, J.R., 1988, 'Triassic evaporites and Plio-Quaternary diapirism in western Greece', *Journal of the Geological Society* 145: 269-82.

268 Underhill, J.R., 1989, 'Late Cenozoic deformation of the Hellenide foreland, Western Greece', *Geological Society of America Bulletin* 101: 613-34.

269. Vallois, R., 1966, *L'architecture hellénique et hellénistique à Délos*. Paris.

270. van Andel, T.H. and Zangger, E., 1990, 'Landscape stability and destabilisation in the prehistory of Greece', in *Man's Role in the Shaping of the Eastern Mediterranean Landscape*, ed. S. Bottema, G. Entjes-Nieborg and W. Van Zeist. Balkema, Rotterdam, pp. 139-57.

271. van Andel, T.H., Runnels, C.N. and Pope, K.O., 1986, 'Five thousand years of land use and abuse in the southern Argolid, Greece', *Hesperia*, 55: 103-28.

272. Varnavas, S.P. and Cronan, D.S., 1991, 'Hydrothermal metallogenic processes off the islands of Nisiros and Kos in the Hellenic volcanic arc', *Marine Geology* 99: 109-33.

273. Vavelidis, M. and Amstutz, G.C., 1983, 'Investigations on the gold occurrence in the Kinyra and Thasos (city) areas on Thasos island', in *Mineral Deposits of the Alps and of the Alpine Epoch in Europe*, ed. H.J. Schneider. Springer-Verlag, Berlin. 385-91.

274. Vavelidis, M. and Amstutz, G.C., 1983, 'New genetic investigations on the Pb-Zn deposits of Thasos (Greece)', in *Mineral Deposits of the Alps and of the Alpine Epoch in Europe*, ed. H.J. Schneider. Springer-Verlag, Berlin. 359-65.

275. Vetters, W., 1990, 'Ancient quarries around Ephesus and examples of ancient stone-technologies', in *Engineering Geology of Ancient Works, Monuments and Historical Sites*, ed. P.G. Marinos and G.C. Koukis. Balkema, Rotterdam, pp. 2067-78.

276. Vita-Finzi, C. and King, G.C.P. 1985, 'The seismicity, geomorphology and structural evolution of the Corinth area of Greece', *Philosophical Transactions of the Royal Society, London*, Series A, 314: 379-407.

277. Vita-Finzi, C., 1969, *The Mediterranean Valleys*, Cambridge University Press.

278. Vitaliano, C.J. and Vitaliano, D.B., 1974, 'Tephra on Crete', *American Journal of Archeology*, 78: 19-24.

279. Voreadis, G.D., 1954, *Geological and Mining Research in Thasos*. IGME, Athens.

280. Vougioukalakis, G., 1992, 'Volcanic stratigraphy and evolution of Nisyros island', *Bulletin of the Geological Society of Greece* 28/2: 239-58.

281. Wade, A., 1932, 'The geology of Zante and its ancient oilfield', *Institute of Petroleum Technologists Journal*, 18: 1-36.

282. Waelkens, M., 1992, 'Bronze age quarries and quarrying techniques in the Eastern Mediterranean and the near East', in *Ancient Stones: Quarrying, Trade and Provenance*, ed. M. Waelkens, N. Herz and L. Moens. Leuven University Press, pp. 5-20.

283. Wagner, G.A. and Weisgerber, G., 1985, *Silber, Blei und Gold auf Sifnos*. Deutschen Bergbau-Museums, Bochum.

284. Wagner, G.A. and Weisgerber, G., 1988, *Antike Edel- und Bunt-Metallgewinnung auf Thasos*, Deutsches Bergbau-Museum, Bochum.

285. Wagner, G.A., Pernicka, E., Gialoglou, G. and Vavelidis, M., 1981, 'Ancient gold mines on Thasos', *Naturwissenschaften* 68: 263-4.

286. Weidman, M. et al., 1984, 'Neogene stratigraphy of the eastern basin, Samos island, Greece', *Geobios* 17/4: 477-90.

287. Wenner, D.B. and Herz, N., 1992, 'Provence signatures for classical marbles', in *Ancient Stones: Quarrying, Trade and Provenance*, ed. M. Waelkens, N. Herz and L. Moens. Leuven University Press, pp. 199-202.

288. Wetzenstein, W., 1975, 'Tektonik und Metallogenese der Insel Milos/Kykladen', *Bulletin of the Geological Society of Greece* 12: 31-9.

289. Whitbred, I.K., 1987, *The application of ceramic petrology to the study of ancient Greek transport amphorae, with special reference to Corinthian amphora production*. PhD thesis, University of Southampton.

290. Wycherly, R.E., 1978, *The Stones of Athens*. Princeton University Press, Princeton.

291. Wyers, G.P. and Barton, M., 1986, 'Petrology and evolution of transitional alkaline-subalkaline lavas from Patmos, Dodecanesos, Greece: evidence for fractional crystallization, magma mixing and assimilation', *Contributions to Mineralogy and Petrology* 93: 297-311.

292. Wyers, G.P. and Barton, M., 1989, 'Polybaric evolution of calc-alkaline magmas from Nisyros, Southeastern Hellenic arc, Greece', *Journal of Petrology* 30: 1-37.

293. Zamani, A., 1979, 'Contribution to the interpretation of the formation and development of the landforms of Meteora', *Annales Géologiques des Pays Helléniques* 30: 281-90.

Index

Subjects covering several pages are referred to in this index by the first page of the section only.